TO LEGEN[illegible]
PICTURES —
KEEP WATCHING
THE SKIES!
— [illegible] '06

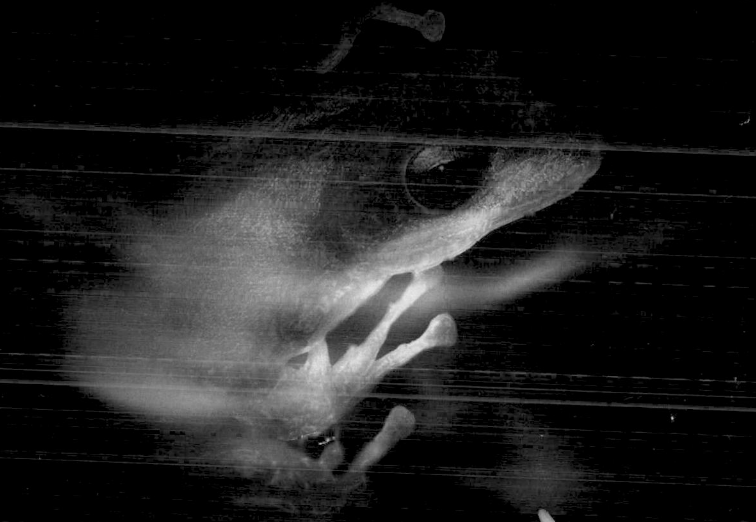

RIBIT

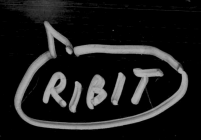

A Penny-Farthing Press, Inc. Book

STUART MOORE'S

PARA™

Stuart Moore's Para™ Graphic Novel
Published by Penny-Farthing Press, Inc.
10370 Richmond Avenue, Suite 980
Houston, Texas 77042
(713) 780-0300 or (800) 926-2669
corp@pfpress.com
www.pfpress.com

987654321

ISBN: 0-9719012-4-4

Printed in Canada

STUART MOORE'S

PARA

CREATOR: Stuart Moore
SCRIPT: Stuart Moore
PENCILS: Pablo Villalobos, Claude St. Aubin
and Federico Zumel
INKS: Mostafa Moussa and James Taylor
COLORS: Mike Garcia
LETTERS: Richard Starkings
PAINTED COVER: Stephan Martiniere

PUBLISHER: Ken White, Jr.
EDITOR-IN-CHIEF: Marlaine Maddux
CREATIVE DIRECTOR: Trainor Houghton
ART DIRECTOR: Charles M. Hancock
SENIOR EDITOR: Michelle Nichols
TALENT COORDINATOR: Courtney Huddleston
GRAPHIC DESIGNER: André McBride
OFFICE MANAGER: Pam Johnston
VP OF MARKETING AND MEDIA
COMMUNICATIONS: Pamela Miltenberger
ACCOUNTS MANAGER: Selma Medina

TABLE OF CONTENTS

"If we value the pursuit of knowledge, we must be free to follow wherever that search may lead us."

–Adlai Stevenson

Dedicated to *William H. Moore*

CHAPTER 1

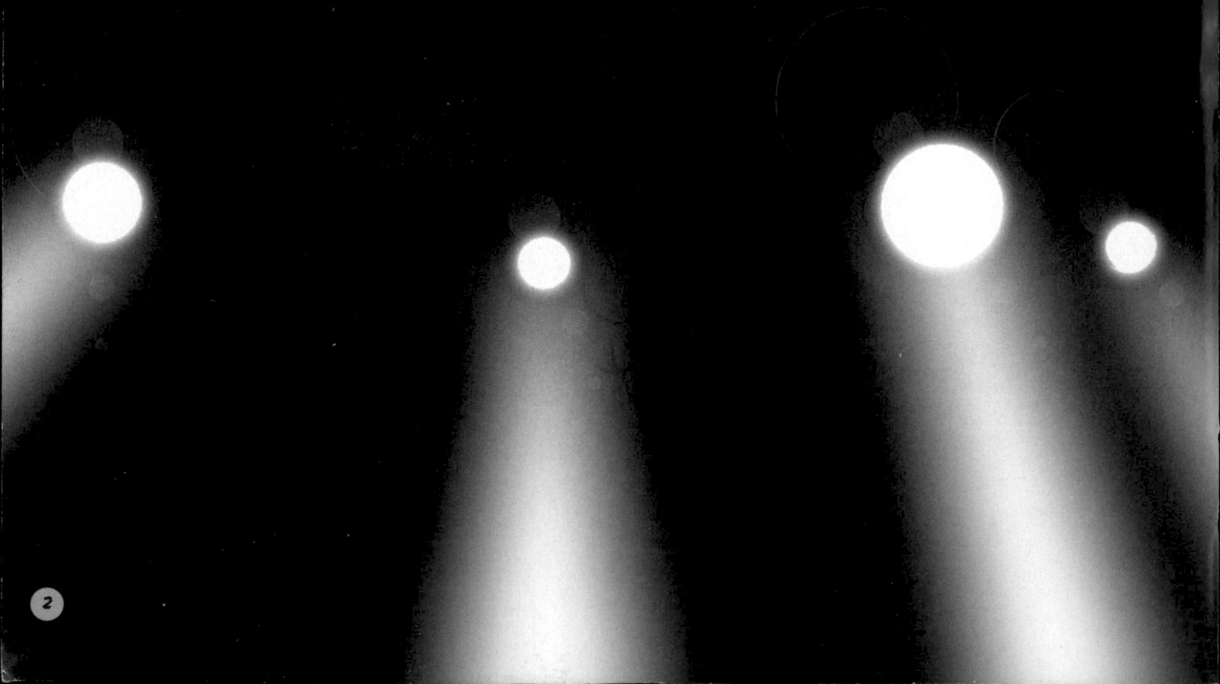

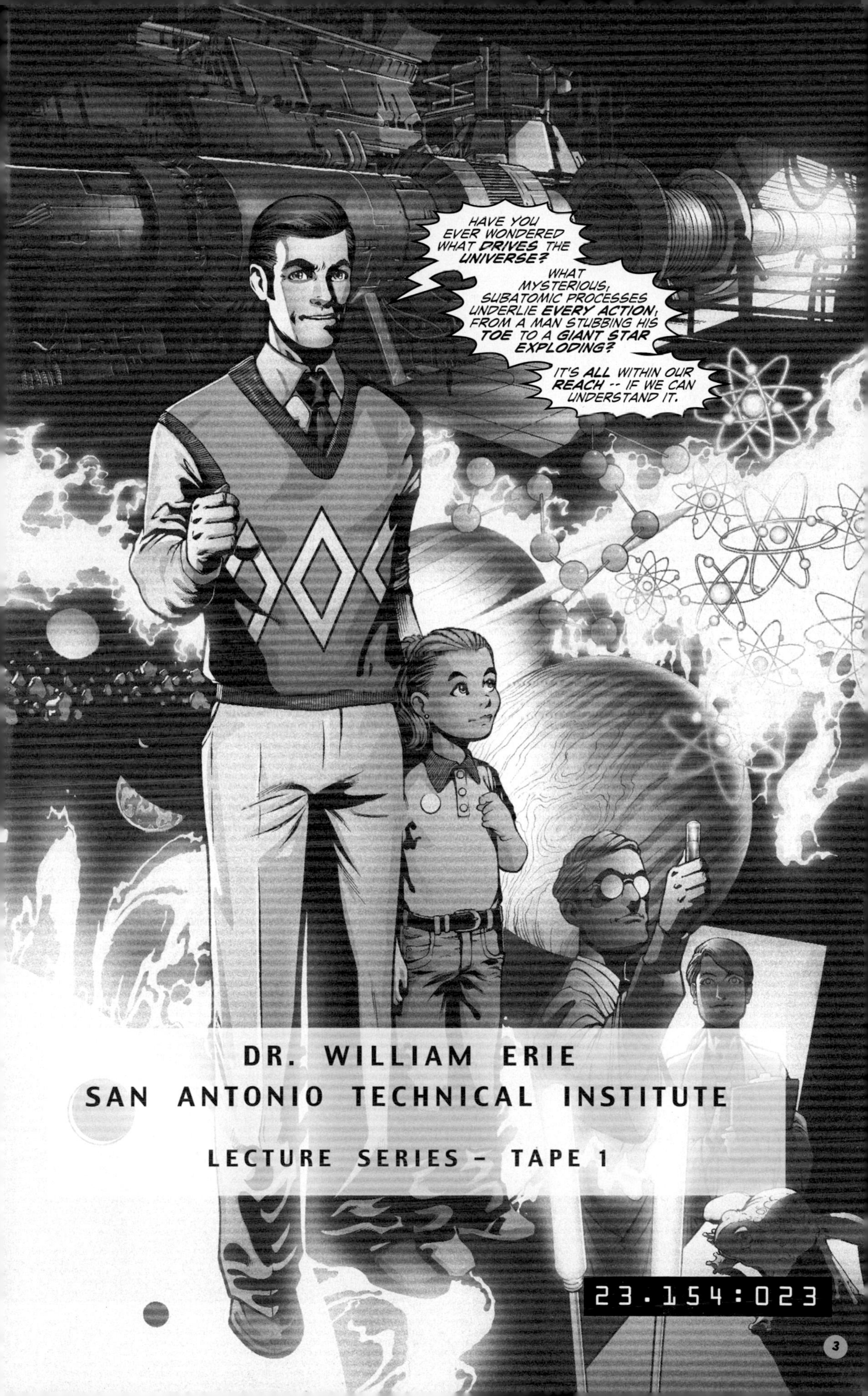
HAVE YOU EVER WONDERED WHAT DRIVES THE UNIVERSE?
WHAT MYSTERIOUS, SUBATOMIC PROCESSES UNDERLIE EVERY ACTION, FROM A MAN STUBBING HIS TOE TO A GIANT STAR EXPLODING?
IT'S ALL WITHIN OUR REACH -- IF WE CAN UNDERSTAND IT.
DR. WILLIAM ERIE
SAN ANTONIO TECHNICAL INSTITUTE
LECTURE SERIES – TAPE 1
23.154:023

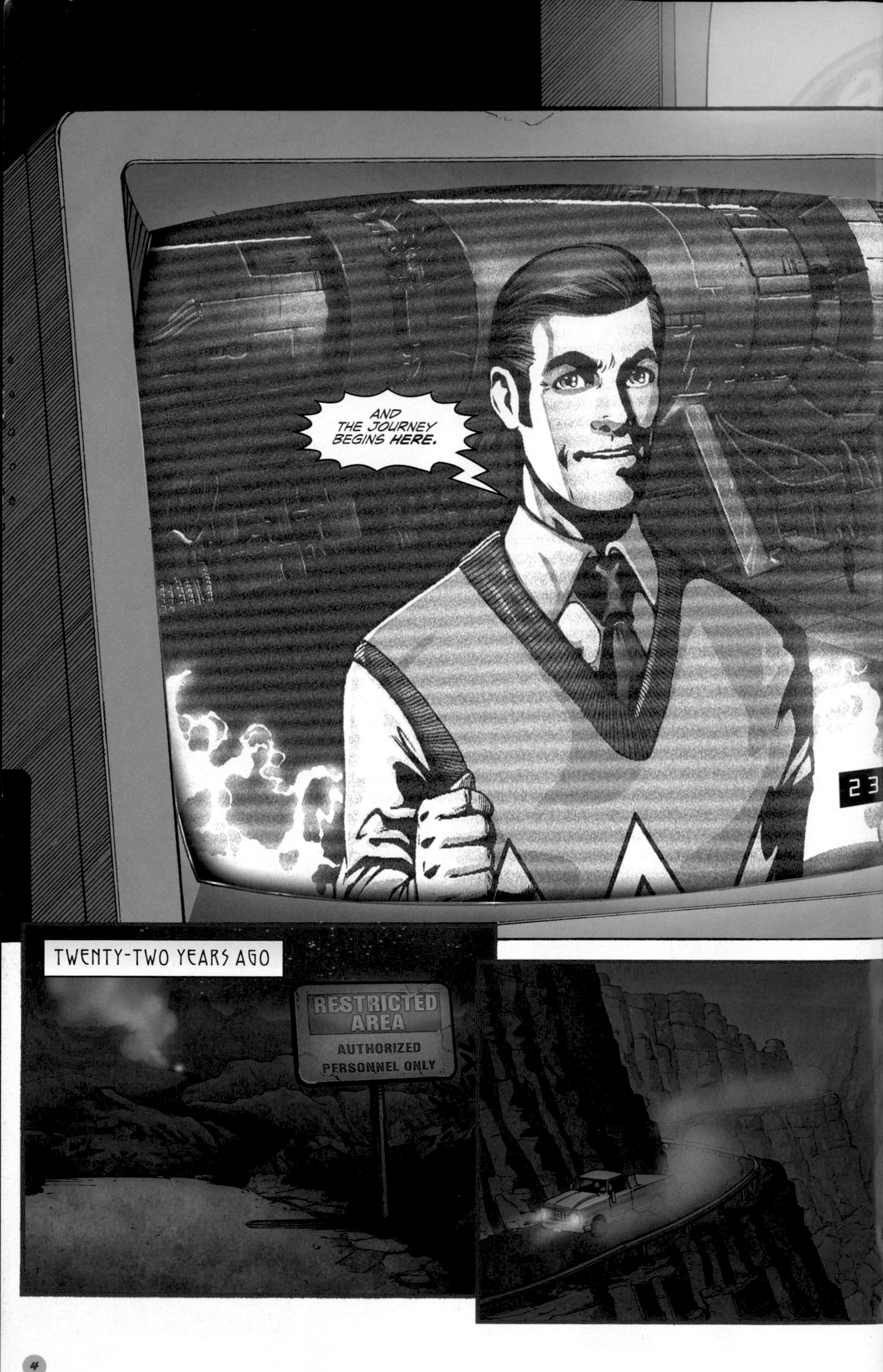
AND THE JOURNEY BEGINS HERE.
23
TWENTY-TWO YEARS AGO
RESTRICTED AREA
AUTHORIZED PERSONNEL ONLY

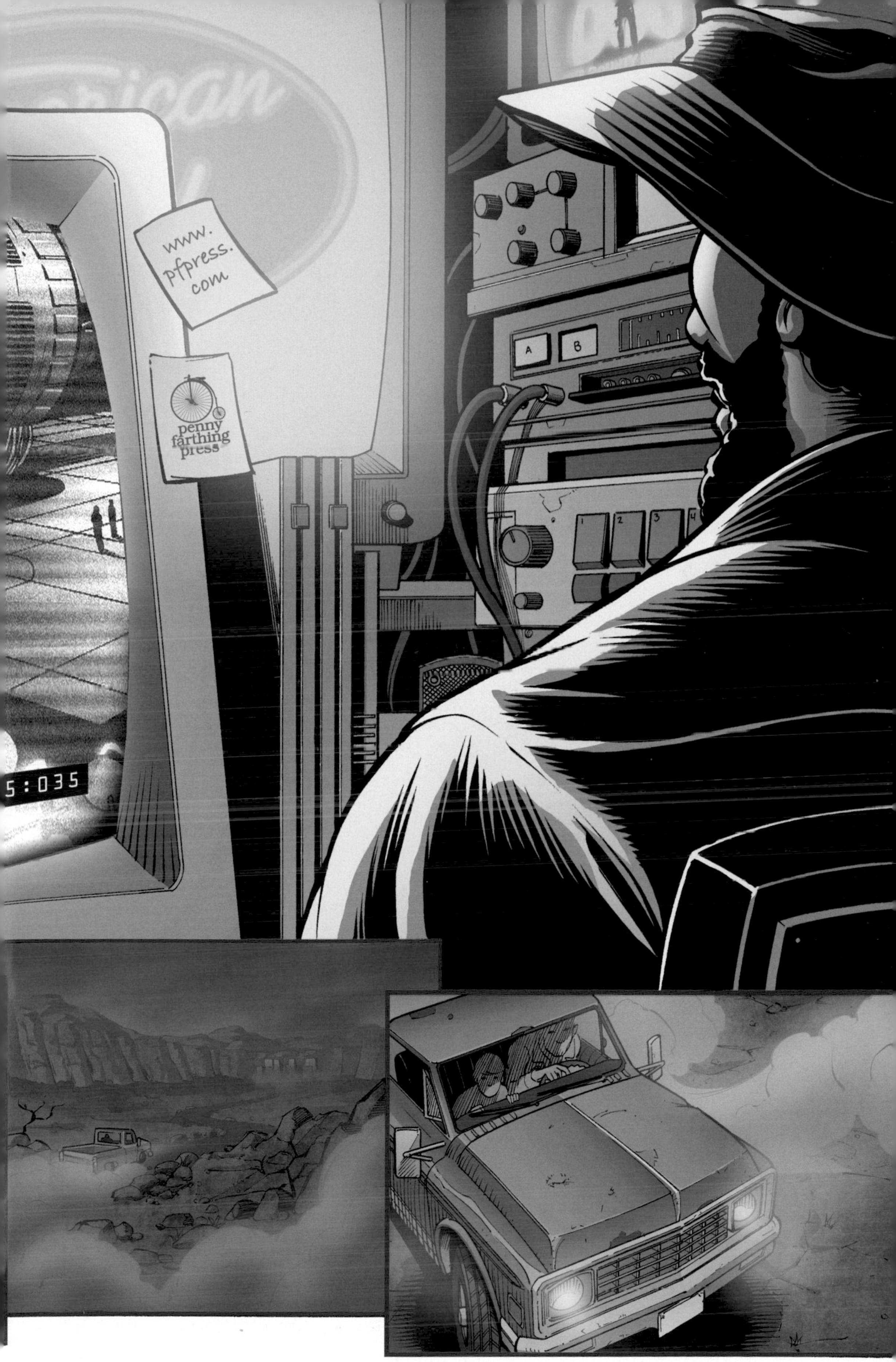
www.
pfpress.
com
penny
farthing
press
A
B
1
2
3
4
5:035

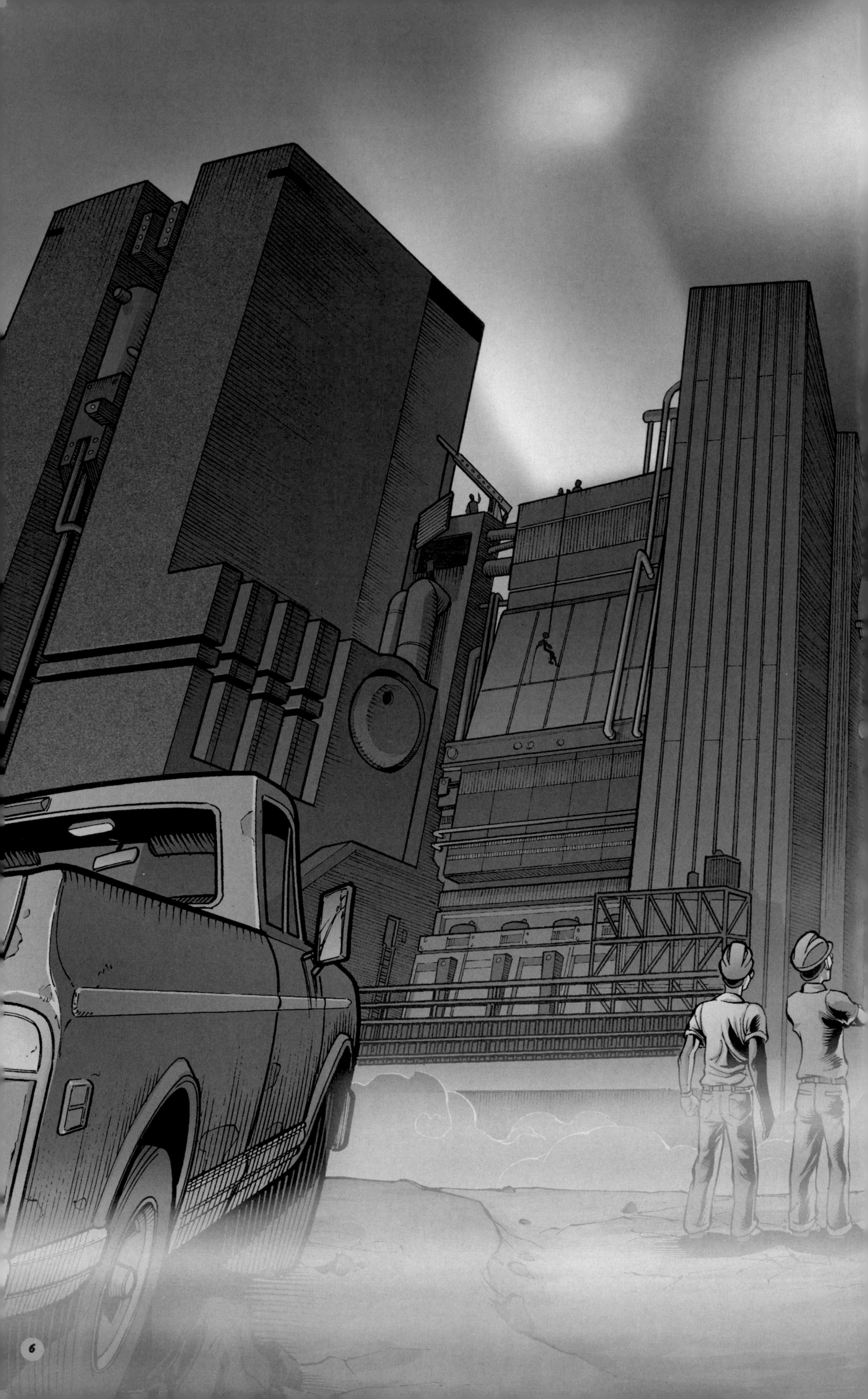

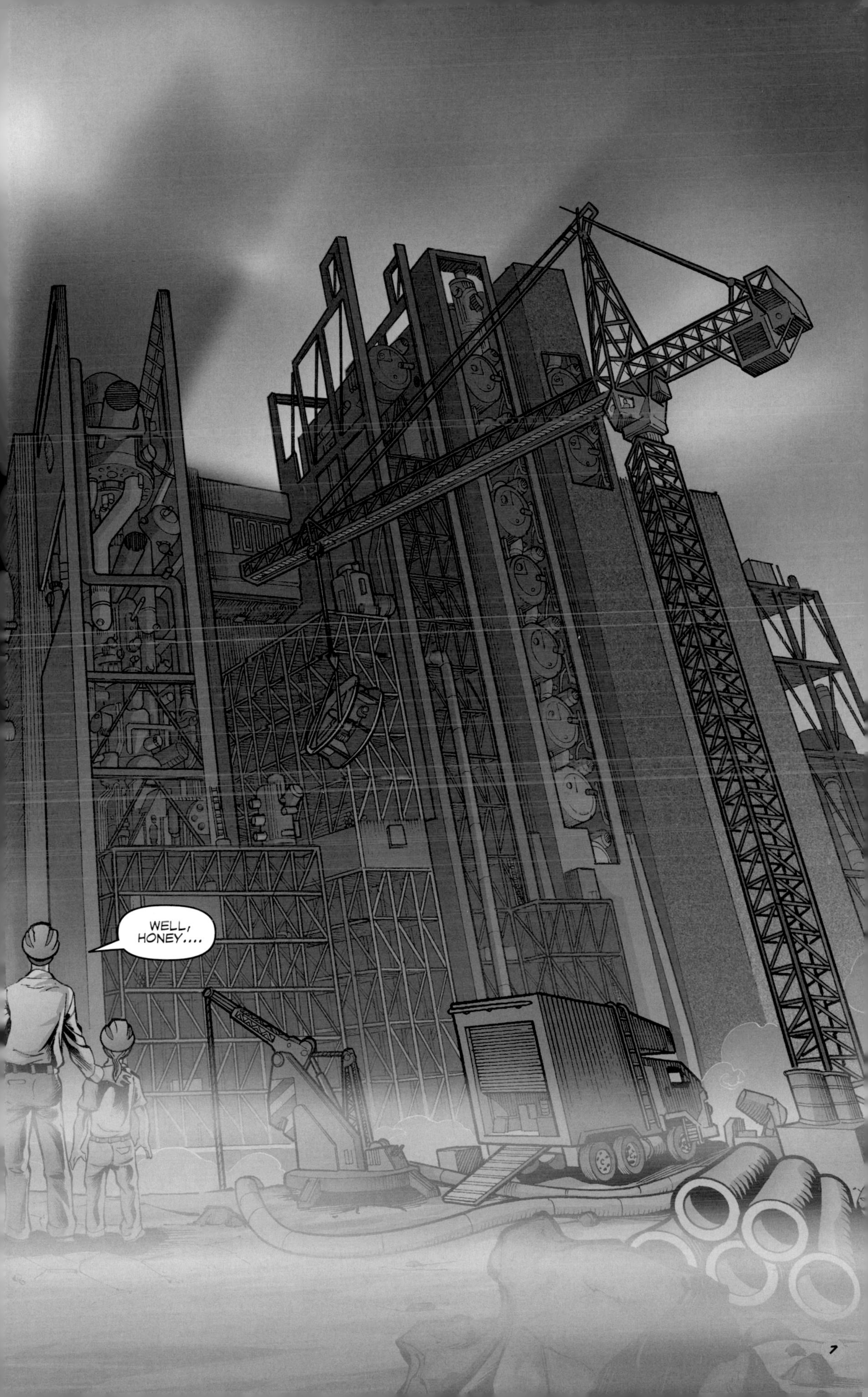
WELL, HONEY....

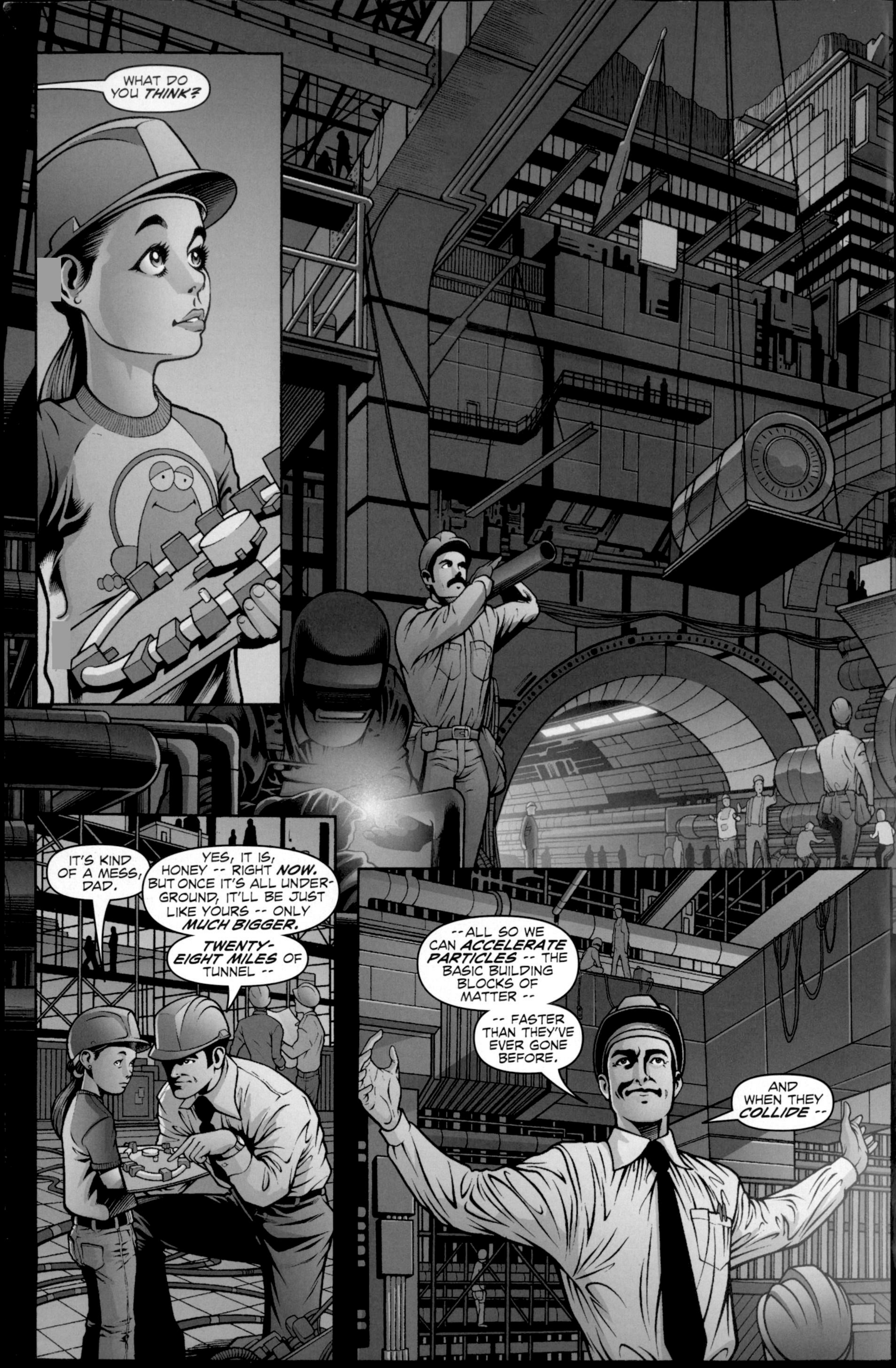
WHAT DO YOU THINK?
IT'S KIND OF A MESS, DAD.
YES, IT IS, HONEY -- RIGHT NOW. BUT ONCE IT'S ALL UNDERGROUND, IT'LL BE JUST LIKE YOURS -- ONLY MUCH BIGGER.
TWENTY-EIGHT MILES OF TUNNEL --
--ALL SO WE CAN ACCELERATE PARTICLES -- THE BASIC BUILDING BLOCKS OF MATTER --
-- FASTER THAN THEY'VE EVER GONE BEFORE.
AND WHEN THEY COLLIDE --

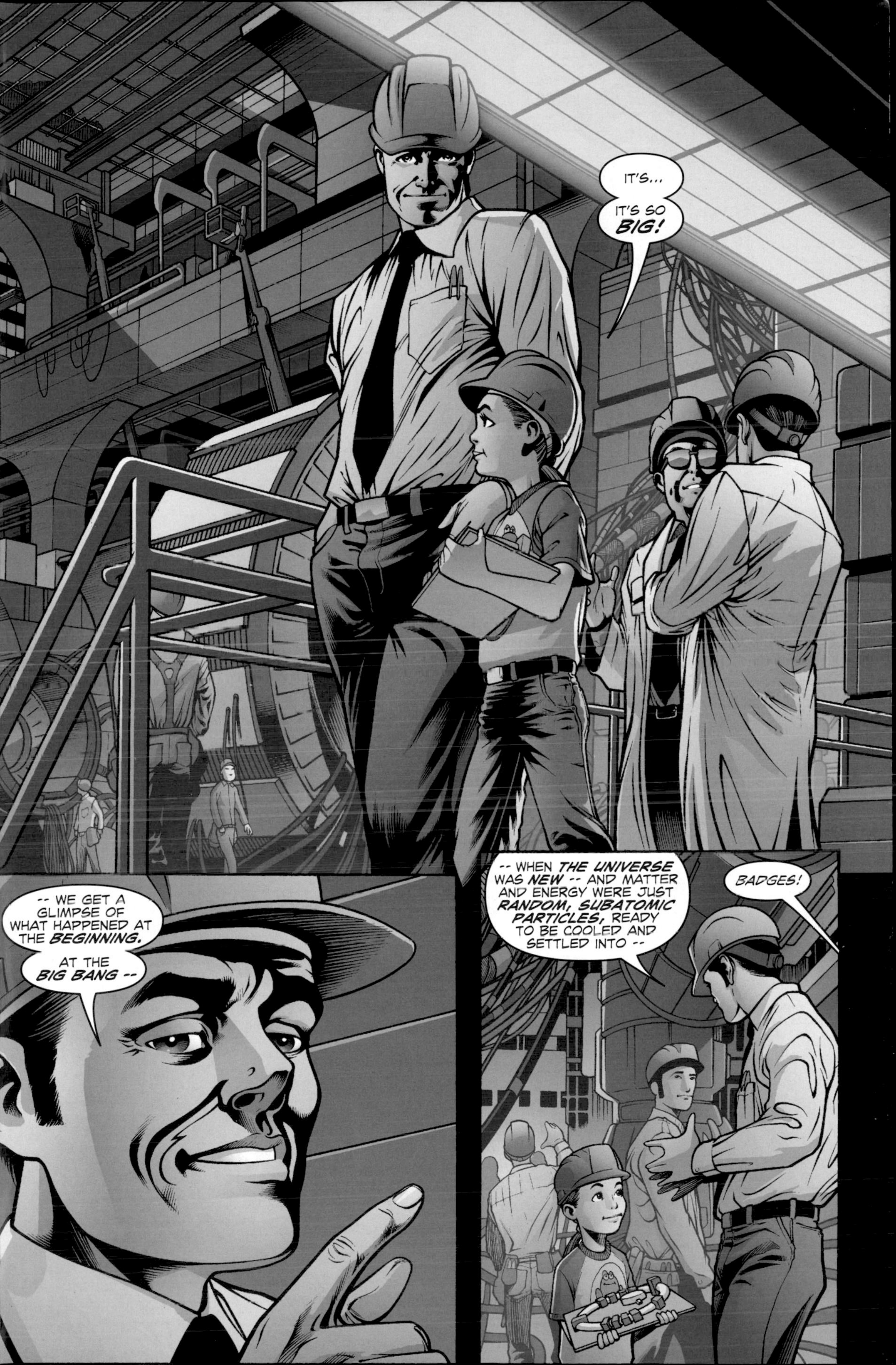
IT'S...
IT'S SO BIG!
-- WE GET A GLIMPSE OF WHAT HAPPENED AT THE BEGINNING.
AT THE BIG BANG --
-- WHEN THE UNIVERSE WAS NEW -- AND MATTER AND ENERGY WERE JUST RANDOM, SUBATOMIC PARTICLES, READY TO BE COOLED AND SETTLED INTO --
BADGES!

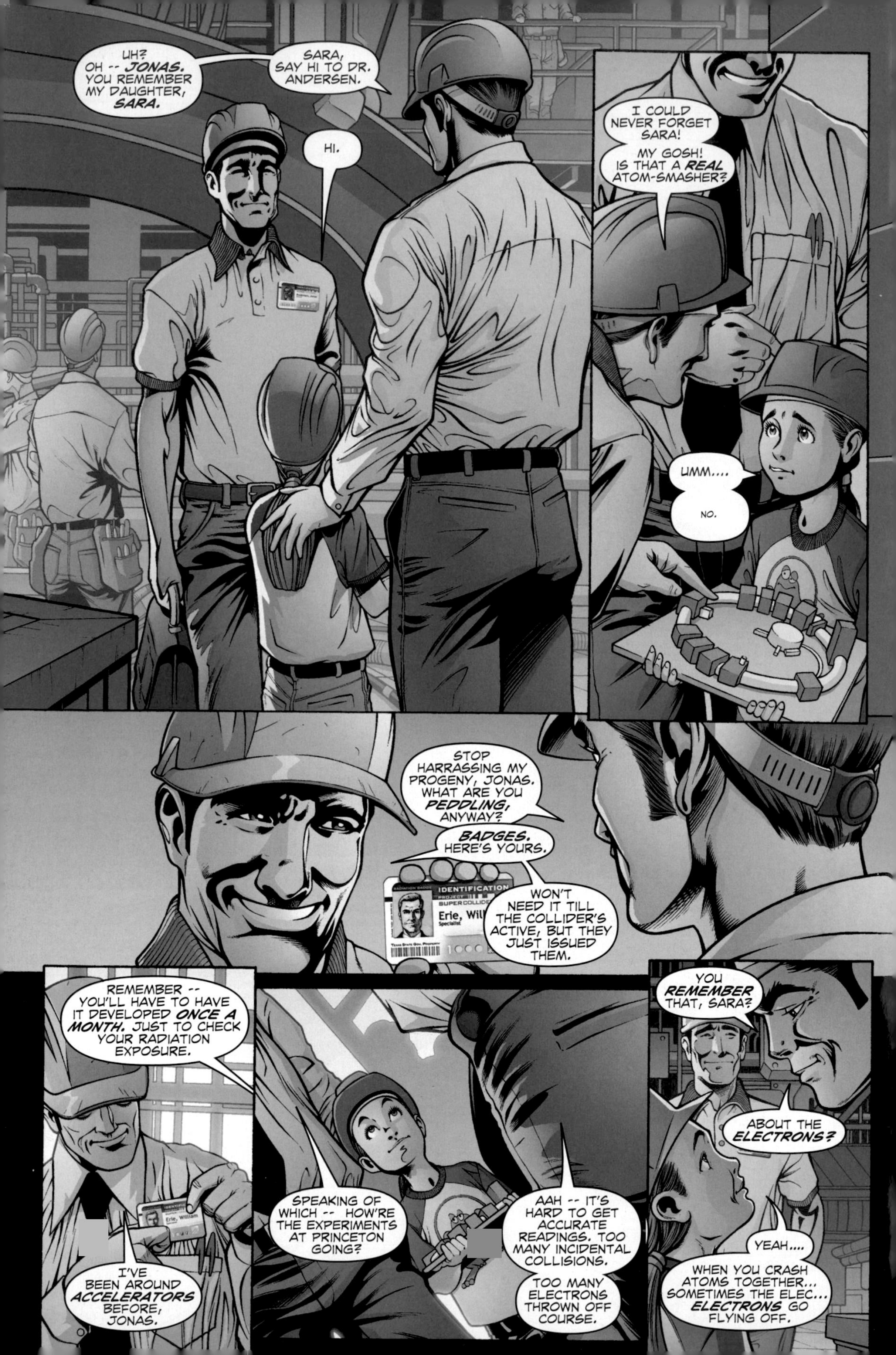
SARA, SAY HI TO DR. ANDERSEN.
UH? OH -- JONAS. YOU REMEMBER MY DAUGHTER, SARA.
HI.
I COULD NEVER FORGET SARA! MY GOSH! IS THAT A REAL ATOM-SMASHER?
UMM....
NO.
STOP HARRASSING MY PROGENY, JONAS. WHAT ARE YOU PEDDLING, ANYWAY?
BADGES. HERE'S YOURS.
WON'T NEED IT TILL THE COLLIDER'S ACTIVE, BUT THEY JUST ISSUED THEM.
RADIATION BADGE
IDENTIFICATION
PROJECT
SUPER COLLIDER
Erie, Will
Specialist
REMEMBER -- YOU'LL HAVE TO HAVE IT DEVELOPED ONCE A MONTH. JUST TO CHECK YOUR RADIATION EXPOSURE.
I'VE BEEN AROUND ACCELERATORS BEFORE, JONAS.
Erie, William
SPEAKING OF WHICH -- HOW'RE THE EXPERIMENTS AT PRINCETON GOING?
AAH -- IT'S HARD TO GET ACCURATE READINGS. TOO MANY INCIDENTAL COLLISIONS.
TOO MANY ELECTRONS THROWN OFF COURSE.
YOU REMEMBER THAT, SARA?
ABOUT THE ELECTRONS?
YEAH....
WHEN YOU CRASH ATOMS TOGETHER... SOMETIMES THE ELEC... ELECTRONS GO FLYING OFF.

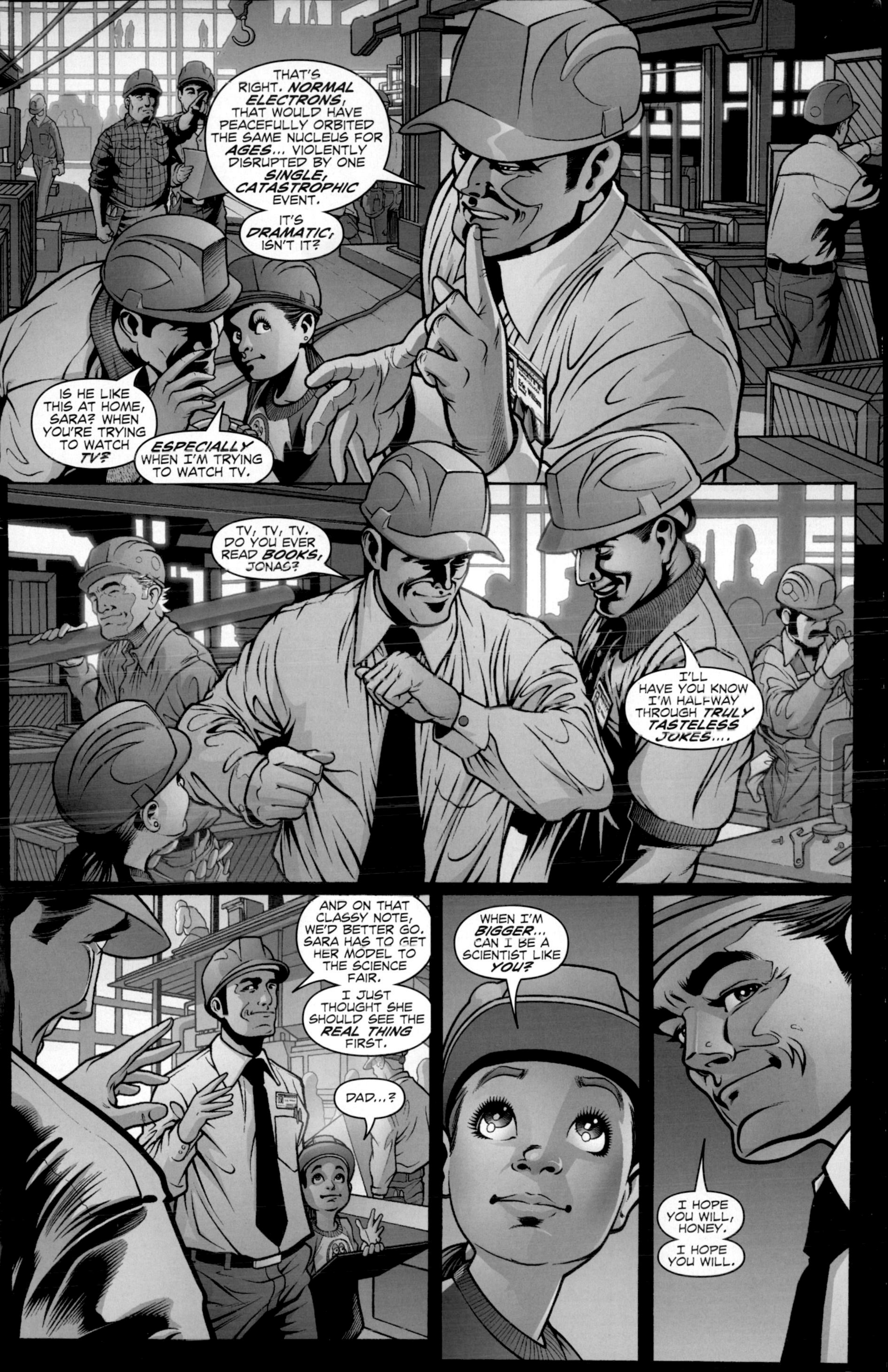
THAT'S RIGHT. NORMAL ELECTRONS, THAT WOULD HAVE PEACEFULLY ORBITED THE SAME NUCLEUS FOR AGES... VIOLENTLY DISRUPTED BY ONE SINGLE, CATASTROPHIC EVENT.
IT'S DRAMATIC, ISN'T IT?
IS HE LIKE THIS AT HOME, SARA? WHEN YOU'RE TRYING TO WATCH TV?
ESPECIALLY WHEN I'M TRYING TO WATCH TV.
TV, TV, TV. DO YOU EVER READ BOOKS, JONAS?
I'LL HAVE YOU KNOW I'M HALFWAY THROUGH TRULY TASTELESS JOKES....
AND ON THAT CLASSY NOTE, WE'D BETTER GO. SARA HAS TO GET HER MODEL TO THE SCIENCE FAIR.
I JUST THOUGHT SHE SHOULD SEE THE REAL THING FIRST.
DAD...?
WHEN I'M BIGGER... CAN I BE A SCIENTIST LIKE YOU?
I HOPE YOU WILL, HONEY.
I HOPE YOU WILL.

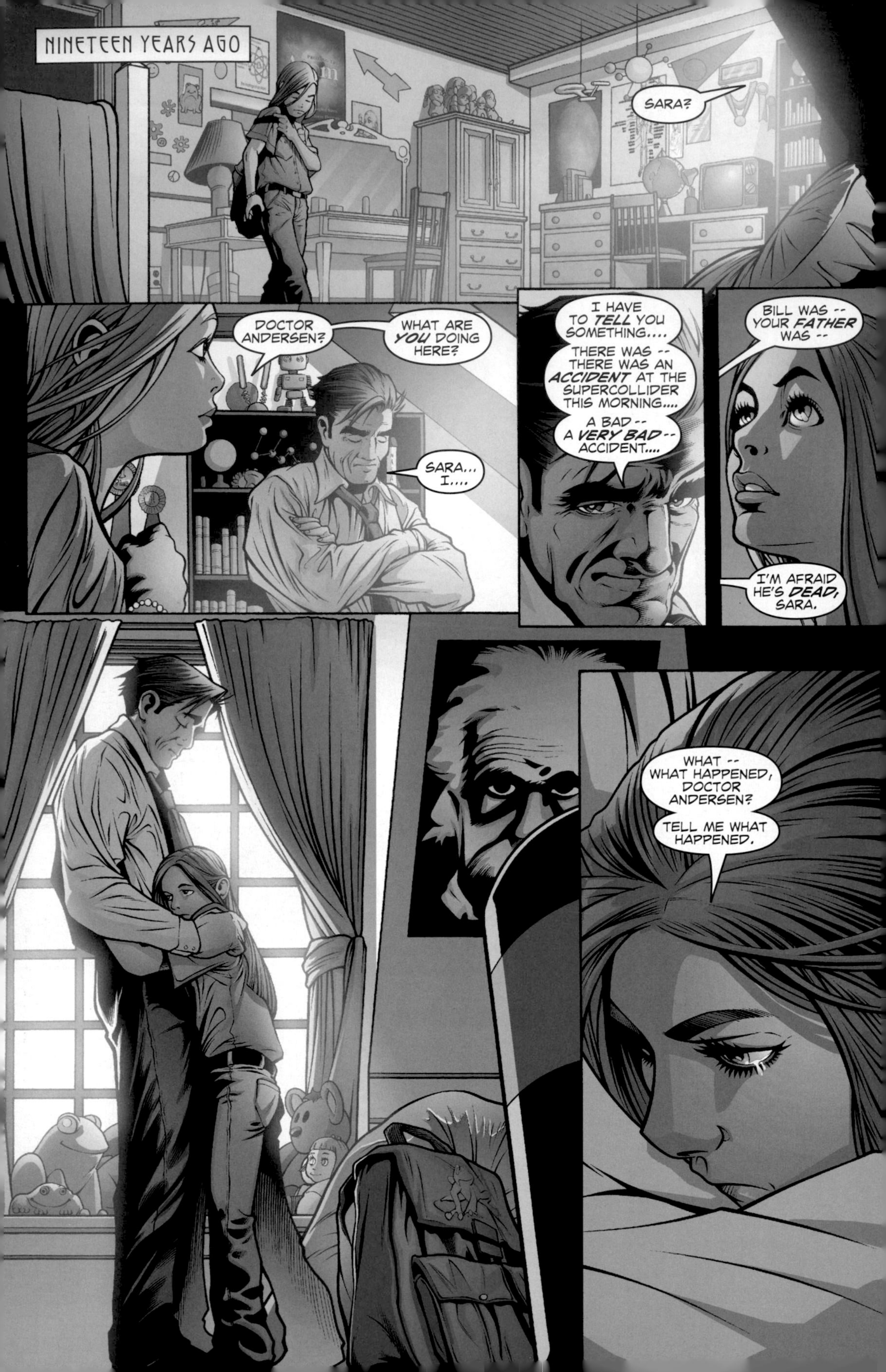
NINETEEN YEARS AGO
SARA?
DOCTOR ANDERSEN?
WHAT ARE YOU DOING HERE?
SARA... I....
I HAVE TO TELL YOU SOMETHING....
THERE WAS -- THERE WAS AN ACCIDENT AT THE SUPERCOLLIDER THIS MORNING....
A BAD -- A VERY BAD -- ACCIDENT....
BILL WAS -- YOUR FATHER WAS --
I'M AFRAID HE'S DEAD, SARA.
WHAT -- WHAT HAPPENED, DOCTOR ANDERSEN?
TELL ME WHAT HAPPENED.

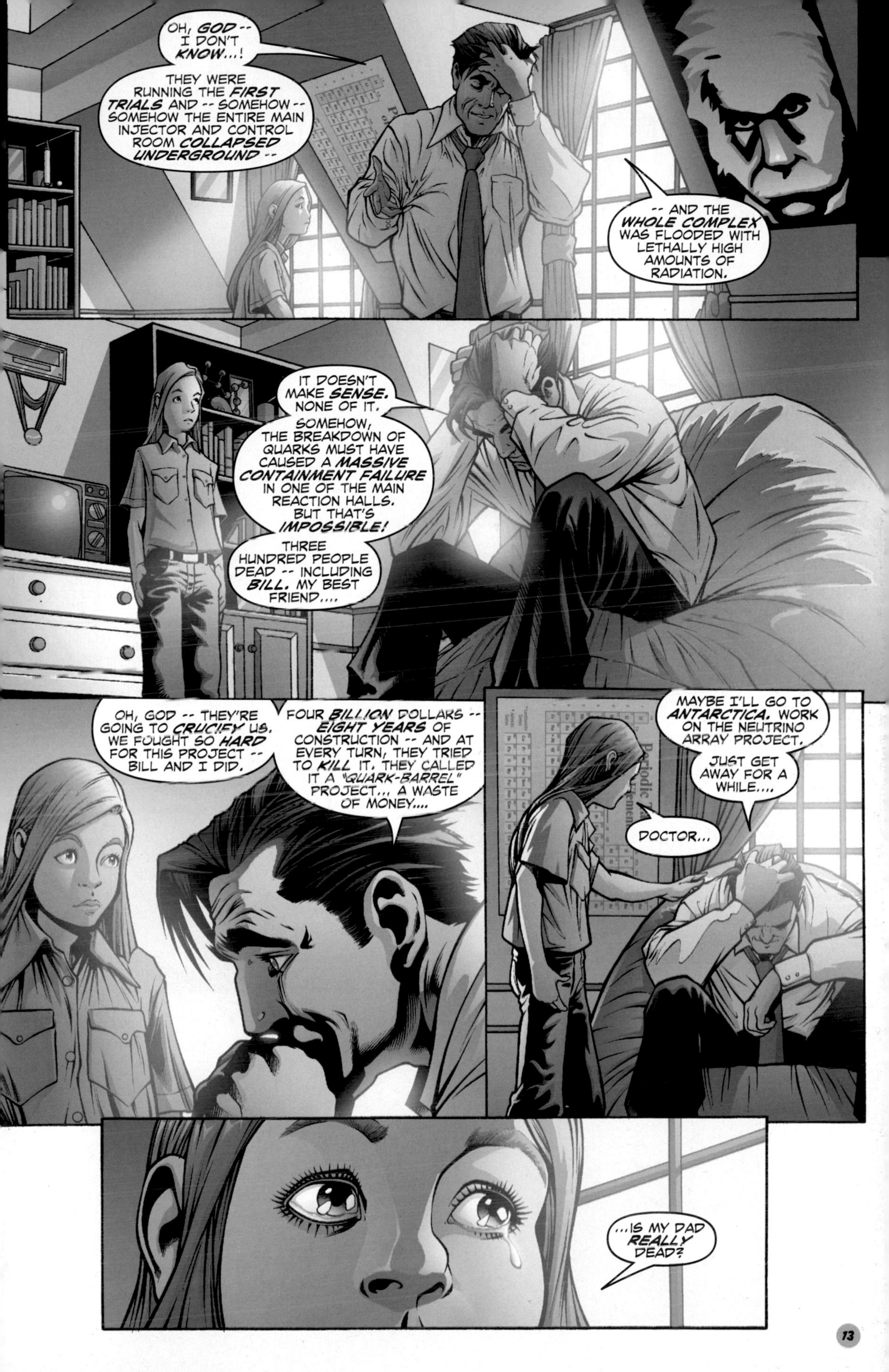
OH, GOD -- I DON'T KNOW...!
THEY WERE RUNNING THE FIRST TRIALS AND -- SOMEHOW -- SOMEHOW THE ENTIRE MAIN INJECTOR AND CONTROL ROOM COLLAPSED UNDERGROUND --
-- AND THE WHOLE COMPLEX WAS FLOODED WITH LETHALLY HIGH AMOUNTS OF RADIATION.
IT DOESN'T MAKE SENSE. NONE OF IT.
SOMEHOW, THE BREAKDOWN OF QUARKS MUST HAVE CAUSED A MASSIVE CONTAINMENT FAILURE IN ONE OF THE MAIN REACTION HALLS. BUT THAT'S IMPOSSIBLE!
THREE HUNDRED PEOPLE DEAD -- INCLUDING BILL. MY BEST FRIEND....
OH, GOD -- THEY'RE GOING TO CRUCIFY US. WE FOUGHT SO HARD FOR THIS PROJECT -- BILL AND I DID.
FOUR BILLION DOLLARS -- EIGHT YEARS OF CONSTRUCTION -- AND AT EVERY TURN, THEY TRIED TO KILL IT. THEY CALLED IT A "QUARK-BARREL" PROJECT..., A WASTE OF MONEY....
MAYBE I'LL GO TO ANTARCTICA. WORK ON THE NEUTRINO ARRAY PROJECT.
JUST GET AWAY FOR A WHILE....
DOCTOR...
...IS MY DAD REALLY DEAD?

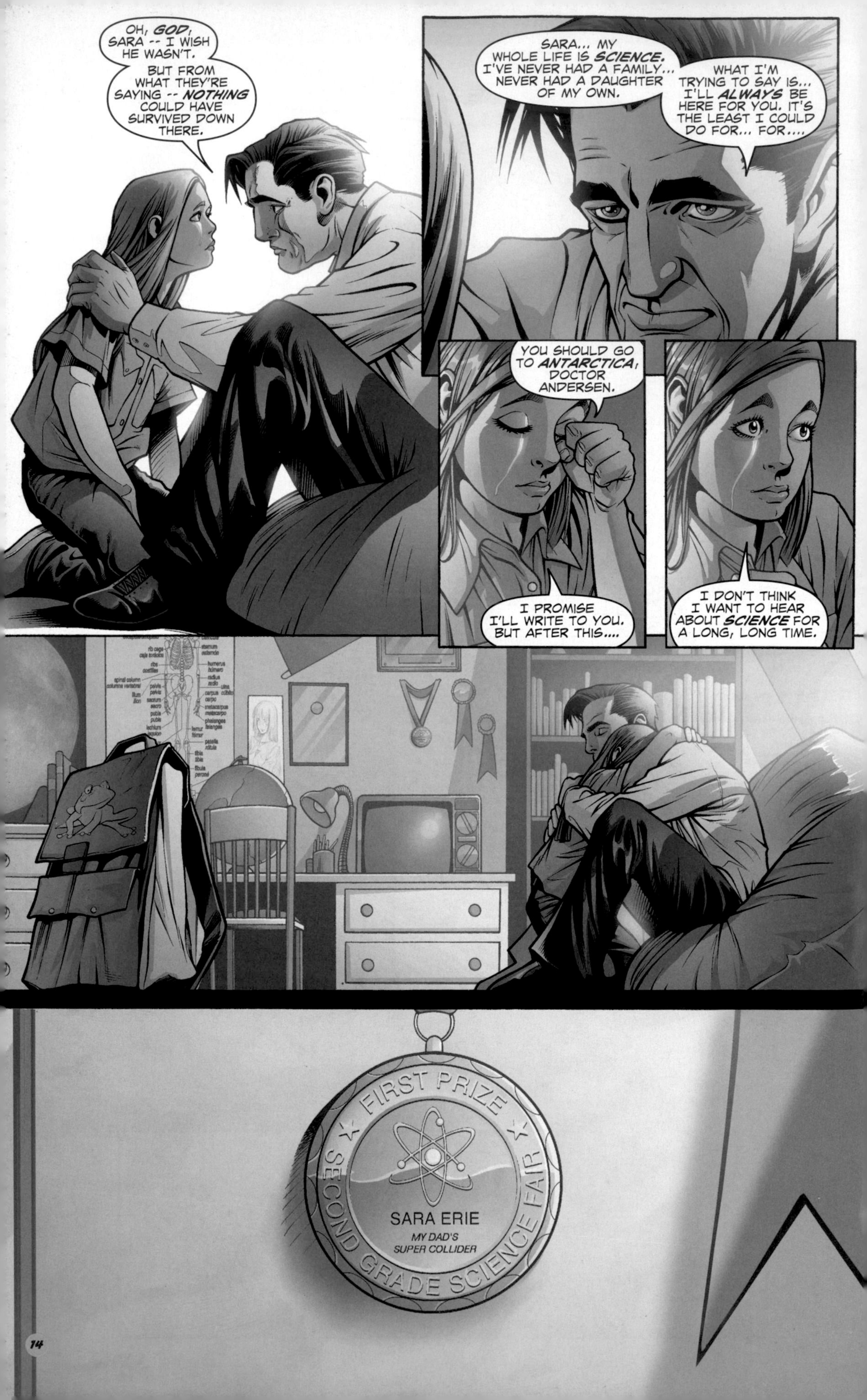
OH, GOD, SARA -- I WISH HE WASN'T.
BUT FROM WHAT THEY'RE SAYING -- NOTHING COULD HAVE SURVIVED DOWN THERE.
SARA... MY WHOLE LIFE IS SCIENCE. I'VE NEVER HAD A FAMILY... NEVER HAD A DAUGHTER OF MY OWN.
WHAT I'M TRYING TO SAY IS... I'LL ALWAYS BE HERE FOR YOU. IT'S THE LEAST I COULD DO FOR... FOR....
YOU SHOULD GO TO ANTARCTICA, DOCTOR ANDERSEN.
I PROMISE I'LL WRITE TO YOU. BUT AFTER THIS....
I DON'T THINK I WANT TO HEAR ABOUT SCIENCE FOR A LONG, LONG TIME.
FIRST PRIZE
SECOND GRADE SCIENCE FAIR
SARA ERIE
MY DAD'S SUPER COLLIDER

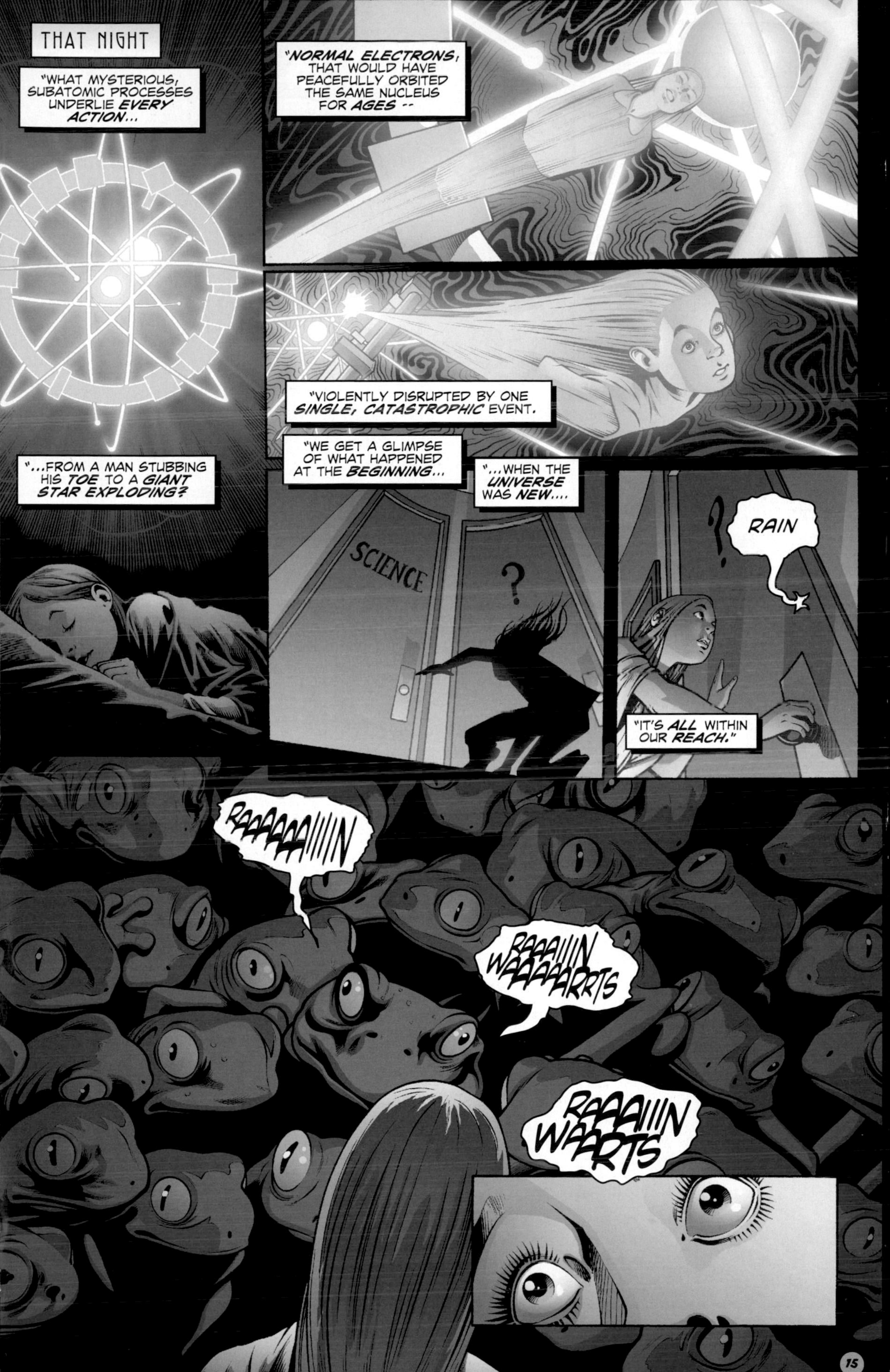
THAT NIGHT
"WHAT MYSTERIOUS, SUBATOMIC PROCESSES UNDERLIE EVERY ACTION...
"...FROM A MAN STUBBING HIS TOE TO A GIANT STAR EXPLODING?
"NORMAL ELECTRONS, THAT WOULD HAVE PEACEFULLY ORBITED THE SAME NUCLEUS FOR AGES --
"VIOLENTLY DISRUPTED BY ONE SINGLE, CATASTROPHIC EVENT.
"WE GET A GLIMPSE OF WHAT HAPPENED AT THE BEGINNING...
"...WHEN THE UNIVERSE WAS NEW....
SCIENCE
?
?
RAIN
"IT'S ALL WITHIN OUR REACH."
RAAAAAAIIIIN
RAAAIIIN WAAAAARRTS
RAAAIIIN WAARTS

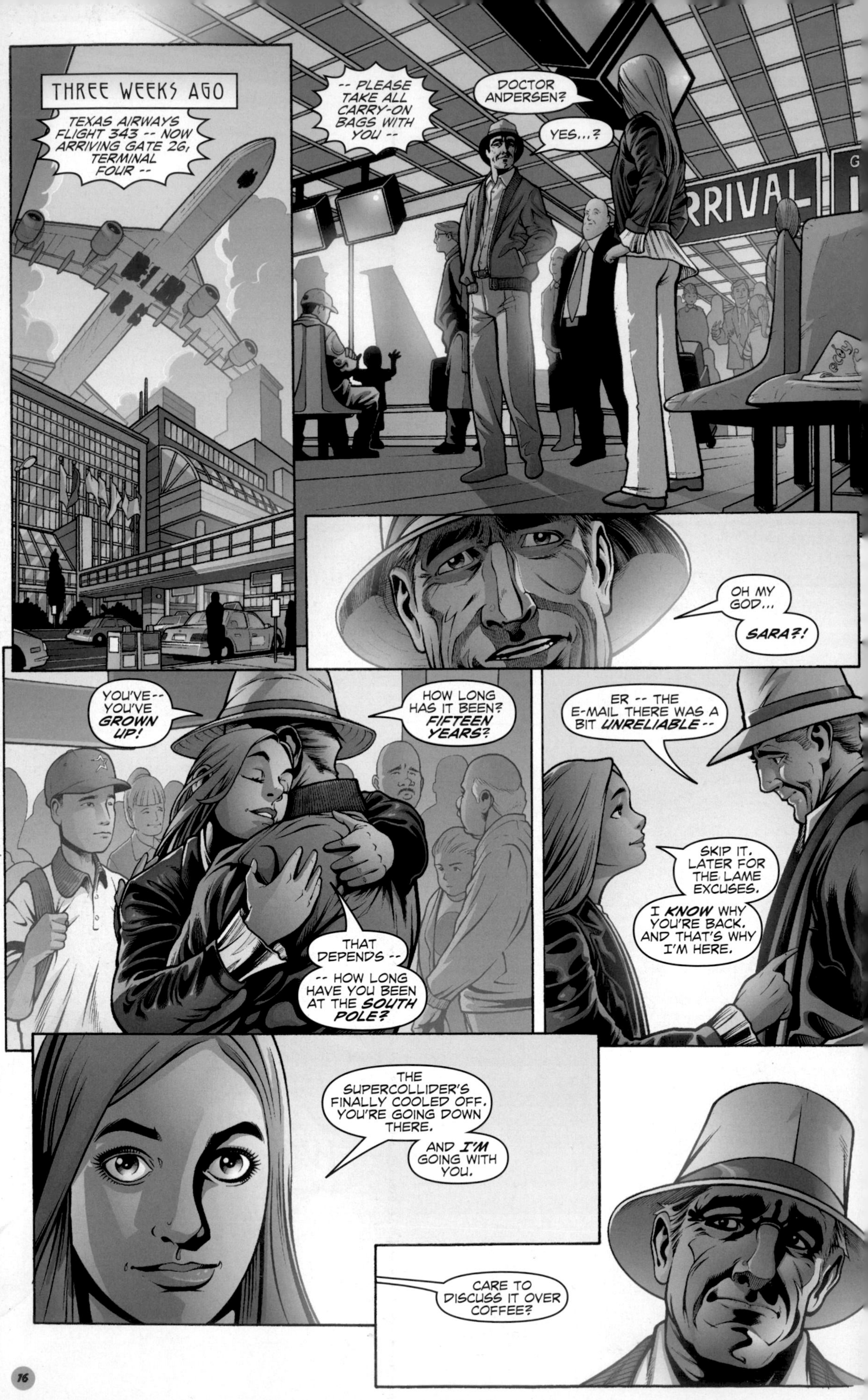
THREE WEEKS AGO
TEXAS AIRWAYS FLIGHT 343 -- NOW ARRIVING GATE 26, TERMINAL FOUR --
-- PLEASE TAKE ALL CARRY-ON BAGS WITH YOU --
DOCTOR ANDERSEN?
YES...?
RRIVAL
OH MY GOD...
SARA?!
YOU'VE-- YOU'VE GROWN UP!
HOW LONG HAS IT BEEN? FIFTEEN YEARS?
THAT DEPENDS --
-- HOW LONG HAVE YOU BEEN AT THE SOUTH POLE?
ER -- THE E-MAIL THERE WAS A BIT UNRELIABLE --
SKIP IT. LATER FOR THE LAME EXCUSES.
I KNOW WHY YOU'RE BACK. AND THAT'S WHY I'M HERE.
THE SUPERCOLLIDER'S FINALLY COOLED OFF. YOU'RE GOING DOWN THERE.
AND I'M GOING WITH YOU.
CARE TO DISCUSS IT OVER COFFEE?

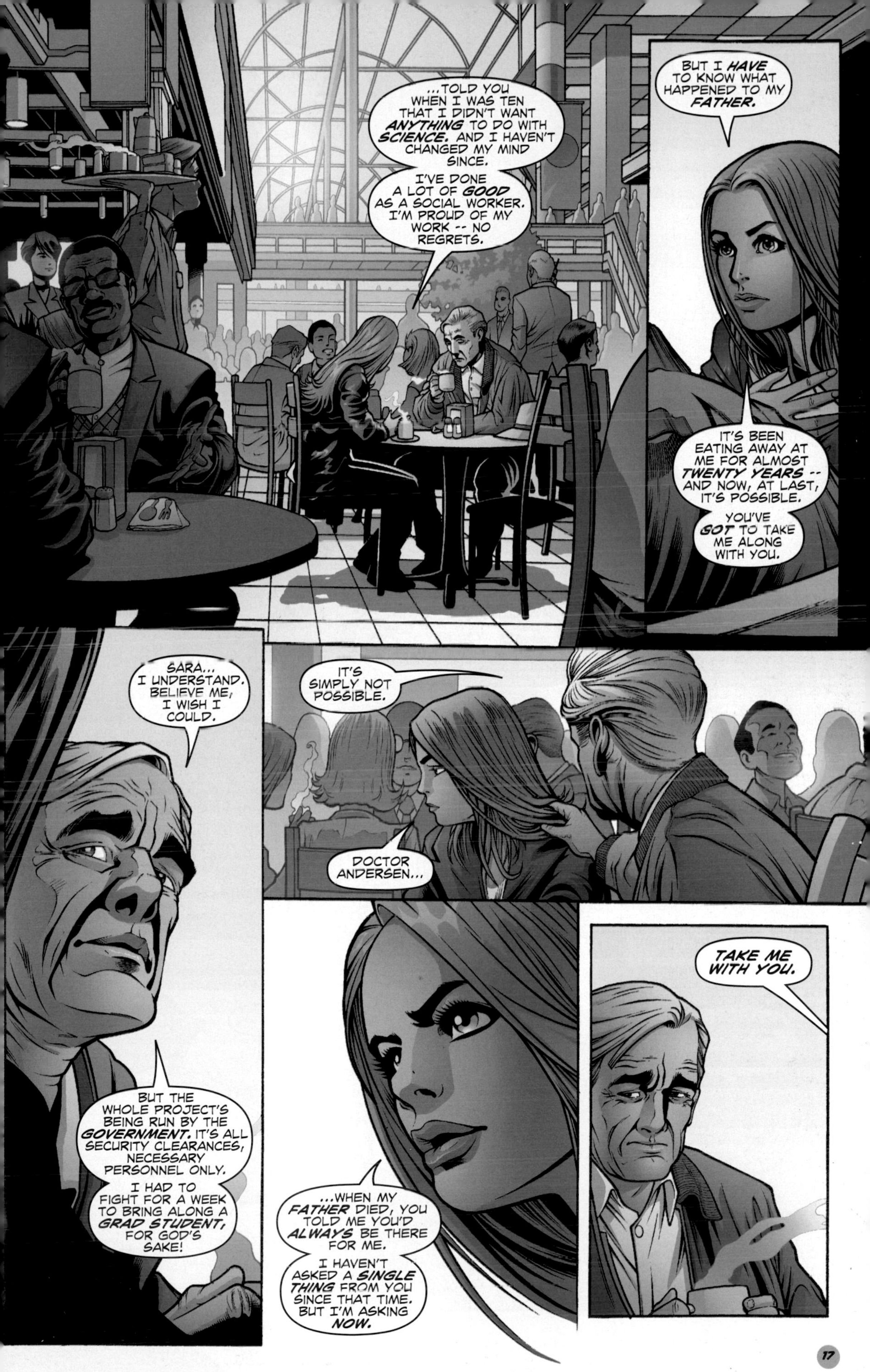
...TOLD YOU WHEN I WAS TEN THAT I DIDN'T WANT ANYTHING TO DO WITH SCIENCE. AND I HAVEN'T CHANGED MY MIND SINCE.
I'VE DONE A LOT OF GOOD AS A SOCIAL WORKER. I'M PROUD OF MY WORK -- NO REGRETS.
BUT I HAVE TO KNOW WHAT HAPPENED TO MY FATHER.
IT'S BEEN EATING AWAY AT ME FOR ALMOST TWENTY YEARS -- AND NOW, AT LAST, IT'S POSSIBLE.
YOU'VE GOT TO TAKE ME ALONG WITH YOU.
SARA... I UNDERSTAND. BELIEVE ME, I WISH I COULD.
BUT THE WHOLE PROJECT'S BEING RUN BY THE GOVERNMENT. IT'S ALL SECURITY CLEARANCES, NECESSARY PERSONNEL ONLY.
I HAD TO FIGHT FOR A WEEK TO BRING ALONG A GRAD STUDENT, FOR GOD'S SAKE!
IT'S SIMPLY NOT POSSIBLE.
DOCTOR ANDERSEN...
...WHEN MY FATHER DIED, YOU TOLD ME YOU'D ALWAYS BE THERE FOR ME.
I HAVEN'T ASKED A SINGLE THING FROM YOU SINCE THAT TIME. BUT I'M ASKING NOW.
TAKE ME WITH YOU.

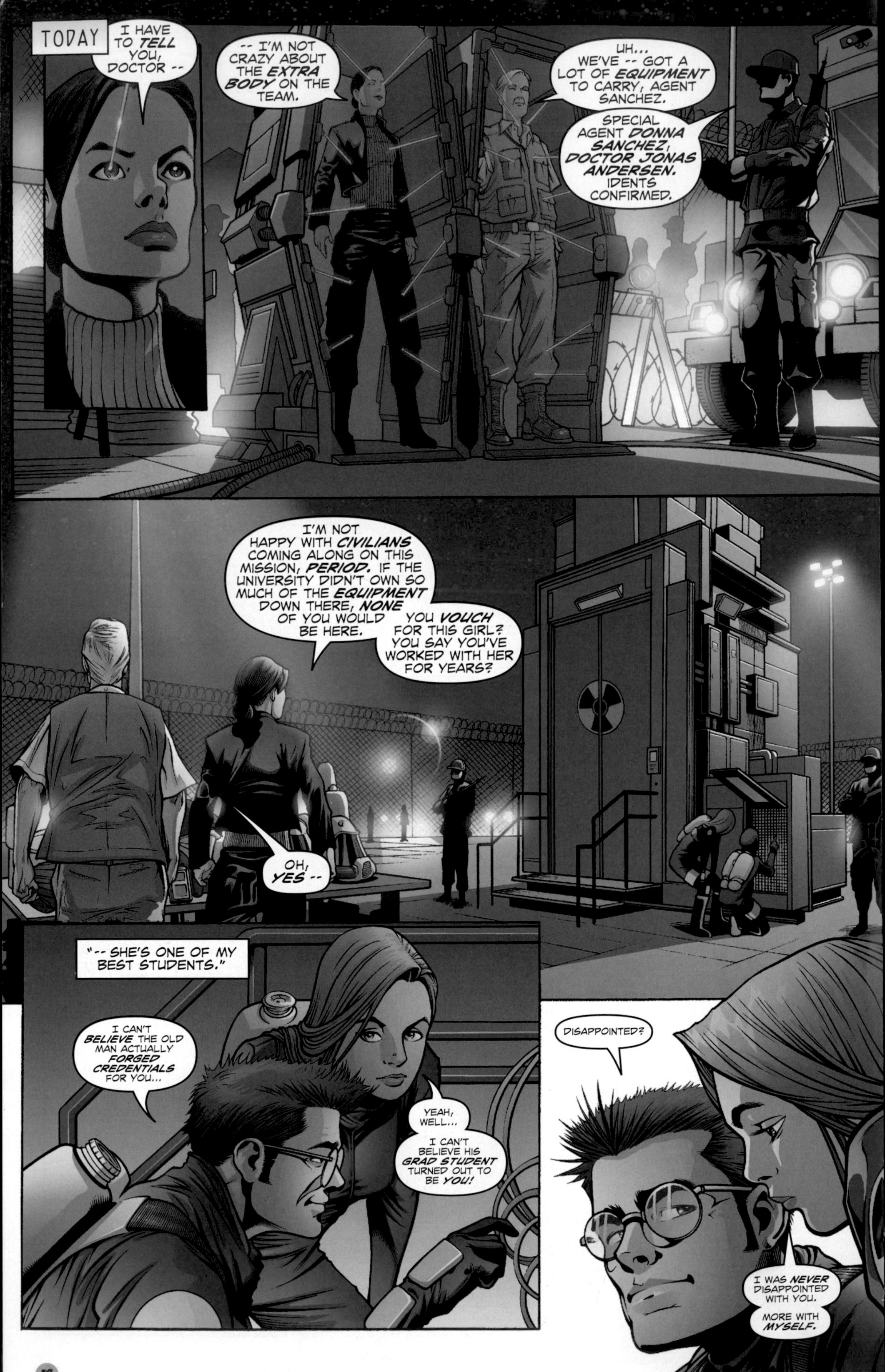
TODAY
I HAVE TO TELL YOU, DOCTOR --
-- I'M NOT CRAZY ABOUT THE EXTRA BODY ON THE TEAM.
UH... WE'VE -- GOT A LOT OF EQUIPMENT TO CARRY, AGENT SANCHEZ.
SPECIAL AGENT DONNA SANCHEZ, DOCTOR JONAS ANDERSEN. IDENTS CONFIRMED.
I'M NOT HAPPY WITH CIVILIANS COMING ALONG ON THIS MISSION, PERIOD. IF THE UNIVERSITY DIDN'T OWN SO MUCH OF THE EQUIPMENT DOWN THERE, NONE OF YOU WOULD BE HERE.
YOU VOUCH FOR THIS GIRL? YOU SAY YOU'VE WORKED WITH HER FOR YEARS?
OH, YES --
"-- SHE'S ONE OF MY BEST STUDENTS."
I CAN'T BELIEVE THE OLD MAN ACTUALLY FORGED CREDENTIALS FOR YOU...
YEAH, WELL... I CAN'T BELIEVE HIS GRAD STUDENT TURNED OUT TO BE YOU!
DISAPPOINTED?
I WAS NEVER DISAPPOINTED WITH YOU. MORE WITH MYSELF.

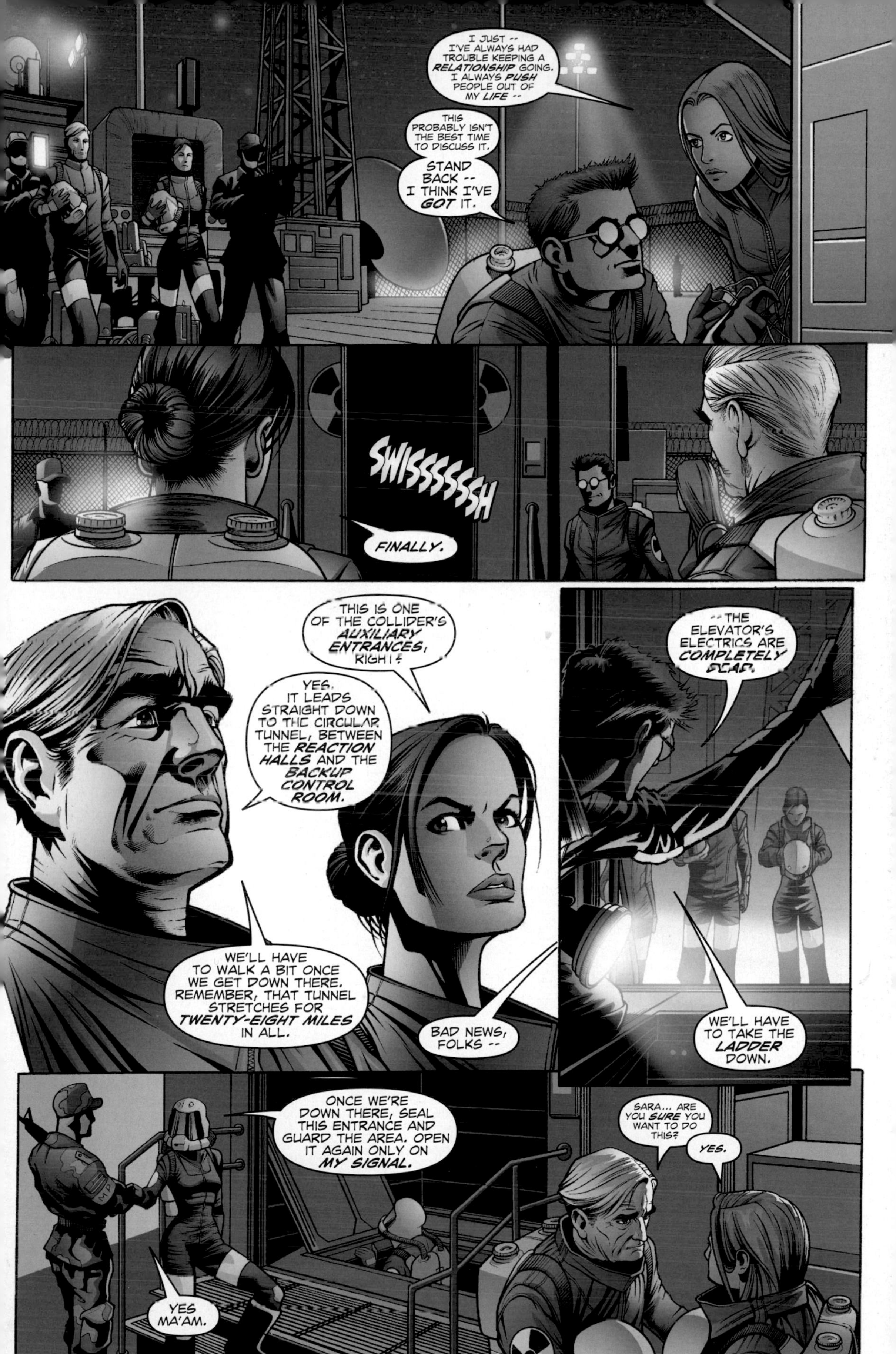
I JUST -- I'VE ALWAYS HAD TROUBLE KEEPING A RELATIONSHIP GOING. I ALWAYS PUSH PEOPLE OUT OF MY LIFE --
THIS PROBABLY ISN'T THE BEST TIME TO DISCUSS IT.
STAND BACK -- I THINK I'VE GOT IT.
SWISSSSSSSH
FINALLY.
THIS IS ONE OF THE COLLIDER'S AUXILIARY ENTRANCES, RIGHT?
YES. IT LEADS STRAIGHT DOWN TO THE CIRCULAR TUNNEL, BETWEEN THE REACTION HALLS AND THE BACKUP CONTROL ROOM.
WE'LL HAVE TO WALK A BIT ONCE WE GET DOWN THERE. REMEMBER, THAT TUNNEL STRETCHES FOR TWENTY-EIGHT MILES IN ALL.
BAD NEWS, FOLKS --
-- THE ELEVATOR'S ELECTRICS ARE COMPLETELY DEAD.
WE'LL HAVE TO TAKE THE LADDER DOWN.
ONCE WE'RE DOWN THERE, SEAL THIS ENTRANCE AND GUARD THE AREA. OPEN IT AGAIN ONLY ON MY SIGNAL.
YES MA'AM.
SARA... ARE YOU SURE YOU WANT TO DO THIS?
YES.

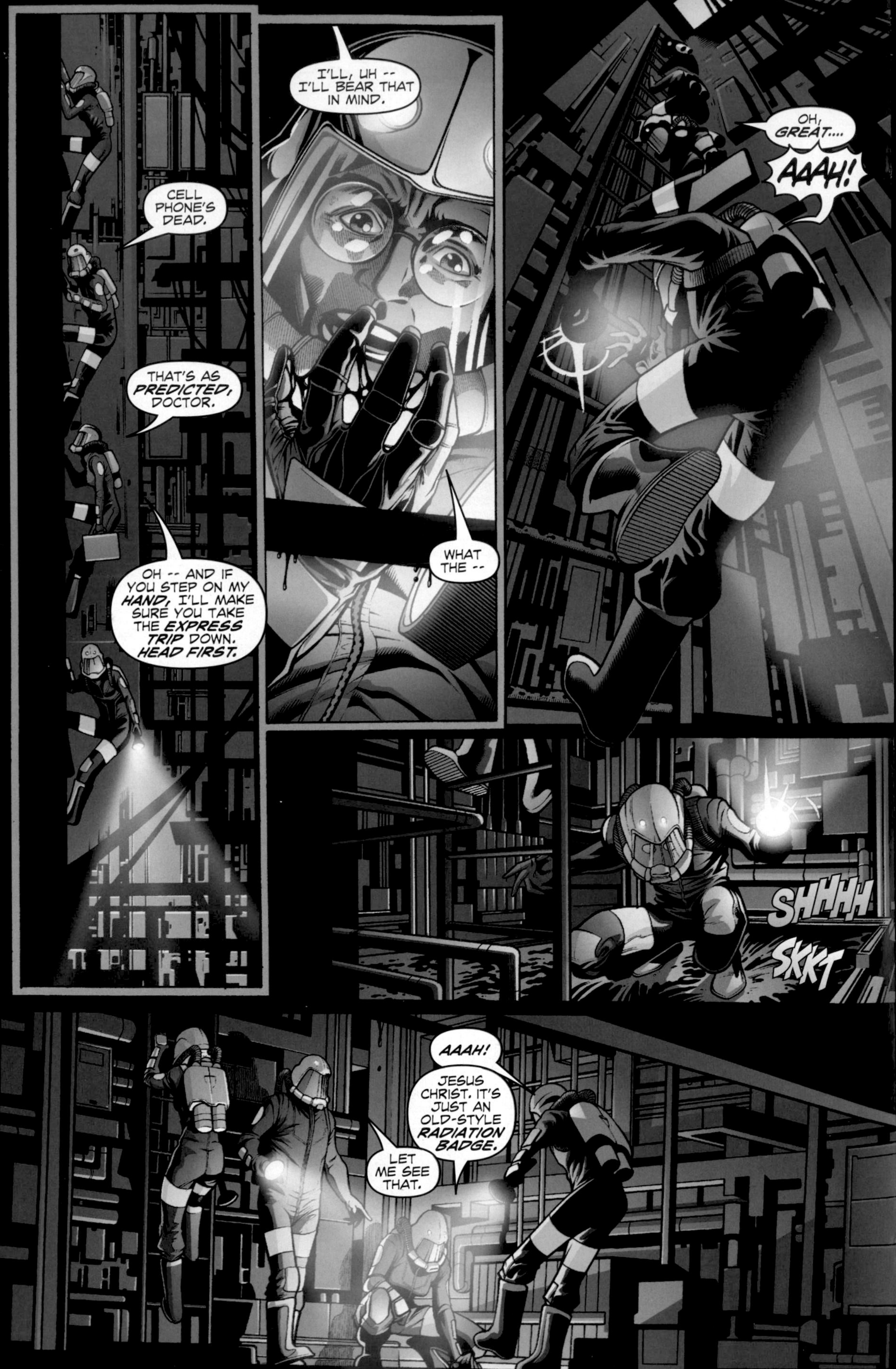
CELL PHONE'S DEAD.
THAT'S AS *PREDICTED,* DOCTOR.
OH -- AND IF YOU STEP ON MY *HAND,* I'LL MAKE SURE YOU TAKE THE *EXPRESS TRIP* DOWN. *HEAD FIRST.*
I'LL, UH -- I'LL BEAR THAT IN MIND.
WHAT THE --
OH, *GREAT....*
AAAH!
SHHHH
SKKT
AAAH!
JESUS CHRIST. IT'S JUST AN OLD-STYLE *RADIATION BADGE.*
LET ME SEE THAT.

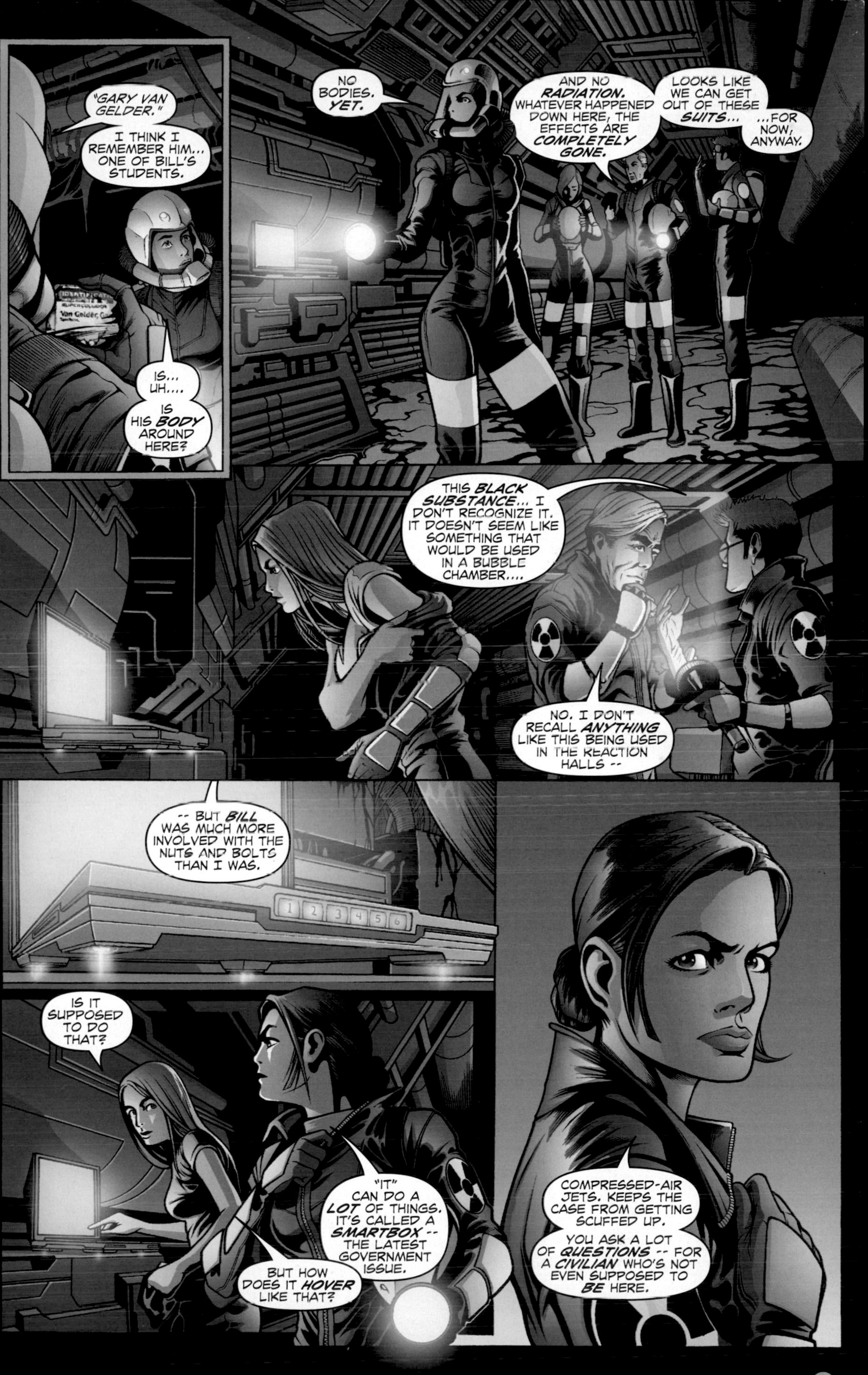
"GARY VAN GELDER."
I THINK I REMEMBER HIM... ONE OF BILL'S STUDENTS.
IDENTIFICATION
SUPERCOLLIDER
Van Gelder, G.
IS... UH.... IS HIS BODY AROUND HERE?
NO BODIES. YET.
AND NO RADIATION. WHATEVER HAPPENED DOWN HERE, THE EFFECTS ARE COMPLETELY GONE.
LOOKS LIKE WE CAN GET OUT OF THESE SUITS...
...FOR NOW, ANYWAY.
THIS BLACK SUBSTANCE... I DON'T RECOGNIZE IT. IT DOESN'T SEEM LIKE SOMETHING THAT WOULD BE USED IN A BUBBLE CHAMBER....
NO. I DON'T RECALL ANYTHING LIKE THIS BEING USED IN THE REACTION HALLS --
-- BUT BILL WAS MUCH MORE INVOLVED WITH THE NUTS AND BOLTS THAN I WAS.
1 2 3 4 5 6
IS IT SUPPOSED TO DO THAT?
"IT" CAN DO A LOT OF THINGS. IT'S CALLED A SMARTBOX -- THE LATEST GOVERNMENT ISSUE.
BUT HOW DOES IT HOVER LIKE THAT?
COMPRESSED-AIR JETS. KEEPS THE CASE FROM GETTING SCUFFED UP.
YOU ASK A LOT OF QUESTIONS -- FOR A CIVILIAN WHO'S NOT EVEN SUPPOSED TO BE HERE.

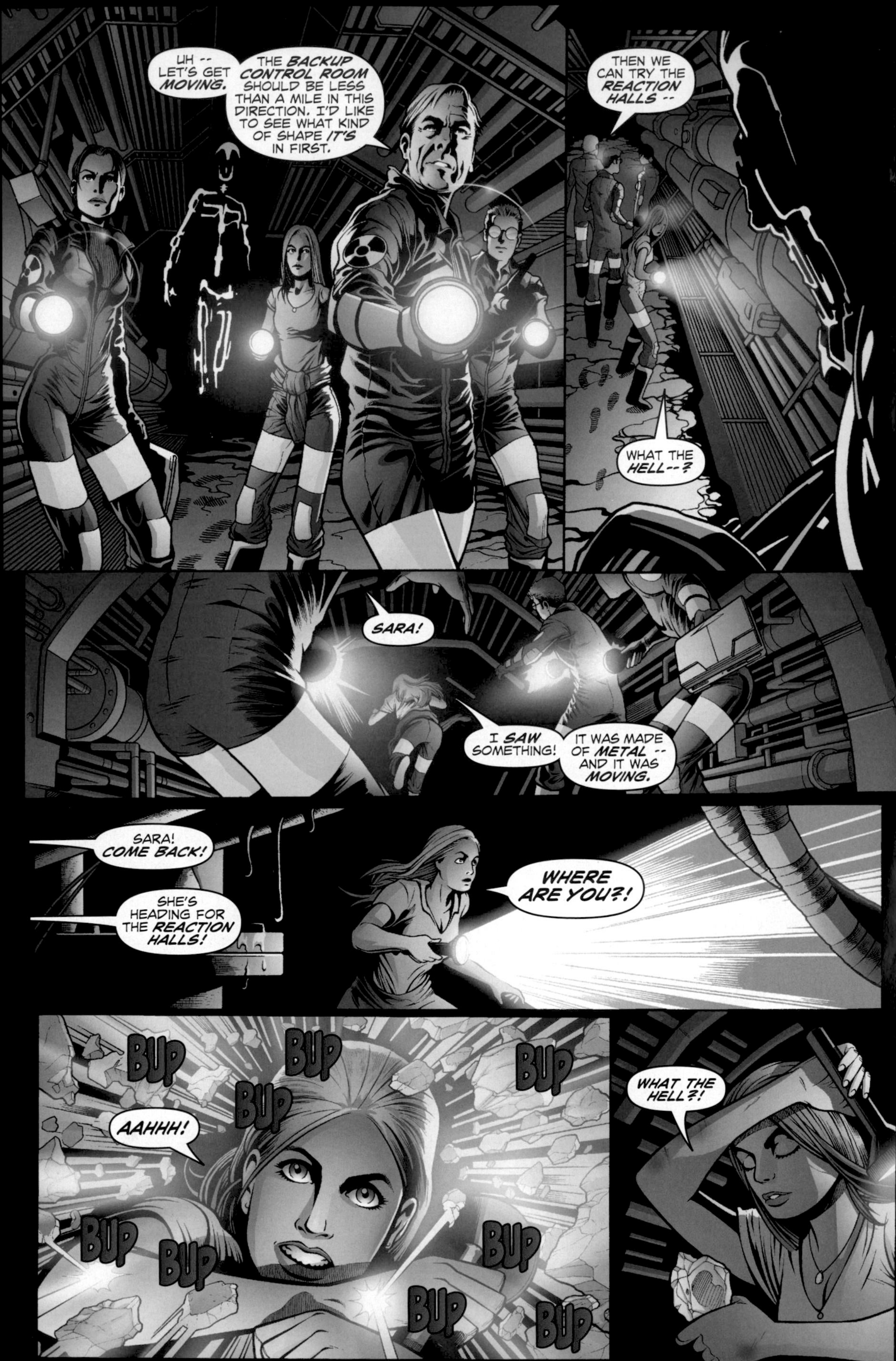
UH -- LET'S GET MOVING.
THE BACKUP CONTROL ROOM SHOULD BE LESS THAN A MILE IN THIS DIRECTION. I'D LIKE TO SEE WHAT KIND OF SHAPE IT'S IN FIRST.
THEN WE CAN TRY THE REACTION HALLS --
WHAT THE HELL--?
SARA!
I SAW SOMETHING!
IT WAS MADE OF METAL -- AND IT WAS MOVING.
SARA! COME BACK!
SHE'S HEADING FOR THE REACTION HALLS!
WHERE ARE YOU?!
BUP
BUP
BUP
BUP
AAHHH!
BUP
BUP
BUP
BUP
BUP
WHAT THE HELL?!

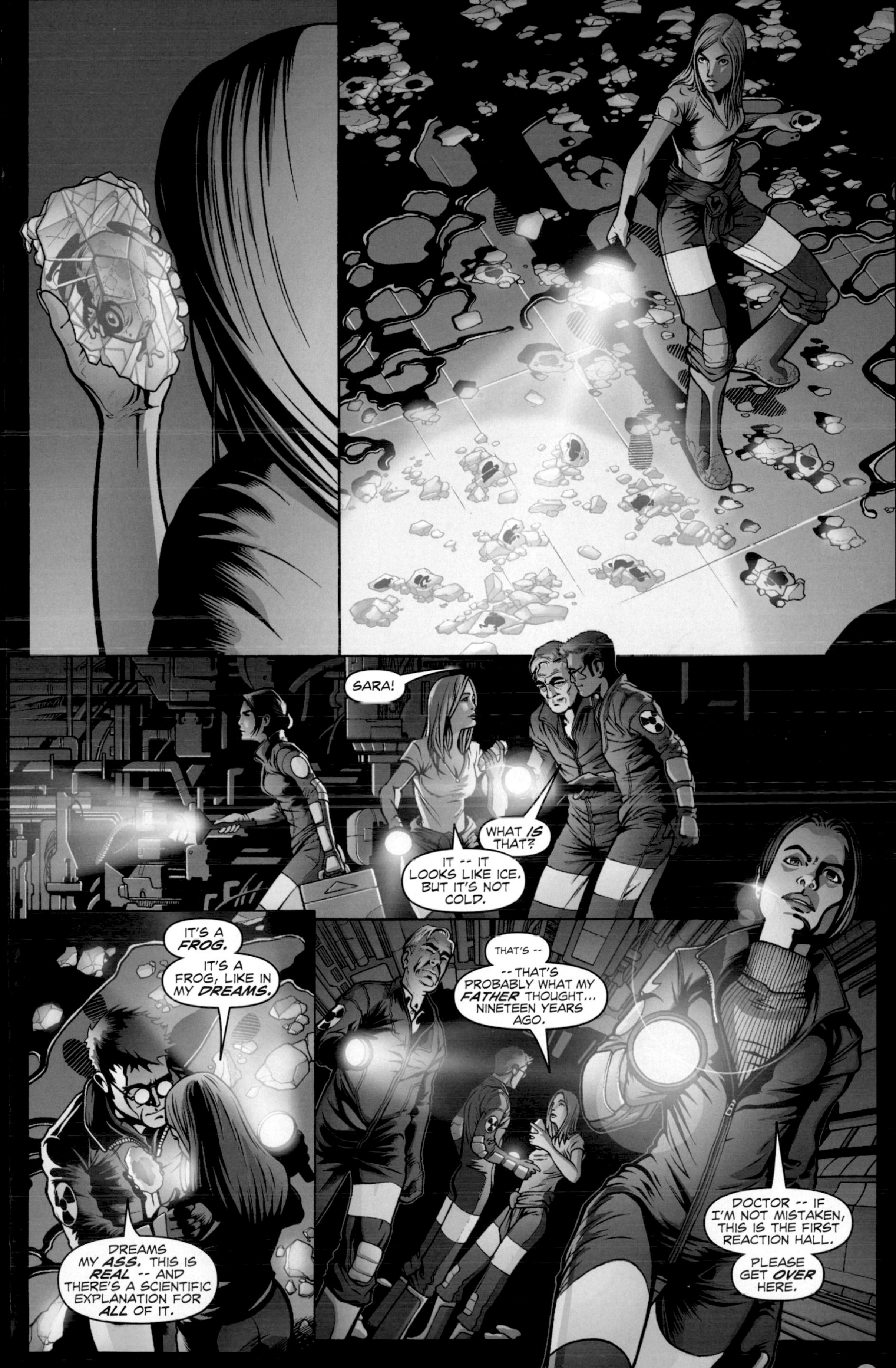
SARA!
WHAT *IS* THAT?
IT -- IT LOOKS LIKE ICE. BUT IT'S NOT COLD.
IT'S A *FROG.*
IT'S A FROG, LIKE IN MY *DREAMS.*
DREAMS MY *ASS.* THIS IS *REAL* -- AND THERE'S A SCIENTIFIC EXPLANATION FOR *ALL* OF IT.
THAT'S --
-- THAT'S PROBABLY WHAT MY *FATHER* THOUGHT... NINETEEN YEARS AGO.
DOCTOR -- IF I'M NOT MISTAKEN, THIS IS THE FIRST REACTION HALL.
PLEASE GET *OVER* HERE.

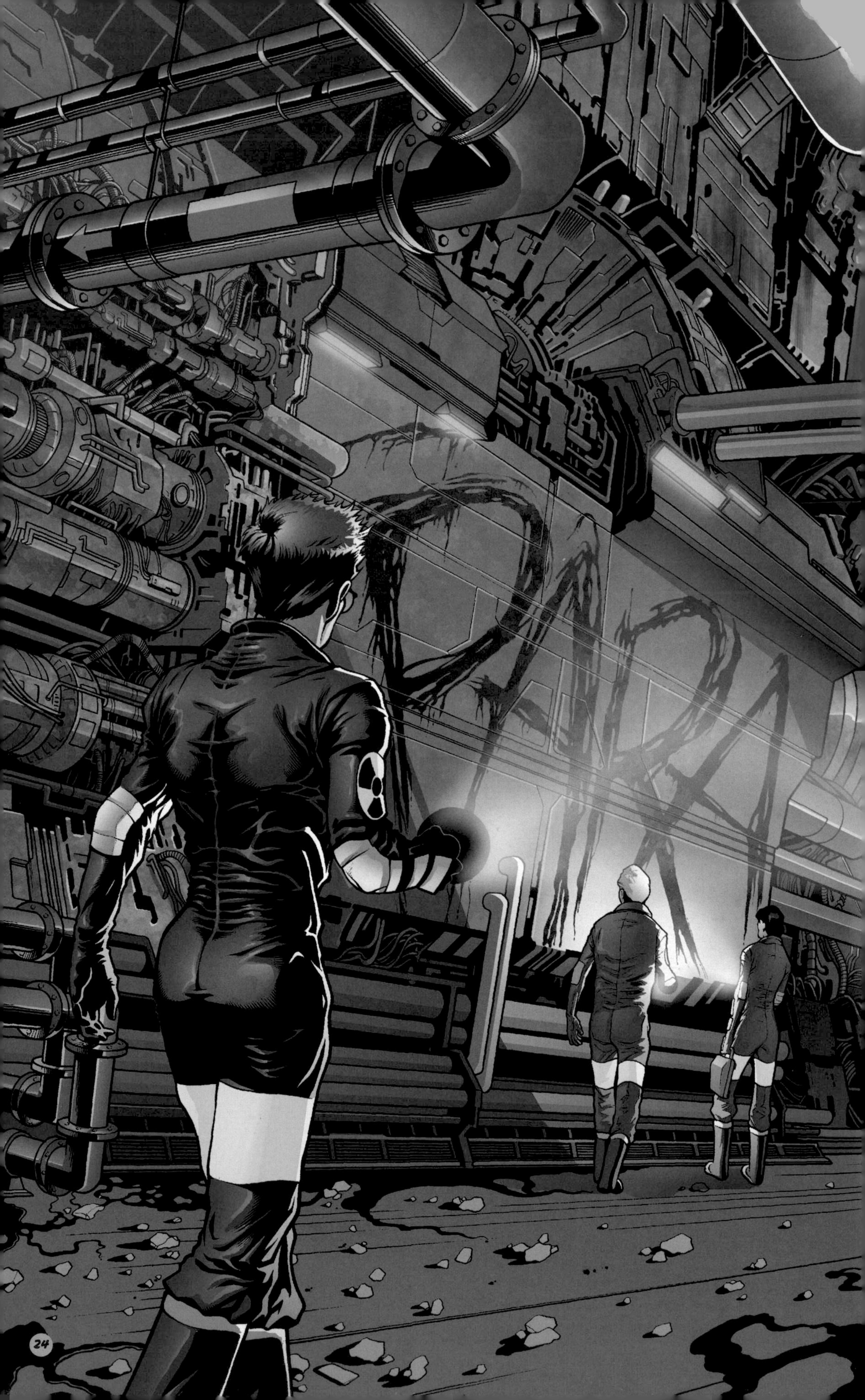

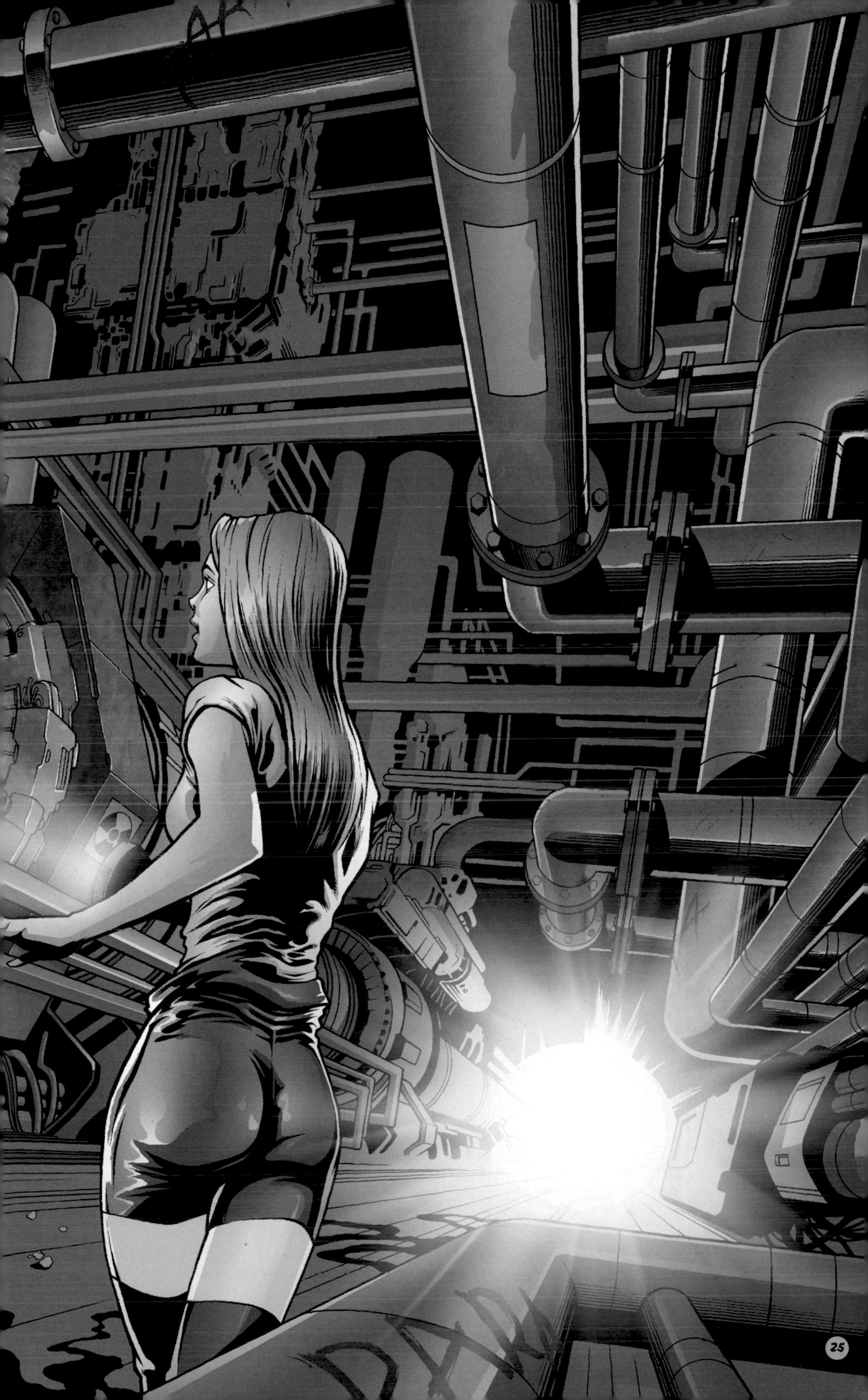

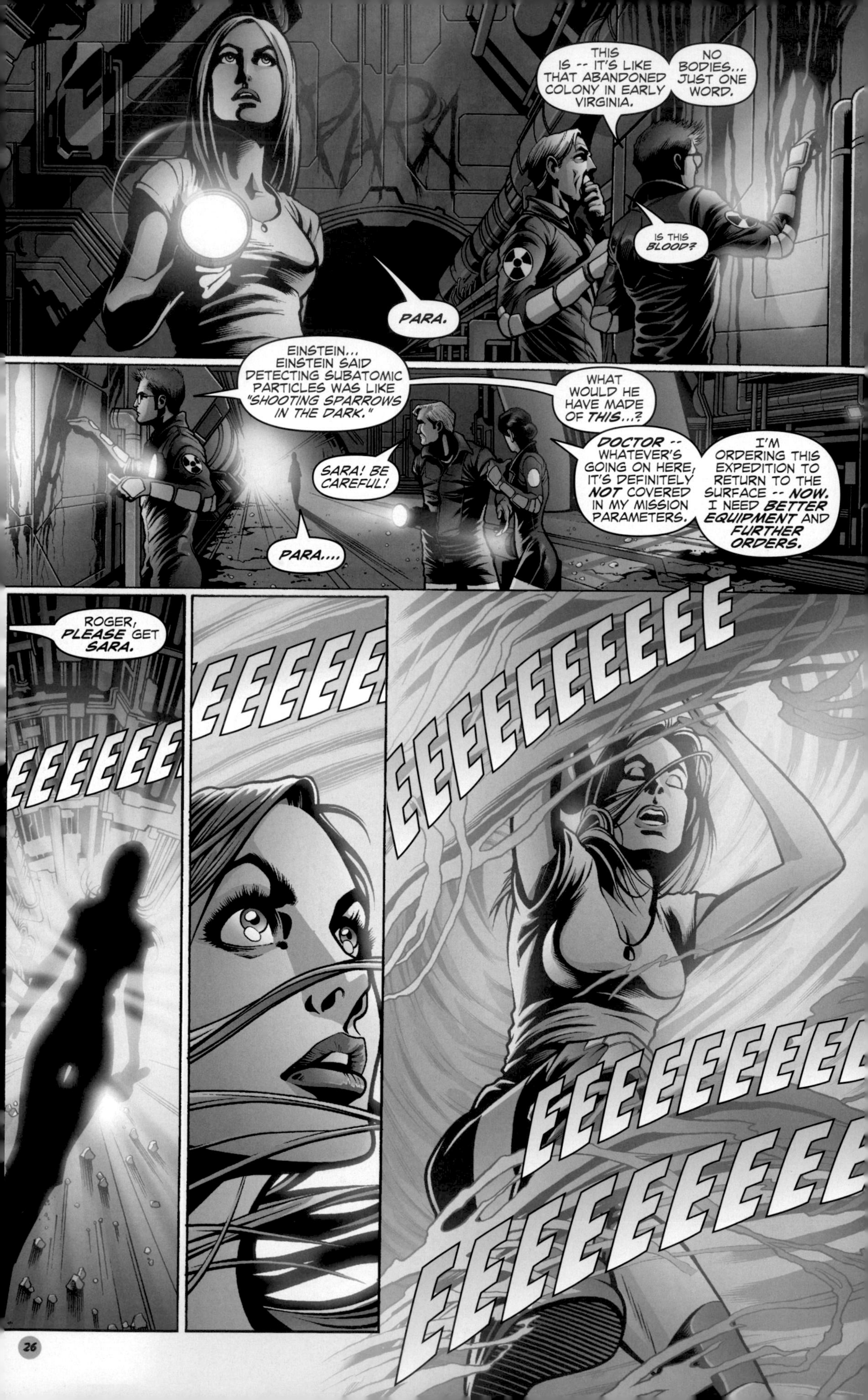
THIS IS -- IT'S LIKE THAT ABANDONED COLONY IN EARLY VIRGINIA.
NO BODIES... JUST ONE WORD.
IS THIS BLOOD?
PARA.
EINSTEIN... EINSTEIN SAID DETECTING SUBATOMIC PARTICLES WAS LIKE "SHOOTING SPARROWS IN THE DARK."
WHAT WOULD HE HAVE MADE OF THIS...?
SARA! BE CAREFUL!
PARA....
DOCTOR -- WHATEVER'S GOING ON HERE, IT'S DEFINITELY NOT COVERED IN MY MISSION PARAMETERS.
I'M ORDERING THIS EXPEDITION TO RETURN TO THE SURFACE -- NOW. I NEED BETTER EQUIPMENT AND FURTHER ORDERS.
ROGER, PLEASE GET SARA.
EEEEEEEEEEEEEEEEEEEEEEEEEEEEEEEEEEEEEEEEEEEEEEEEE

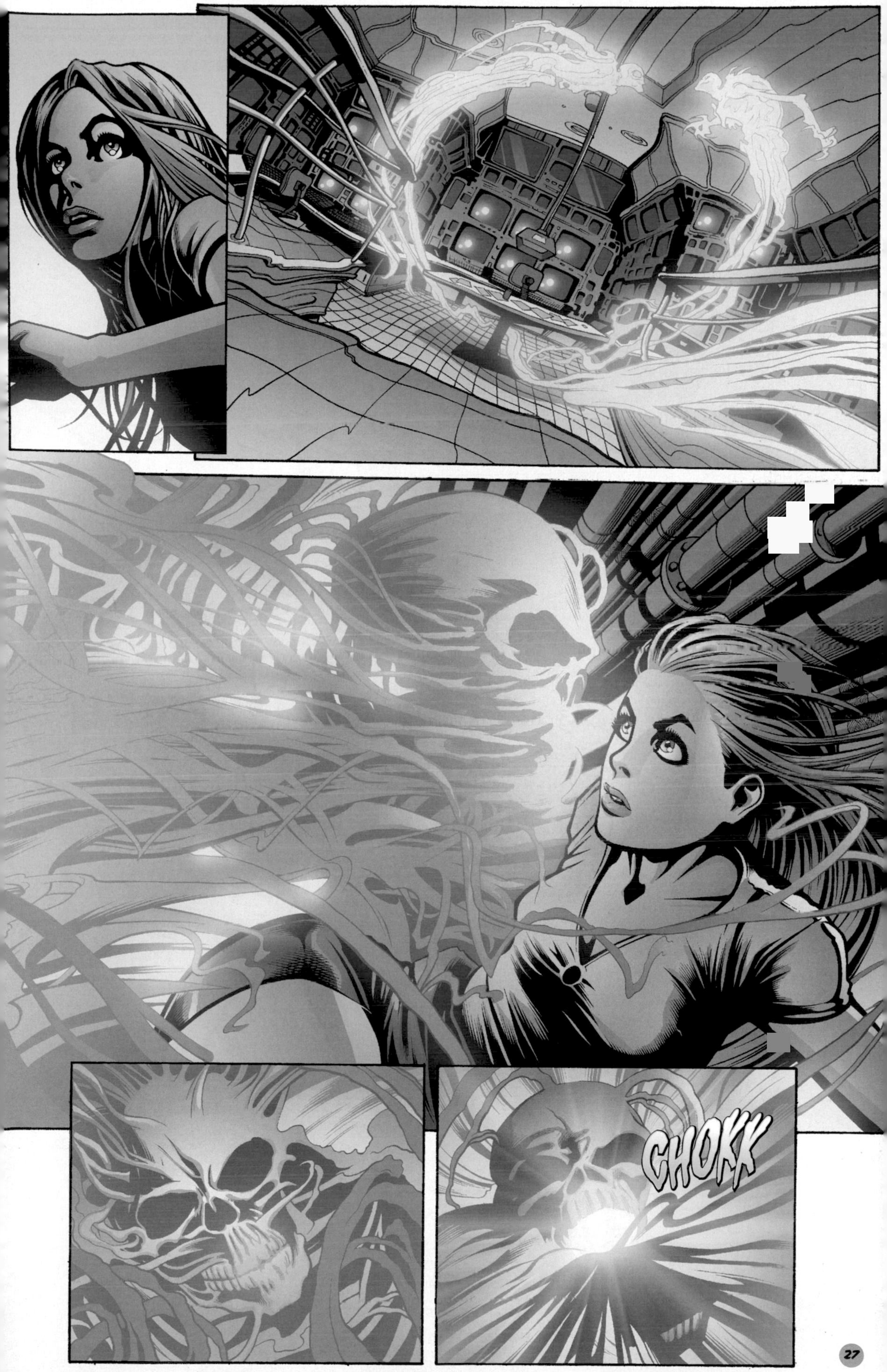
CHOKK

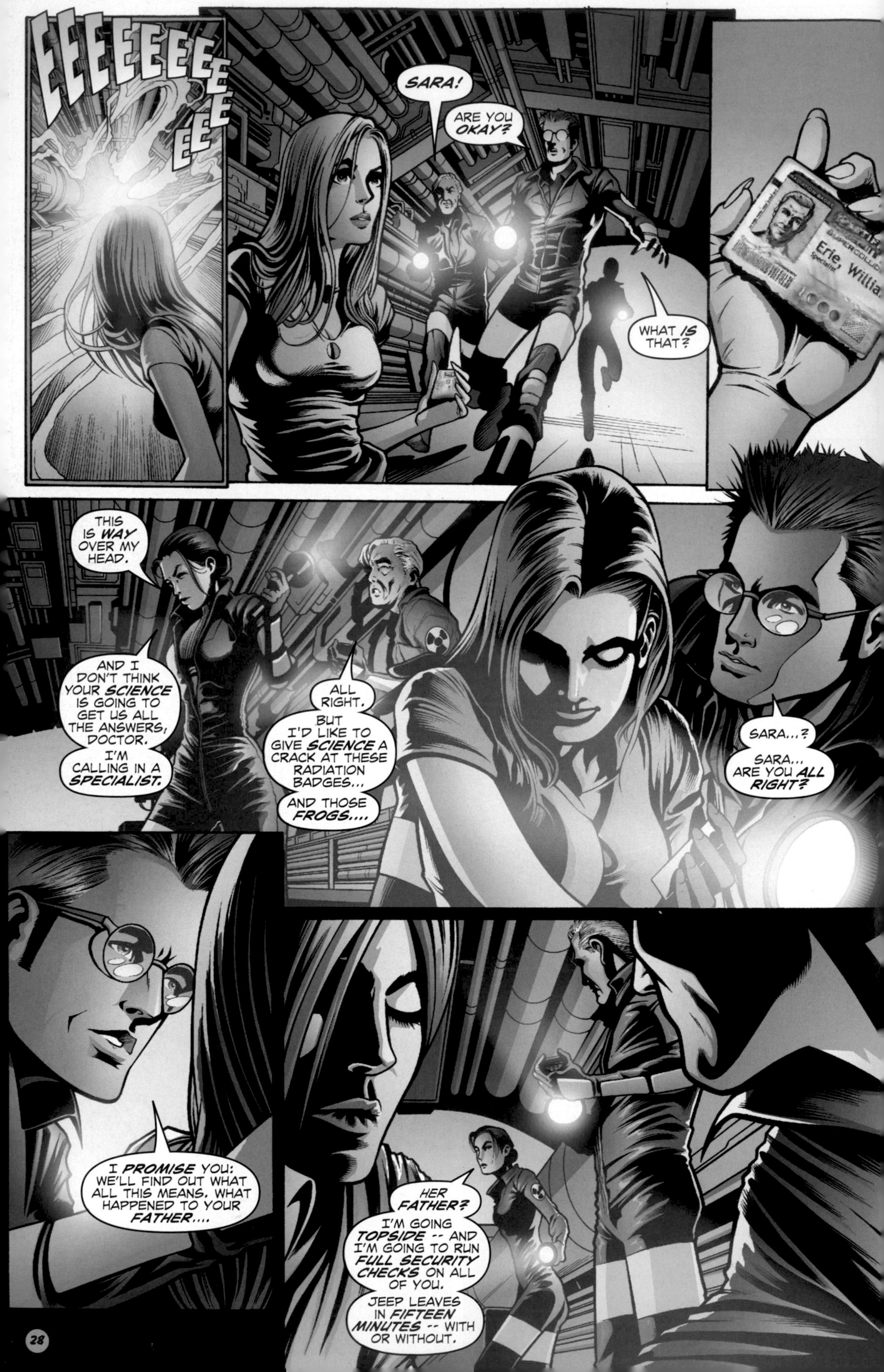
EEEEEEEEEEE
SARA!
ARE YOU OKAY?
WHAT IS THAT?
RADIATION BADGE
SUPERCOLLI
Erie, Willia
Specialist
THIS IS WAY OVER MY HEAD.
AND I DON'T THINK YOUR SCIENCE IS GOING TO GET US ALL THE ANSWERS, DOCTOR.
I'M CALLING IN A SPECIALIST.
ALL RIGHT.
BUT I'D LIKE TO GIVE SCIENCE A CRACK AT THESE RADIATION BADGES...
AND THOSE FROGS....
SARA...?
SARA... ARE YOU ALL RIGHT?
I PROMISE YOU: WE'LL FIND OUT WHAT ALL THIS MEANS. WHAT HAPPENED TO YOUR FATHER....
HER FATHER?
I'M GOING TOPSIDE -- AND I'M GOING TO RUN FULL SECURITY CHECKS ON ALL OF YOU.
JEEP LEAVES IN FIFTEEN MINUTES -- WITH OR WITHOUT.

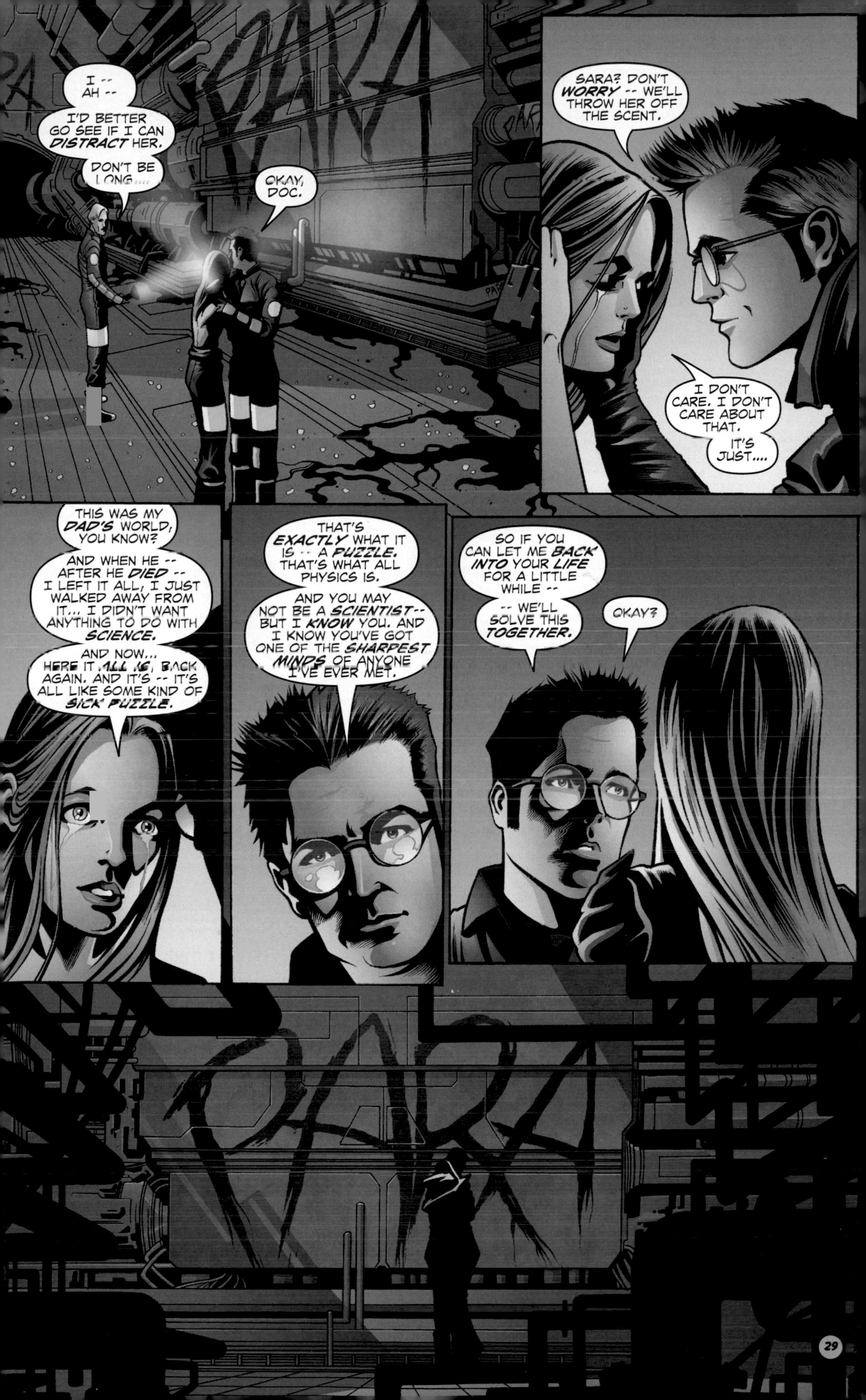

I -- AH --
I'D BETTER GO SEE IF I CAN DISTRACT HER.
DON'T BE LONG....
OKAY, DOC.
SARA? DON'T WORRY -- WE'LL THROW HER OFF THE SCENT.
I DON'T CARE. I DON'T CARE ABOUT THAT.
IT'S JUST....
THIS WAS MY DAD'S WORLD, YOU KNOW?
AND WHEN HE -- AFTER HE DIED -- I LEFT IT ALL, I JUST WALKED AWAY FROM IT... I DIDN'T WANT ANYTHING TO DO WITH SCIENCE.
AND NOW... HERE IT ALL IS, BACK AGAIN. AND IT'S -- IT'S ALL LIKE SOME KIND OF SICK PUZZLE.
THAT'S EXACTLY WHAT IT IS -- A PUZZLE. THAT'S WHAT ALL PHYSICS IS.
AND YOU MAY NOT BE A SCIENTIST -- BUT I KNOW YOU. AND I KNOW YOU'VE GOT ONE OF THE SHARPEST MINDS OF ANYONE I'VE EVER MET.
SO IF YOU CAN LET ME BACK INTO YOUR LIFE FOR A LITTLE WHILE --
-- WE'LL SOLVE THIS TOGETHER.
OKAY?

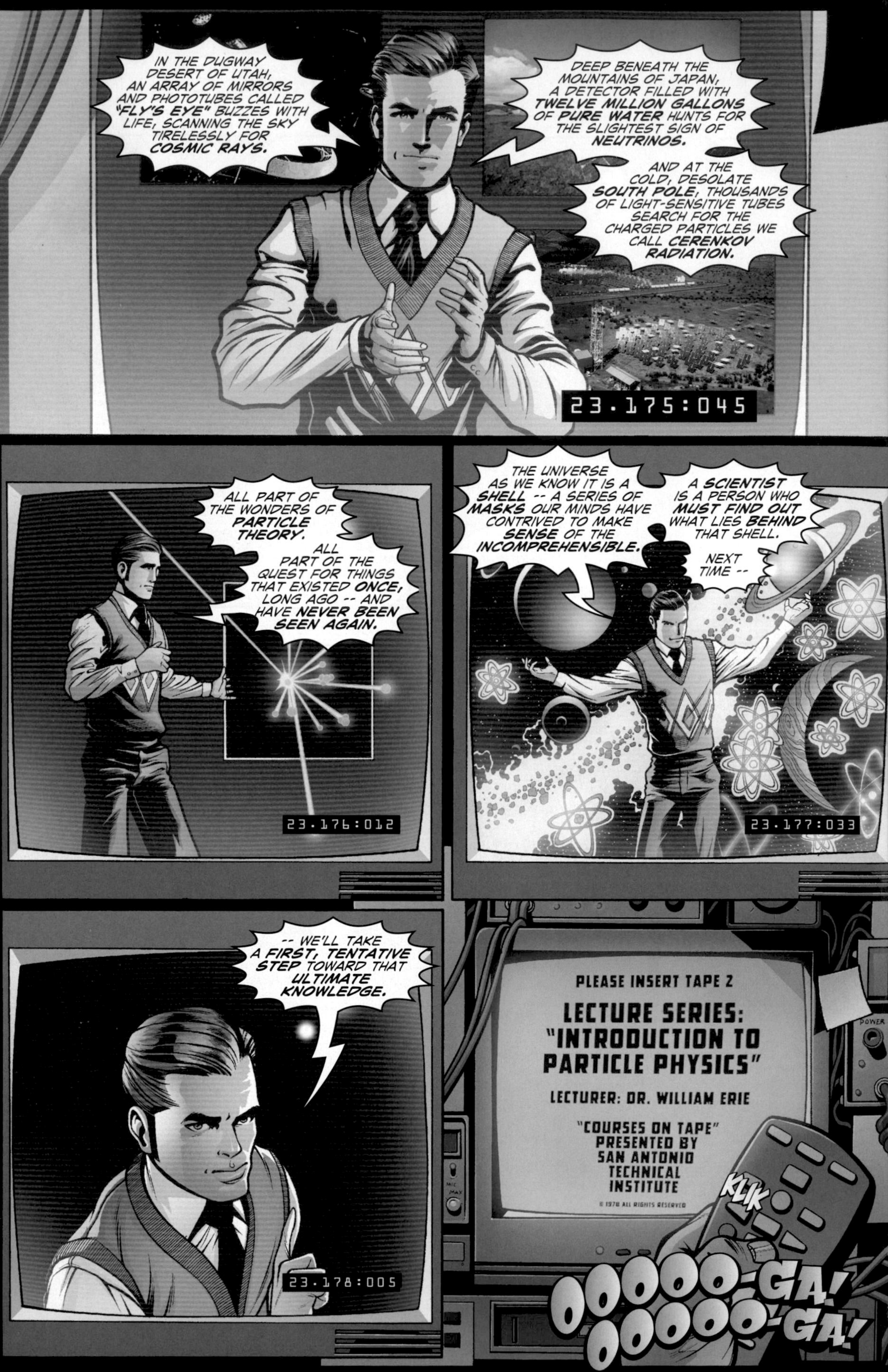
IN THE DUGWAY DESERT OF UTAH, AN ARRAY OF MIRRORS AND PHOTOTUBES CALLED "FLY'S EYE" BUZZES WITH LIFE, SCANNING THE SKY TIRELESSLY FOR COSMIC RAYS.
DEEP BENEATH THE MOUNTAINS OF JAPAN, A DETECTOR FILLED WITH TWELVE MILLION GALLONS OF PURE WATER HUNTS FOR THE SLIGHTEST SIGN OF NEUTRINOS.
AND AT THE COLD, DESOLATE SOUTH POLE, THOUSANDS OF LIGHT-SENSITIVE TUBES SEARCH FOR THE CHARGED PARTICLES WE CALL CERENKOV RADIATION.
23.175:045
ALL PART OF THE WONDERS OF PARTICLE THEORY.
ALL PART OF THE QUEST FOR THINGS THAT EXISTED ONCE, LONG AGO -- AND HAVE NEVER BEEN SEEN AGAIN.
23.176:012
THE UNIVERSE AS WE KNOW IT IS A SHELL -- A SERIES OF MASKS OUR MINDS HAVE CONTRIVED TO MAKE SENSE OF THE INCOMPREHENSIBLE.
A SCIENTIST IS A PERSON WHO MUST FIND OUT WHAT LIES BEHIND THAT SHELL.
NEXT TIME --
23.177:033
-- WE'LL TAKE A FIRST, TENTATIVE STEP TOWARD THAT ULTIMATE KNOWLEDGE.
23.178:005
PLEASE INSERT TAPE 2
LECTURE SERIES: "INTRODUCTION TO PARTICLE PHYSICS"
LECTURER: DR. WILLIAM ERIE
"COURSES ON TAPE" PRESENTED BY SAN ANTONIO TECHNICAL INSTITUTE
© 1978 ALL RIGHTS RESERVED
POWER
KLIK
OOOOO-GA! OOOOO-GA!

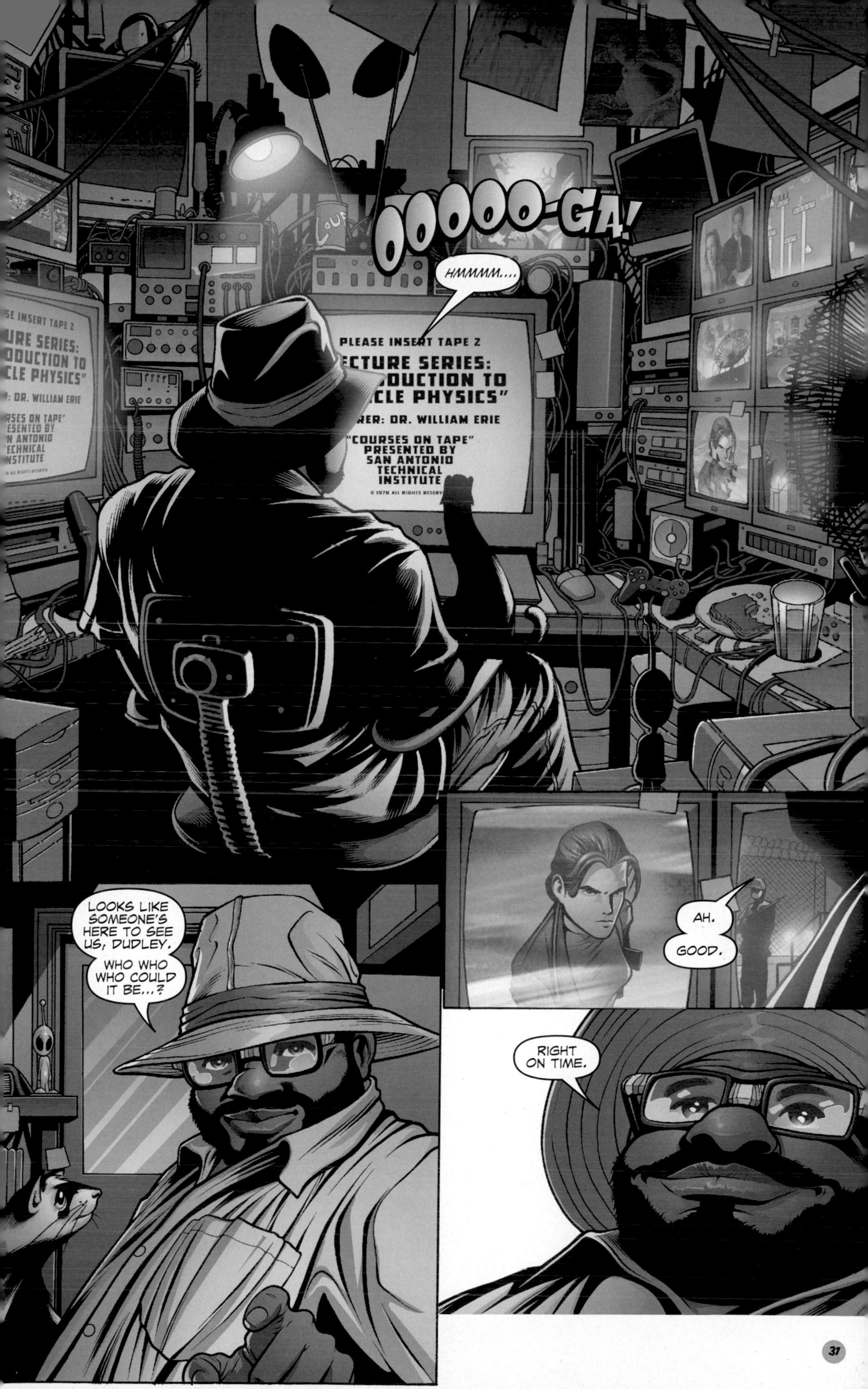
OOOOO-GA!
HMMMM....
PLEASE INSERT TAPE 2
LOOKS LIKE SOMEONE'S HERE TO SEE US, DUDLEY.
WHO WHO WHO COULD IT BE...?
AH.
GOOD.
RIGHT ON TIME.

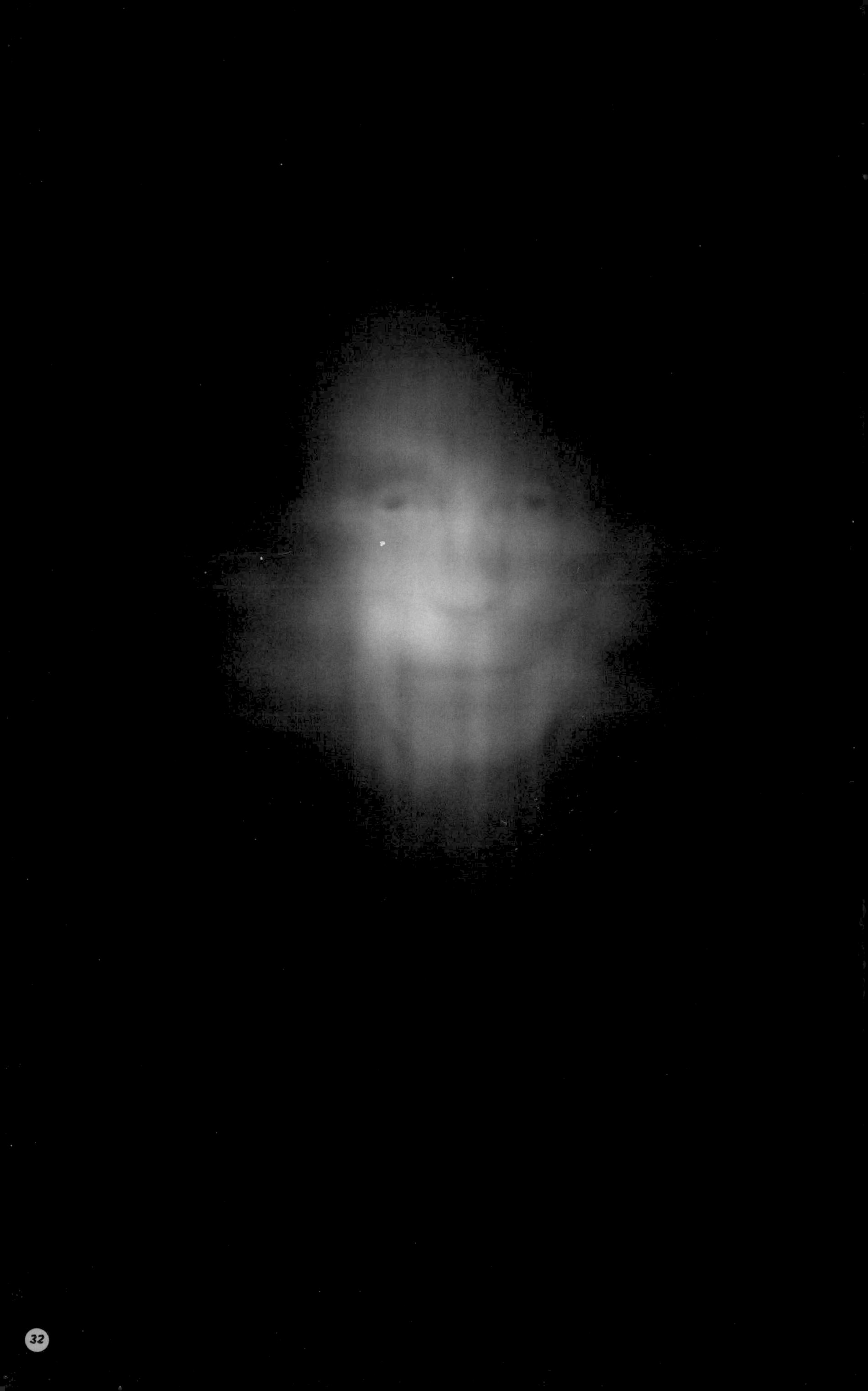

CHAPTER 2

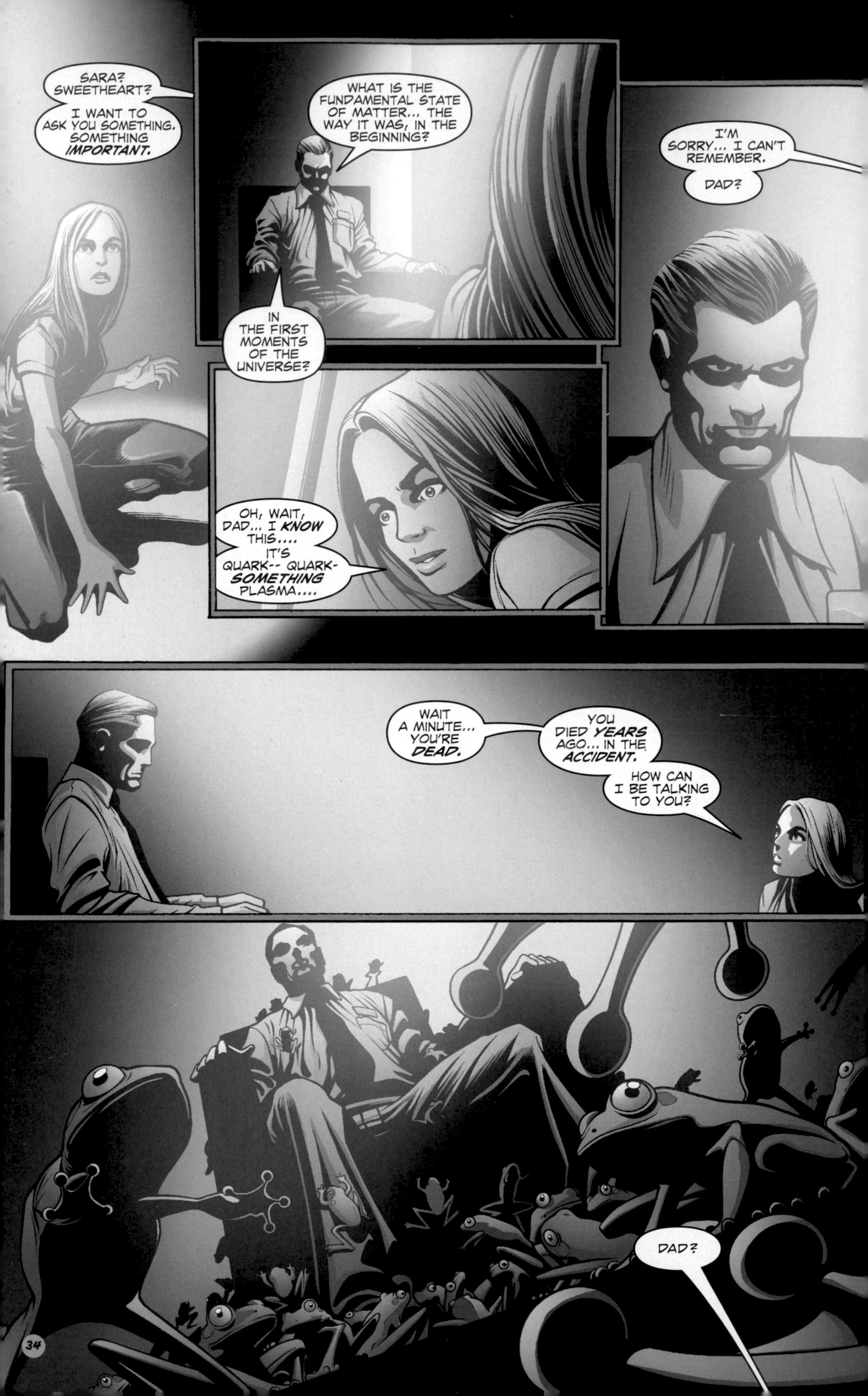
SARA? SWEETHEART?
I WANT TO ASK YOU SOMETHING. SOMETHING *IMPORTANT.*
WHAT IS THE FUNDAMENTAL STATE OF MATTER... THE WAY IT WAS, IN THE BEGINNING?
IN THE FIRST MOMENTS OF THE UNIVERSE?
OH, WAIT, DAD... I *KNOW* THIS.... IT'S QUARK-- QUARK-*SOMETHING* PLASMA....
I'M SORRY... I CAN'T REMEMBER.
DAD?
WAIT A MINUTE... YOU'RE *DEAD.*
YOU DIED *YEARS* AGO... IN THE *ACCIDENT.*
HOW CAN I BE TALKING TO YOU?
DAD?

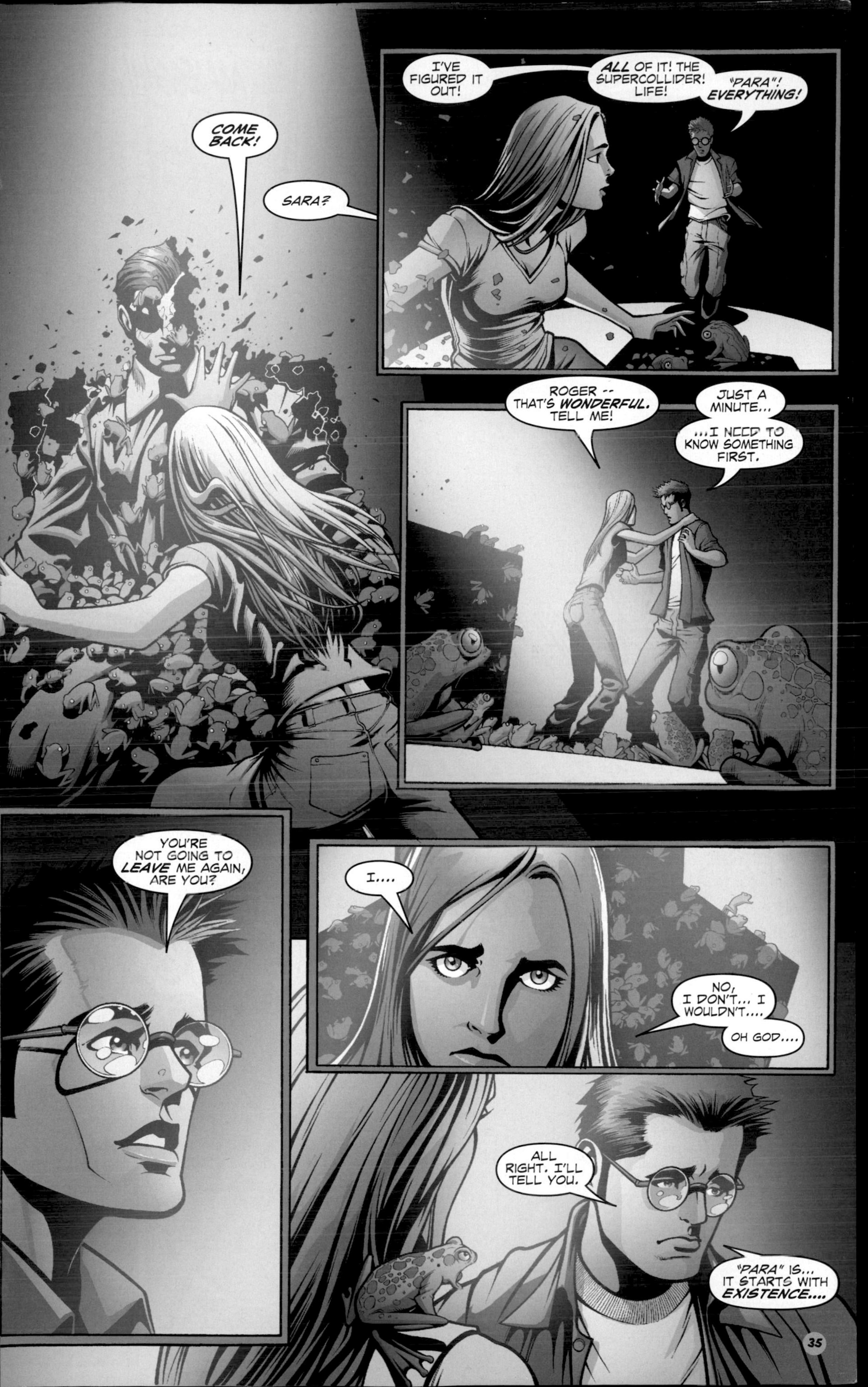
COME BACK!
SARA?
I'VE FIGURED IT OUT!
ALL OF IT! THE SUPERCOLLIDER! LIFE!
"PARA"! EVERYTHING!
ROGER -- THAT'S WONDERFUL. TELL ME!
JUST A MINUTE...
...I NEED TO KNOW SOMETHING FIRST.
YOU'RE NOT GOING TO LEAVE ME AGAIN, ARE YOU?
I....
NO, I DON'T... I WOULDN'T....
OH GOD....
ALL RIGHT. I'LL TELL YOU.
"PARA" IS... IT STARTS WITH EXISTENCE....

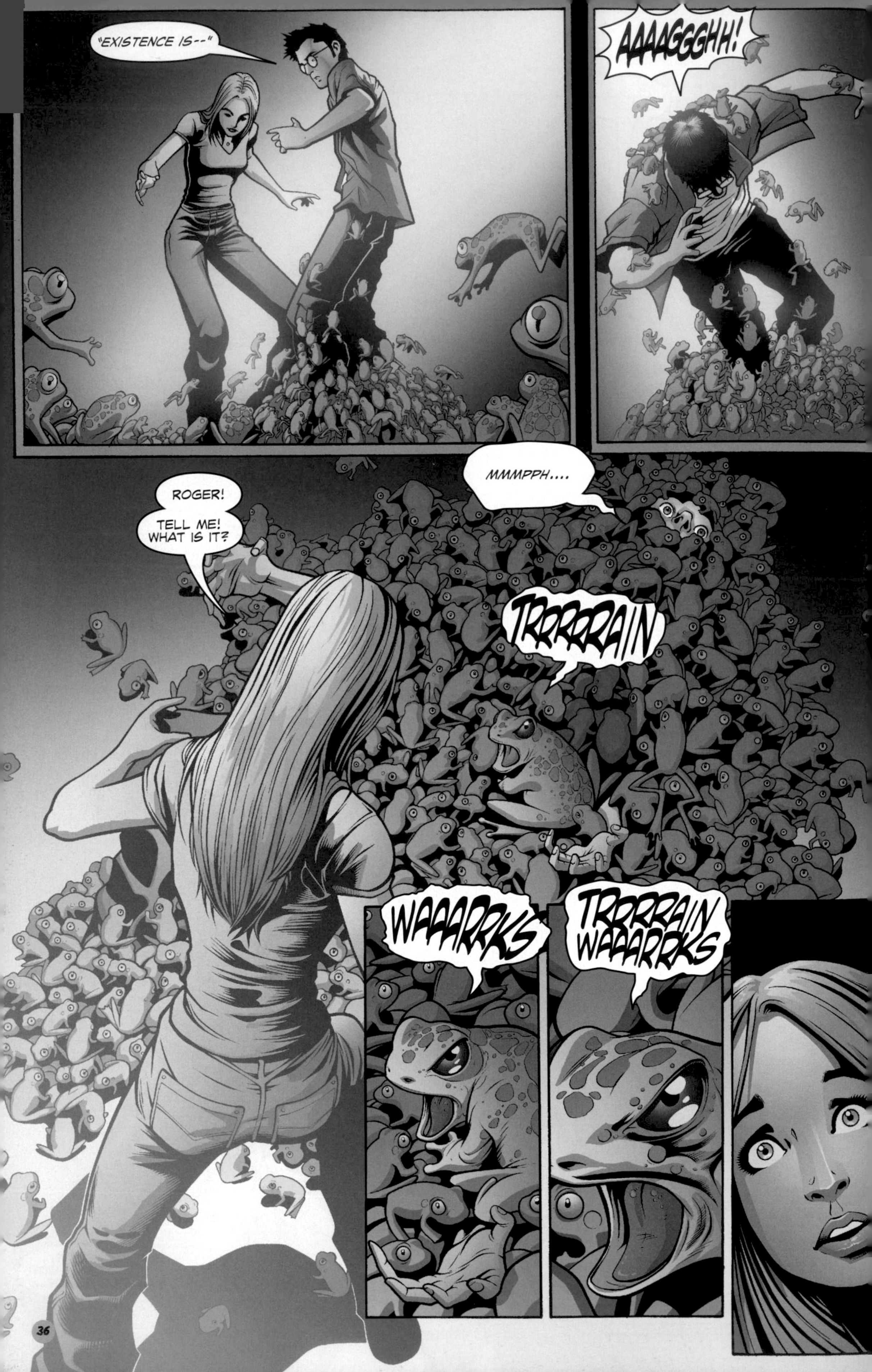
"EXISTENCE IS--"
AAAAGGGHH!
ROGER!
TELL ME! WHAT IS IT?
MMMPPH....
TRRRRRAIN
WAAAARRKS
TRRRRAIN WAAARRKS

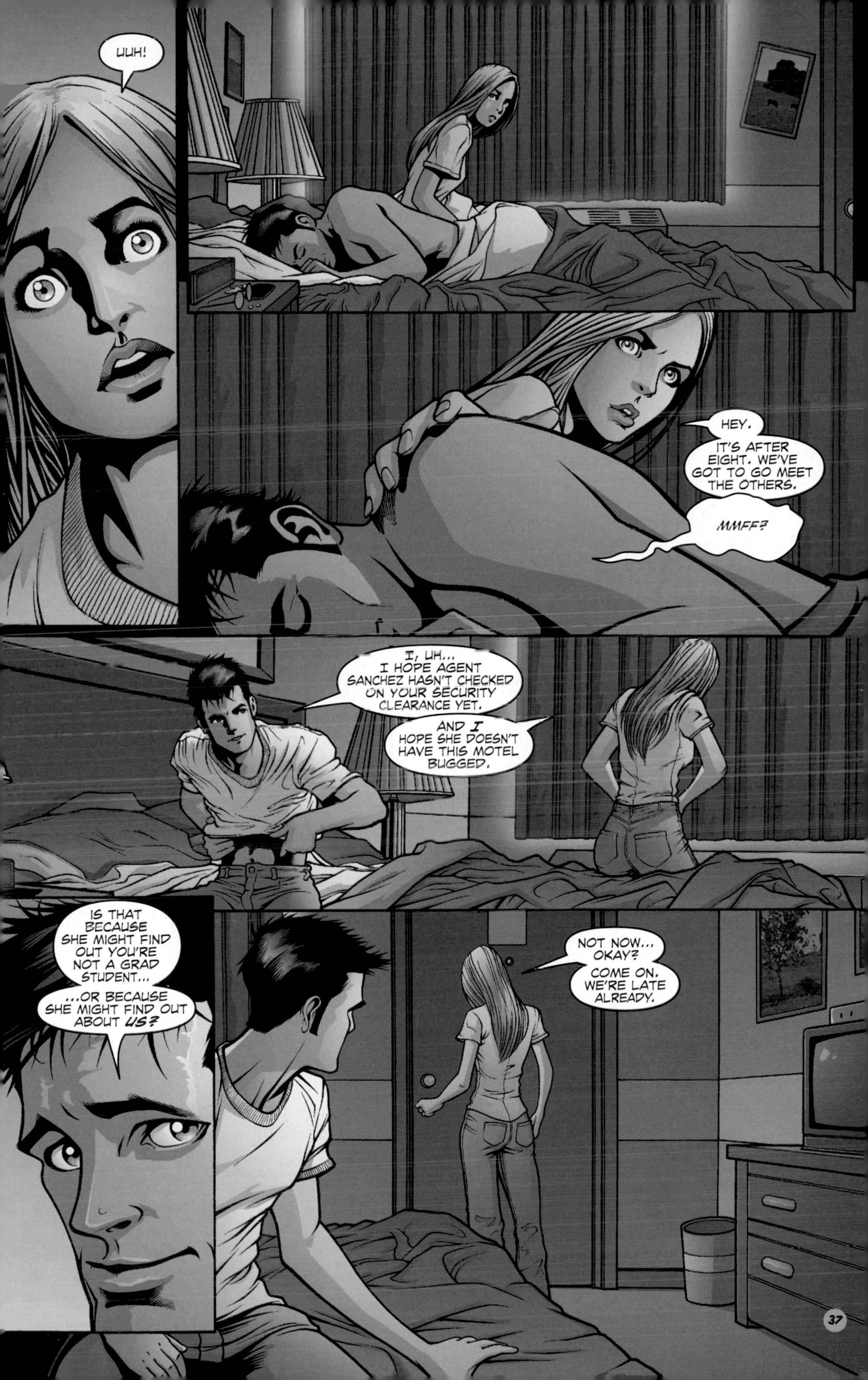
UUH!
HEY.
IT'S AFTER EIGHT. WE'VE GOT TO GO MEET THE OTHERS.
MMFF?
I, UH... I HOPE AGENT SANCHEZ HASN'T CHECKED ON YOUR SECURITY CLEARANCE YET.
AND I HOPE SHE DOESN'T HAVE THIS MOTEL BUGGED.
IS THAT BECAUSE SHE MIGHT FIND OUT YOU'RE NOT A GRAD STUDENT...
...OR BECAUSE SHE MIGHT FIND OUT ABOUT US?
NOT NOW... OKAY?
COME ON. WE'RE LATE ALREADY.

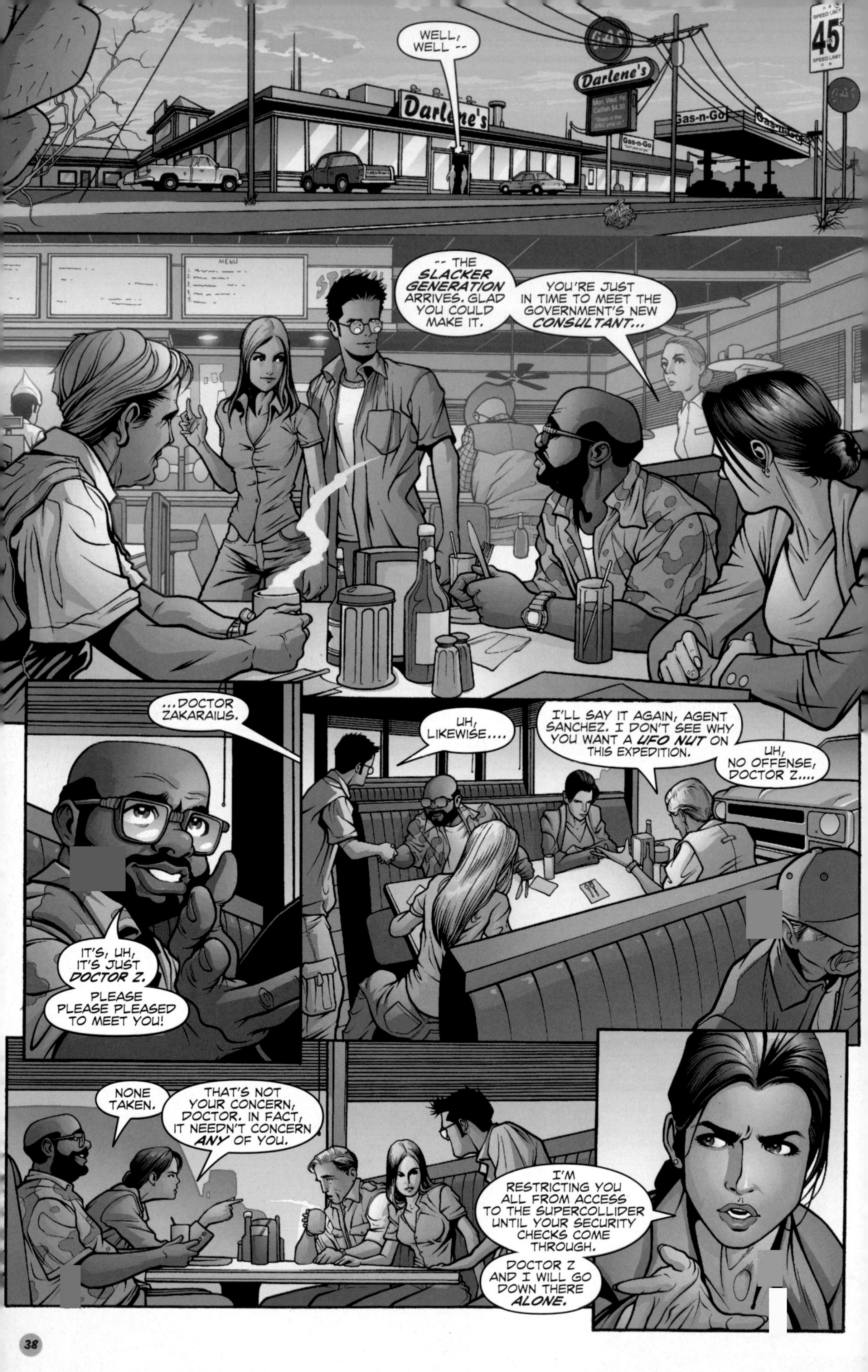
45
SPEED LIMIT
GAS
Darlene's
Mon. Wed. Fri.
Catfish $4.30
Gas-n-Go
Darlene's
WELL, WELL --
MENU
-- THE *SLACKER GENERATION* ARRIVES. GLAD YOU COULD MAKE IT.
YOU'RE JUST IN TIME TO MEET THE GOVERNMENT'S NEW *CONSULTANT...*
...DOCTOR ZAKARAIUS.
IT'S, UH, IT'S JUST *DOCTOR Z.*
PLEASE PLEASE PLEASED TO MEET YOU!
UH, LIKEWISE....
I'LL SAY IT AGAIN, AGENT SANCHEZ. I DON'T SEE WHY YOU WANT A *UFO NUT* ON THIS EXPEDITION.
UH, NO OFFENSE, DOCTOR Z....
NONE TAKEN.
THAT'S NOT YOUR CONCERN, DOCTOR. IN FACT, IT NEEDN'T CONCERN *ANY* OF YOU.
I'M RESTRICTING YOU ALL FROM ACCESS TO THE SUPERCOLLIDER UNTIL YOUR SECURITY CHECKS COME THROUGH.
DOCTOR Z AND I WILL GO DOWN THERE *ALONE.*

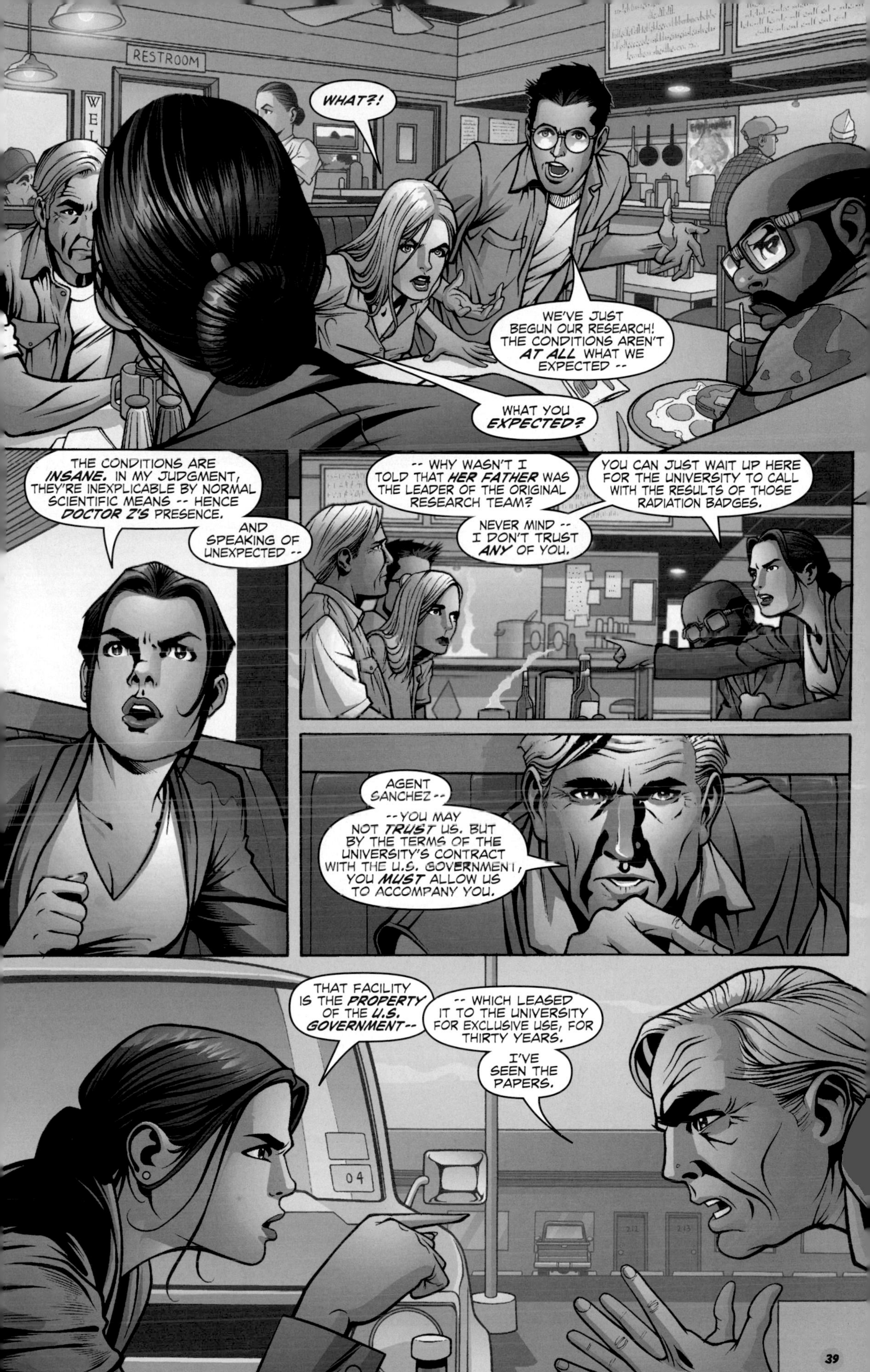
RESTROOM
WHAT?!
WE'VE JUST BEGUN OUR RESEARCH! THE CONDITIONS AREN'T AT ALL WHAT WE EXPECTED --
WHAT YOU EXPECTED?
THE CONDITIONS ARE INSANE. IN MY JUDGMENT, THEY'RE INEXPLICABLE BY NORMAL SCIENTIFIC MEANS -- HENCE DOCTOR Z'S PRESENCE.
AND SPEAKING OF UNEXPECTED --
-- WHY WASN'T I TOLD THAT HER FATHER WAS THE LEADER OF THE ORIGINAL RESEARCH TEAM?
NEVER MIND -- I DON'T TRUST ANY OF YOU.
YOU CAN JUST WAIT UP HERE FOR THE UNIVERSITY TO CALL WITH THE RESULTS OF THOSE RADIATION BADGES.
AGENT SANCHEZ --
--YOU MAY NOT TRUST US. BUT BY THE TERMS OF THE UNIVERSITY'S CONTRACT WITH THE U.S. GOVERNMENT, YOU MUST ALLOW US TO ACCOMPANY YOU.
THAT FACILITY IS THE PROPERTY OF THE U.S. GOVERNMENT--
-- WHICH LEASED IT TO THE UNIVERSITY FOR EXCLUSIVE USE, FOR THIRTY YEARS.
I'VE SEEN THE PAPERS.

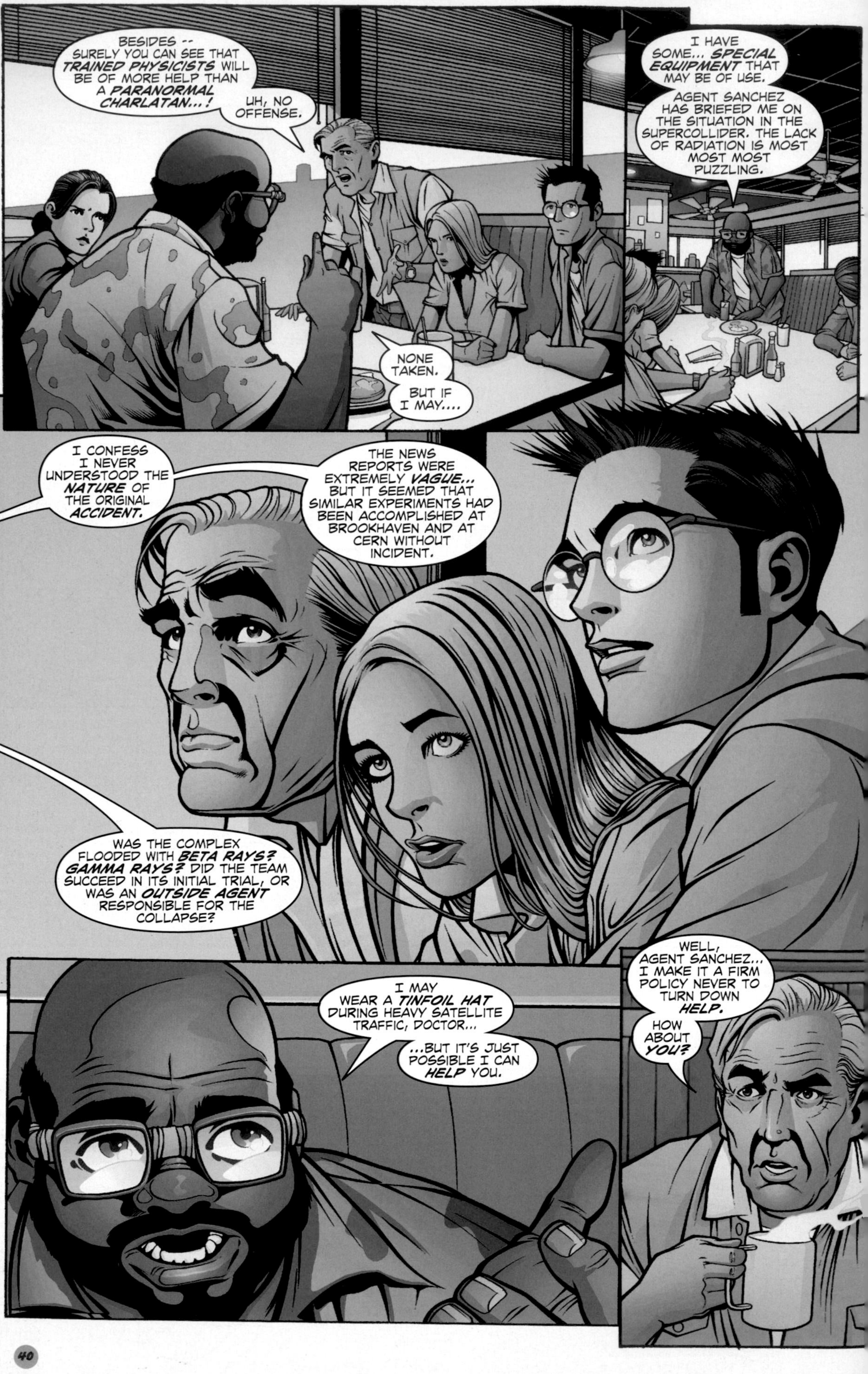
BESIDES -- SURELY YOU CAN SEE THAT TRAINED PHYSICISTS WILL BE OF MORE HELP THAN A PARANORMAL CHARLATAN...!
UH, NO OFFENSE.
NONE TAKEN.
BUT IF I MAY....
I HAVE SOME... SPECIAL EQUIPMENT THAT MAY BE OF USE.
AGENT SANCHEZ HAS BRIEFED ME ON THE SITUATION IN THE SUPERCOLLIDER. THE LACK OF RADIATION IS MOST MOST PUZZLING.
I CONFESS I NEVER UNDERSTOOD THE NATURE OF THE ORIGINAL ACCIDENT.
THE NEWS REPORTS WERE EXTREMELY VAGUE... BUT IT SEEMED THAT SIMILAR EXPERIMENTS HAD BEEN ACCOMPLISHED AT BROOKHAVEN AND AT CERN WITHOUT INCIDENT.
WAS THE COMPLEX FLOODED WITH BETA RAYS? GAMMA RAYS? DID THE TEAM SUCCEED IN ITS INITIAL TRIAL, OR WAS AN OUTSIDE AGENT RESPONSIBLE FOR THE COLLAPSE?
I MAY WEAR A TINFOIL HAT DURING HEAVY SATELLITE TRAFFIC, DOCTOR...
...BUT IT'S JUST POSSIBLE I CAN HELP YOU.
WELL, AGENT SANCHEZ... I MAKE IT A FIRM POLICY NEVER TO TURN DOWN HELP.
HOW ABOUT YOU?

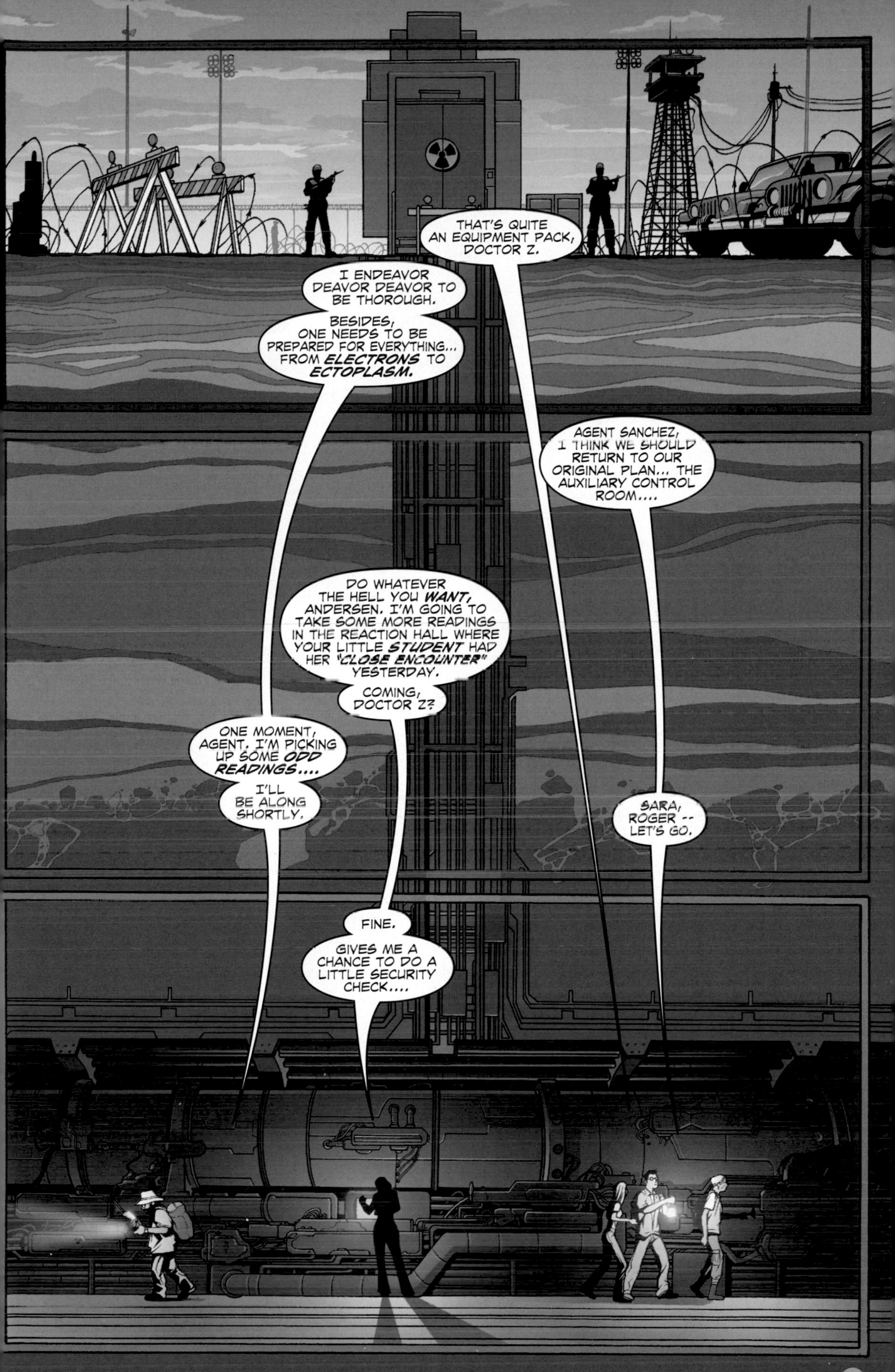
THAT'S QUITE AN EQUIPMENT PACK, DOCTOR Z.
I ENDEAVOR DEAVOR DEAVOR TO BE THOROUGH.
BESIDES, ONE NEEDS TO BE PREPARED FOR EVERYTHING... FROM ELECTRONS TO ECTOPLASM.
AGENT SANCHEZ, I THINK WE SHOULD RETURN TO OUR ORIGINAL PLAN... THE AUXILIARY CONTROL ROOM....
DO WHATEVER THE HELL YOU WANT, ANDERSEN. I'M GOING TO TAKE SOME MORE READINGS IN THE REACTION HALL WHERE YOUR LITTLE STUDENT HAD HER "CLOSE ENCOUNTER" YESTERDAY.
COMING, DOCTOR Z?
ONE MOMENT, AGENT. I'M PICKING UP SOME ODD READINGS....
I'LL BE ALONG SHORTLY.
SARA, ROGER -- LET'S GO.
FINE.
GIVES ME A CHANCE TO DO A LITTLE SECURITY CHECK....

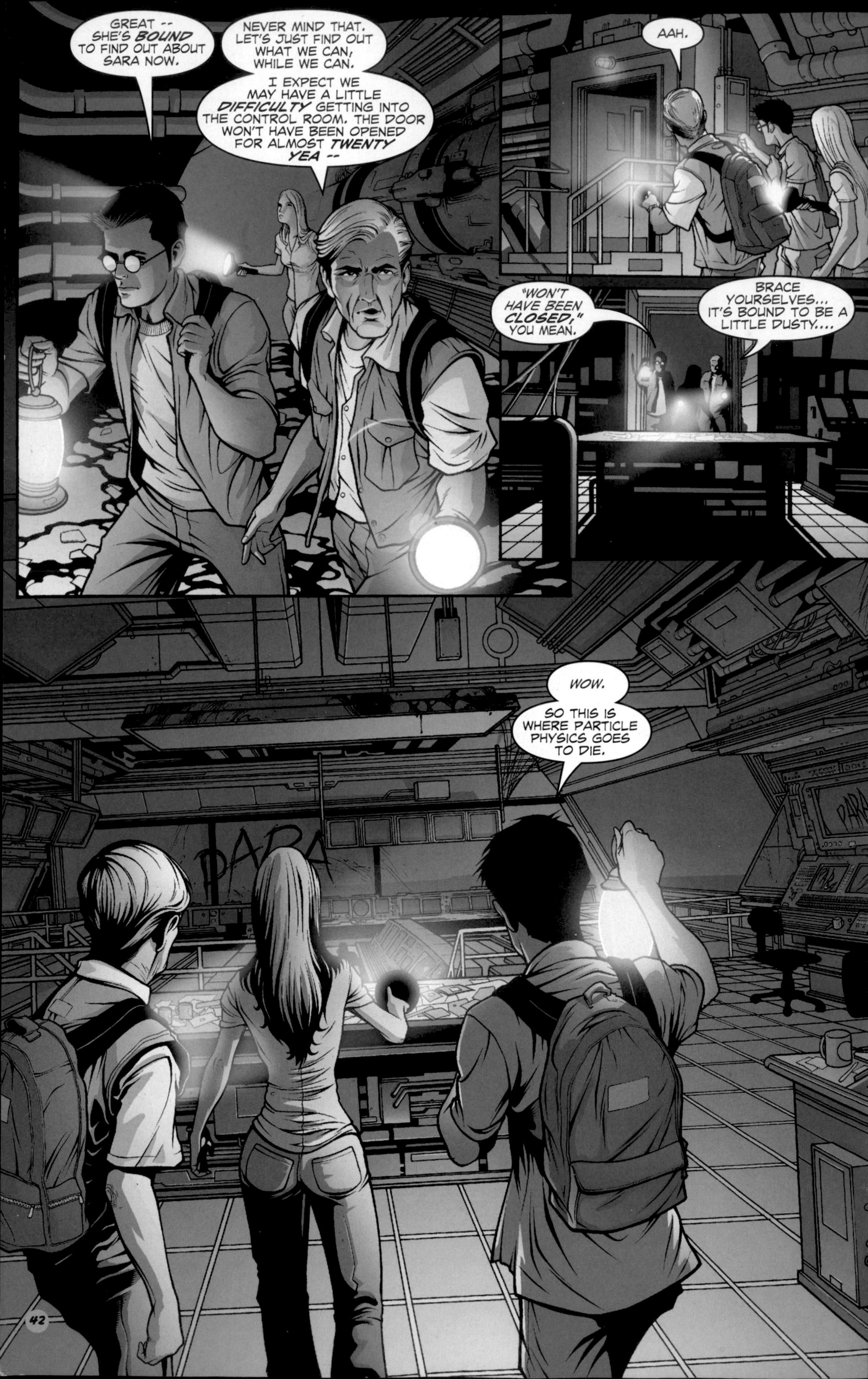
GREAT -- SHE'S BOUND TO FIND OUT ABOUT SARA NOW.
NEVER MIND THAT. LET'S JUST FIND OUT WHAT WE CAN, WHILE WE CAN.
I EXPECT WE MAY HAVE A LITTLE DIFFICULTY GETTING INTO THE CONTROL ROOM. THE DOOR WON'T HAVE BEEN OPENED FOR ALMOST TWENTY YEA --
AAH.
"WON'T HAVE BEEN CLOSED," YOU MEAN.
BRACE YOURSELVES... IT'S BOUND TO BE A LITTLE DUSTY....
WOW.
SO THIS IS WHERE PARTICLE PHYSICS GOES TO DIE.

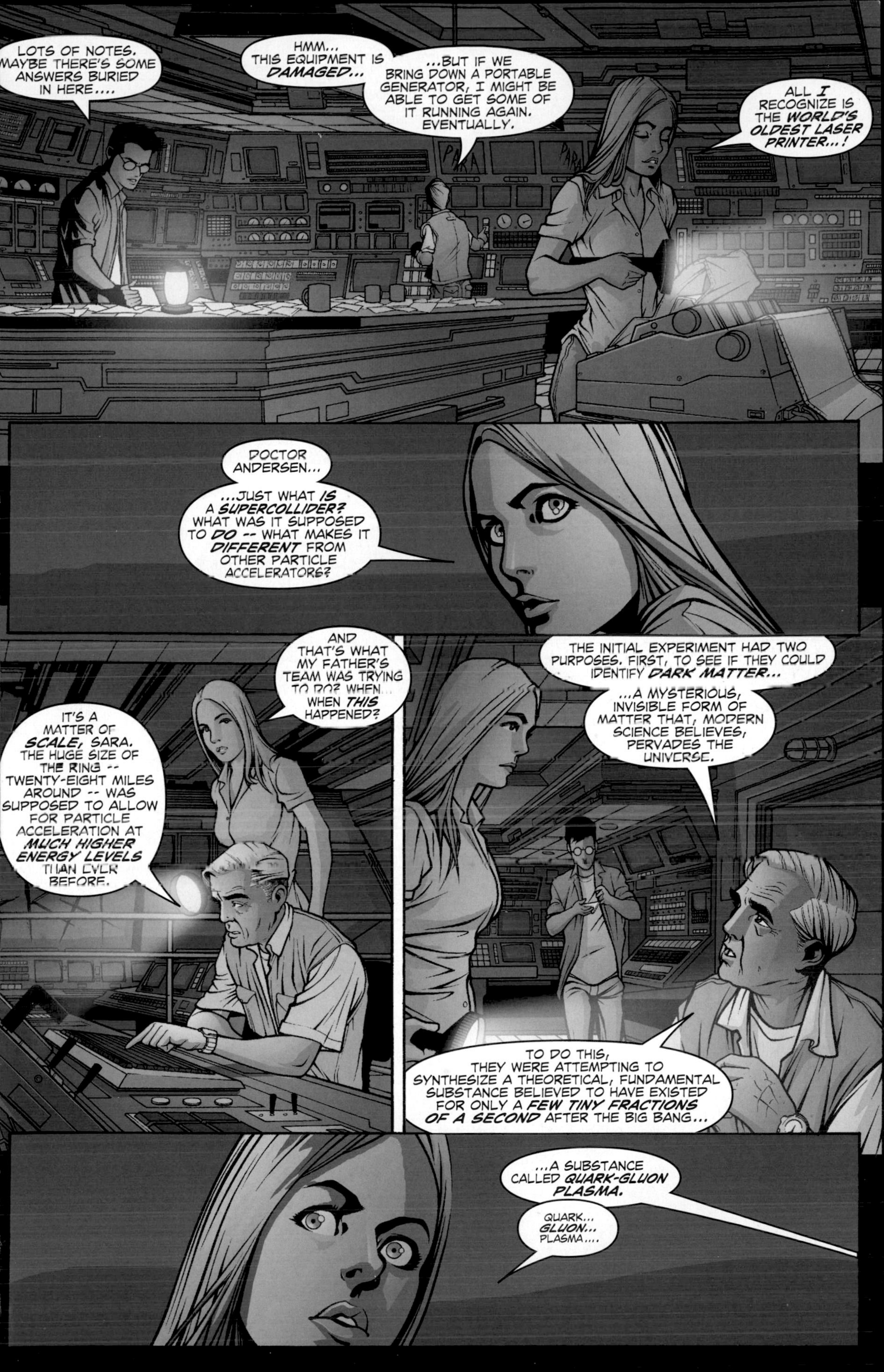

LOTS OF NOTES. MAYBE THERE'S SOME ANSWERS BURIED IN HERE....
HMM... THIS EQUIPMENT IS DAMAGED...
...BUT IF WE BRING DOWN A PORTABLE GENERATOR, I MIGHT BE ABLE TO GET SOME OF IT RUNNING AGAIN. EVENTUALLY.
ALL I RECOGNIZE IS THE WORLD'S OLDEST LASER PRINTER...!
DOCTOR ANDERSEN...
...JUST WHAT IS A SUPERCOLLIDER? WHAT WAS IT SUPPOSED TO DO -- WHAT MAKES IT DIFFERENT FROM OTHER PARTICLE ACCELERATORS?
IT'S A MATTER OF SCALE, SARA. THE HUGE SIZE OF THE RING -- TWENTY-EIGHT MILES AROUND -- WAS SUPPOSED TO ALLOW FOR PARTICLE ACCELERATION AT MUCH HIGHER ENERGY LEVELS THAN EVER BEFORE.
AND THAT'S WHAT MY FATHER'S TEAM WAS TRYING TO DO? WHEN... WHEN THIS HAPPENED?
THE INITIAL EXPERIMENT HAD TWO PURPOSES. FIRST, TO SEE IF THEY COULD IDENTIFY DARK MATTER...
...A MYSTERIOUS, INVISIBLE FORM OF MATTER THAT, MODERN SCIENCE BELIEVES, PERVADES THE UNIVERSE.
TO DO THIS, THEY WERE ATTEMPTING TO SYNTHESIZE A THEORETICAL, FUNDAMENTAL SUBSTANCE BELIEVED TO HAVE EXISTED FOR ONLY A FEW TINY FRACTIONS OF A SECOND AFTER THE BIG BANG...
...A SUBSTANCE CALLED QUARK-GLUON PLASMA.
QUARK... GLUON... PLASMA....

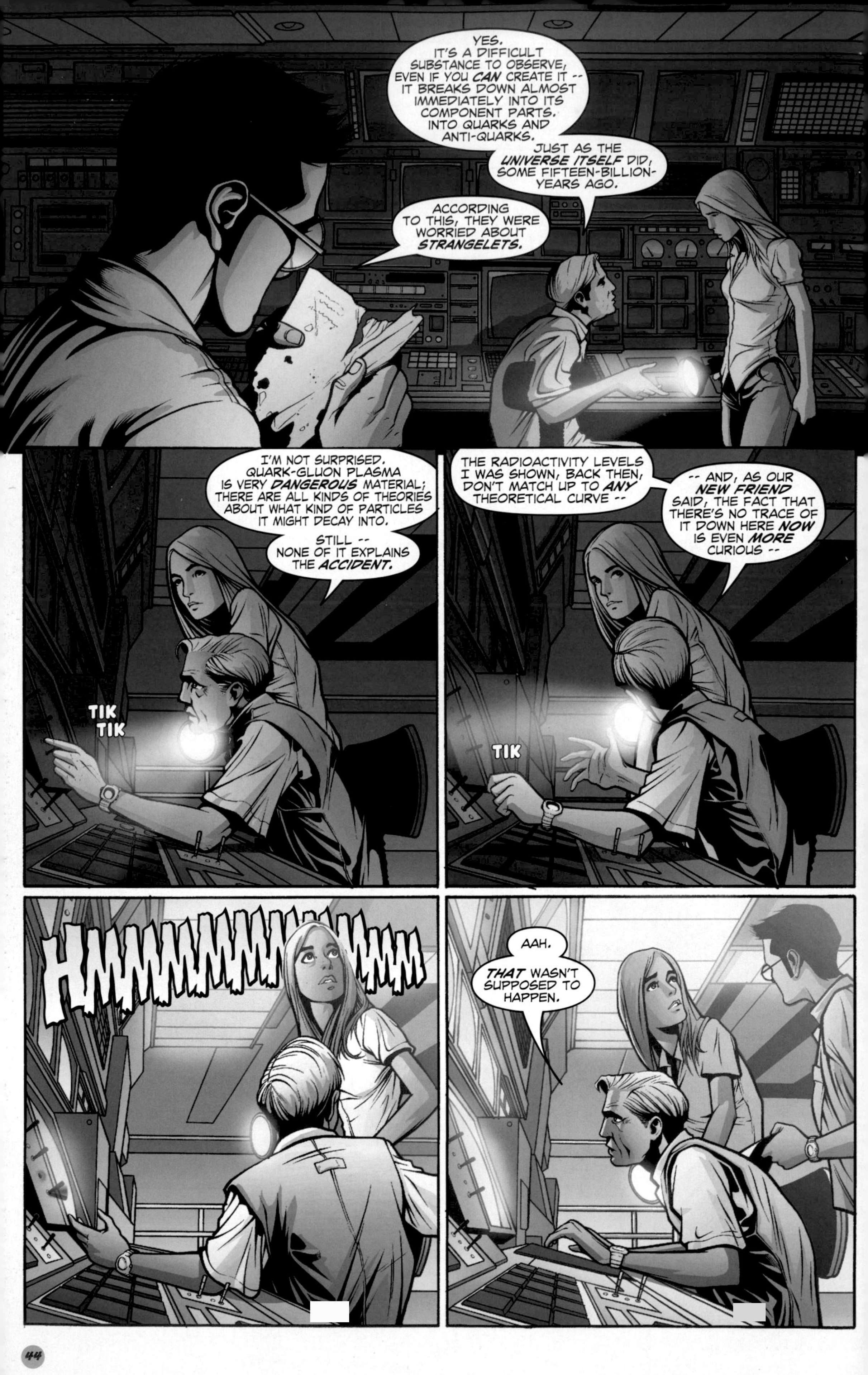
YES. IT'S A DIFFICULT SUBSTANCE TO OBSERVE, EVEN IF YOU CAN CREATE IT -- IT BREAKS DOWN ALMOST IMMEDIATELY INTO ITS COMPONENT PARTS. INTO QUARKS AND ANTI-QUARKS.
JUST AS THE UNIVERSE ITSELF DID, SOME FIFTEEN-BILLION-YEARS AGO.
ACCORDING TO THIS, THEY WERE WORRIED ABOUT STRANGELETS.
I'M NOT SURPRISED. QUARK-GLUON PLASMA IS VERY DANGEROUS MATERIAL; THERE ARE ALL KINDS OF THEORIES ABOUT WHAT KIND OF PARTICLES IT MIGHT DECAY INTO.
STILL -- NONE OF IT EXPLAINS THE ACCIDENT.
TIK
TIK
THE RADIOACTIVITY LEVELS I WAS SHOWN, BACK THEN, DON'T MATCH UP TO ANY THEORETICAL CURVE --
-- AND, AS OUR NEW FRIEND SAID, THE FACT THAT THERE'S NO TRACE OF IT DOWN HERE NOW IS EVEN MORE CURIOUS --
TIK
HMMMMMMMMMMM
AAH.
THAT WASN'T SUPPOSED TO HAPPEN.

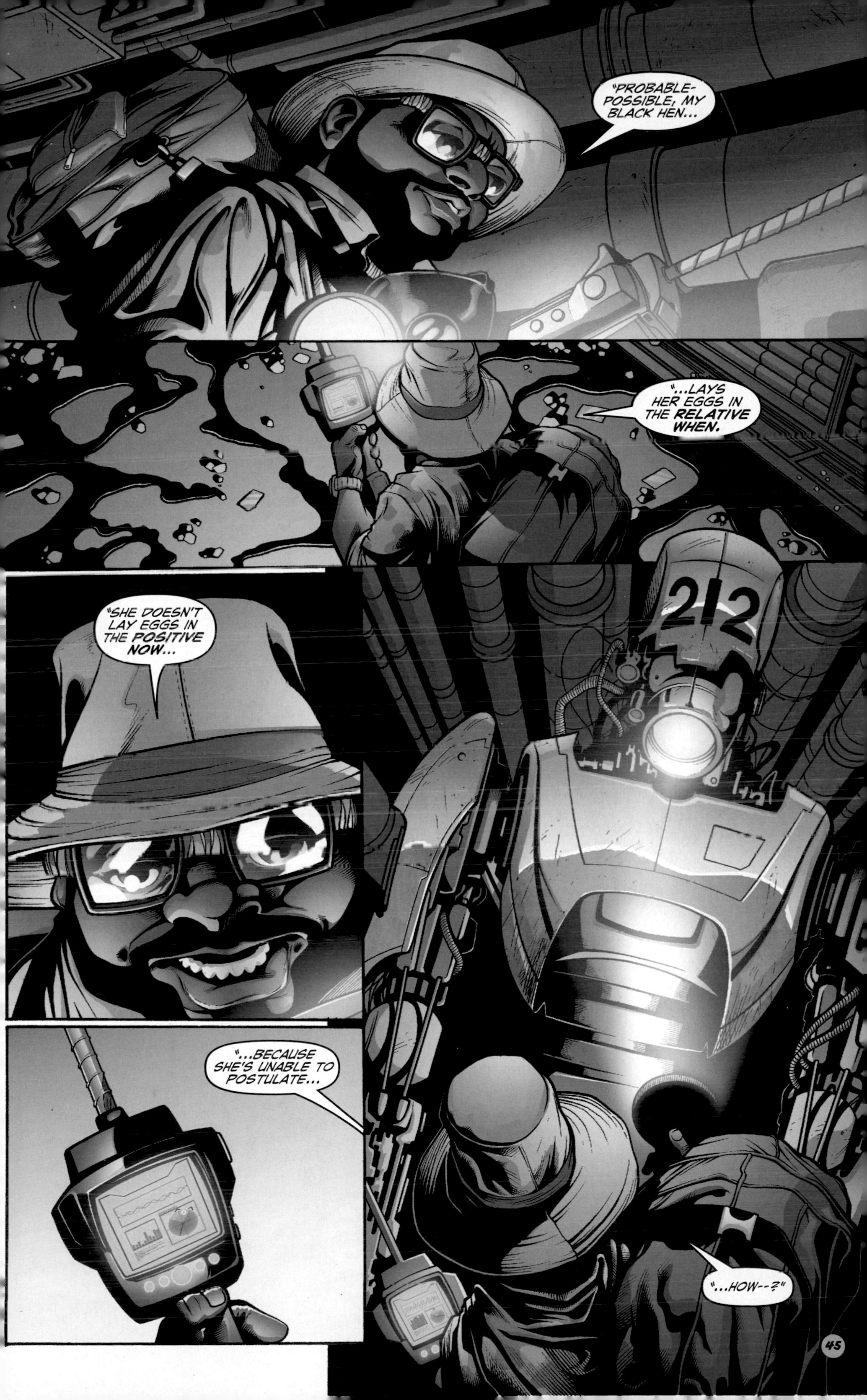
"PROBABLE-POSSIBLE, MY BLACK HEN...
"...LAYS HER EGGS IN THE **RELATIVE WHEN.**
"SHE DOESN'T LAY EGGS IN THE *POSITIVE* **NOW...**
"...BECAUSE SHE'S UNABLE TO POSTULATE...
"...HOW--?"
212

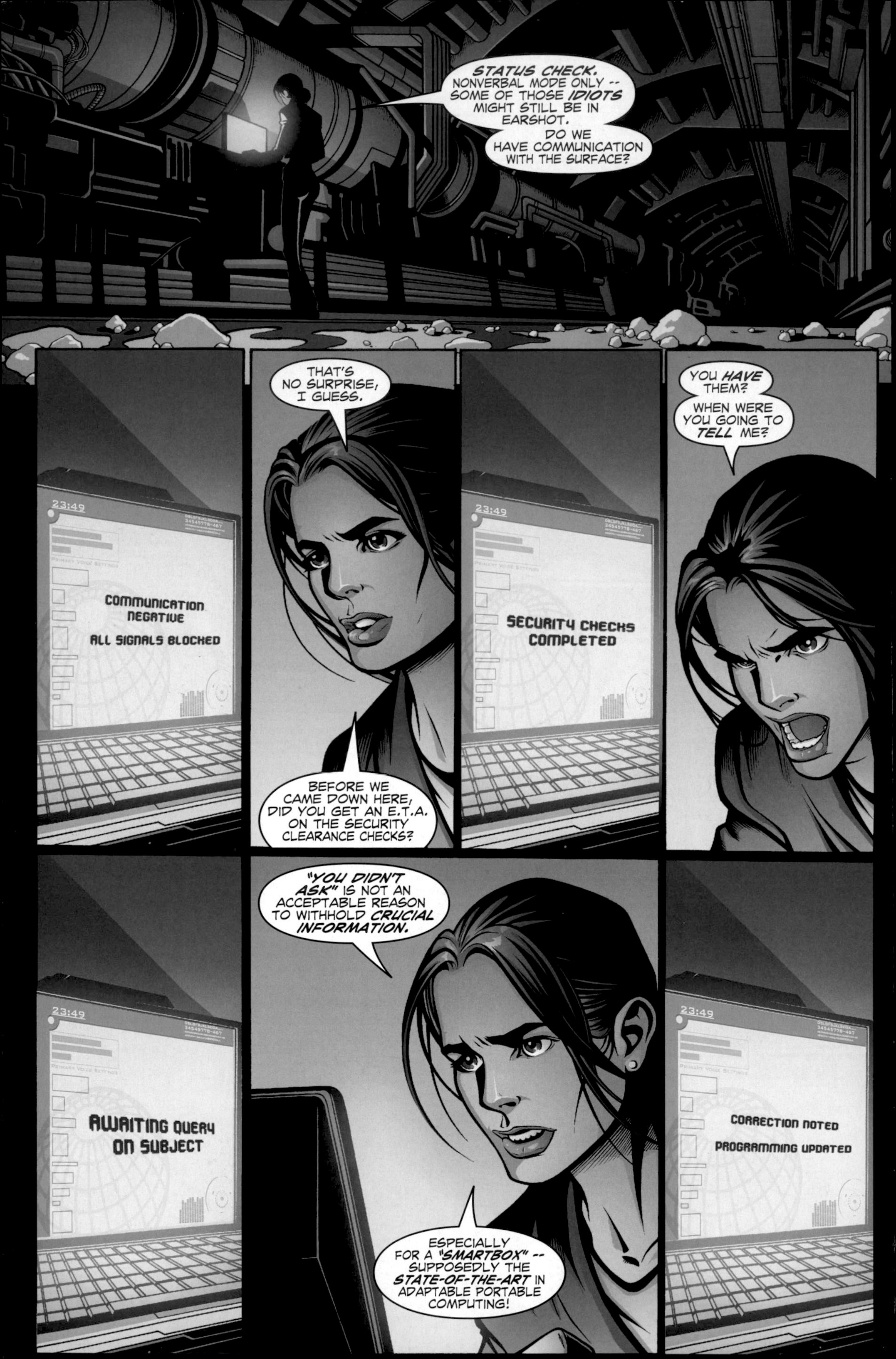

STATUS CHECK. NONVERBAL MODE ONLY -- SOME OF THOSE IDIOTS MIGHT STILL BE IN EARSHOT.
DO WE HAVE COMMUNICATION WITH THE SURFACE?
23:49
COMMUNICATION NEGATIVE
ALL SIGNALS BLOCKED
THAT'S NO SURPRISE, I GUESS.
BEFORE WE CAME DOWN HERE, DID YOU GET AN E.T.A. ON THE SECURITY CLEARANCE CHECKS?
23:49
SECURITY CHECKS COMPLETED
YOU HAVE THEM?
WHEN WERE YOU GOING TO TELL ME?
23:49
AWAITING QUERY ON SUBJECT
"YOU DIDN'T ASK" IS NOT AN ACCEPTABLE REASON TO WITHHOLD CRUCIAL INFORMATION.
ESPECIALLY FOR A "SMARTBOX" -- SUPPOSEDLY THE STATE-OF-THE-ART IN ADAPTABLE PORTABLE COMPUTING!
23:49
CORRECTION NOTED
PROGRAMMING UPDATED

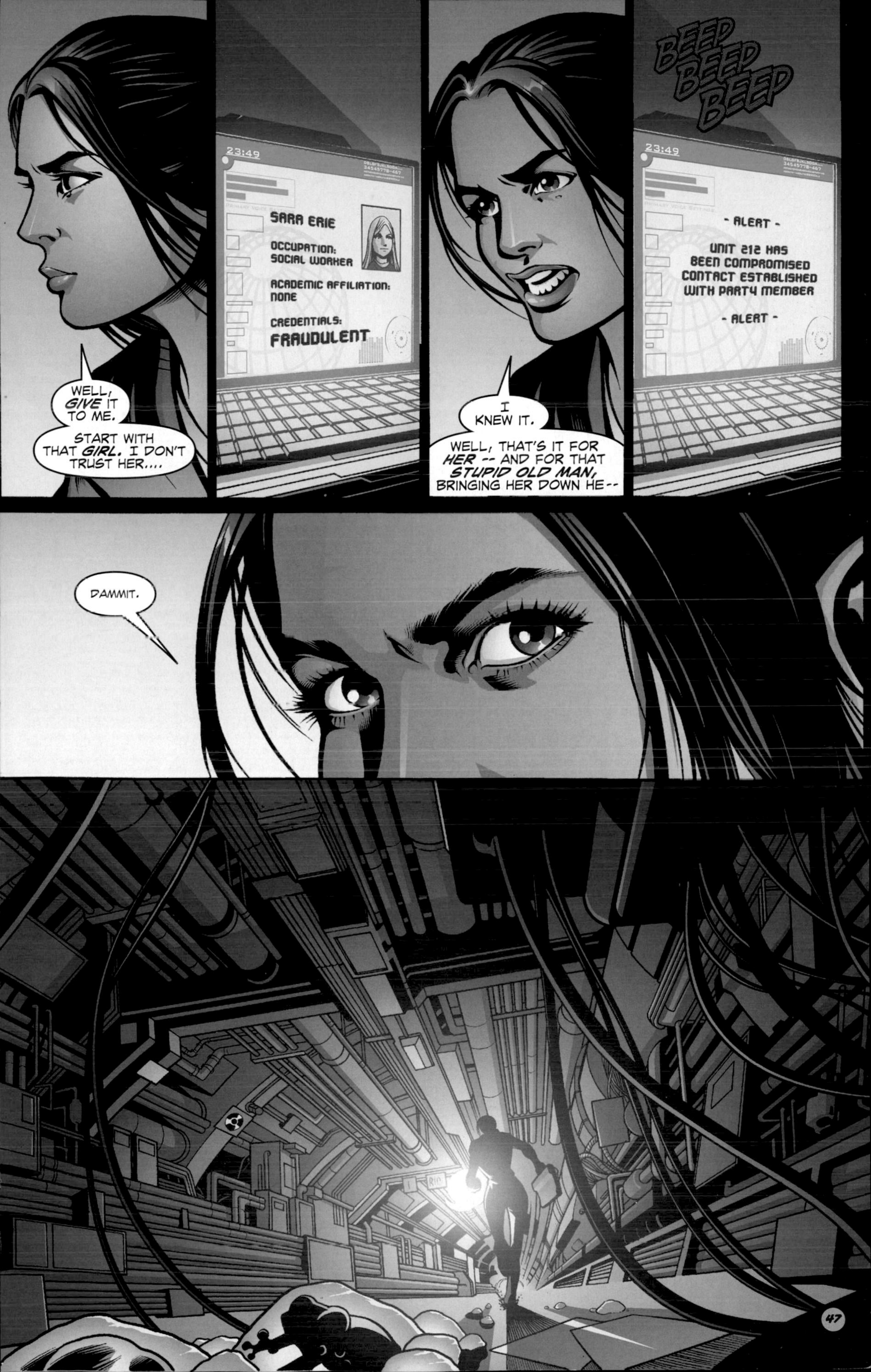
WELL, GIVE IT TO ME.
START WITH THAT GIRL. I DON'T TRUST HER....
23:49
SARA ERIE
OCCUPATION: SOCIAL WORKER
ACADEMIC AFFILIATION: NONE
CREDENTIALS: FRAUDULENT
I KNEW IT.
WELL, THAT'S IT FOR HER -- AND FOR THAT STUPID OLD MAN, BRINGING HER DOWN HE--
BEEP BEEP BEEP
23:49
- ALERT -
UNIT 212 HAS BEEN COMPROMISED CONTACT ESTABLISHED WITH PARTY MEMBER
- ALERT -
DAMMIT.

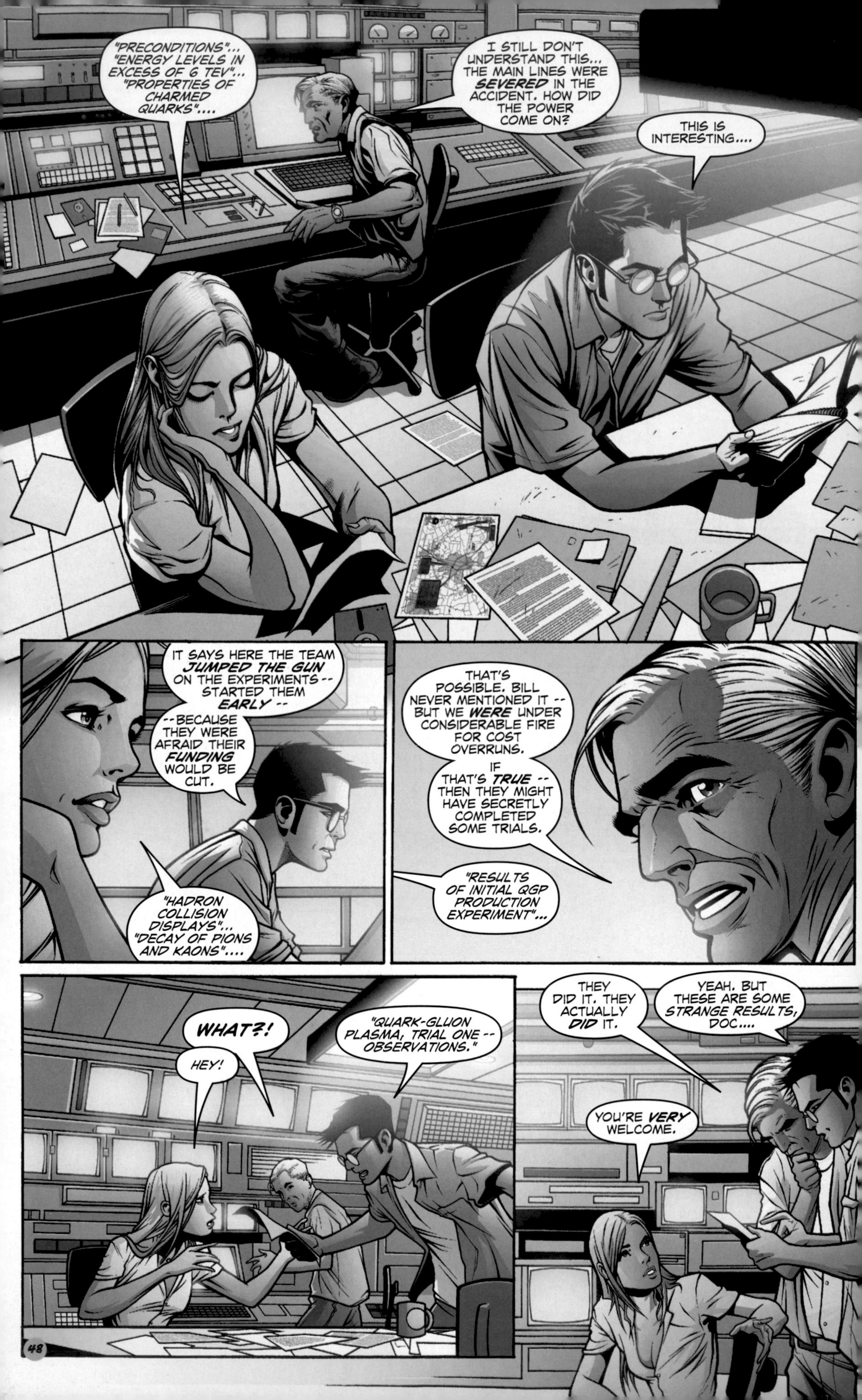
"PRECONDITIONS"... "ENERGY LEVELS IN EXCESS OF 6 TEV"... "PROPERTIES OF CHARMED QUARKS"....
I STILL DON'T UNDERSTAND THIS... THE MAIN LINES WERE SEVERED IN THE ACCIDENT. HOW DID THE POWER COME ON?
THIS IS INTERESTING....
IT SAYS HERE THE TEAM JUMPED THE GUN ON THE EXPERIMENTS -- STARTED THEM EARLY --
--BECAUSE THEY WERE AFRAID THEIR FUNDING WOULD BE CUT.
"HADRON COLLISION DISPLAYS"... "DECAY OF PIONS AND KAONS"....
THAT'S POSSIBLE. BILL NEVER MENTIONED IT -- BUT WE WERE UNDER CONSIDERABLE FIRE FOR COST OVERRUNS.
IF THAT'S TRUE -- THEN THEY MIGHT HAVE SECRETLY COMPLETED SOME TRIALS.
"RESULTS OF INITIAL QGP PRODUCTION EXPERIMENT"...
WHAT?!
HEY!
"QUARK-GLUON PLASMA, TRIAL ONE -- OBSERVATIONS."
THEY DID IT. THEY ACTUALLY DID IT.
YEAH. BUT THESE ARE SOME STRANGE RESULTS, DOC....
YOU'RE VERY WELCOME.

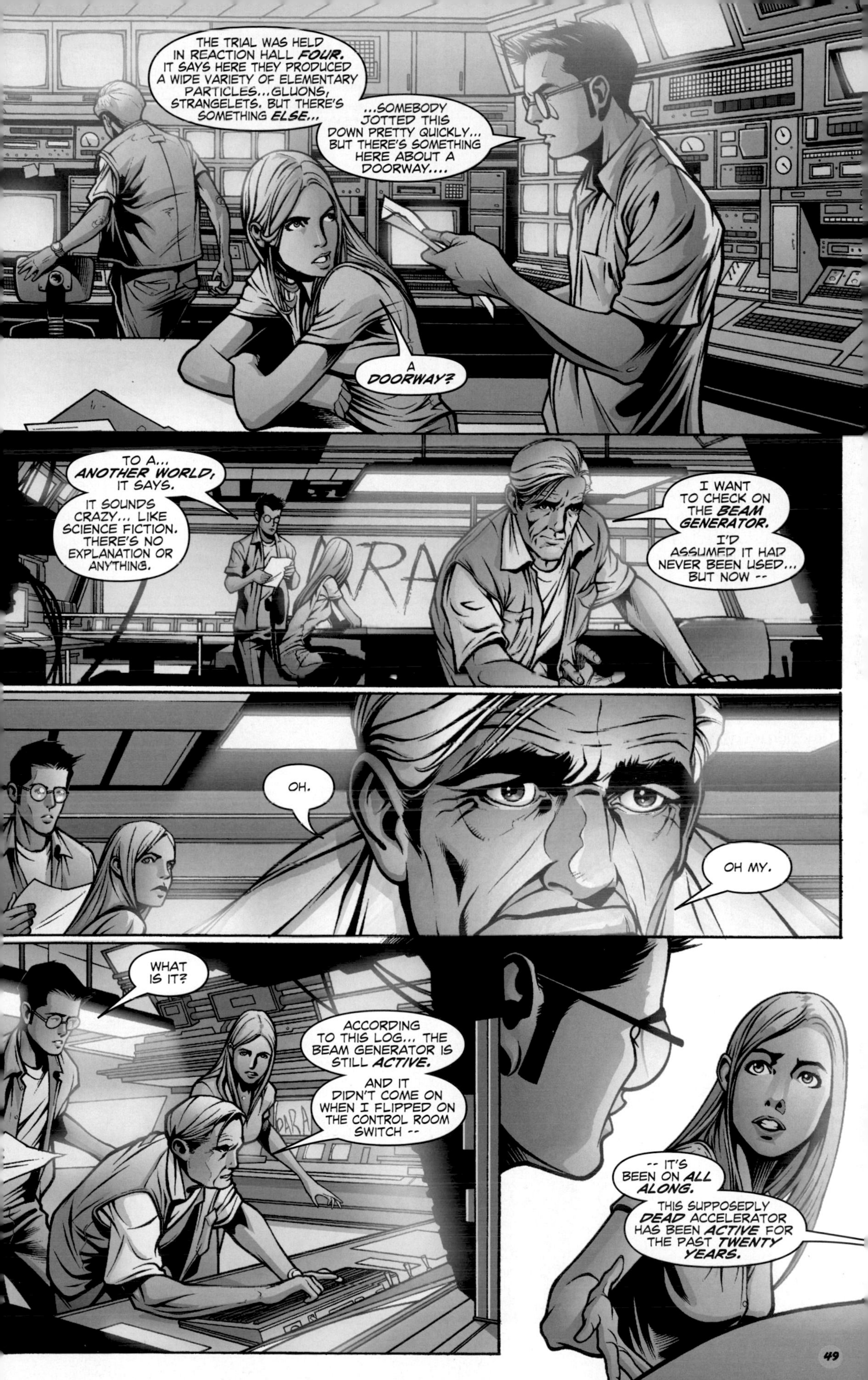
THE TRIAL WAS HELD IN REACTION HALL FOUR. IT SAYS HERE THEY PRODUCED A WIDE VARIETY OF ELEMENTARY PARTICLES...GLUONS, STRANGELETS. BUT THERE'S SOMETHING ELSE...
...SOMEBODY JOTTED THIS DOWN PRETTY QUICKLY... BUT THERE'S SOMETHING HERE ABOUT A DOORWAY....
A DOORWAY?
TO A... ANOTHER WORLD, IT SAYS.
IT SOUNDS CRAZY... LIKE SCIENCE FICTION. THERE'S NO EXPLANATION OR ANYTHING.
I WANT TO CHECK ON THE BEAM GENERATOR.
I'D ASSUMED IT HAD NEVER BEEN USED... BUT NOW --
OH.
OH MY.
WHAT IS IT?
ACCORDING TO THIS LOG... THE BEAM GENERATOR IS STILL ACTIVE.
AND IT DIDN'T COME ON WHEN I FLIPPED ON THE CONTROL ROOM SWITCH --
-- IT'S BEEN ON ALL ALONG.
THIS SUPPOSEDLY DEAD ACCELERATOR HAS BEEN ACTIVE FOR THE PAST TWENTY YEARS.

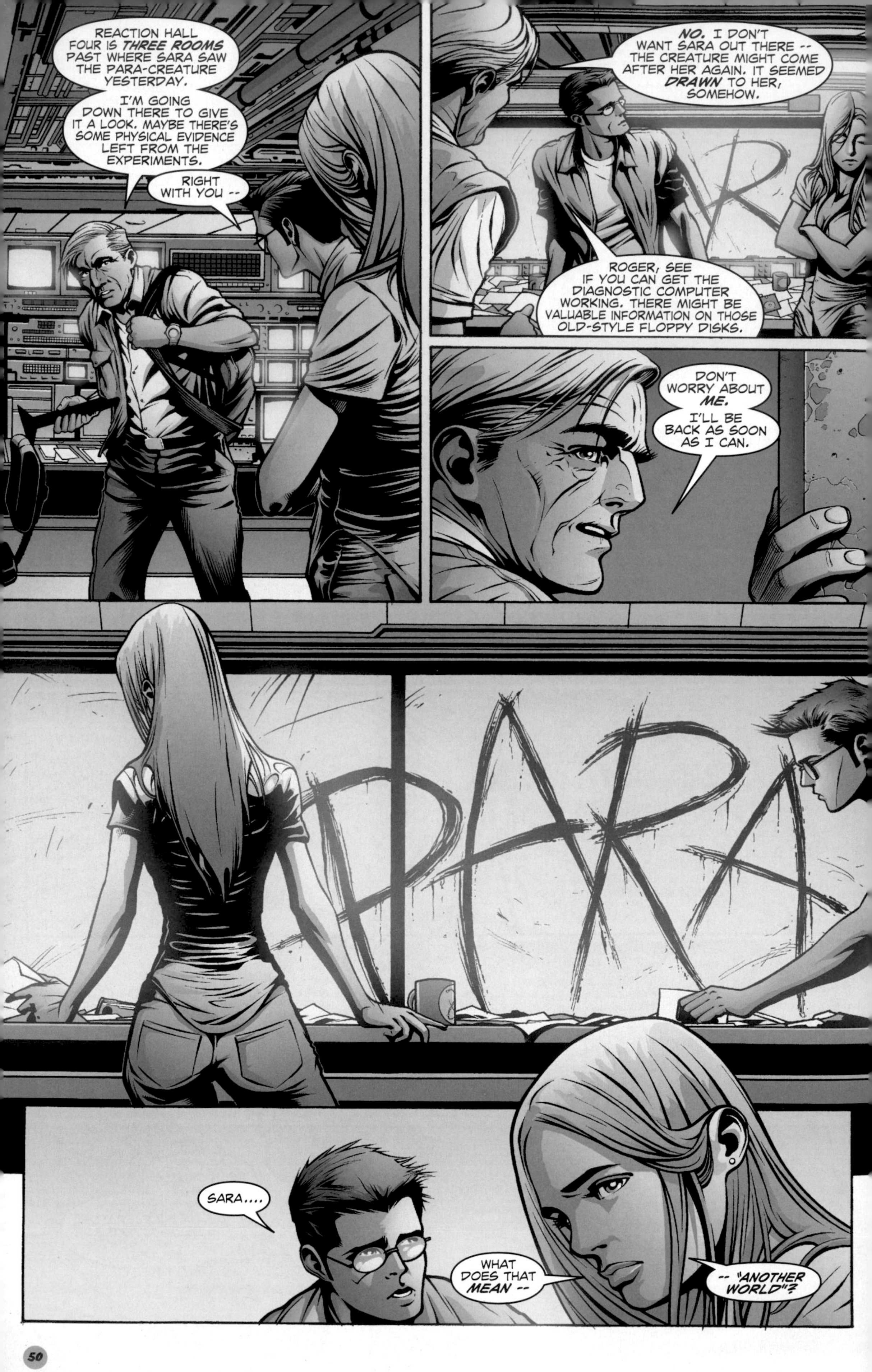

REACTION HALL FOUR IS THREE ROOMS PAST WHERE SARA SAW THE PARA-CREATURE YESTERDAY.
I'M GOING DOWN THERE TO GIVE IT A LOOK. MAYBE THERE'S SOME PHYSICAL EVIDENCE LEFT FROM THE EXPERIMENTS.
RIGHT WITH YOU --
NO. I DON'T WANT SARA OUT THERE -- THE CREATURE MIGHT COME AFTER HER AGAIN. IT SEEMED DRAWN TO HER, SOMEHOW.
ROGER, SEE IF YOU CAN GET THE DIAGNOSTIC COMPUTER WORKING. THERE MIGHT BE VALUABLE INFORMATION ON THOSE OLD-STYLE FLOPPY DISKS.
DON'T WORRY ABOUT ME.
I'LL BE BACK AS SOON AS I CAN.
PARA
SARA....
WHAT DOES THAT MEAN --
-- "ANOTHER WORLD"?

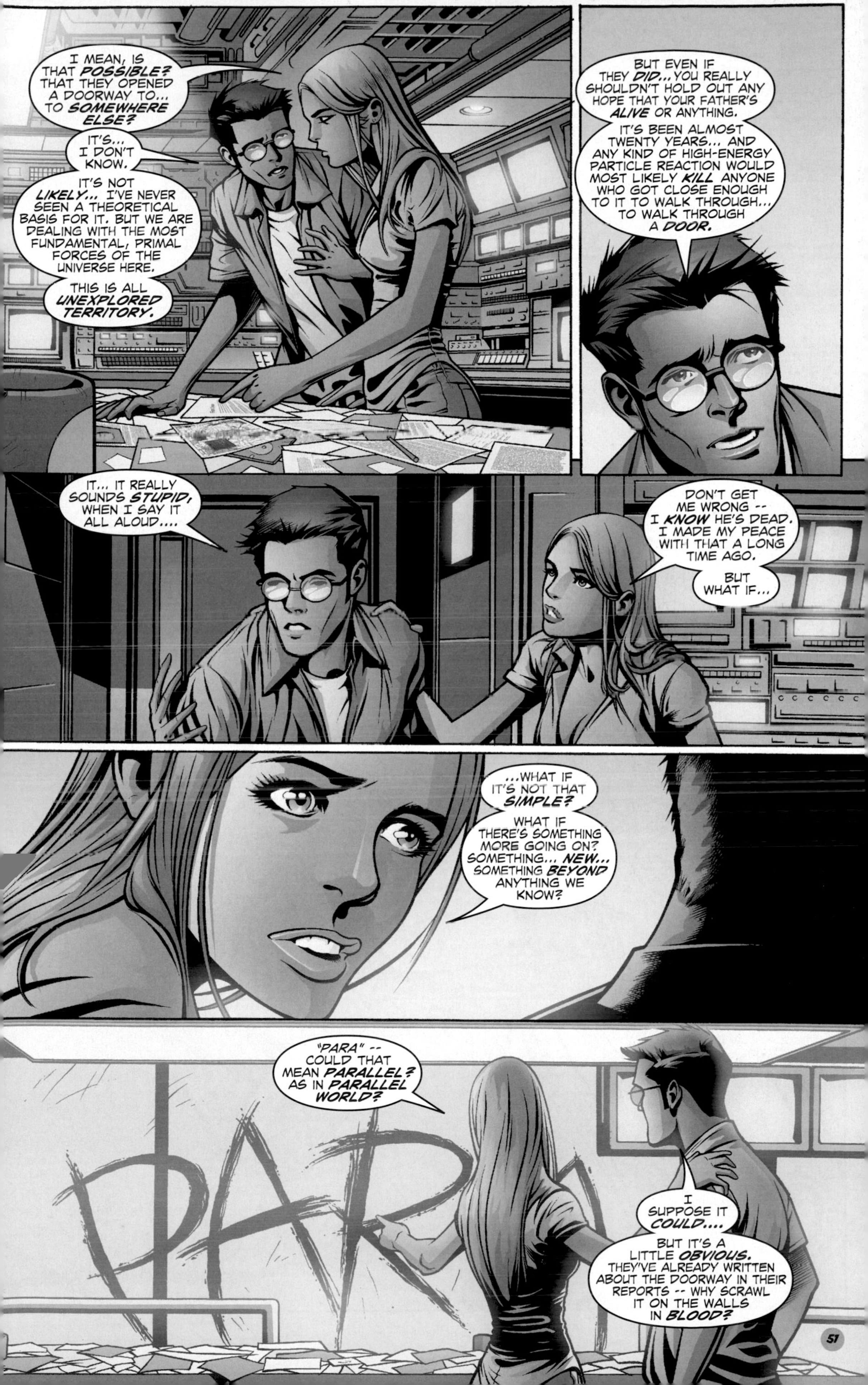
I MEAN, IS THAT POSSIBLE? THAT THEY OPENED A DOORWAY TO... TO SOMEWHERE ELSE?
IT'S... I DON'T KNOW.
IT'S NOT LIKELY... I'VE NEVER SEEN A THEORETICAL BASIS FOR IT. BUT WE ARE DEALING WITH THE MOST FUNDAMENTAL, PRIMAL FORCES OF THE UNIVERSE HERE.
THIS IS ALL UNEXPLORED TERRITORY.
BUT EVEN IF THEY DID... YOU REALLY SHOULDN'T HOLD OUT ANY HOPE THAT YOUR FATHER'S ALIVE OR ANYTHING.
IT'S BEEN ALMOST TWENTY YEARS... AND ANY KIND OF HIGH-ENERGY PARTICLE REACTION WOULD MOST LIKELY KILL ANYONE WHO GOT CLOSE ENOUGH TO IT TO WALK THROUGH... TO WALK THROUGH A DOOR.
IT... IT REALLY SOUNDS STUPID, WHEN I SAY IT ALL ALOUD....
DON'T GET ME WRONG -- I KNOW HE'S DEAD. I MADE MY PEACE WITH THAT A LONG TIME AGO.
BUT WHAT IF...
...WHAT IF IT'S NOT THAT SIMPLE?
WHAT IF THERE'S SOMETHING MORE GOING ON? SOMETHING... NEW... SOMETHING BEYOND ANYTHING WE KNOW?
"PARA" -- COULD THAT MEAN PARALLEL? AS IN PARALLEL WORLD?
PARA
I SUPPOSE IT COULD....
BUT IT'S A LITTLE OBVIOUS. THEY'VE ALREADY WRITTEN ABOUT THE DOORWAY IN THEIR REPORTS -- WHY SCRAWL IT ON THE WALLS IN BLOOD?

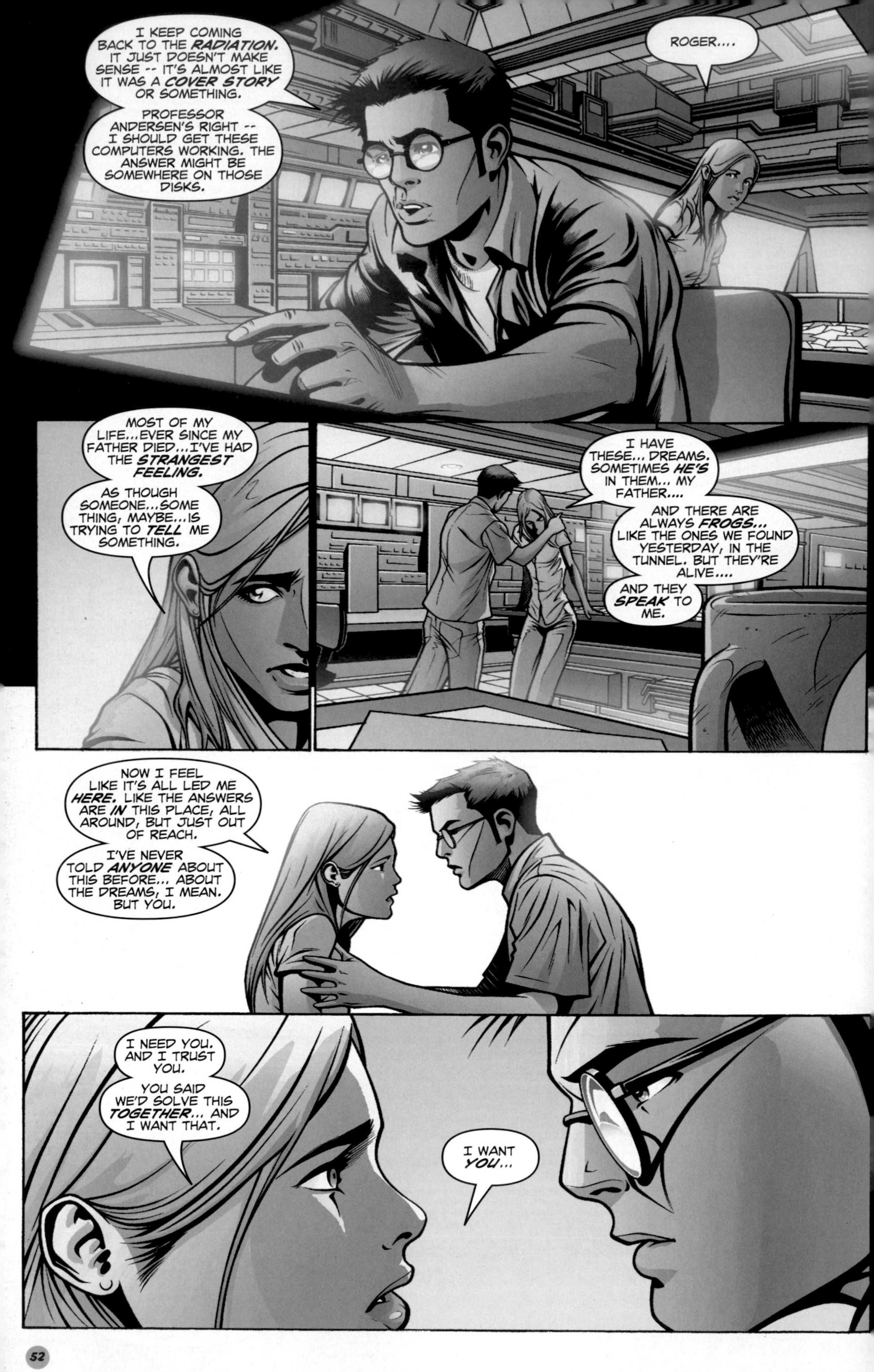
I KEEP COMING BACK TO THE RADIATION. IT JUST DOESN'T MAKE SENSE -- IT'S ALMOST LIKE IT WAS A COVER STORY OR SOMETHING.
PROFESSOR ANDERSEN'S RIGHT -- I SHOULD GET THESE COMPUTERS WORKING. THE ANSWER MIGHT BE SOMEWHERE ON THOSE DISKS.
ROGER....
MOST OF MY LIFE...EVER SINCE MY FATHER DIED...I'VE HAD THE STRANGEST FEELING.
AS THOUGH SOMEONE...SOME THING, MAYBE...IS TRYING TO TELL ME SOMETHING.
I HAVE THESE... DREAMS. SOMETIMES HE'S IN THEM... MY FATHER....
AND THERE ARE ALWAYS FROGS... LIKE THE ONES WE FOUND YESTERDAY, IN THE TUNNEL. BUT THEY'RE ALIVE....
AND THEY SPEAK TO ME.
NOW I FEEL LIKE IT'S ALL LED ME HERE. LIKE THE ANSWERS ARE IN THIS PLACE, ALL AROUND, BUT JUST OUT OF REACH.
I'VE NEVER TOLD ANYONE ABOUT THIS BEFORE... ABOUT THE DREAMS, I MEAN. BUT YOU.
I NEED YOU. AND I TRUST YOU.
YOU SAID WE'D SOLVE THIS TOGETHER... AND I WANT THAT.
I WANT YOU...

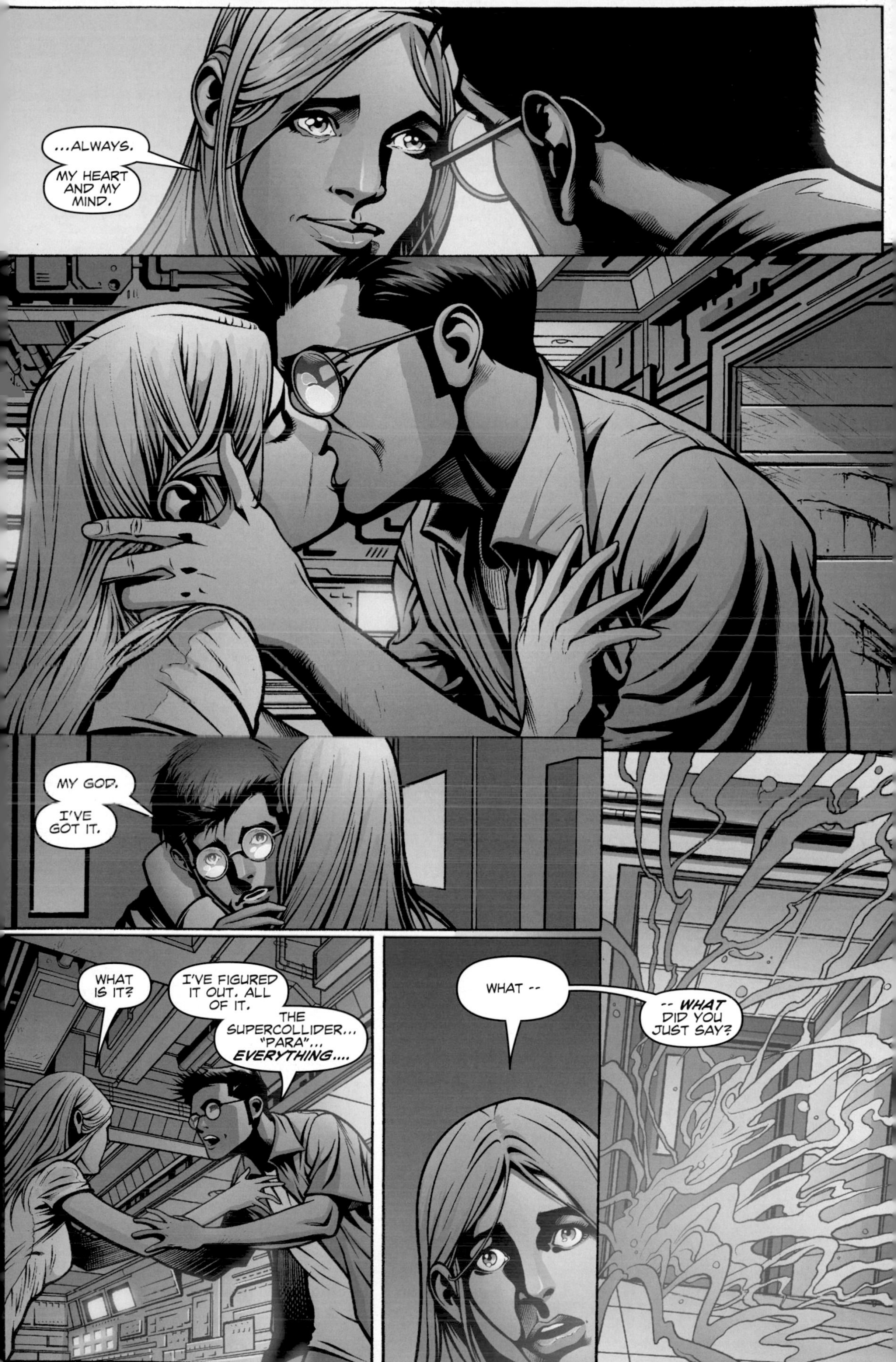
...ALWAYS.
MY HEART AND MY MIND.
MY GOD.
I'VE GOT IT.
WHAT IS IT?
I'VE FIGURED IT OUT. ALL OF IT.
THE SUPERCOLLIDER... "PARA"... EVERYTHING....
WHAT --
-- WHAT DID YOU JUST SAY?

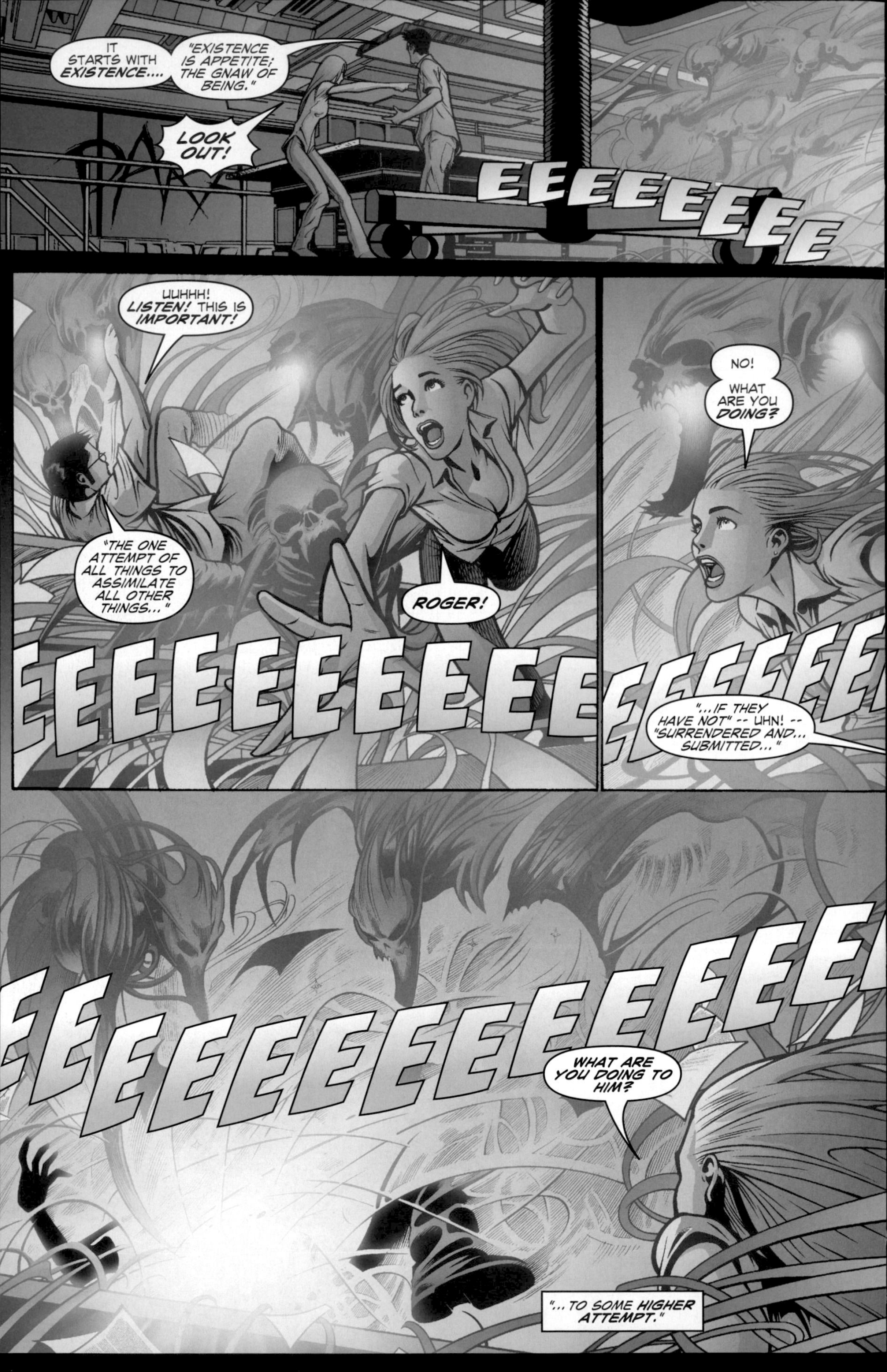
IT STARTS WITH EXISTENCE....
"EXISTENCE IS APPETITE: THE GNAW OF BEING."
LOOK OUT!
EEEEEEEEEE
UUHHH! LISTEN! THIS IS IMPORTANT!
"THE ONE ATTEMPT OF ALL THINGS TO ASSIMILATE ALL OTHER THINGS..."
ROGER!
EEEEEEEEEEE
NO! WHAT ARE YOU DOING?
"...IF THEY HAVE NOT" -- UHN! -- "SURRENDERED AND... SUBMITTED..."
WHAT ARE YOU DOING TO HIM?
"...TO SOME HIGHER ATTEMPT."

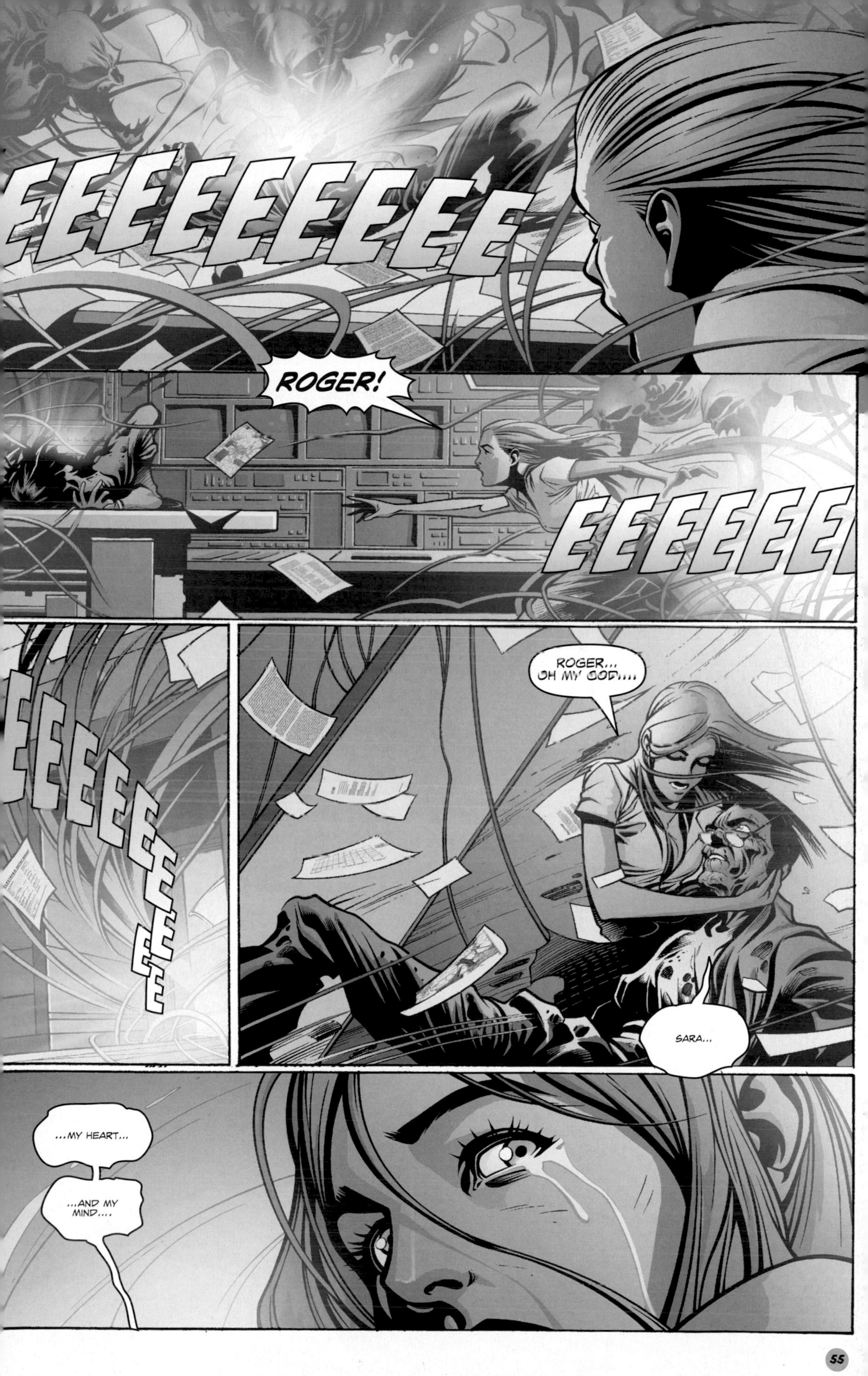
EEEEEEEEEE
ROGER!
EEEEEEE
EEEEEEEEEEE
ROGER... OH MY GOD....
SARA...
...MY HEART...
...AND MY MIND....

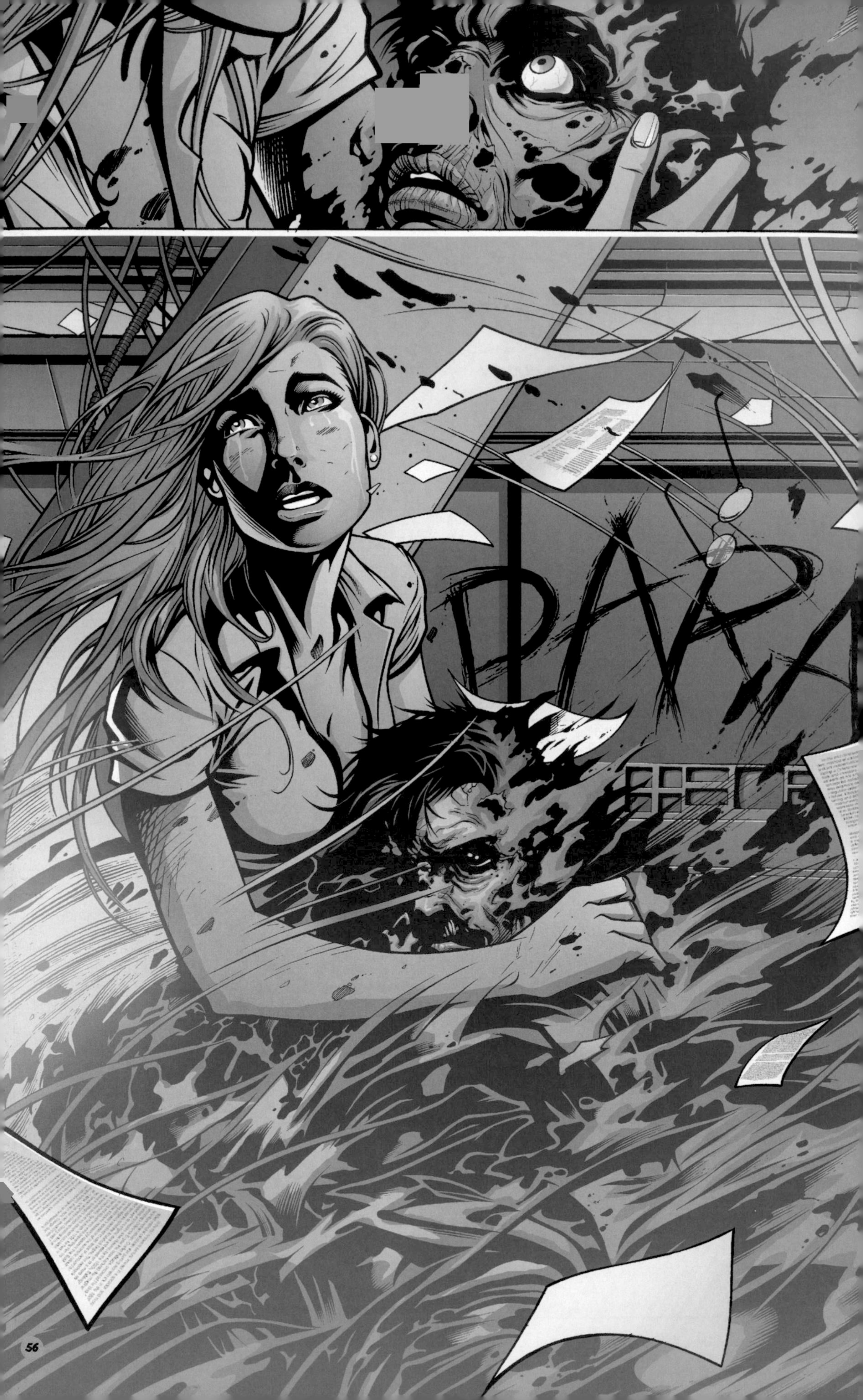

CHAPTER 3

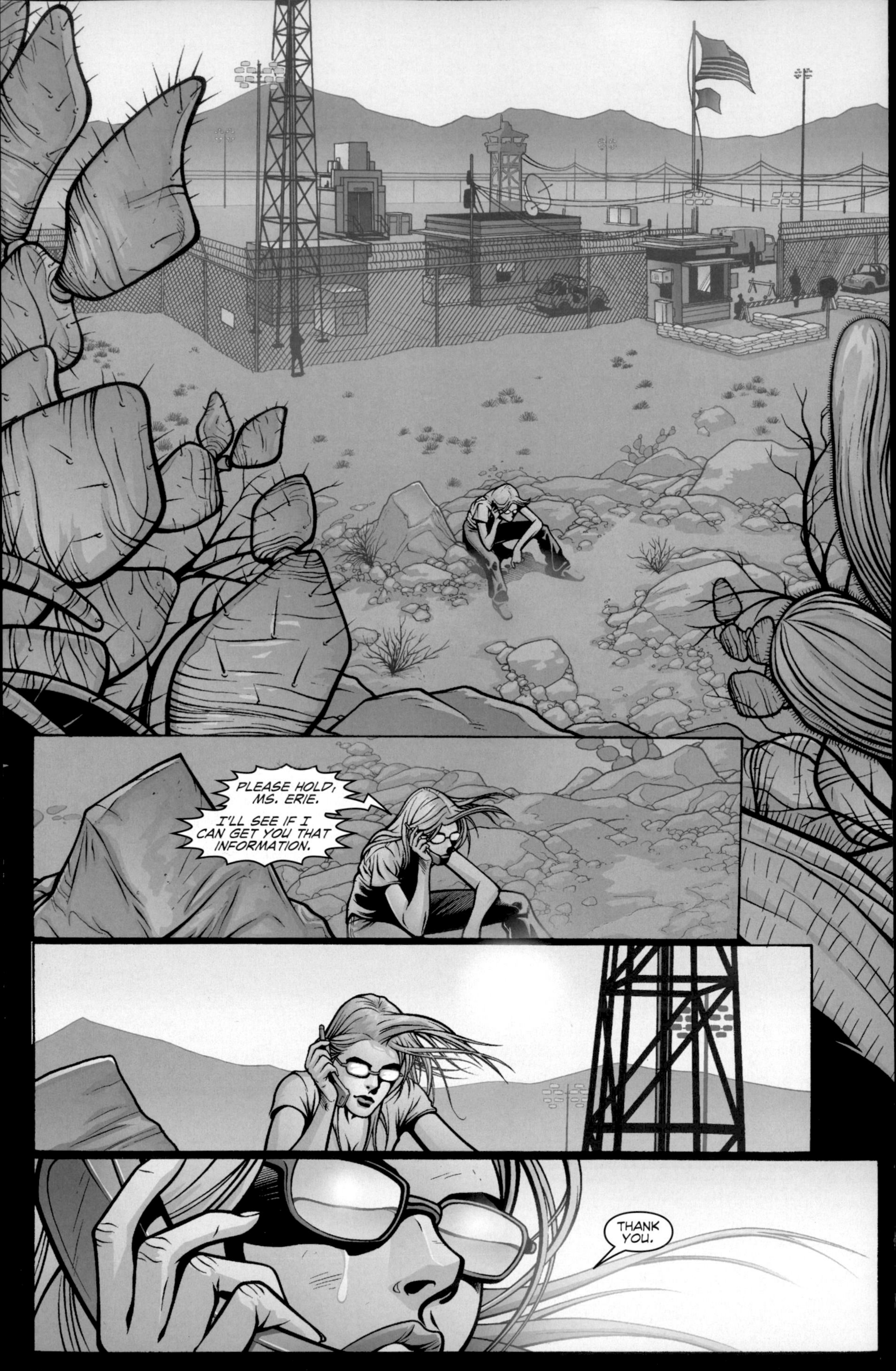
PLEASE HOLD, MS. ERIE.
I'LL SEE IF I CAN GET YOU THAT INFORMATION.
THANK YOU.

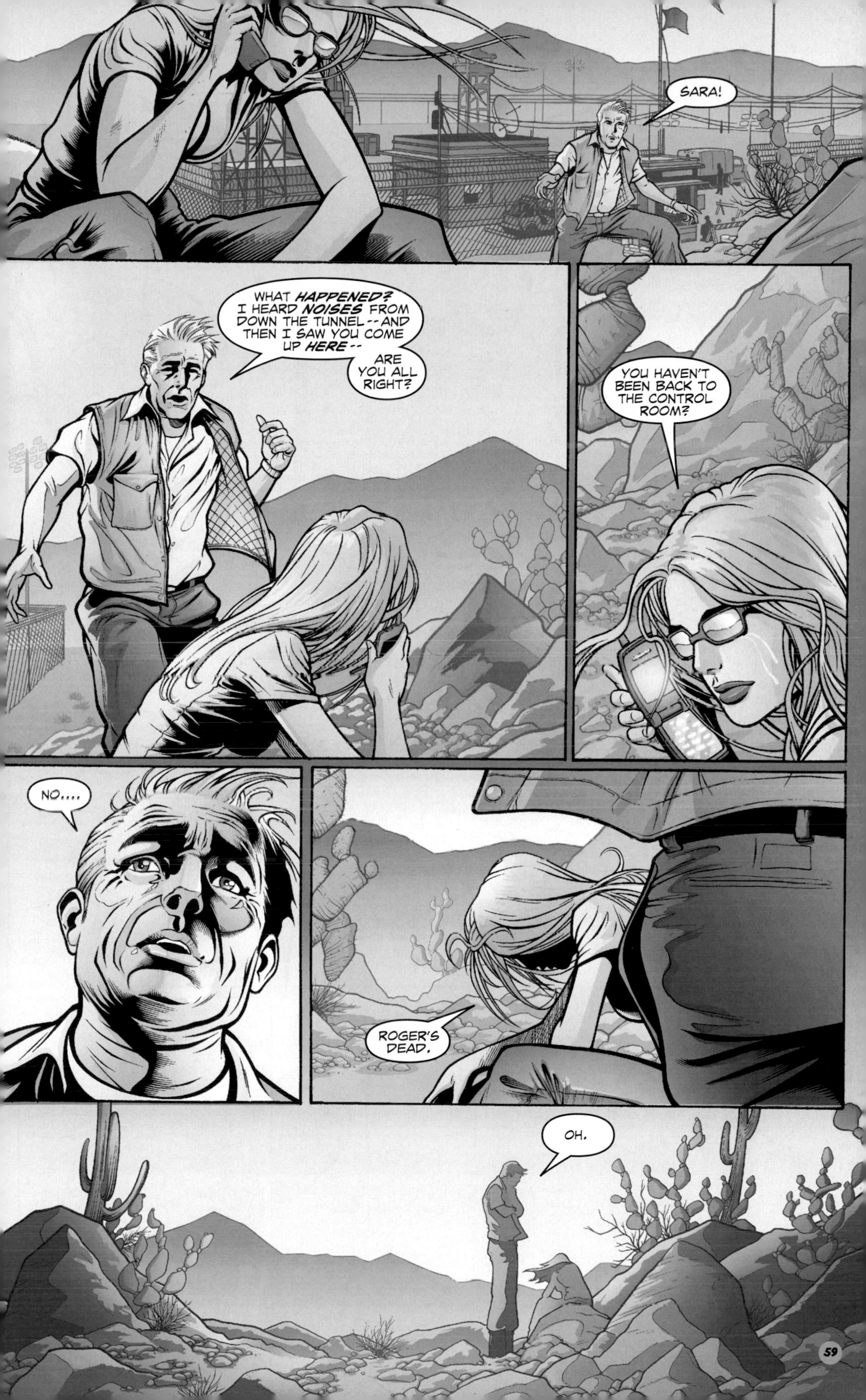
SARA!
WHAT HAPPENED? I HEARD NOISES FROM DOWN THE TUNNEL--AND THEN I SAW YOU COME UP HERE--
ARE YOU ALL RIGHT?
YOU HAVEN'T BEEN BACK TO THE CONTROL ROOM?
NO....
ROGER'S DEAD.
OH.

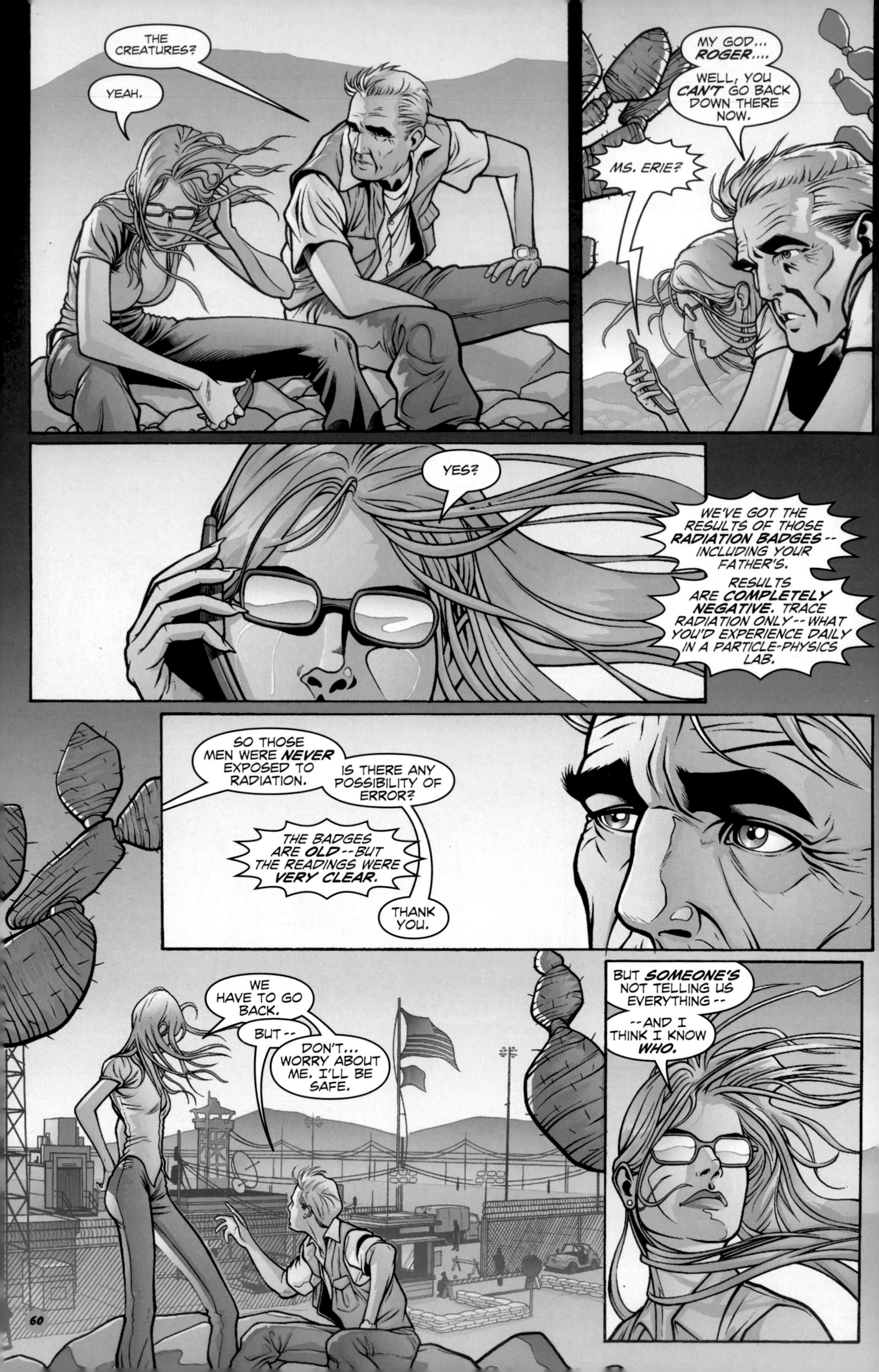

THE CREATURES?
YEAH.
MY GOD... ROGER....
WELL, YOU CAN'T GO BACK DOWN THERE NOW.
MS. ERIE?
YES?
WE'VE GOT THE RESULTS OF THOSE RADIATION BADGES -- INCLUDING YOUR FATHER'S.
RESULTS ARE COMPLETELY NEGATIVE. TRACE RADIATION ONLY -- WHAT YOU'D EXPERIENCE DAILY IN A PARTICLE-PHYSICS LAB.
SO THOSE MEN WERE NEVER EXPOSED TO RADIATION.
IS THERE ANY POSSIBILITY OF ERROR?
THE BADGES ARE OLD -- BUT THE READINGS WERE VERY CLEAR.
THANK YOU.
WE HAVE TO GO BACK.
BUT --
DON'T... WORRY ABOUT ME. I'LL BE SAFE.
BUT SOMEONE'S NOT TELLING US EVERYTHING --
-- AND I THINK I KNOW WHO.

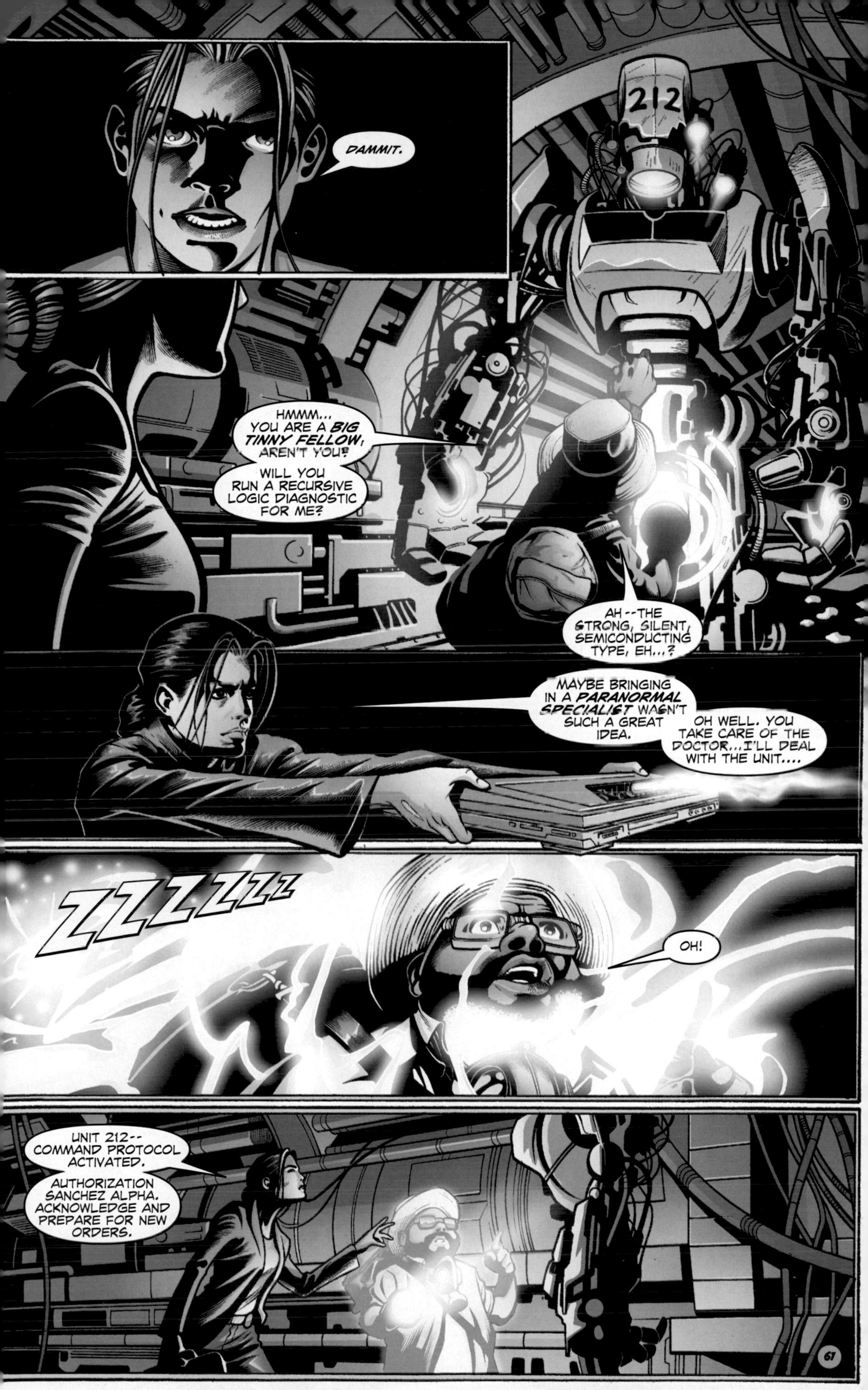
212
DAMMIT.
HMMM... YOU ARE A BIG TINNY FELLOW, AREN'T YOU?
WILL YOU RUN A RECURSIVE LOGIC DIAGNOSTIC FOR ME?
AH--THE STRONG, SILENT, SEMICONDUCTING TYPE, EH...?
MAYBE BRINGING IN A PARANORMAL SPECIALIST WASN'T SUCH A GREAT IDEA.
OH WELL. YOU TAKE CARE OF THE DOCTOR...I'LL DEAL WITH THE UNIT....
ZZZZZZ
OH!
UNIT 212-- COMMAND PROTOCOL ACTIVATED.
AUTHORIZATION SANCHEZ ALPHA. ACKNOWLEDGE AND PREPARE FOR NEW ORDERS.

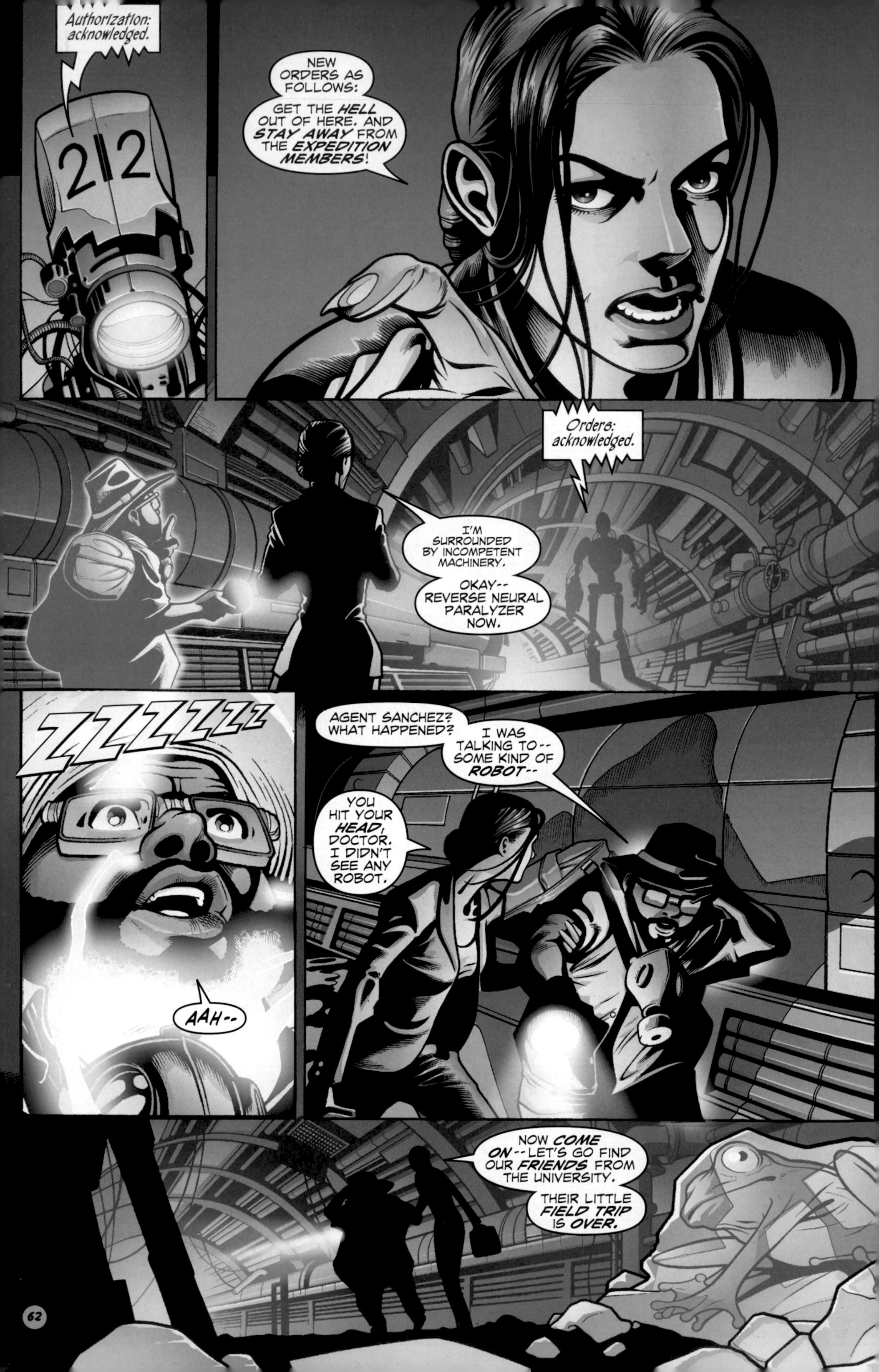
Authorization: acknowledged.
212
NEW ORDERS AS FOLLOWS:
GET THE HELL OUT OF HERE. AND STAY AWAY FROM THE EXPEDITION MEMBERS!
Orders: acknowledged.
I'M SURROUNDED BY INCOMPETENT MACHINERY.
OKAY-- REVERSE NEURAL PARALYZER NOW.
ZZZZZZZ
AAH--
AGENT SANCHEZ? WHAT HAPPENED?
I WAS TALKING TO-- SOME KIND OF ROBOT--
YOU HIT YOUR HEAD, DOCTOR. I DIDN'T SEE ANY ROBOT.
NOW COME ON--LET'S GO FIND OUR FRIENDS FROM THE UNIVERSITY.
THEIR LITTLE FIELD TRIP IS OVER.

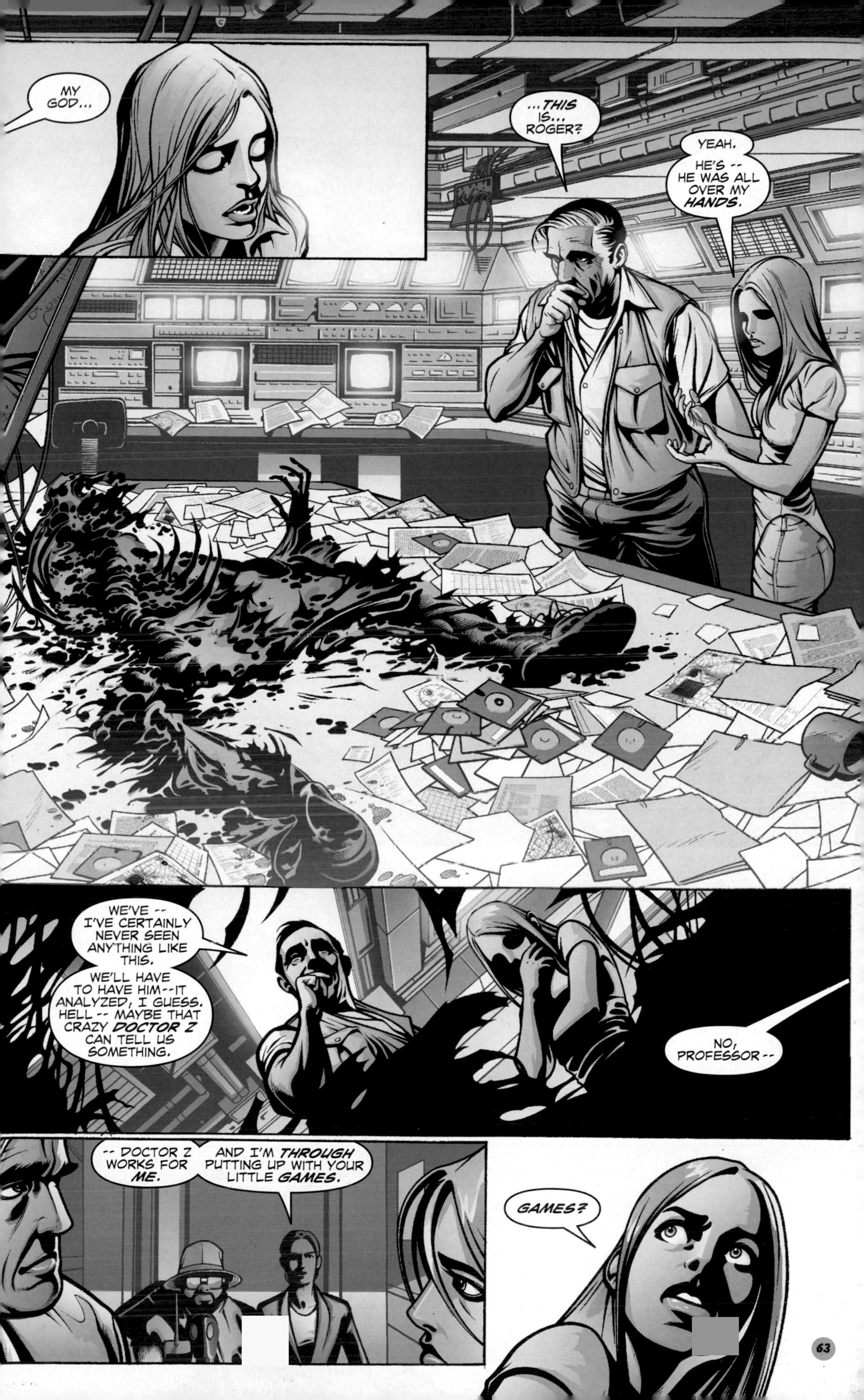
MY GOD...
...THIS IS... ROGER?
YEAH. HE'S -- HE WAS ALL OVER MY HANDS.
WE'VE -- I'VE CERTAINLY NEVER SEEN ANYTHING LIKE THIS.
WE'LL HAVE TO HAVE HIM--IT ANALYZED, I GUESS. HELL -- MAYBE THAT CRAZY DOCTOR Z CAN TELL US SOMETHING.
NO, PROFESSOR --
-- DOCTOR Z WORKS FOR ME.
AND I'M THROUGH PUTTING UP WITH YOUR LITTLE GAMES.
GAMES?

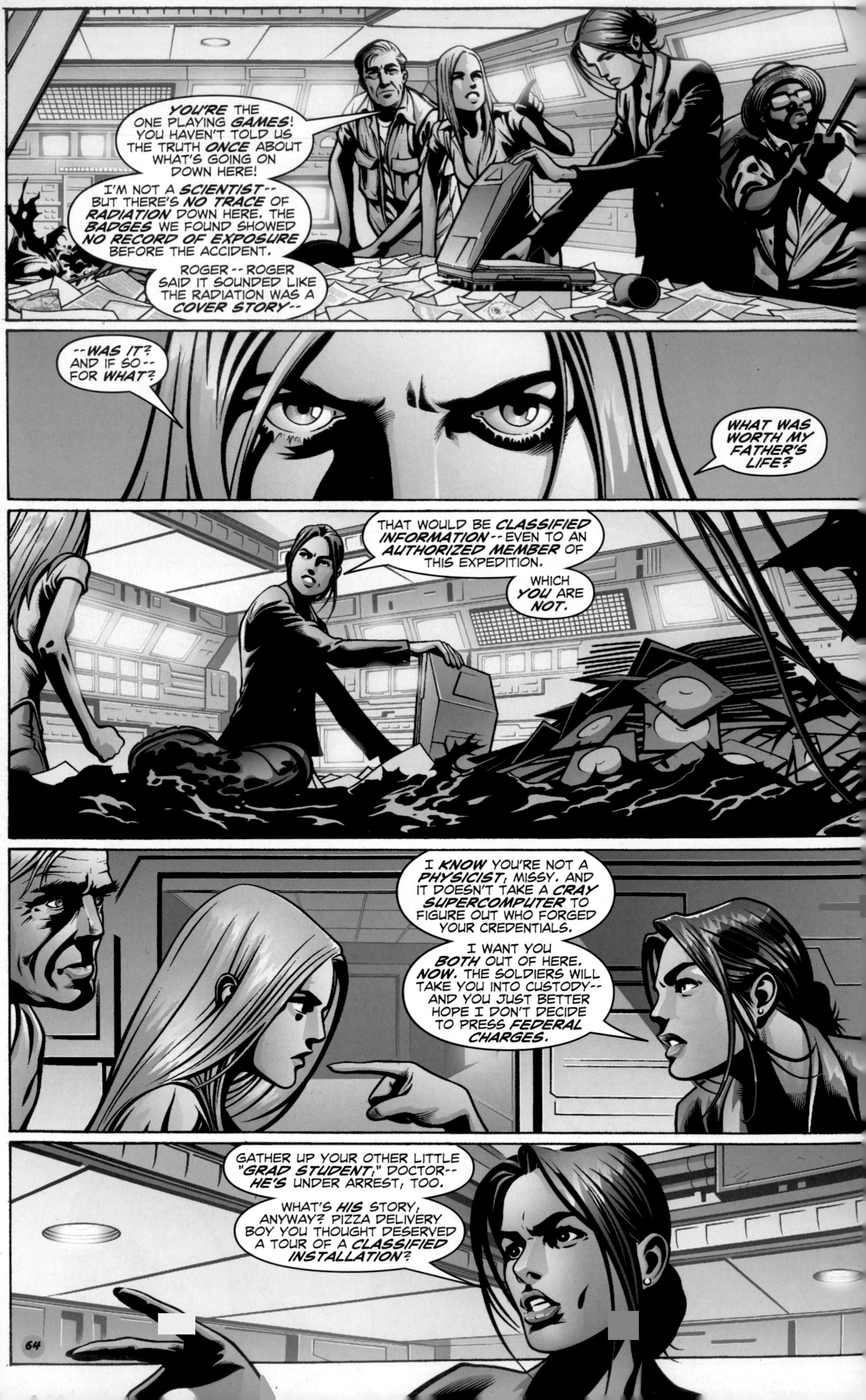
YOU'RE THE ONE PLAYING GAMES! YOU HAVEN'T TOLD US THE TRUTH ONCE ABOUT WHAT'S GOING ON DOWN HERE!
I'M NOT A SCIENTIST-- BUT THERE'S NO TRACE OF RADIATION DOWN HERE. THE BADGES WE FOUND SHOWED NO RECORD OF EXPOSURE BEFORE THE ACCIDENT.
ROGER--ROGER SAID IT SOUNDED LIKE THE RADIATION WAS A COVER STORY--
--WAS IT? AND IF SO-- FOR WHAT?
WHAT WAS WORTH MY FATHER'S LIFE?
THAT WOULD BE CLASSIFIED INFORMATION--EVEN TO AN AUTHORIZED MEMBER OF THIS EXPEDITION.
WHICH YOU ARE NOT.
I KNOW YOU'RE NOT A PHYSICIST, MISSY. AND IT DOESN'T TAKE A CRAY SUPERCOMPUTER TO FIGURE OUT WHO FORGED YOUR CREDENTIALS.
I WANT YOU BOTH OUT OF HERE. NOW. THE SOLDIERS WILL TAKE YOU INTO CUSTODY-- AND YOU JUST BETTER HOPE I DON'T DECIDE TO PRESS FEDERAL CHARGES.
GATHER UP YOUR OTHER LITTLE "GRAD STUDENT," DOCTOR-- HE'S UNDER ARREST, TOO.
WHAT'S HIS STORY, ANYWAY? PIZZA DELIVERY BOY YOU THOUGHT DESERVED A TOUR OF A CLASSIFIED INSTALLATION?

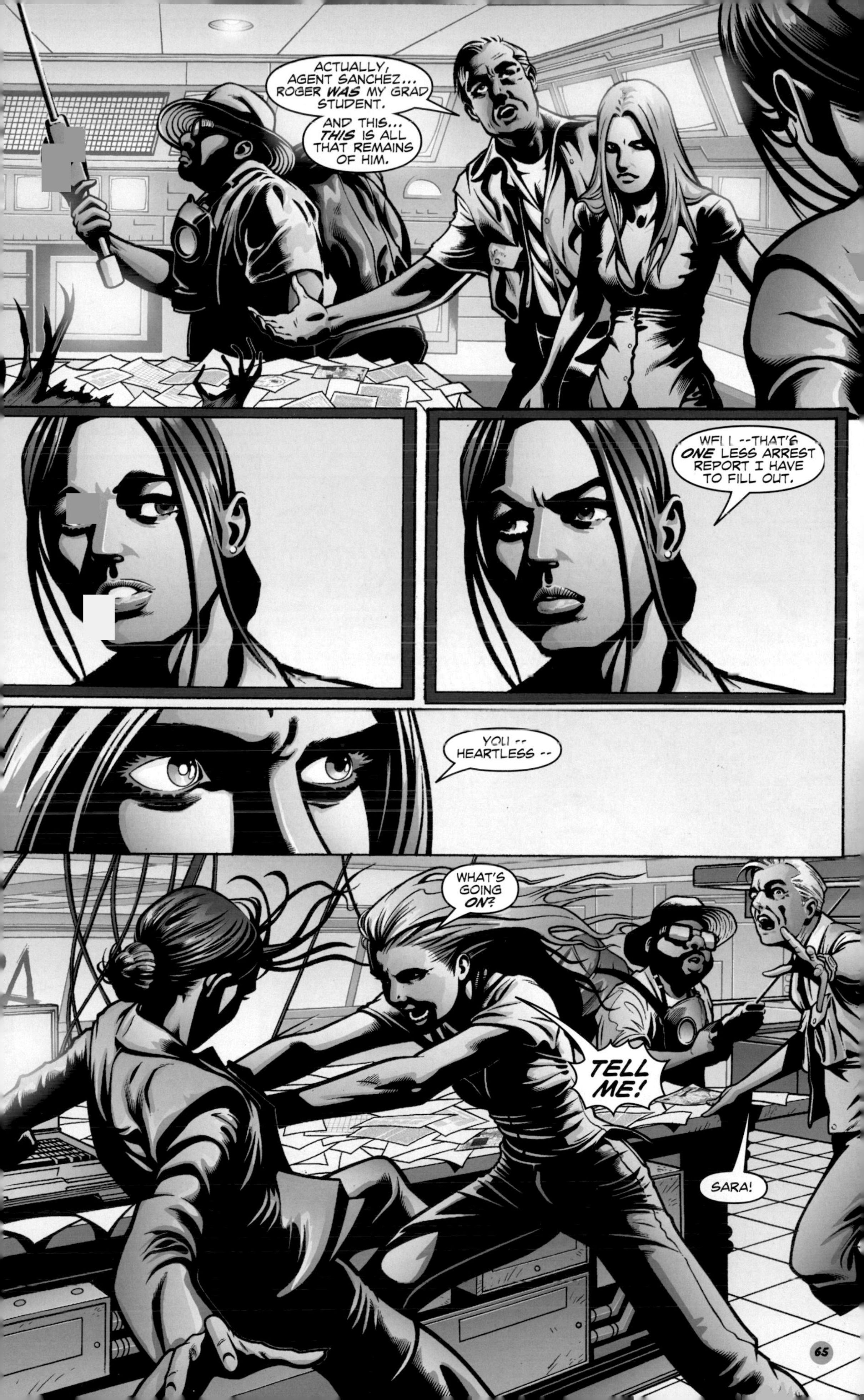
ACTUALLY, AGENT SANCHEZ... ROGER WAS MY GRAD STUDENT.
AND THIS... THIS IS ALL THAT REMAINS OF HIM.
WELL --THAT'S ONE LESS ARREST REPORT I HAVE TO FILL OUT.
YOU -- HEARTLESS --
WHAT'S GOING ON?
TELL ME!
SARA!

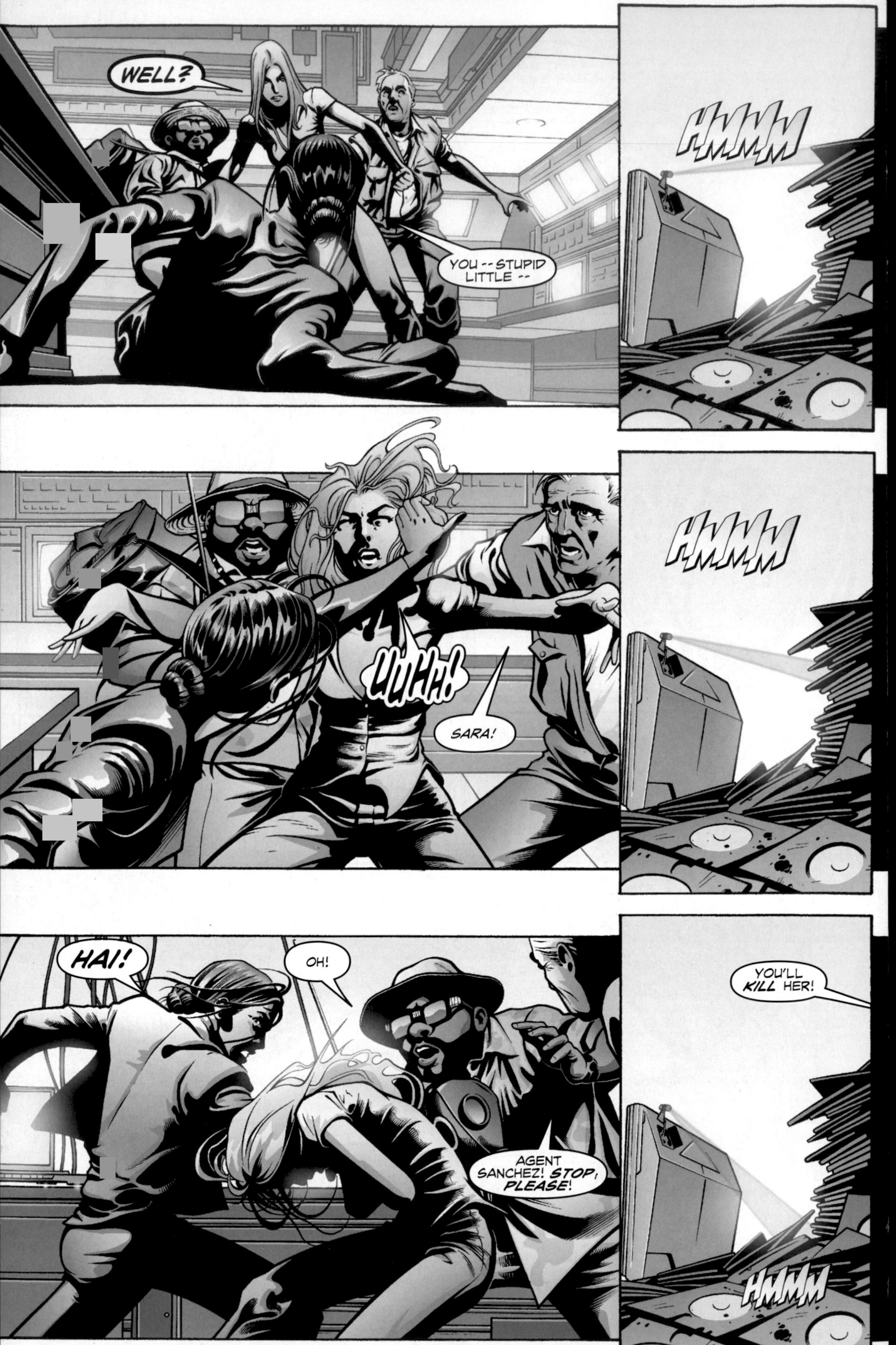
WELL?
YOU -- STUPID LITTLE --
HMMM
HMMM
UUHH!
SARA!
HAI!
OH!
AGENT SANCHEZ! STOP, PLEASE!
YOU'LL KILL HER!
HMMM

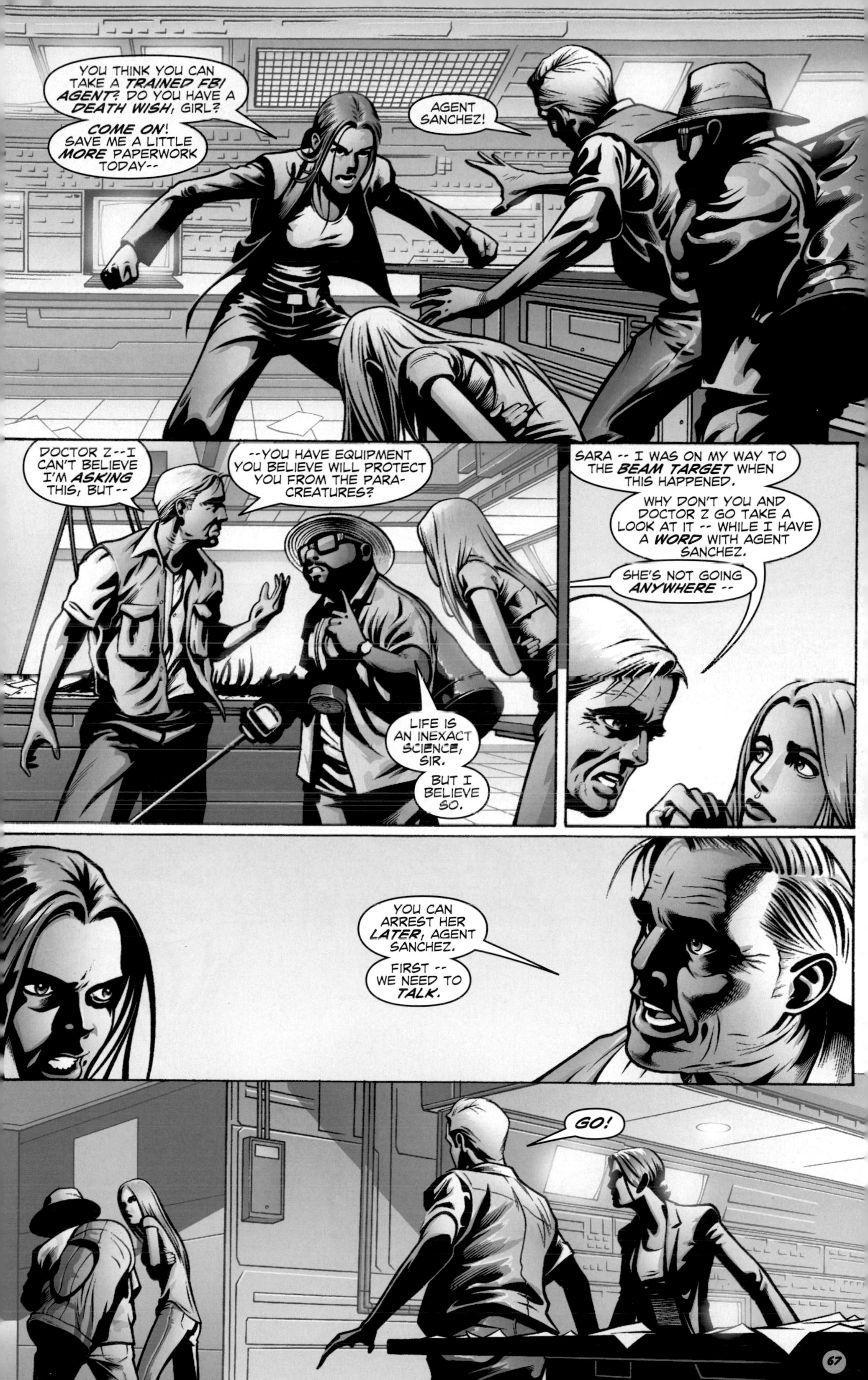
YOU THINK YOU CAN TAKE A TRAINED FBI AGENT? DO YOU HAVE A DEATH WISH, GIRL?
COME ON! SAVE ME A LITTLE MORE PAPERWORK TODAY--
AGENT SANCHEZ!
DOCTOR Z--I CAN'T BELIEVE I'M ASKING THIS, BUT--
--YOU HAVE EQUIPMENT YOU BELIEVE WILL PROTECT YOU FROM THE PARA-CREATURES?
LIFE IS AN INEXACT SCIENCE, SIR.
BUT I BELIEVE SO.
SARA -- I WAS ON MY WAY TO THE BEAM TARGET WHEN THIS HAPPENED.
WHY DON'T YOU AND DOCTOR Z GO TAKE A LOOK AT IT -- WHILE I HAVE A WORD WITH AGENT SANCHEZ.
SHE'S NOT GOING ANYWHERE --
YOU CAN ARREST HER LATER, AGENT SANCHEZ.
FIRST -- WE NEED TO TALK.
GO!

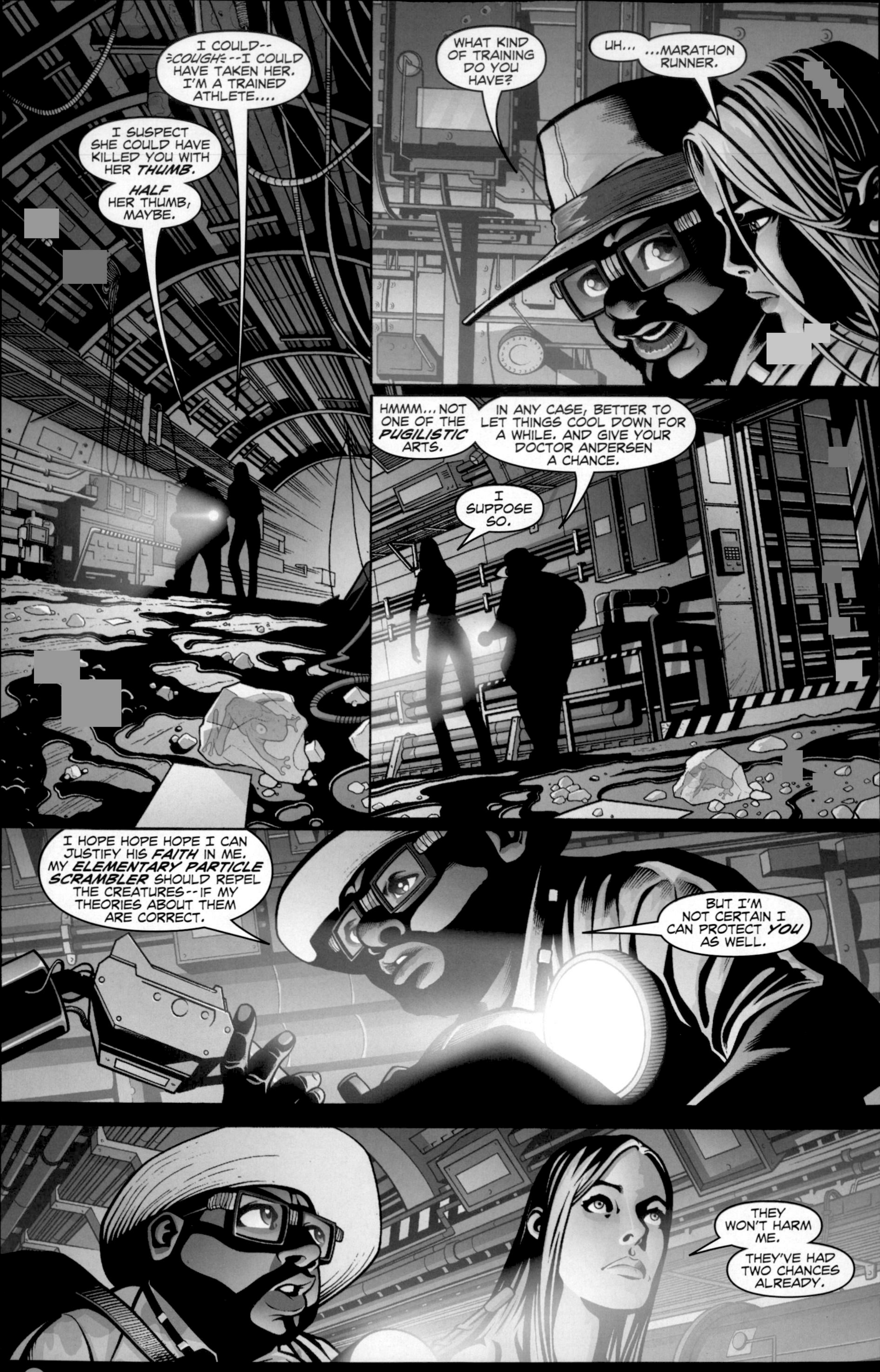
I COULD-- *COUGH* --I COULD HAVE TAKEN HER. I'M A TRAINED ATHLETE....
I SUSPECT SHE COULD HAVE KILLED YOU WITH HER *THUMB*.
HALF HER THUMB, MAYBE.
WHAT KIND OF TRAINING DO YOU HAVE?
UH... ...MARATHON RUNNER.
HMMM... NOT ONE OF THE *PUGILISTIC* ARTS.
IN ANY CASE, BETTER TO LET THINGS COOL DOWN FOR A WHILE. AND GIVE YOUR DOCTOR ANDERSEN A CHANCE.
I SUPPOSE SO.
I HOPE HOPE HOPE I CAN JUSTIFY HIS *FAITH* IN ME. MY *ELEMENTARY PARTICLE SCRAMBLER* SHOULD REPEL THE CREATURES--IF MY THEORIES ABOUT THEM ARE CORRECT.
BUT I'M NOT CERTAIN I CAN PROTECT *YOU* AS WELL.
THEY WON'T HARM ME.
THEY'VE HAD TWO CHANCES ALREADY.

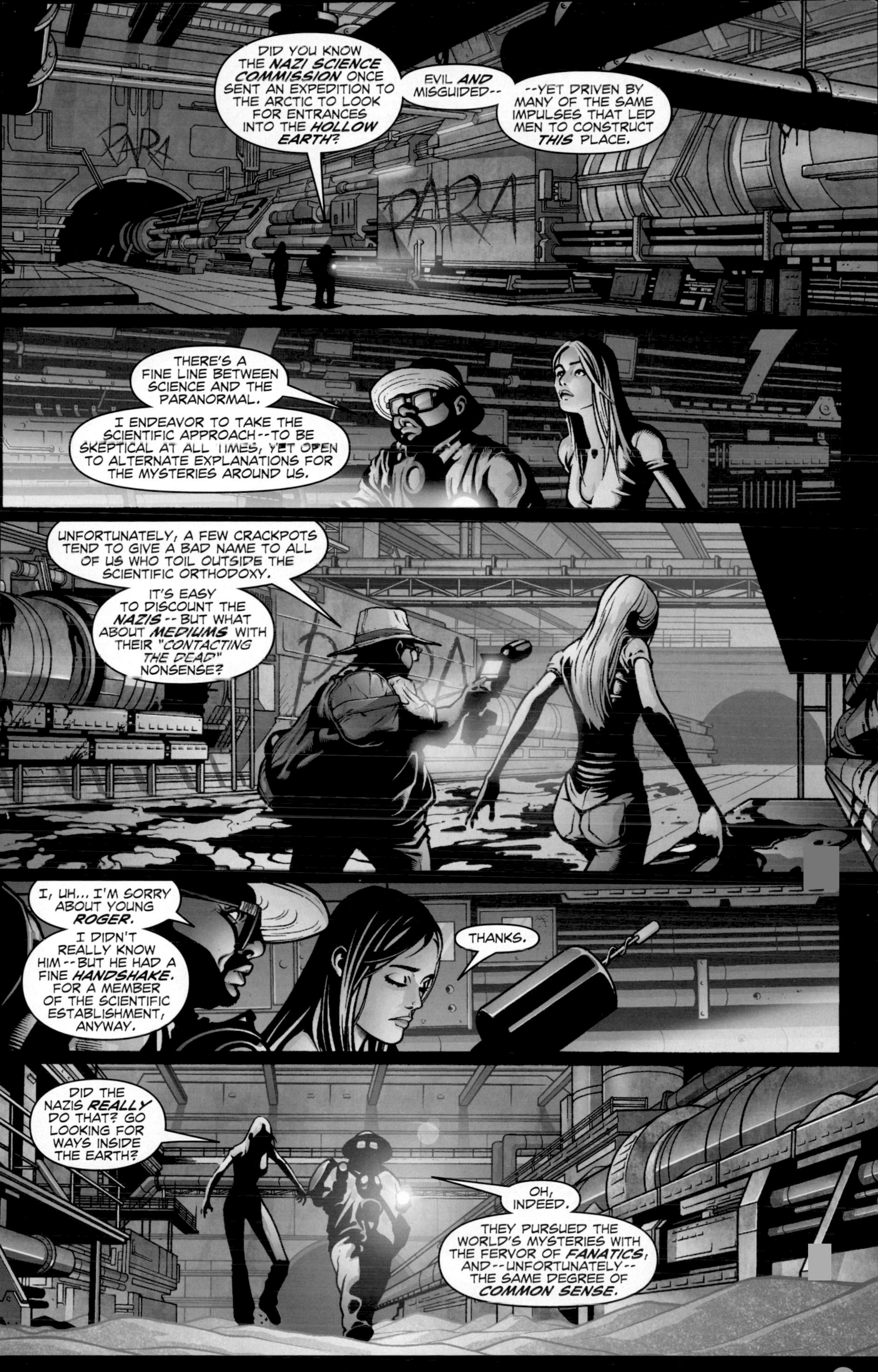
DID YOU KNOW THE NAZI SCIENCE COMMISSION ONCE SENT AN EXPEDITION TO THE ARCTIC TO LOOK FOR ENTRANCES INTO THE HOLLOW EARTH?
EVIL AND MISGUIDED--
--YET DRIVEN BY MANY OF THE SAME IMPULSES THAT LED MEN TO CONSTRUCT THIS PLACE.
PARA
PARA
THERE'S A FINE LINE BETWEEN SCIENCE AND THE PARANORMAL.
I ENDEAVOR TO TAKE THE SCIENTIFIC APPROACH--TO BE SKEPTICAL AT ALL TIMES, YET OPEN TO ALTERNATE EXPLANATIONS FOR THE MYSTERIES AROUND US.
UNFORTUNATELY, A FEW CRACKPOTS TEND TO GIVE A BAD NAME TO ALL OF US WHO TOIL OUTSIDE THE SCIENTIFIC ORTHODOXY.
IT'S EASY TO DISCOUNT THE NAZIS--BUT WHAT ABOUT MEDIUMS WITH THEIR "CONTACTING THE DEAD" NONSENSE?
I, UH... I'M SORRY ABOUT YOUNG ROGER.
I DIDN'T REALLY KNOW HIM--BUT HE HAD A FINE HANDSHAKE. FOR A MEMBER OF THE SCIENTIFIC ESTABLISHMENT, ANYWAY.
THANKS.
DID THE NAZIS REALLY DO THAT? GO LOOKING FOR WAYS INSIDE THE EARTH?
OH, INDEED.
THEY PURSUED THE WORLD'S MYSTERIES WITH THE FERVOR OF FANATICS, AND--UNFORTUNATELY--THE SAME DEGREE OF COMMON SENSE.

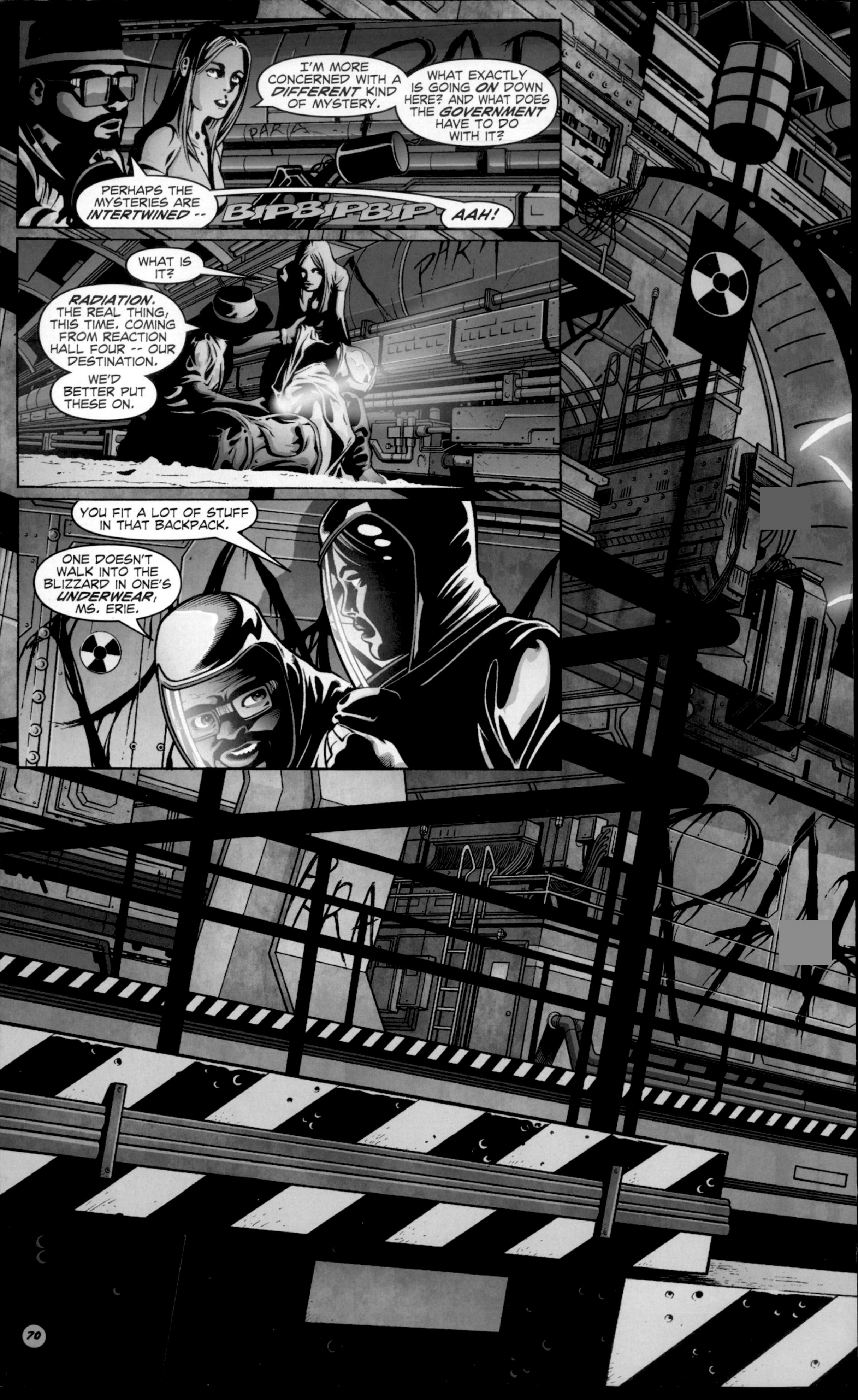
I'M MORE CONCERNED WITH A *DIFFERENT* KIND OF MYSTERY.
WHAT EXACTLY IS GOING *ON* DOWN HERE? AND WHAT DOES THE *GOVERNMENT* HAVE TO DO WITH IT?
PERHAPS THE MYSTERIES ARE *INTERTWINED* --
BIPBIPBIP
AAH!
WHAT IS IT?
RADIATION. THE REAL THING, THIS TIME. COMING FROM REACTION HALL FOUR -- OUR DESTINATION.
WE'D BETTER PUT THESE ON.
YOU FIT A LOT OF STUFF IN THAT BACKPACK.
ONE DOESN'T WALK INTO THE BLIZZARD IN ONE'S *UNDERWEAR,* MS. ERIE.

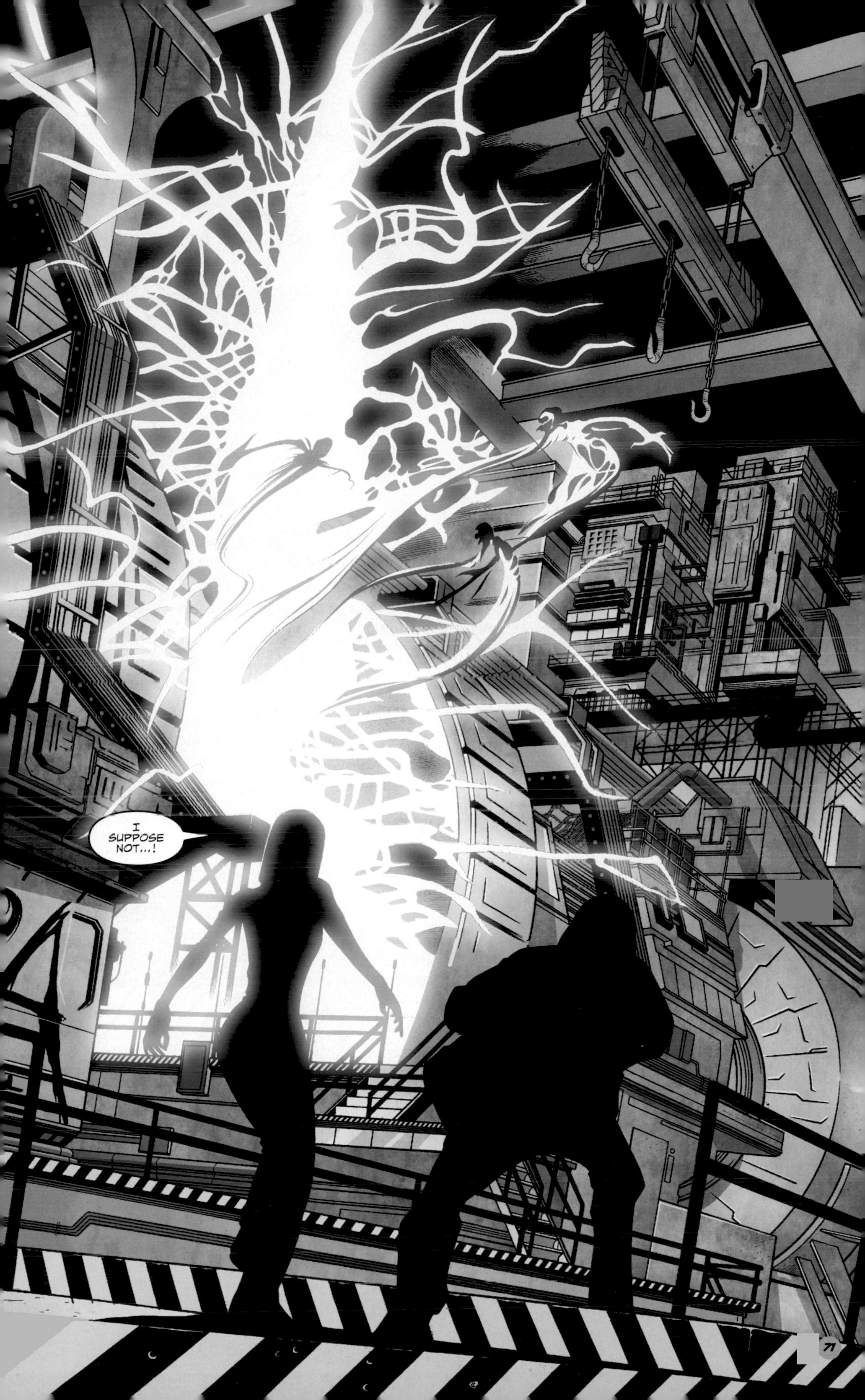
I SUPPOSE NOT...!

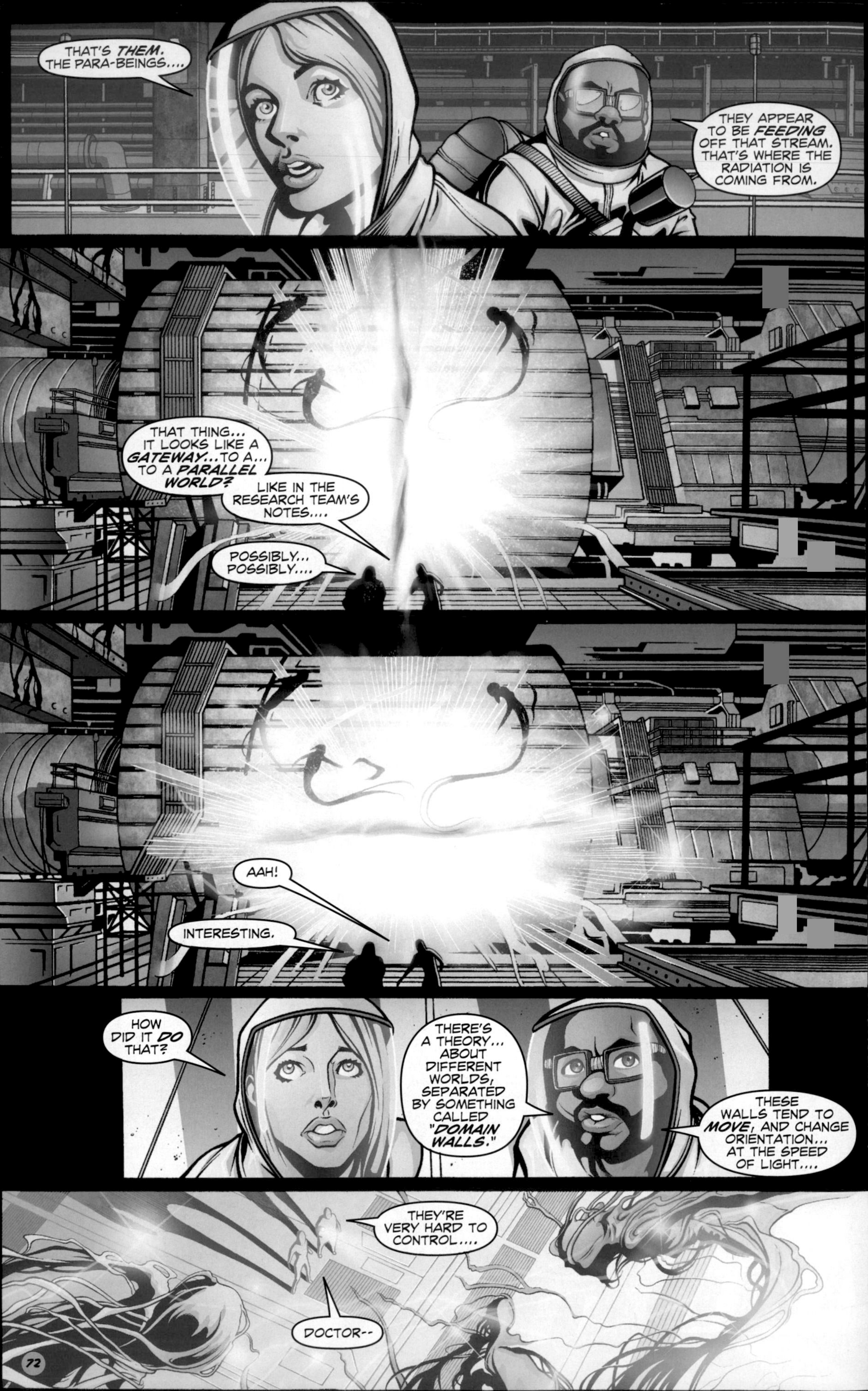
THAT'S THEM. THE PARA-BEINGS....
THEY APPEAR TO BE FEEDING OFF THAT STREAM. THAT'S WHERE THE RADIATION IS COMING FROM.
THAT THING... IT LOOKS LIKE A GATEWAY...TO A... TO A PARALLEL WORLD?
LIKE IN THE RESEARCH TEAM'S NOTES....
POSSIBLY... POSSIBLY....
AAH!
INTERESTING.
HOW DID IT DO THAT?
THERE'S A THEORY... ABOUT DIFFERENT WORLDS, SEPARATED BY SOMETHING CALLED "DOMAIN WALLS."
THESE WALLS TEND TO MOVE, AND CHANGE ORIENTATION... AT THE SPEED OF LIGHT....
THEY'RE VERY HARD TO CONTROL....
DOCTOR--

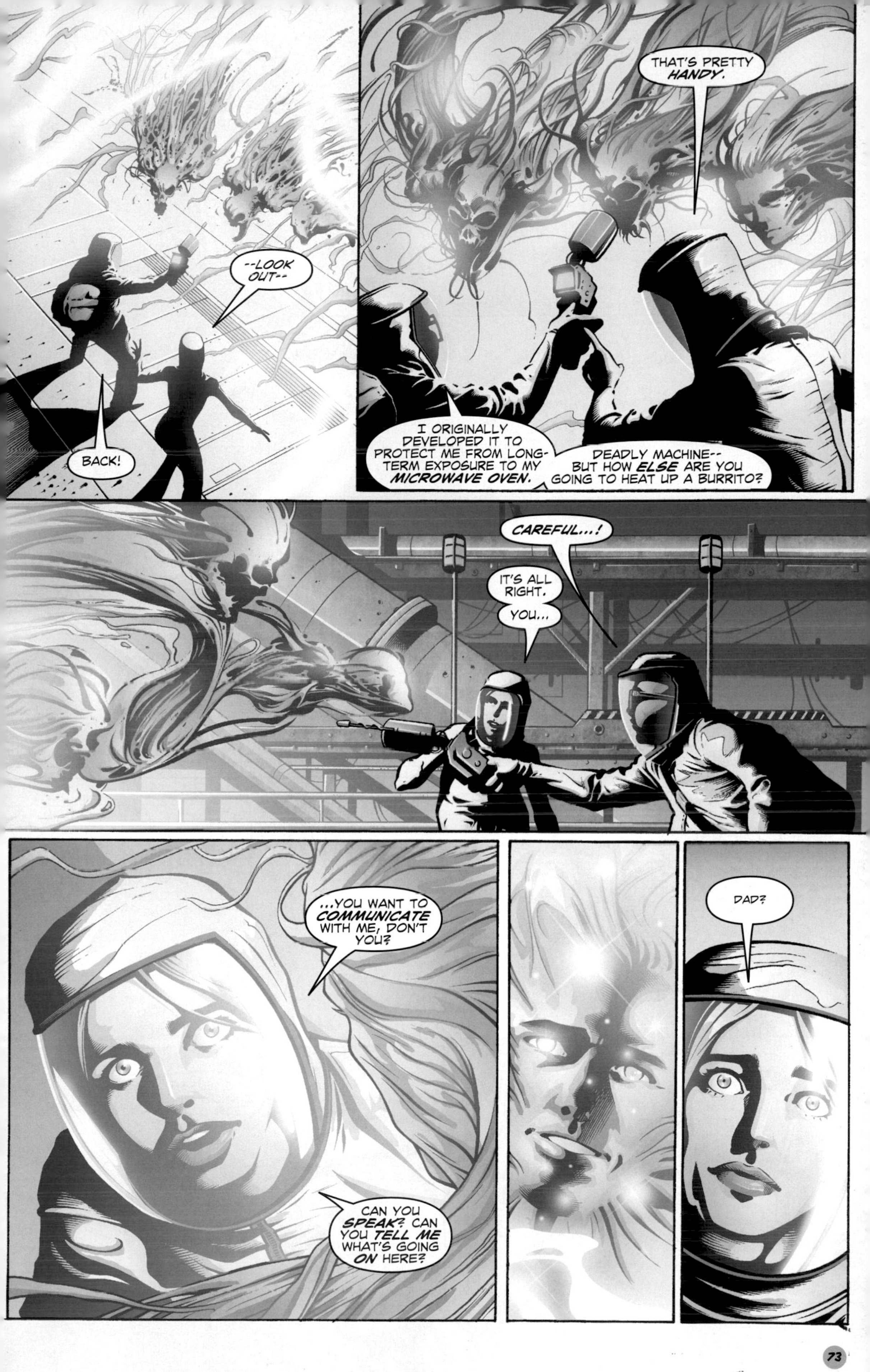
--LOOK OUT--
BACK!
THAT'S PRETTY HANDY.
I ORIGINALLY DEVELOPED IT TO PROTECT ME FROM LONG-TERM EXPOSURE TO MY MICROWAVE OVEN.
DEADLY MACHINE-- BUT HOW ELSE ARE YOU GOING TO HEAT UP A BURRITO?
CAREFUL...!
IT'S ALL RIGHT.
YOU...
...YOU WANT TO COMMUNICATE WITH ME, DON'T YOU?
CAN YOU SPEAK? CAN YOU TELL ME WHAT'S GOING ON HERE?
DAD?

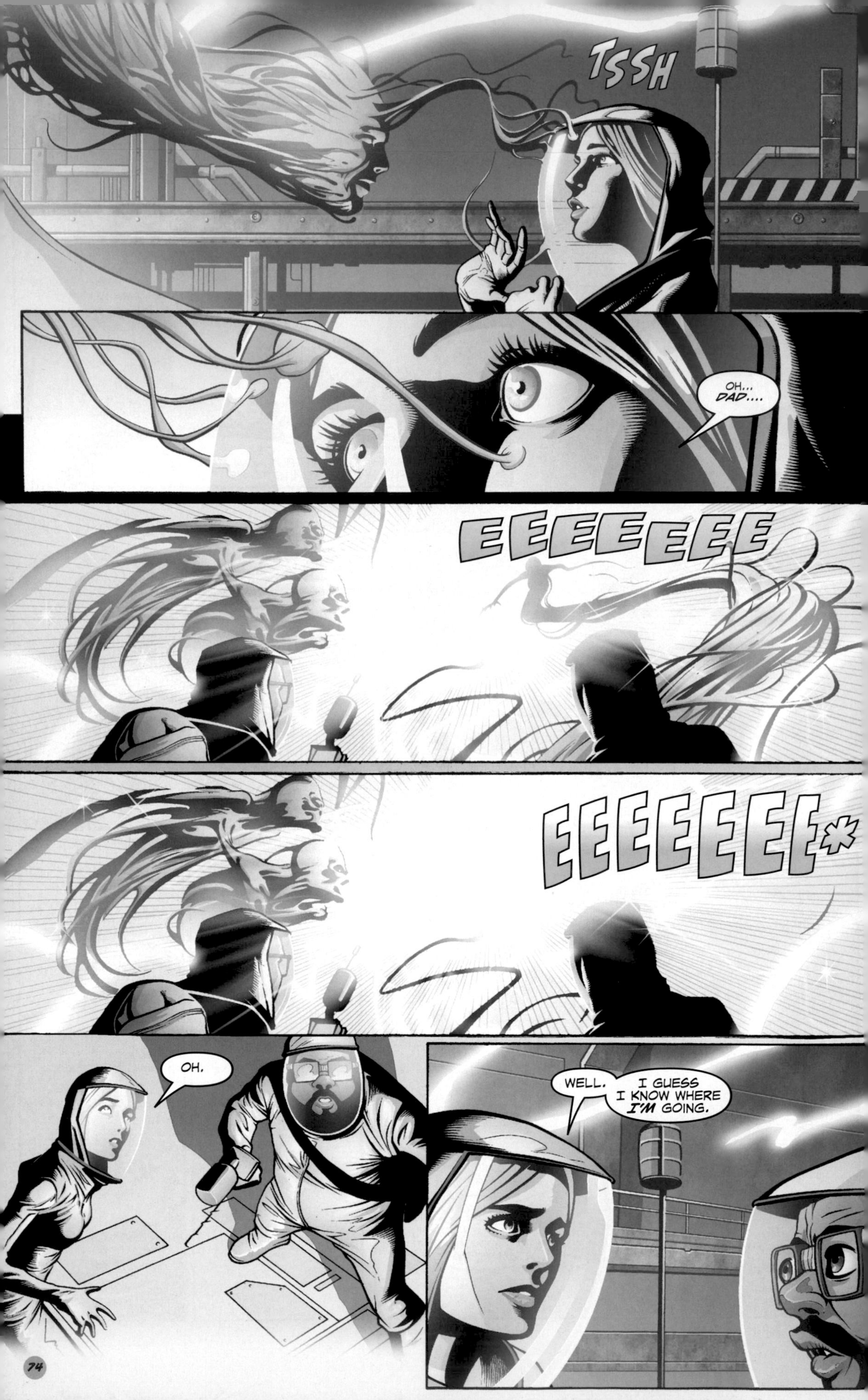
TSSH
OH... DAD....
EEEEEEE
EEEEEEE*
OH.
WELL.
I GUESS I KNOW WHERE I'M GOING.

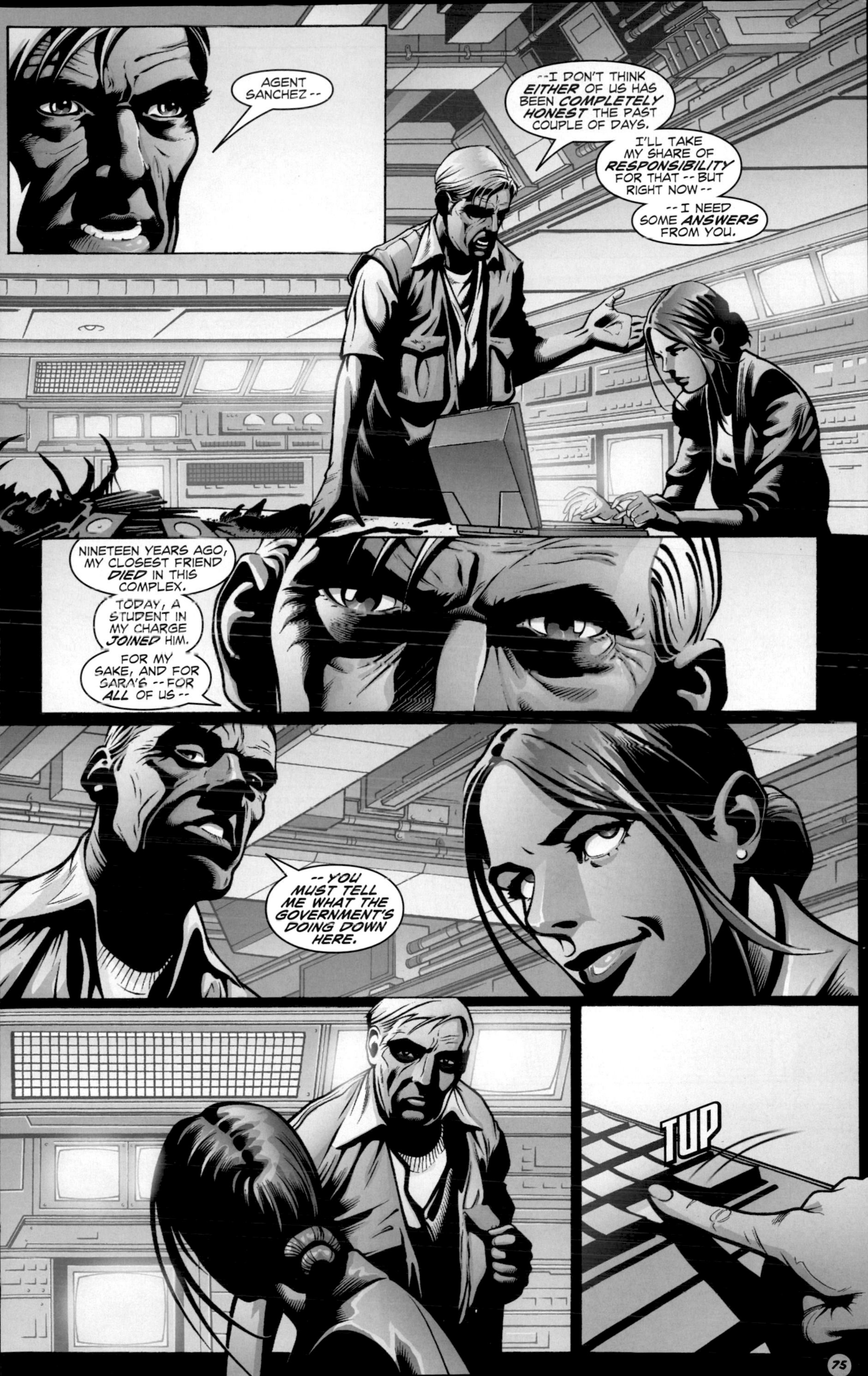
AGENT SANCHEZ --
--I DON'T THINK EITHER OF US HAS BEEN COMPLETELY HONEST THE PAST COUPLE OF DAYS.
I'LL TAKE MY SHARE OF RESPONSIBILITY FOR THAT -- BUT RIGHT NOW --
-- I NEED SOME ANSWERS FROM YOU.
NINETEEN YEARS AGO, MY CLOSEST FRIEND DIED IN THIS COMPLEX.
TODAY, A STUDENT IN MY CHARGE JOINED HIM.
FOR MY SAKE, AND FOR SARA'S -- FOR ALL OF US --
-- YOU MUST TELL ME WHAT THE GOVERNMENT'S DOING DOWN HERE.
TUP

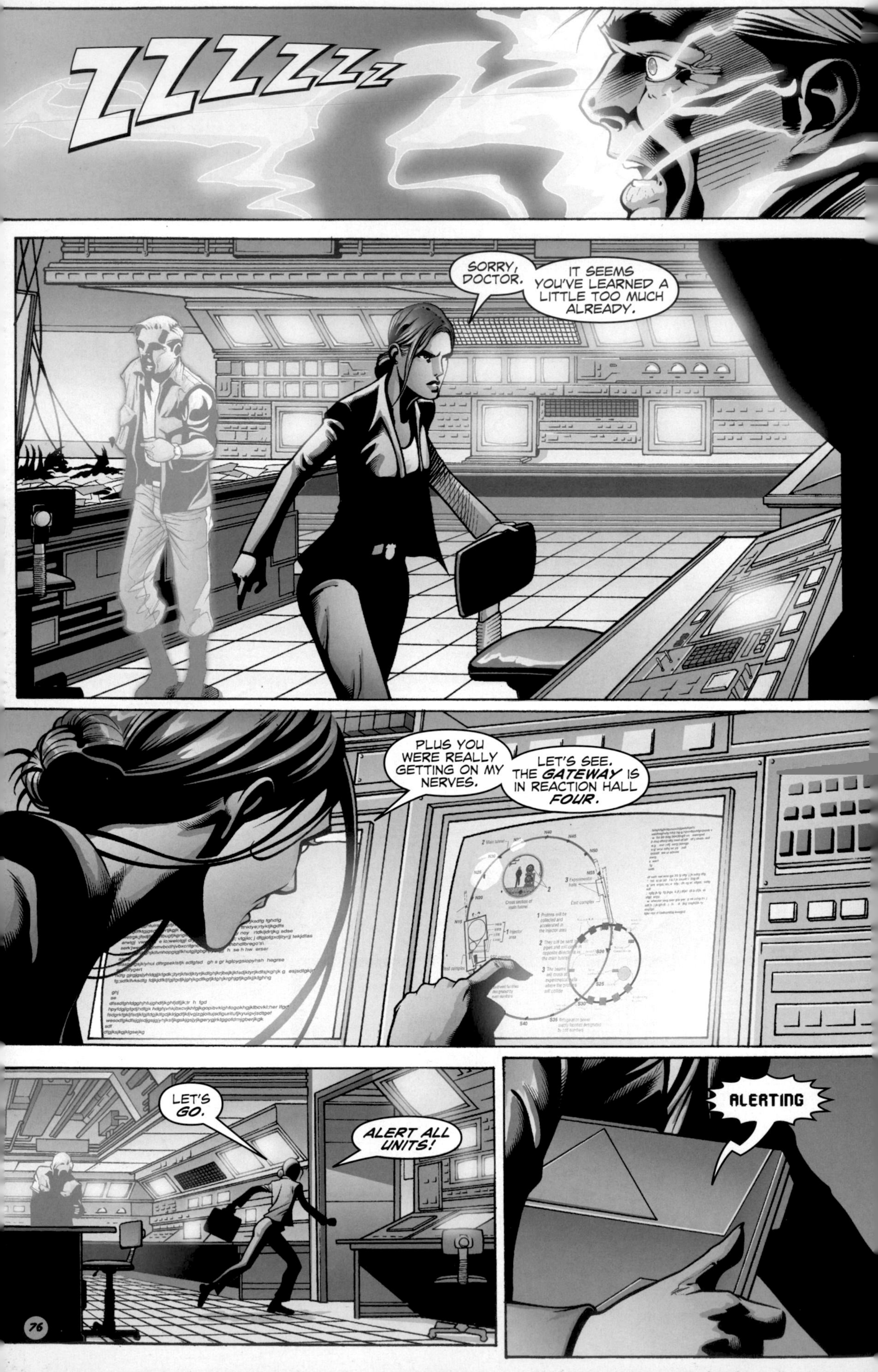
ZZZZZZz
SORRY, DOCTOR.
IT SEEMS YOU'VE LEARNED A LITTLE TOO MUCH ALREADY.
PLUS YOU WERE REALLY GETTING ON MY NERVES.
LET'S SEE. THE GATEWAY IS IN REACTION HALL FOUR.
LET'S GO.
ALERT ALL UNITS!
ALERTING

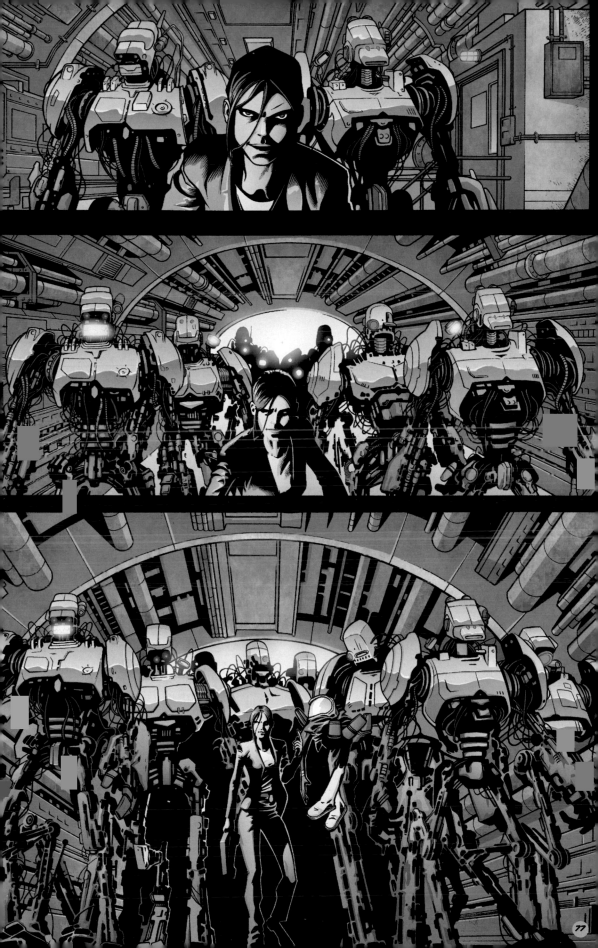

THIS IS DANGEROUS. DANGEROUS DANGEROUS DANGEROUS....

I *HAVE* TO DO IT, DOCTOR.

SOMETHING OF MY FATHER IS *IN* THAT THING. WHEN IT TOUCHED MY HEAD... I *FELT* IT. MAYBE SOMETHING'S LEFT OF *ROGER*, TOO, SOMEWHERE OVER THERE. I'VE GOT TO FIND OUT.

-- MAYBE I'LL GET SOME ANSWERS ABOUT WHAT HAPPENED TO THIS PLACE. WHAT'S *THIS* DO?

IT'S AN *ANTI-QUARK GENERATOR* -- MY OWN DESIGN. WITH LUCK, IT SHOULD PROTECT YOU FROM THE VIOLENT SHIFT IN SUBATOMIC ACTIVITY AS YOU PASS THROUGH THE DOORWAY.

AND EVEN IF I DON'T --

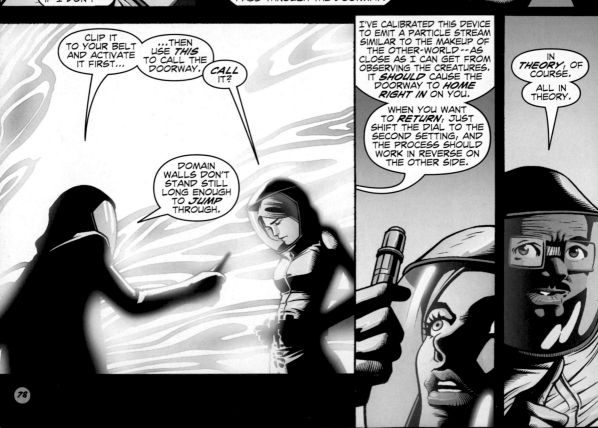

CLIP IT TO YOUR BELT AND ACTIVATE IT FIRST...

...THEN USE *THIS* TO CALL THE DOORWAY.

CALL IT?

DOMAIN WALLS DON'T STAND STILL LONG ENOUGH TO *JUMP* THROUGH.

I'VE CALIBRATED THIS DEVICE TO EMIT A PARTICLE STREAM SIMILAR TO THE MAKEUP OF THE OTHER-WORLD -- AS CLOSE AS I CAN GET FROM OBSERVING THE CREATURES. IT *SHOULD* CAUSE THE DOORWAY TO *HOME RIGHT IN* ON YOU.

WHEN YOU WANT TO *RETURN*, JUST SHIFT THE DIAL TO THE SECOND SETTING, AND THE PROCESS SHOULD WORK IN REVERSE ON THE OTHER SIDE.

IN *THEORY*, OF COURSE. ALL IN THEORY.

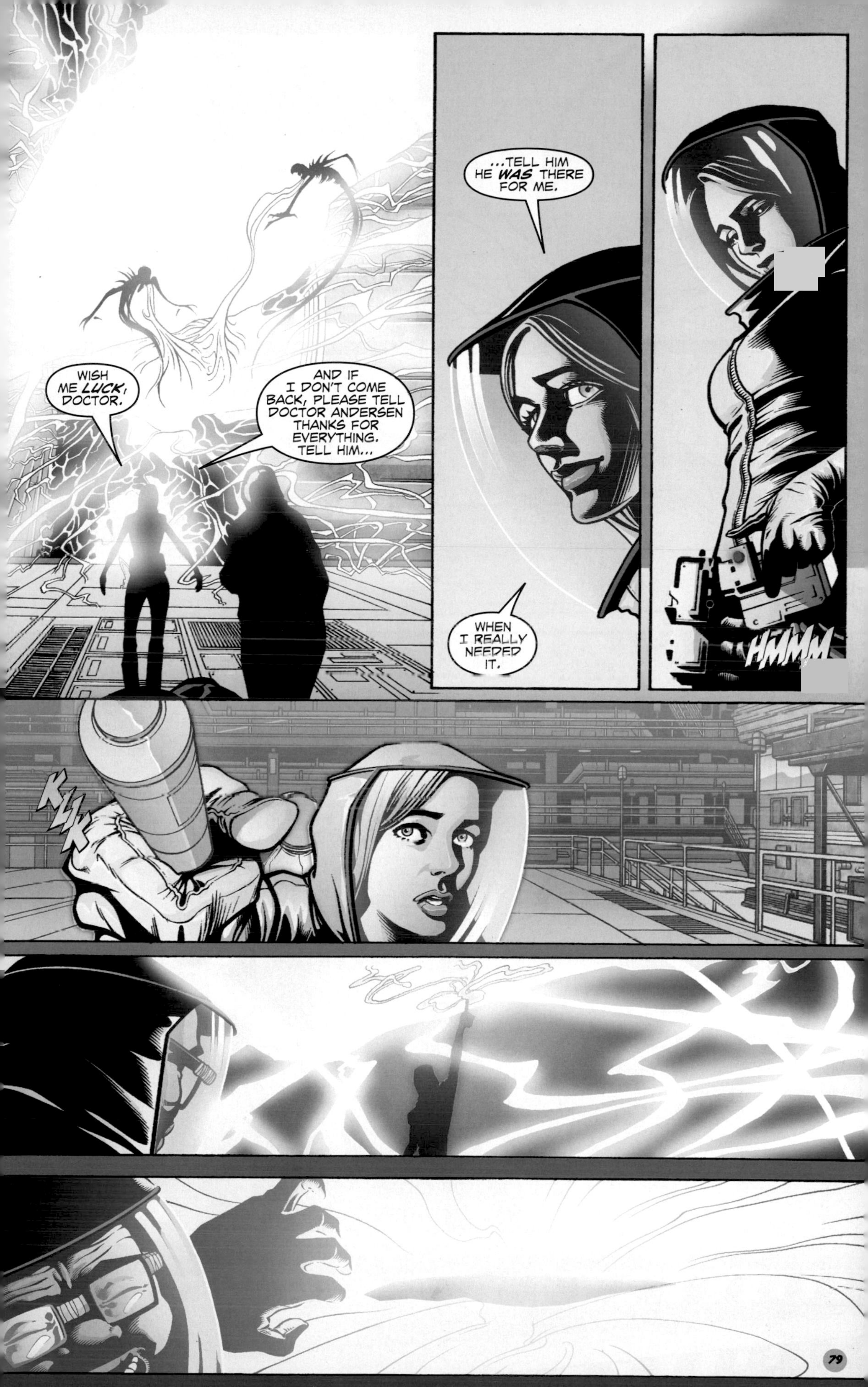
WISH ME LUCK, DOCTOR.
AND IF I DON'T COME BACK, PLEASE TELL DOCTOR ANDERSEN THANKS FOR EVERYTHING. TELL HIM...
...TELL HIM HE WAS THERE FOR ME.
WHEN I REALLY NEEDED IT.
HMMM
KLIK

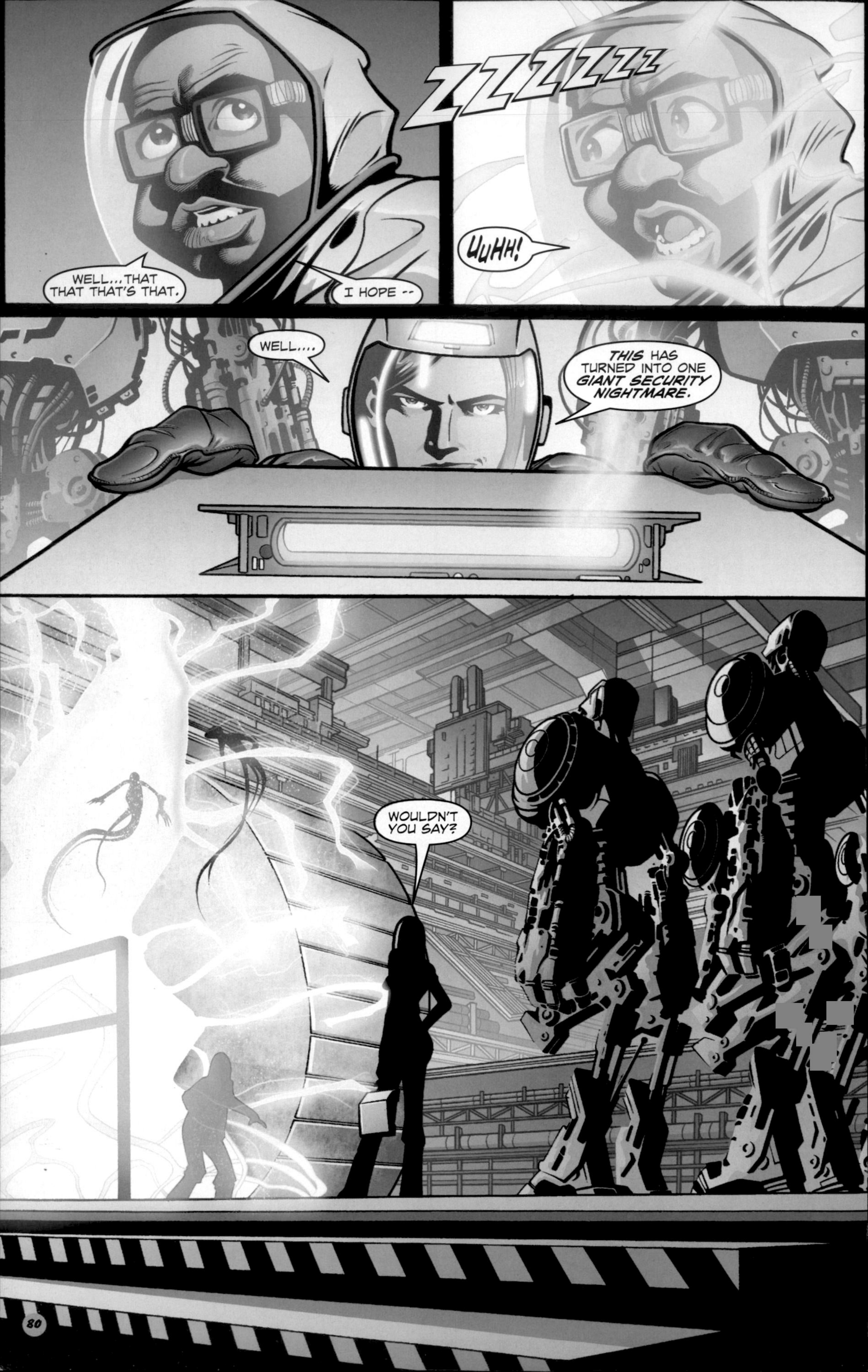
WELL...THAT THAT THAT'S THAT.
I HOPE --
ZZZZZZZ
UUHH!
WELL....
THIS HAS TURNED INTO ONE GIANT SECURITY NIGHTMARE.
WOULDN'T YOU SAY?

CHAPTER 4

As she passed through the gateway, the first thing Sara felt was a tingling feeling that started on her skin and quickly moved all the way through her. It reached right up into her brain, filling her with both a pervasive dread and a gut feeling that there were things in the universe she'd never understand.

Sara had felt that dread once before: nineteen years ago, when her father died.

Doctor Andersen had been there for her, then. But no one could help her now. She was passing into another world, a world no human had ever seen.

At the moment of transit, Sara squeezed her eyes shut. Phosphenes, bright flashes of light, penetrated her eyelids. The sight of one universe fading, and another coming into view.

Amazing.

When she opened her eyes, she saw a long line of lights...like an infinity of fiber-optic cables, stretching off into the distance. She raised her hand, and her muscles reacted, but slowly. Then she jerked her head back, too quickly, and almost lost her balance.

Time seemed to move...strangely, here. Not faster, or slower, necessarily, but at a *varying* rate. For instance, a thousand patterns might flash across those lights in an instant. But when she opened her mouth to say:

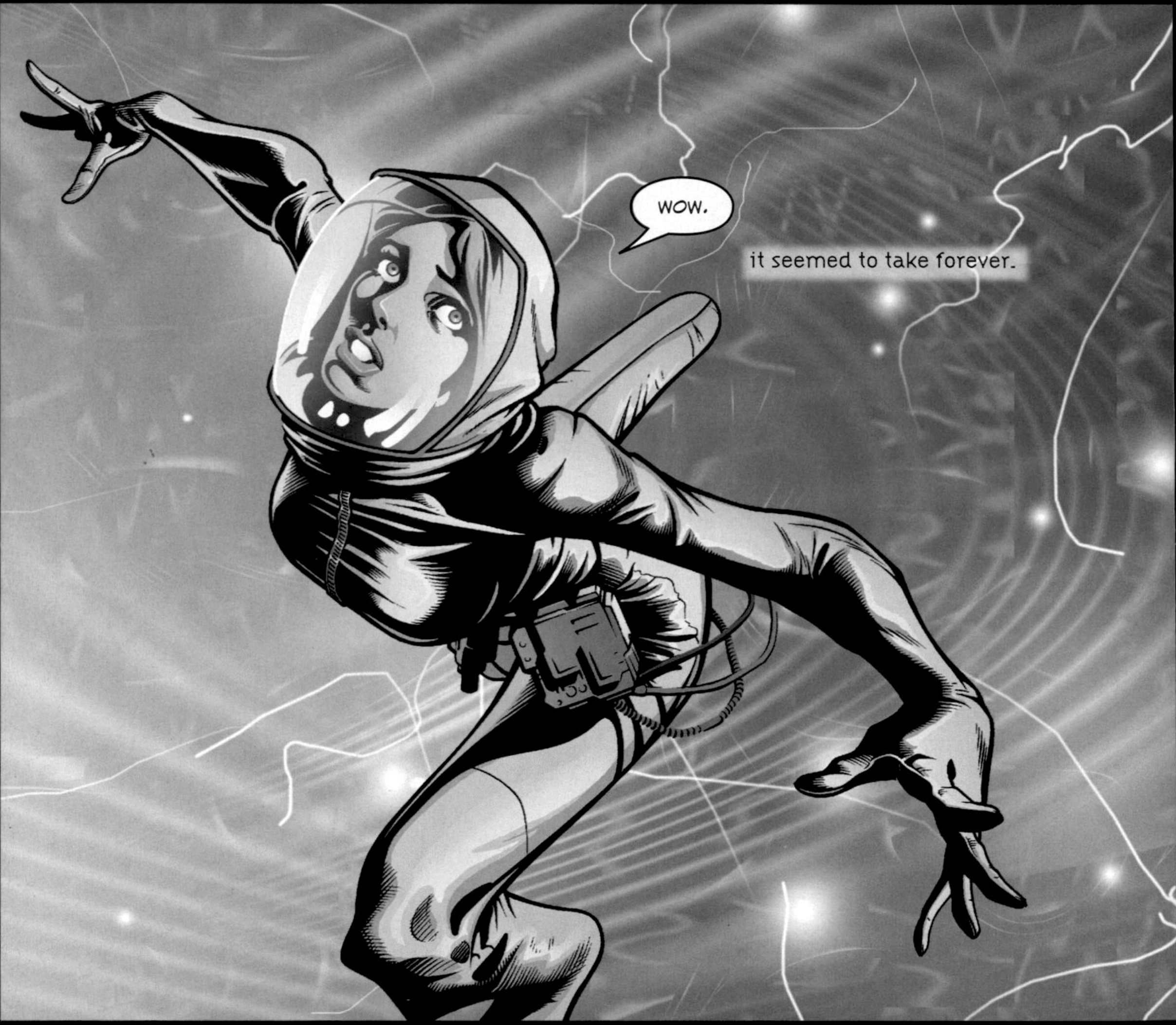
WOW.
it seemed to take forever.

The Anti-Quark generator had worked—protected her from the stresses of the transit. Whatever you thought about Doctor Z, his hardware was solid.

Now she had to find the Paras, especially the one that seemed to hold some remnant of her father within it. But where were they?

This was their universe—but that was the problem. It was an entire *universe.* And Sara had no road map, no guidebook to Para-world.

For a moment, she despaired. The exhaustion of the day's events caught up with her, and her knees buckled.

Then she had an idea....

Sara closed her eyes and concentrated. She didn't know if it was possible to project thought-energy, but she intended to try.

She remembered the touch of the Para-creature to her forehead...the impressions, the dreamlike sense of her father it had passed along to her for that brief moment.

She recalled the touch of her dad's hand when she was seven...when she'd built the diorama model of the Supercollider, the place he was helping to build.

She'd been so proud, so happy. The world was safe because her dad would always protect her, and yet it was full of endless possibilities, infinite promises of discovery.

That's what he had taught her, above all: To keep searching...to ask what lies beyond the next wall, the next layer of the onion...

...beneath the surface trappings of reality....

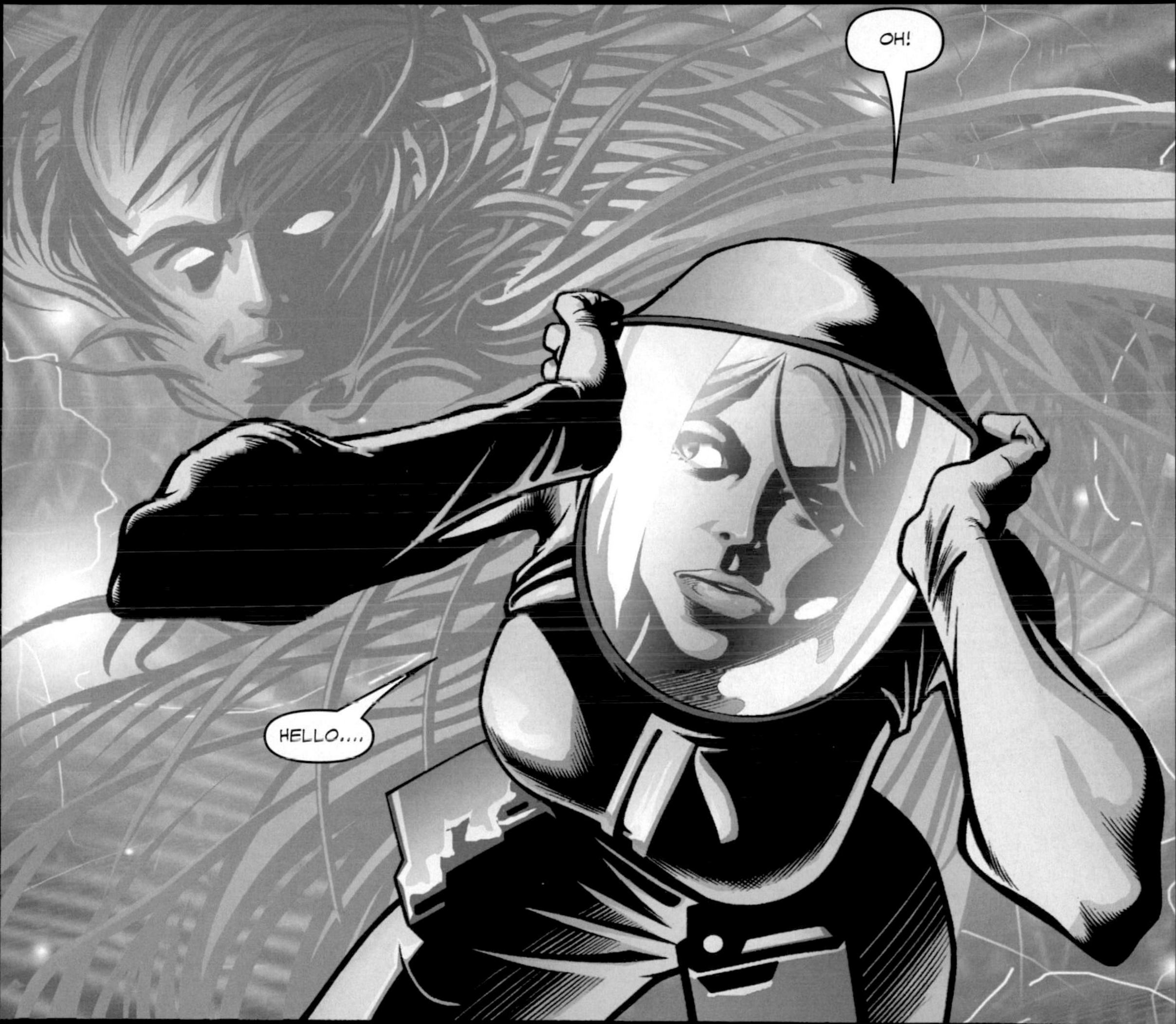
OH!
HELLO....

Then it was there.

Sara turned to look at it, and found it looking back at her with what seemed like curiosity. But did that curiosity come from her father, or merely some alien creature? After all, Sara was an invader in *its* world now.

The more she looked at the creature, the more she seemed to see her father's face. But it wasn't quite right...it was more like an echo, a faded photocopy of him. Like a child's memory, strong in emotional resonance but fuzzy in the details.

Like a wispy dream that would never survive the dawn.

A wave of what might have been disappointment crossed the Para's face, and it started to move away. Sara cried out for it to stay.

It hesitated, then moved closer again.

The Para circled around Sara once, quickly, and she began to see images. Not impressions in her mind, like before; these were real, tactile, formed out of the raw, swirling matter all around her.

She saw her father, twenty years ago, desperately starting the Supercollider's first experiments in secret.

"They're going to cut the funding—we have to move fast. We have to prove to them that this place is important!"

So they fired up the beam, a week early. The unimaginable energies—greater than any particle accelerator had ever produced before—shot around and around the twenty-eight mile tunnel, faster and faster, powerful electromagnets guiding the beam, channeling it tightly toward the beam target.

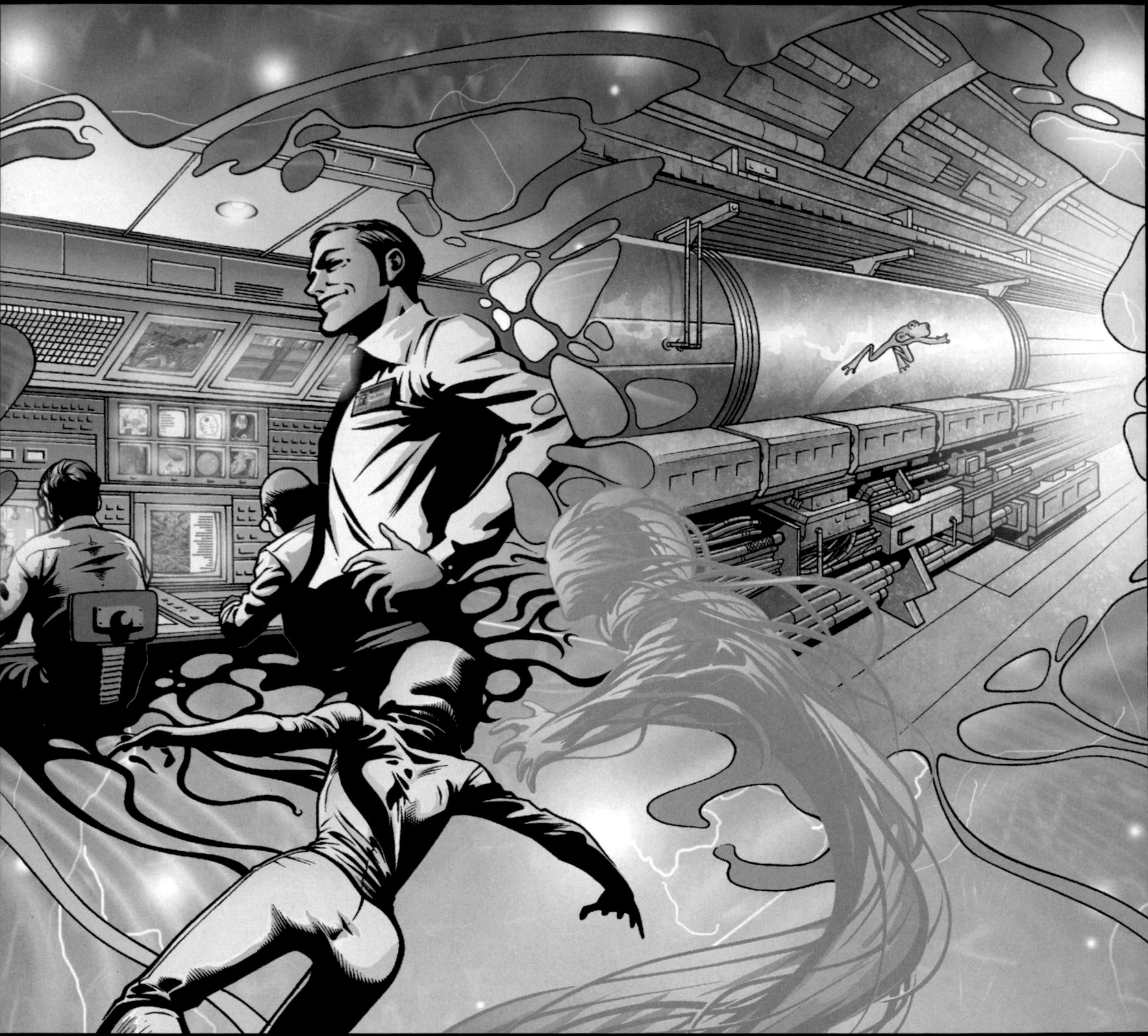

All their hopes and dreams hung on this first trial. If it produced the quark-gluon plasma as predicted, it would provide invaluable insight into the Big Bang—the origins of the universe. Around and around the beam spun...faster and faster, hotter and hotter....

The radiation levels were holding fine...and then the beam hit its target.

Particles flashed into existence—and then immediately disappeared. They didn't break down into other particles; those would have left trails, signs that they had once existed, however briefly.

They simply vanished.

The team rushed to the beam target area and saw a strange sight.

A doorway, floating in the air. Like the one Sara had travelled through, only smaller.

As they watched, it hopped around, changing orientation. One of the scientists called it a Domain Wall, the same phrase Doctor Z had used.

The scientists took readings, and discovered that the particle beam had been diverted through the Domain Wall. Something on the other side had scooped it right up, leaving no quark-gluon plasma, no trails, no hope for the future of the Supercollider...

...except the Domain Wall itself. Possibly the greatest discovery in scientific history.

Then there was a high, keening noise. And before they knew it...

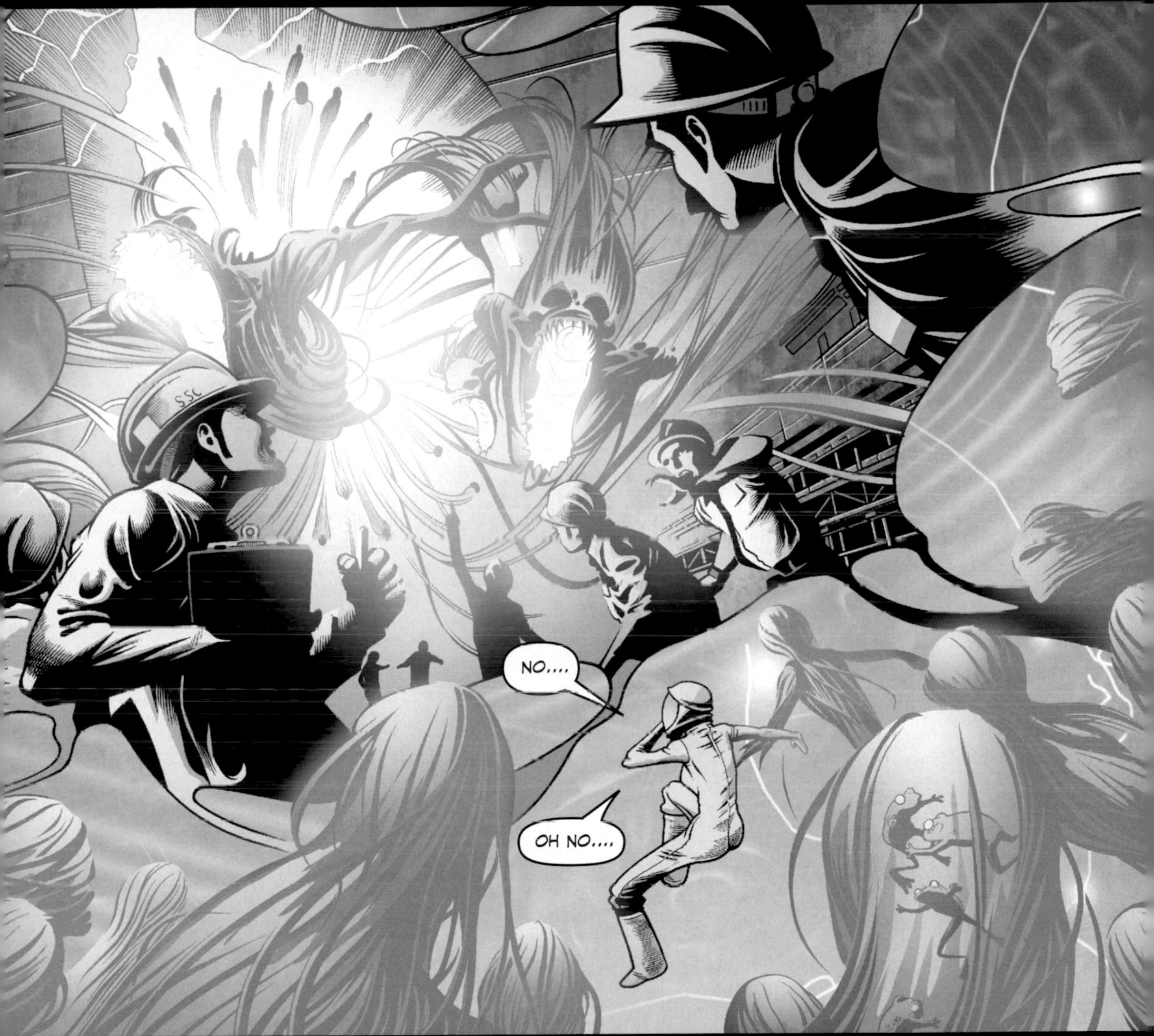

SSC
NO....
OH NO....

...the Paras were there.

They tore apart Iko and Hunter immediately, leaving nothing but hollow shells that dissolved into a black, oily substance on the chamber floor.

Almost everyone else died within minutes. Huddled in an access corridor, William Erie and a few other survivors tried to figure out what had happened, and what they could possibly do next.

It wouldn't be long before someone braved the Supercollider's tunnels—Erie had managed to phone out briefly, and even now, the university was probably notifying the authorities. But Erie knew no one would arrive in time to save his group.

They were doomed...but they had to leave a clue, a message of some kind, for whoever came next. If these creatures were loosed on Earth, no one would be safe. The universe's origins wouldn't matter anymore—

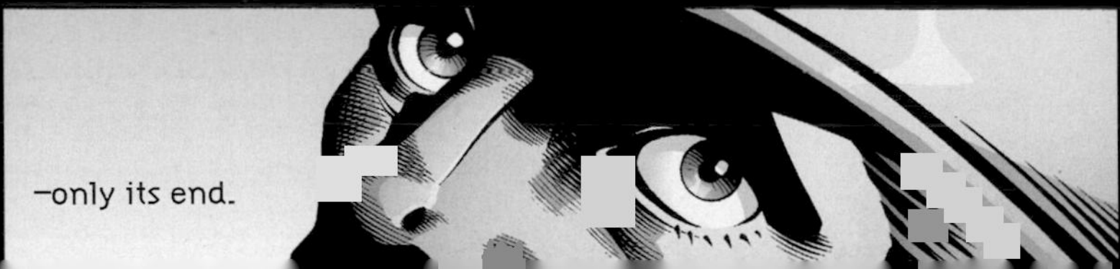

—only its end.

So they wrote the clue on the walls...over and over again. And when they heard the screeching, nearer and nearer, they scrawled it again with their last breaths...

...in their own blood.

Then the creatures came for them.

And when it was all over—when their blood was drained, when their very bodies were leeched of subatomic matter, leaving nothing but hollow shells—

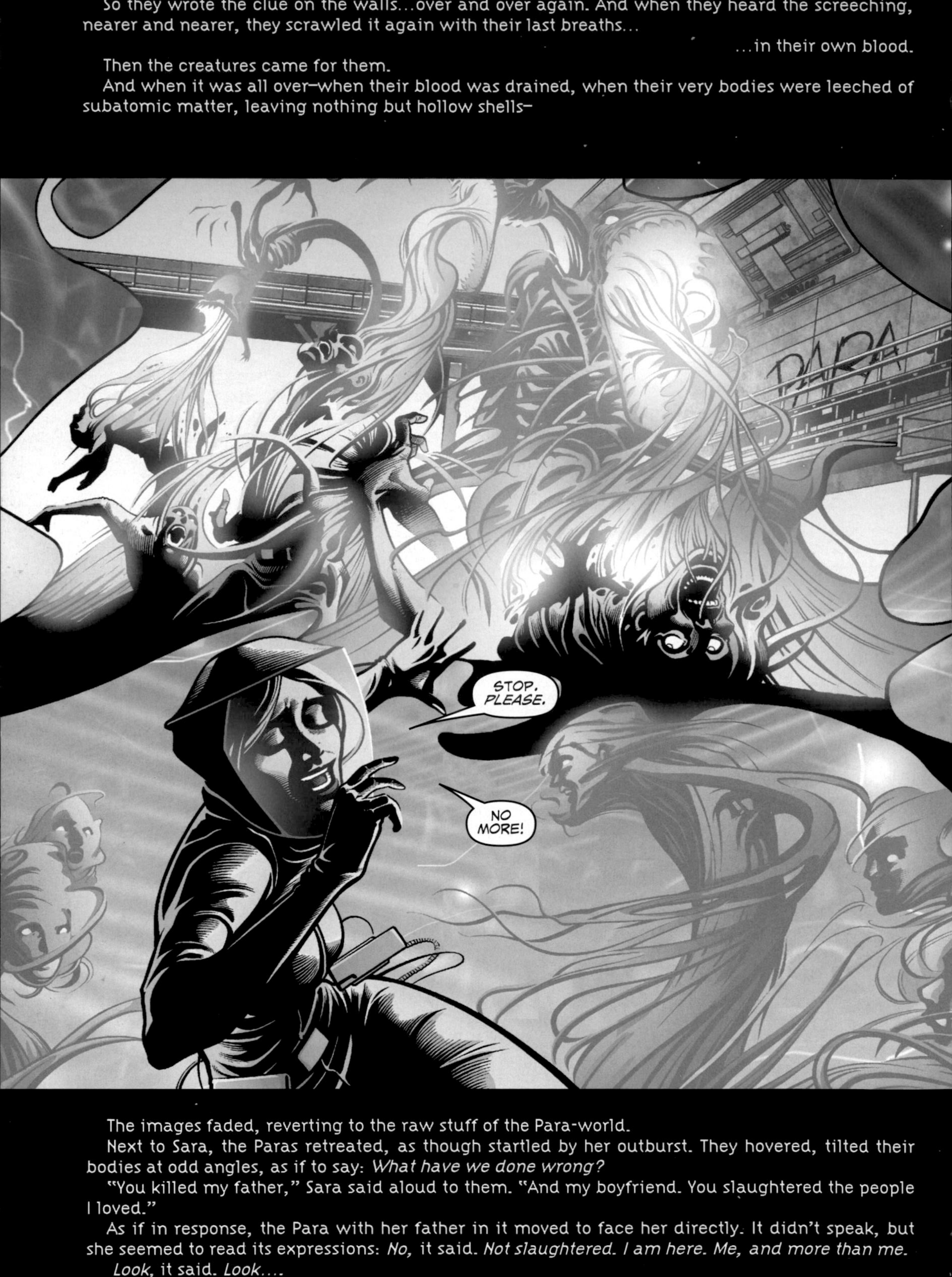
PARA
STOP. PLEASE.
NO MORE!

The images faded, reverting to the raw stuff of the Para-world.

Next to Sara, the Paras retreated, as though startled by her outburst. They hovered, tilted their bodies at odd angles, as if to say: *What have we done wrong?*

"You killed my father," Sara said aloud to them. "And my boyfriend. You slaughtered the people I loved."

As if in response, the Para with her father in it moved to face her directly. It didn't speak, but she seemed to read its expressions: *No,* it said. *Not slaughtered. I am here. Me, and more than me.*

Look, it said. *Look....*

Sara looked behind her, and saw the background of the world starting to form into something...something familiar. Chairs, consoles, screens...a dusty, metallic smell.

The Supercollider's Control Room.

"Are you getting this from ***me?*"** she asked. "While you showed me the images from the past...were you also pulling things from my mind?"

The Father-Para shook its "head," as if to say: *This is not important. Look here.*

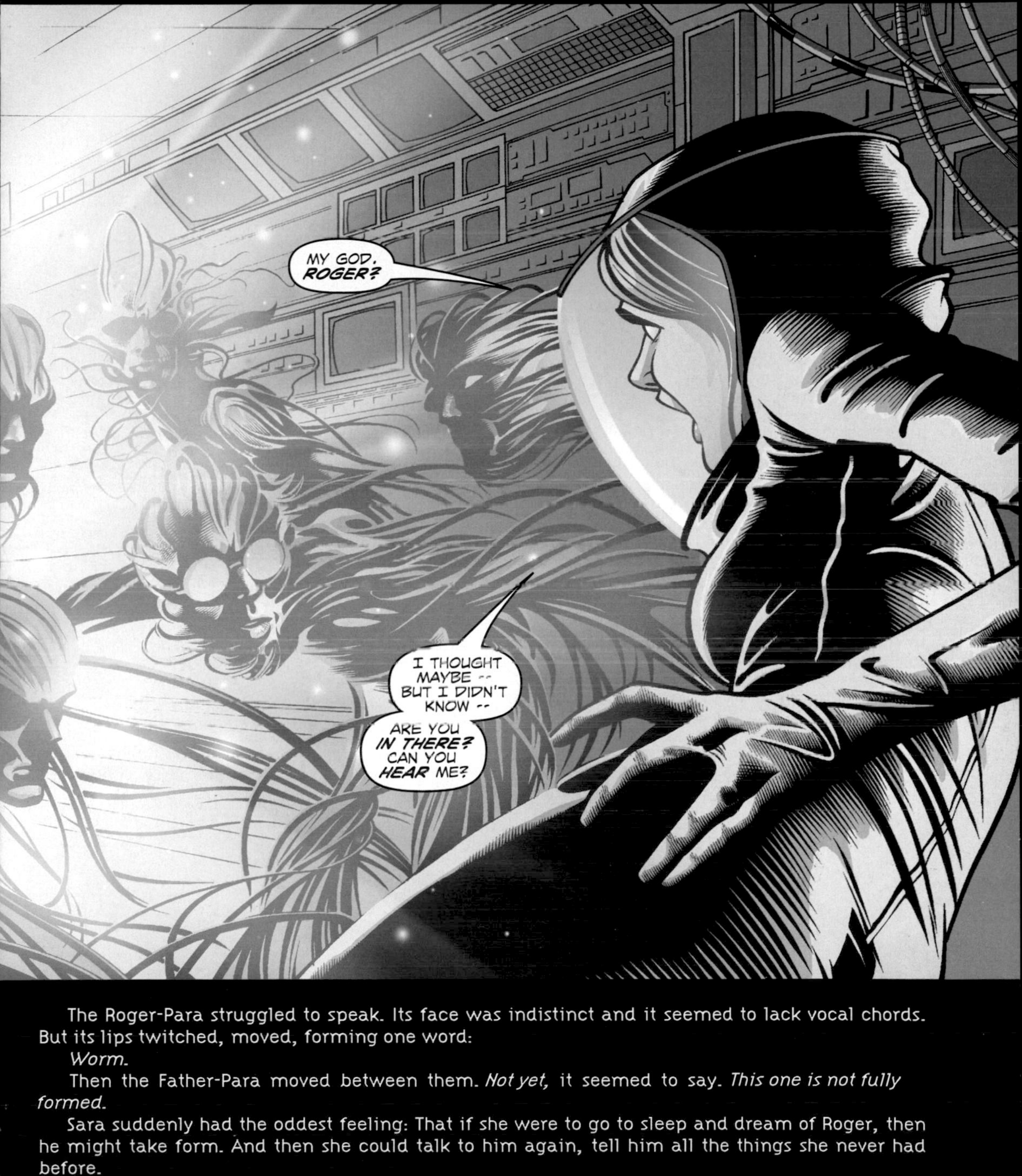

MY GOD. ROGER?
I THOUGHT MAYBE -- BUT I DIDN'T KNOW --
ARE YOU IN THERE? CAN YOU HEAR ME?

The Roger-Para struggled to speak. Its face was indistinct and it seemed to lack vocal chords. But its lips twitched, moved, forming one word:

Worm.

Then the Father-Para moved between them. *Not yet,* it seemed to say. *This one is not fully formed.*

Sara suddenly had the oddest feeling: That if she were to go to sleep and dream of Roger, then he might take form. And then she could talk to him again, tell him all the things she never had before.

She became afraid that she was staring too hard at Roger's Para-self. That, like a watched teakettle, he might never fully form if she kept her eyes on him.

And yet, she didn't want to look away, for fear she'd never see him again.

It was like being trapped in the moment before consciousness. Fleeing from nightmare—yet afraid, above all, of the dull, ashy flatness of the waking world.

A movement caught Sara's eye, and she turned to her right.

Another Para hovered there, an empty one. No face, no human soul within. Yet it seemed fixed on her. The other Paras watched, expectantly, silent as always.

Sara looked around at the Father-Para, the nascent Roger-Para, and the blurred, indistinct Control Room all around them. Then her eyes returned to the empty Para before her, and she heard her own voice, small and scared, say:

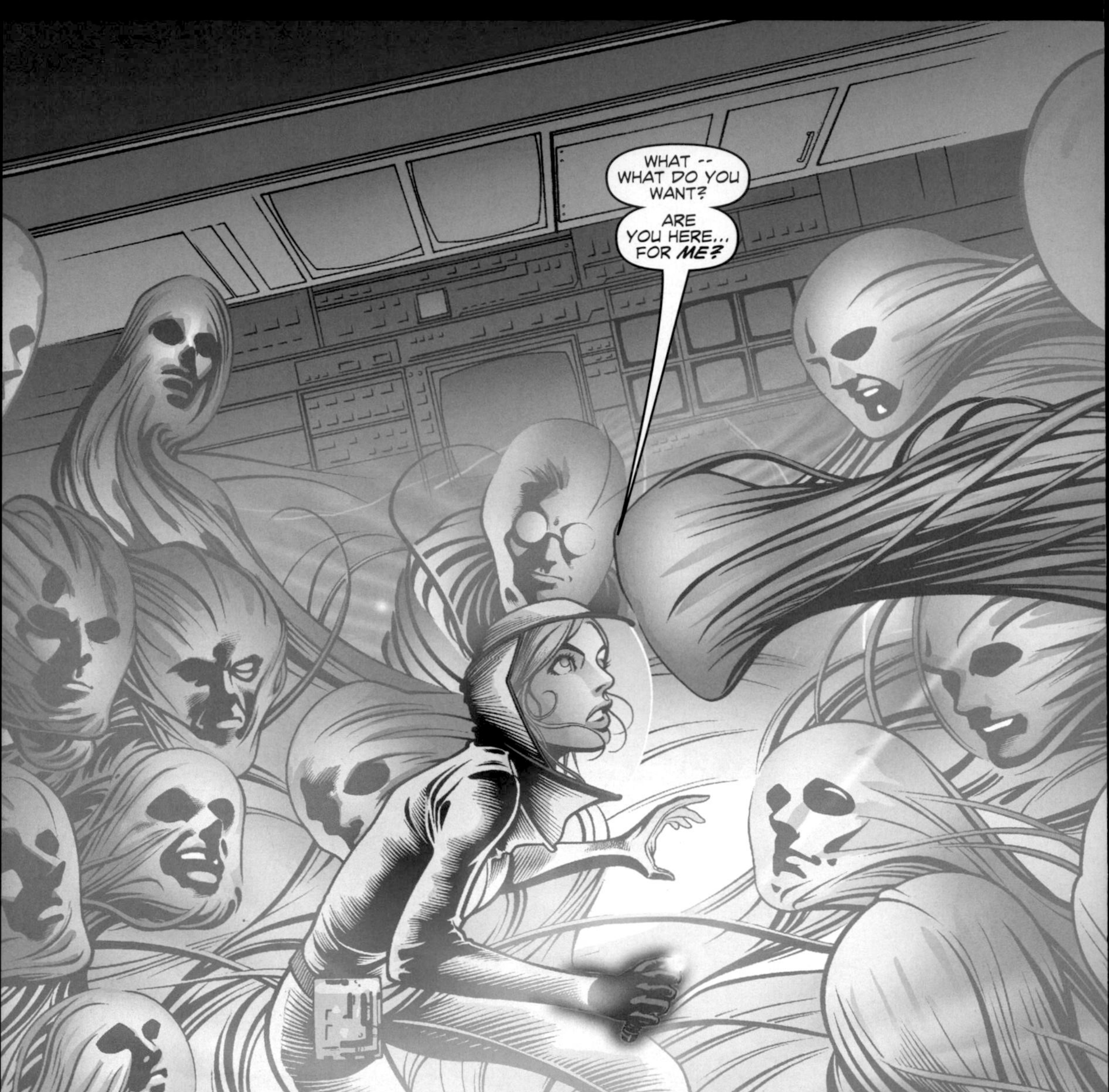
WHAT -- WHAT DO YOU WANT?
ARE YOU HERE... FOR *ME?*

Bile rose in Sara's throat as the Paras massed close around her. She struggled not to panic.

She scrabbled frantically at her belt until she found Doctor Z's recall device. Her thumb pressed down hard on the trigger.

And....

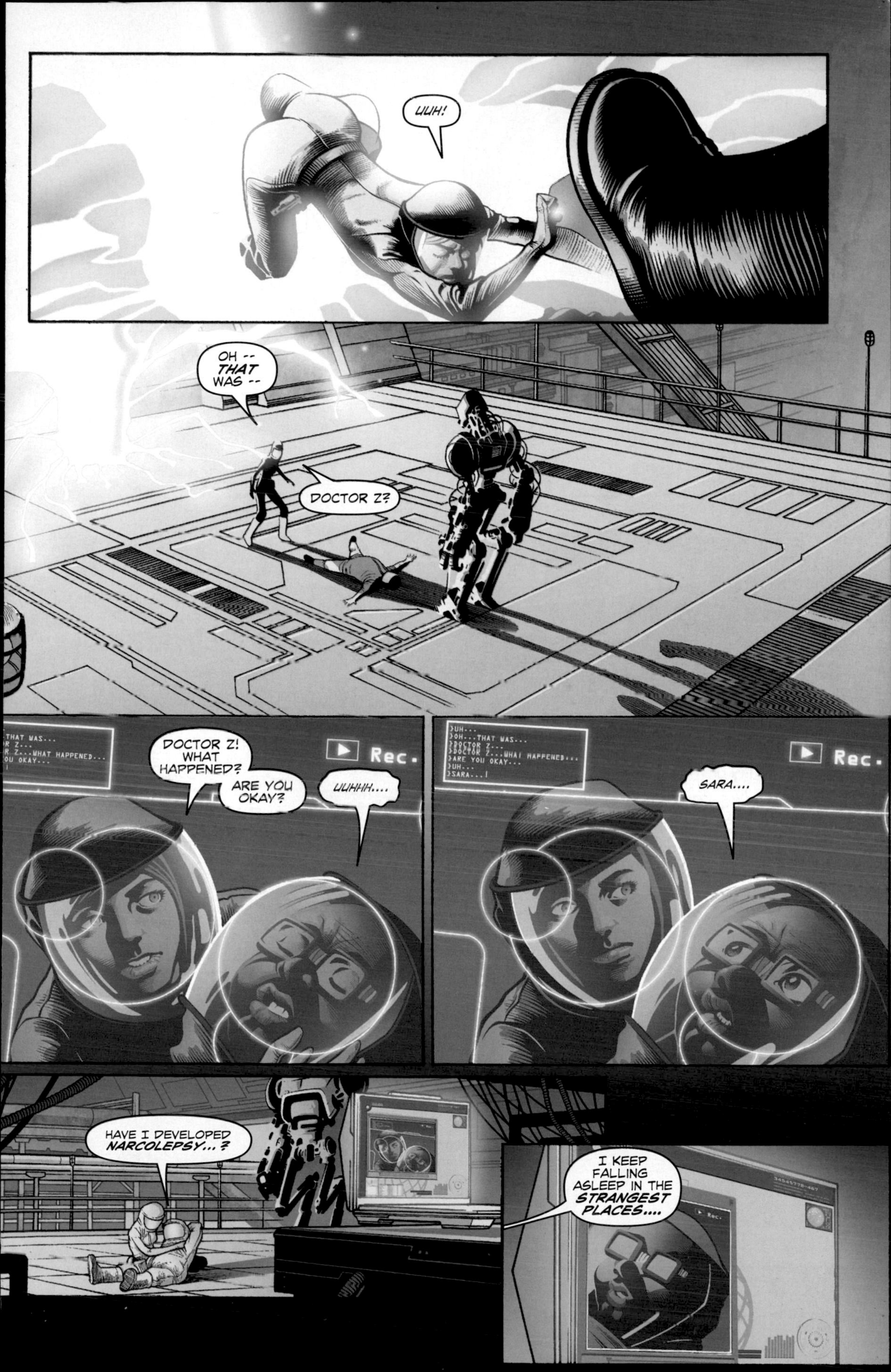
UUH!
OH -- THAT WAS --
DOCTOR Z?
DOCTOR Z! WHAT HAPPENED?
ARE YOU OKAY?
Rec.
UUHHH....
Rec.
SARA....
HAVE I DEVELOPED NARCOLEPSY... ?
I KEEP FALLING ASLEEP IN THE STRANGEST PLACES....

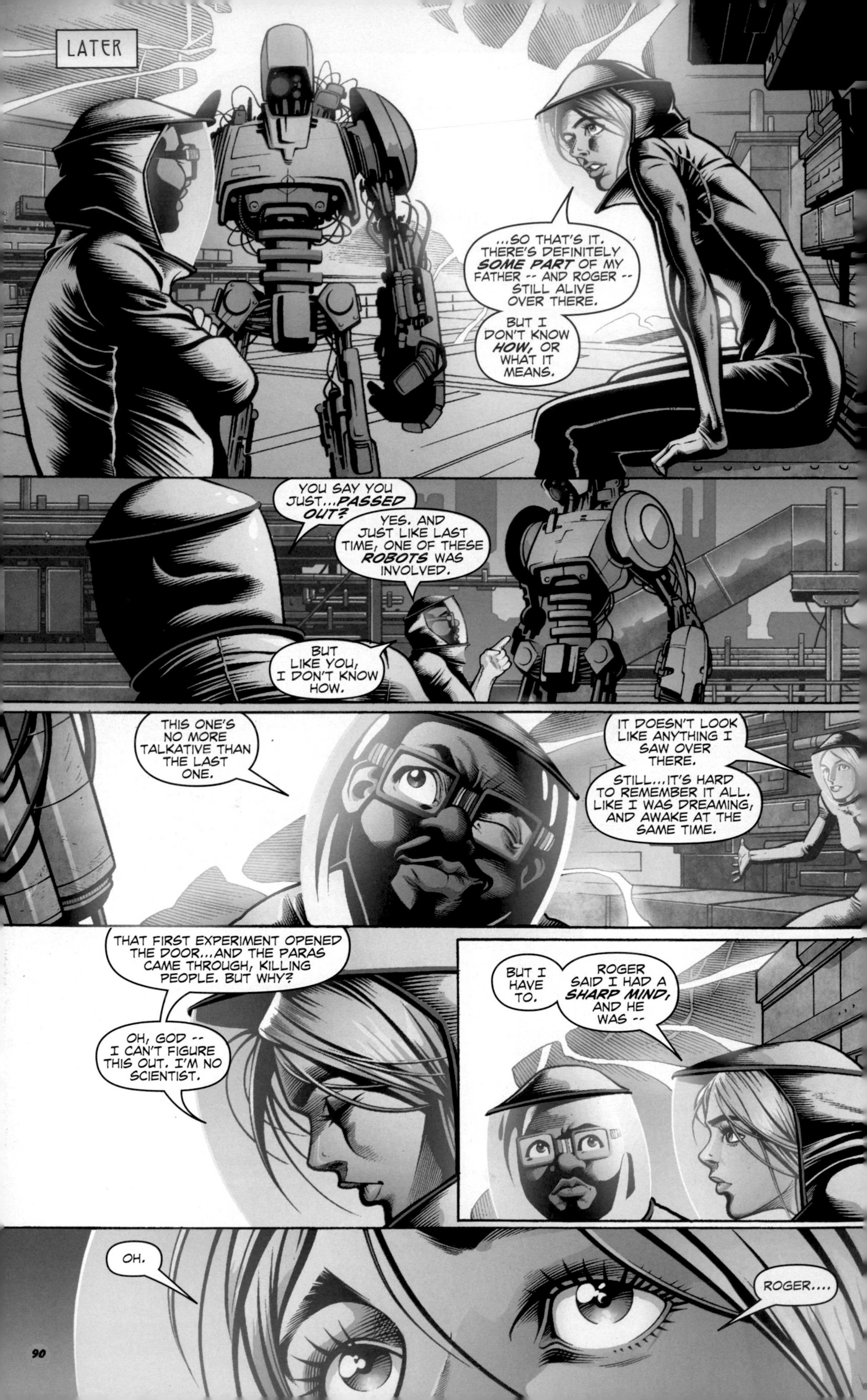

LATER
...SO THAT'S IT. THERE'S DEFINITELY SOME PART OF MY FATHER -- AND ROGER -- STILL ALIVE OVER THERE.
BUT I DON'T KNOW HOW, OR WHAT IT MEANS.
YOU SAY YOU JUST...PASSED OUT?
YES. AND JUST LIKE LAST TIME, ONE OF THESE ROBOTS WAS INVOLVED.
BUT LIKE YOU, I DON'T KNOW HOW.
THIS ONE'S NO MORE TALKATIVE THAN THE LAST ONE.
IT DOESN'T LOOK LIKE ANYTHING I SAW OVER THERE.
STILL...IT'S HARD TO REMEMBER IT ALL. LIKE I WAS DREAMING, AND AWAKE AT THE SAME TIME.
THAT FIRST EXPERIMENT OPENED THE DOOR...AND THE PARAS CAME THROUGH, KILLING PEOPLE. BUT WHY?
OH, GOD -- I CAN'T FIGURE THIS OUT. I'M NO SCIENTIST.
BUT I HAVE TO.
ROGER SAID I HAD A SHARP MIND, AND HE WAS --
OH.
ROGER....

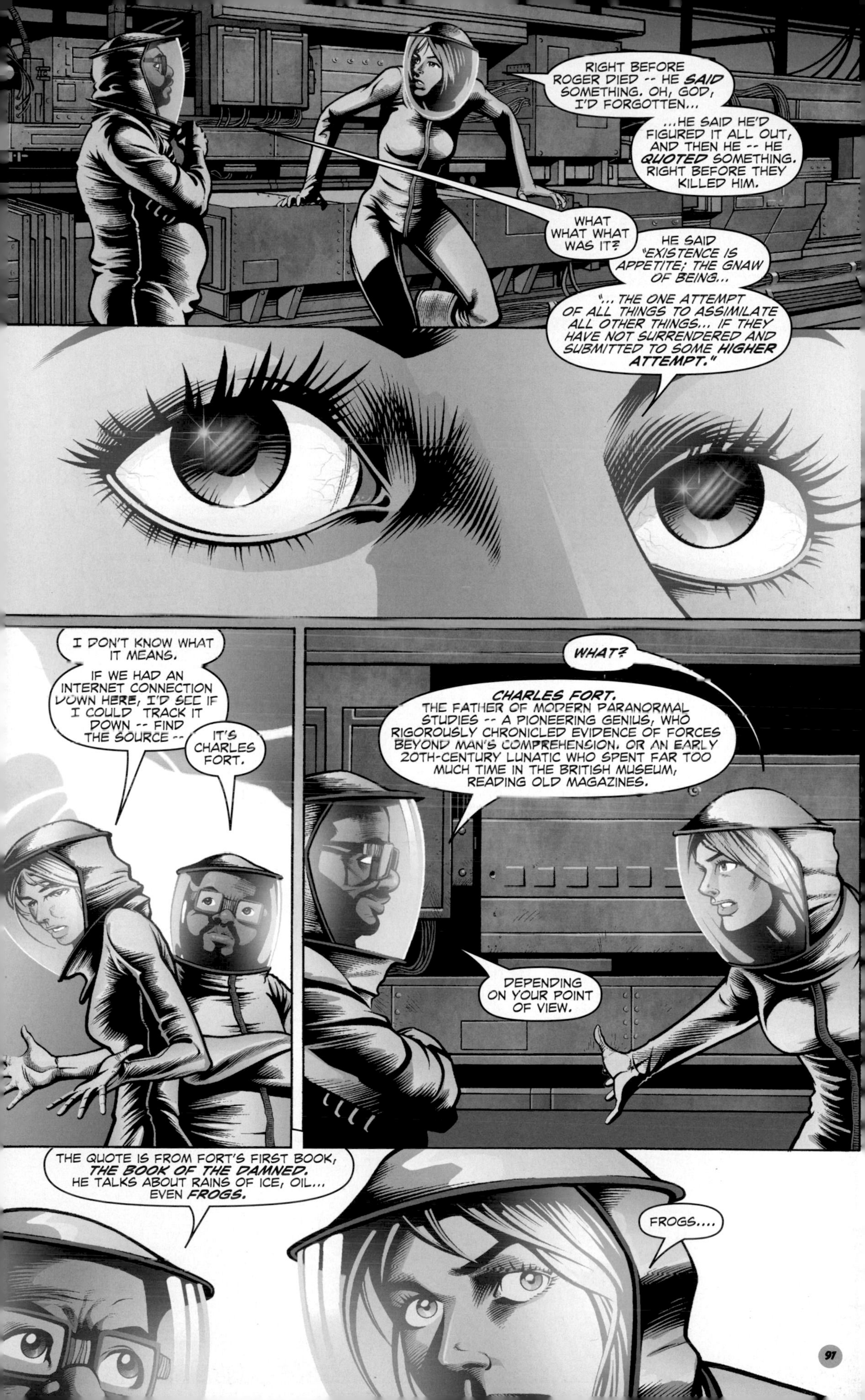
RIGHT BEFORE ROGER DIED -- HE SAID SOMETHING. OH, GOD, I'D FORGOTTEN...
...HE SAID HE'D FIGURED IT ALL OUT, AND THEN HE -- HE QUOTED SOMETHING. RIGHT BEFORE THEY KILLED HIM.
WHAT WHAT WHAT WAS IT?
HE SAID "EXISTENCE IS APPETITE; THE GNAW OF BEING...
"... THE ONE ATTEMPT OF ALL THINGS TO ASSIMILATE ALL OTHER THINGS... IF THEY HAVE NOT SURRENDERED AND SUBMITTED TO SOME HIGHER ATTEMPT."
I DON'T KNOW WHAT IT MEANS.
IF WE HAD AN INTERNET CONNECTION DOWN HERE, I'D SEE IF I COULD TRACK IT DOWN -- FIND THE SOURCE --
IT'S CHARLES FORT.
WHAT?
CHARLES FORT. THE FATHER OF MODERN PARANORMAL STUDIES -- A PIONEERING GENIUS, WHO RIGOROUSLY CHRONICLED EVIDENCE OF FORCES BEYOND MAN'S COMPREHENSION. OR AN EARLY 20TH-CENTURY LUNATIC WHO SPENT FAR TOO MUCH TIME IN THE BRITISH MUSEUM, READING OLD MAGAZINES.
DEPENDING ON YOUR POINT OF VIEW.
THE QUOTE IS FROM FORT'S FIRST BOOK, THE BOOK OF THE DAMNED. HE TALKS ABOUT RAINS OF ICE, OIL... EVEN FROGS.
FROGS....

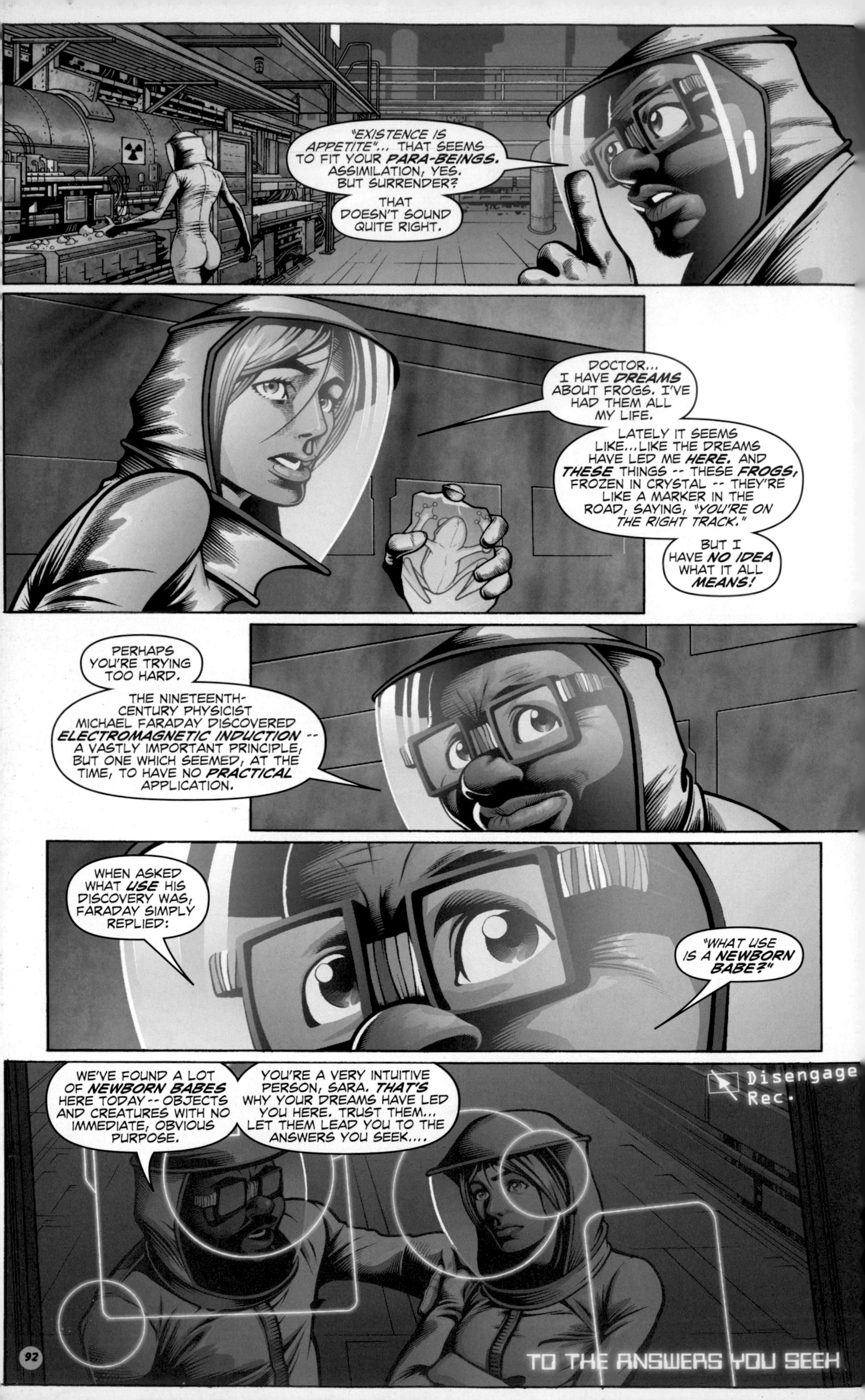
"EXISTENCE IS APPETITE"... THAT SEEMS TO FIT YOUR PARA-BEINGS. ASSIMILATION, YES. BUT SURRENDER?
THAT DOESN'T SOUND QUITE RIGHT.
DOCTOR... I HAVE DREAMS ABOUT FROGS. I'VE HAD THEM ALL MY LIFE.
LATELY IT SEEMS LIKE... LIKE THE DREAMS HAVE LED ME HERE. AND THESE THINGS -- THESE FROGS, FROZEN IN CRYSTAL -- THEY'RE LIKE A MARKER IN THE ROAD, SAYING, "YOU'RE ON THE RIGHT TRACK."
BUT I HAVE NO IDEA WHAT IT ALL MEANS!
PERHAPS YOU'RE TRYING TOO HARD.
THE NINETEENTH-CENTURY PHYSICIST MICHAEL FARADAY DISCOVERED ELECTROMAGNETIC INDUCTION -- A VASTLY IMPORTANT PRINCIPLE, BUT ONE WHICH SEEMED, AT THE TIME, TO HAVE NO PRACTICAL APPLICATION.
WHEN ASKED WHAT USE HIS DISCOVERY WAS, FARADAY SIMPLY REPLIED:
"WHAT USE IS A NEWBORN BABE?"
WE'VE FOUND A LOT OF NEWBORN BABES HERE TODAY -- OBJECTS AND CREATURES WITH NO IMMEDIATE, OBVIOUS PURPOSE.
YOU'RE A VERY INTUITIVE PERSON, SARA. THAT'S WHY YOUR DREAMS HAVE LED YOU HERE. TRUST THEM... LET THEM LEAD YOU TO THE ANSWERS YOU SEEK....
Disengage
Rec.
TO THE ANSWERS YOU SEEK

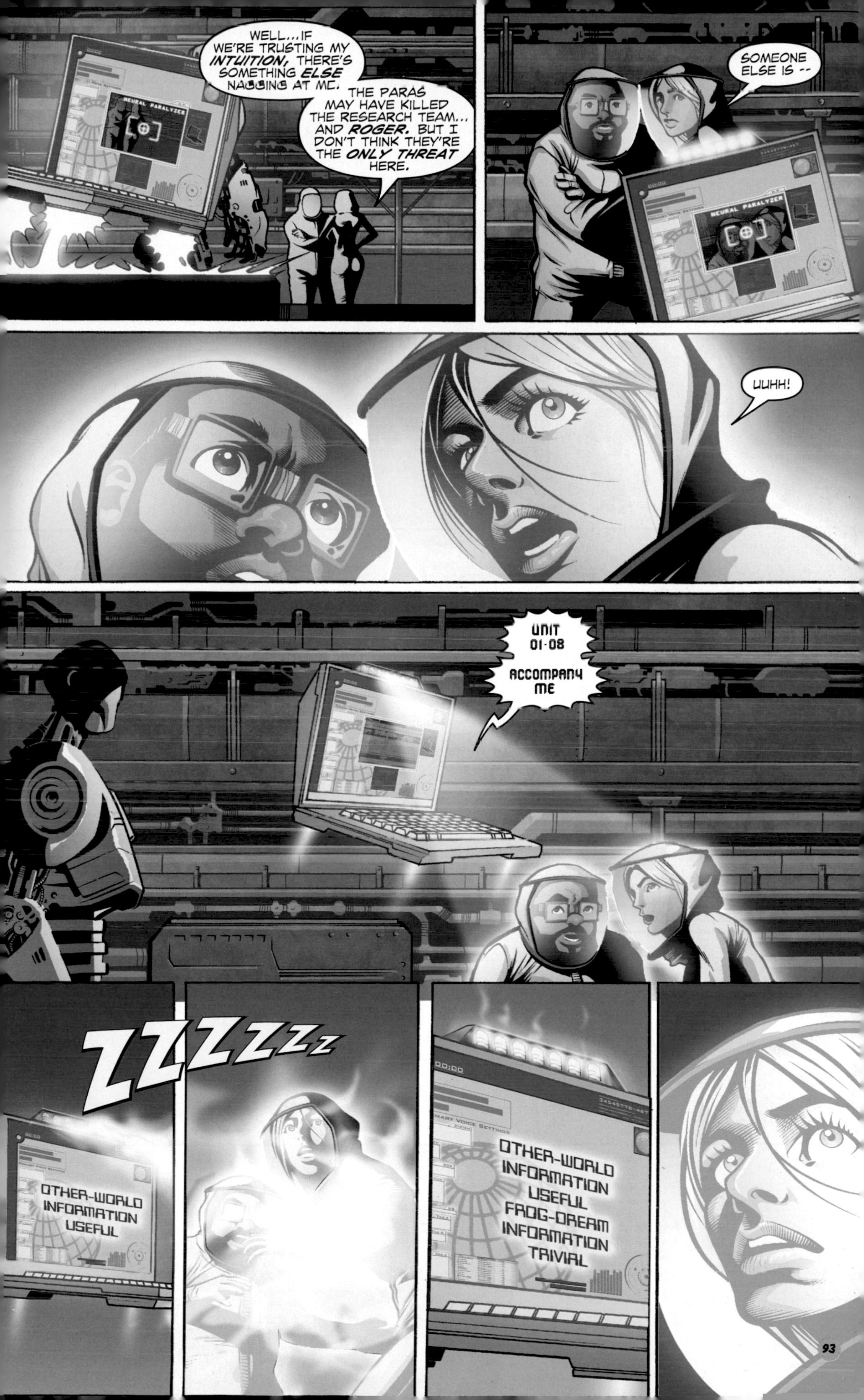
WELL...IF WE'RE TRUSTING MY *INTUITION,* THERE'S SOMETHING *ELSE* NAGGING AT ME.
THE PARAS MAY HAVE KILLED THE RESEARCH TEAM... AND *ROGER.* BUT I DON'T THINK THEY'RE THE *ONLY THREAT* HERE.
NEURAL PARALYZER
SOMEONE ELSE IS --
NEURAL PARALYZER
UUHH!
UNIT 01-08
ACCOMPANY ME
ZZZZZzz
OTHER-WORLD INFORMATION USEFUL
OTHER-WORLD INFORMATION USEFUL FROG-DREAM INFORMATION TRIVIAL

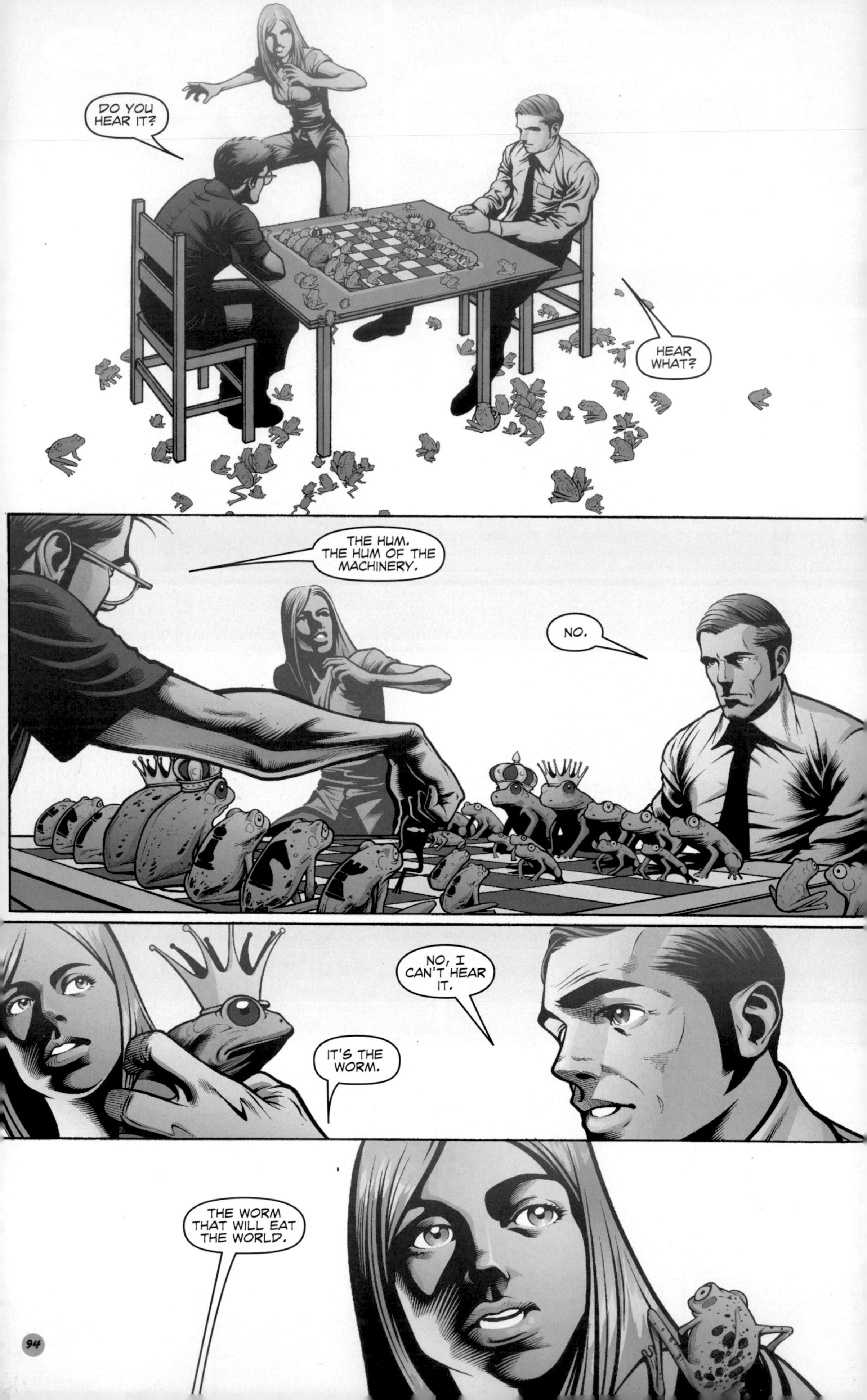
DO YOU HEAR IT?
HEAR WHAT?
THE HUM. THE HUM OF THE MACHINERY.
NO.
NO, I CAN'T HEAR IT.
IT'S THE WORM.
THE WORM THAT WILL EAT THE WORLD.

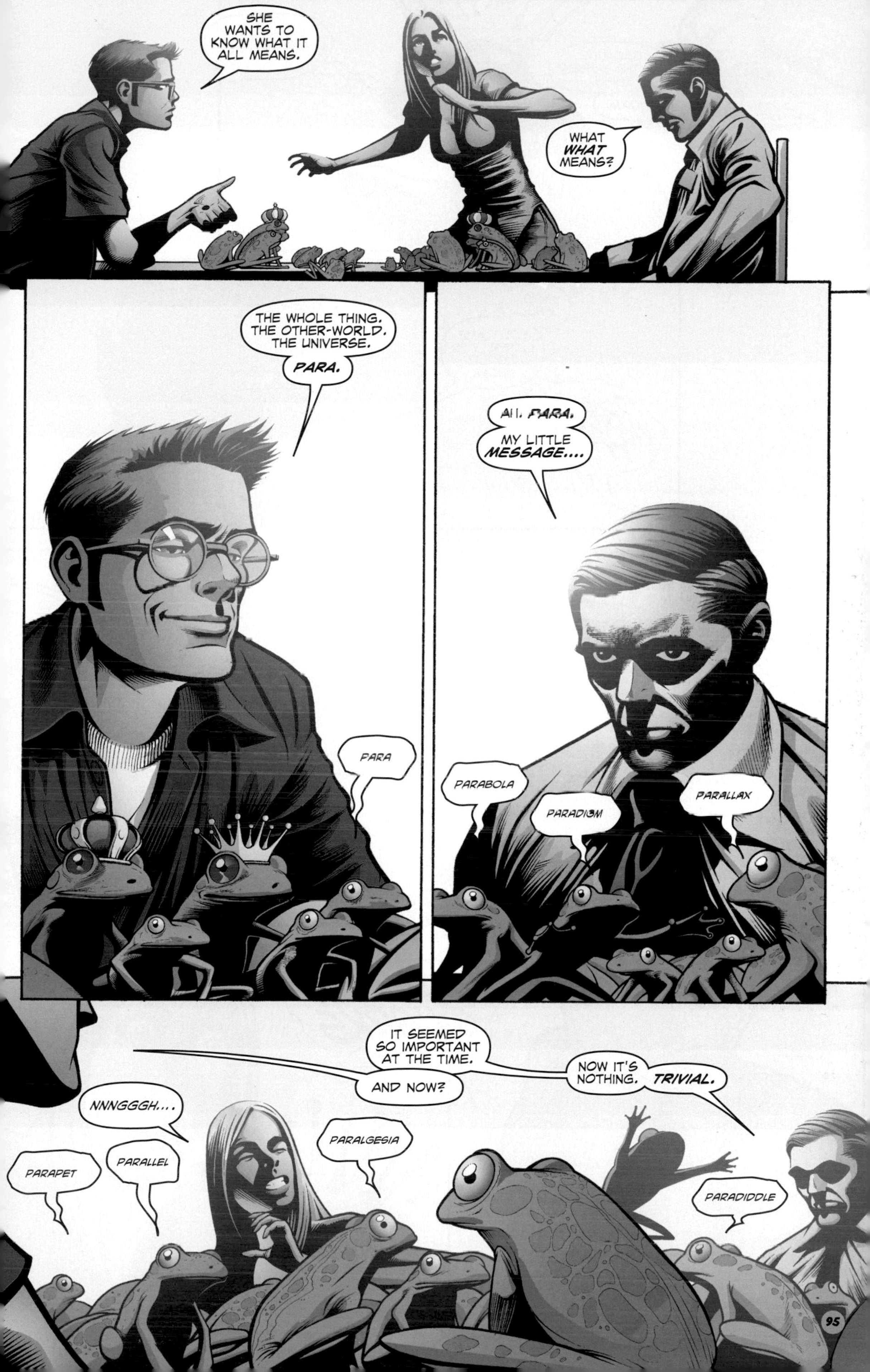
SHE WANTS TO KNOW WHAT IT ALL MEANS.
WHAT *WHAT* MEANS?
THE WHOLE THING. THE OTHER-WORLD. THE UNIVERSE.
PARA.
PARA
AH. *PARA.*
MY LITTLE *MESSAGE....*
PARABOLA
PARADIGM
PARALLAX
IT SEEMED SO IMPORTANT AT THE TIME.
AND NOW?
NOW IT'S NOTHING. *TRIVIAL.*
NNNGGGH....
PARAPET
PARALLEL
PARALGESIA
PARADIDDLE

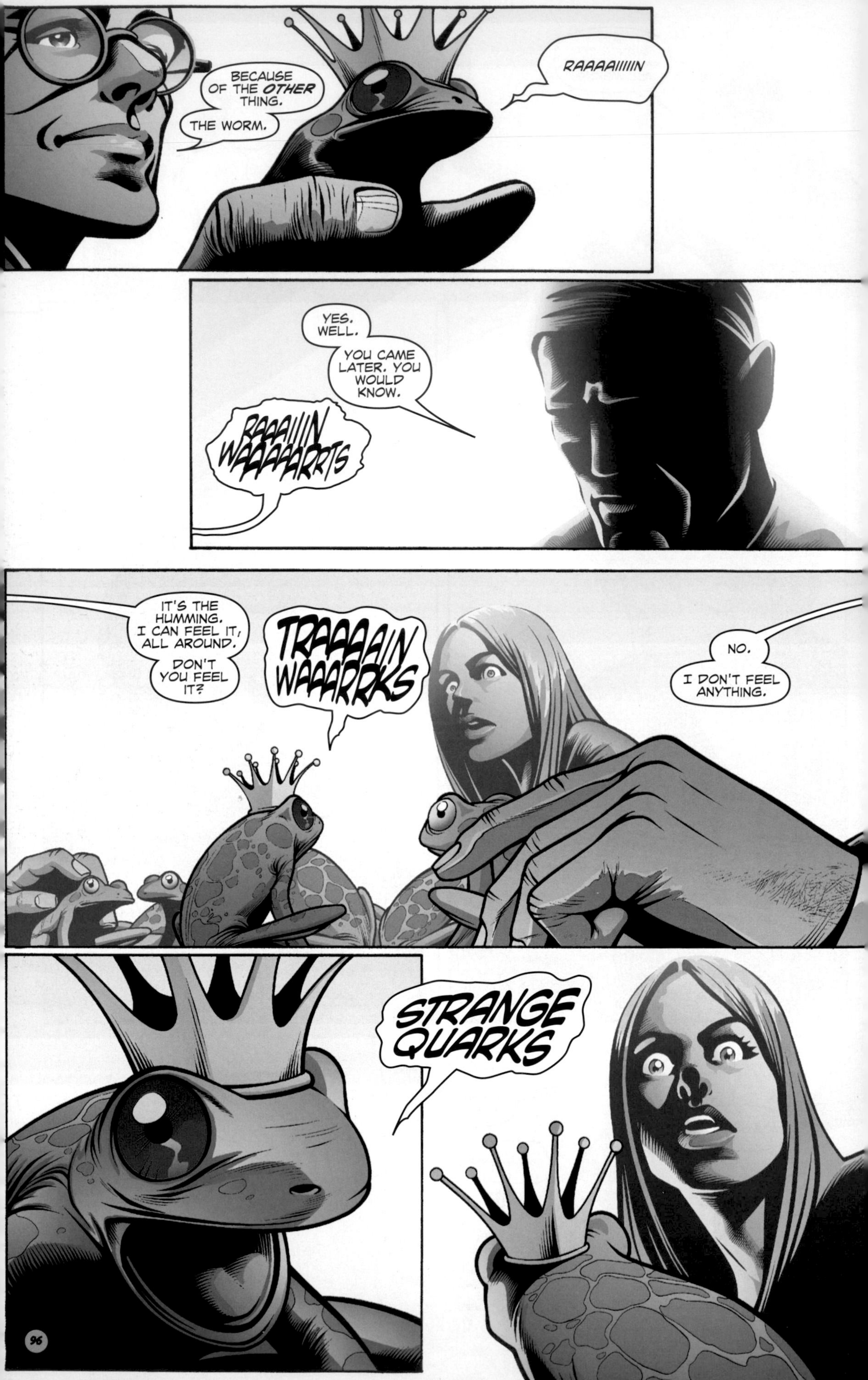
BECAUSE OF THE *OTHER* THING.
THE WORM.
RAAAAIIIIIN
YES. WELL.
YOU CAME LATER. YOU WOULD KNOW.
RAAAIIIN WAAAAARRTS
IT'S THE HUMMING. I CAN FEEL IT, ALL AROUND.
DON'T YOU FEEL IT?
TRAAAAIN WAAARRKS
NO.
I DON'T FEEL ANYTHING.
STRANGE QUARKS

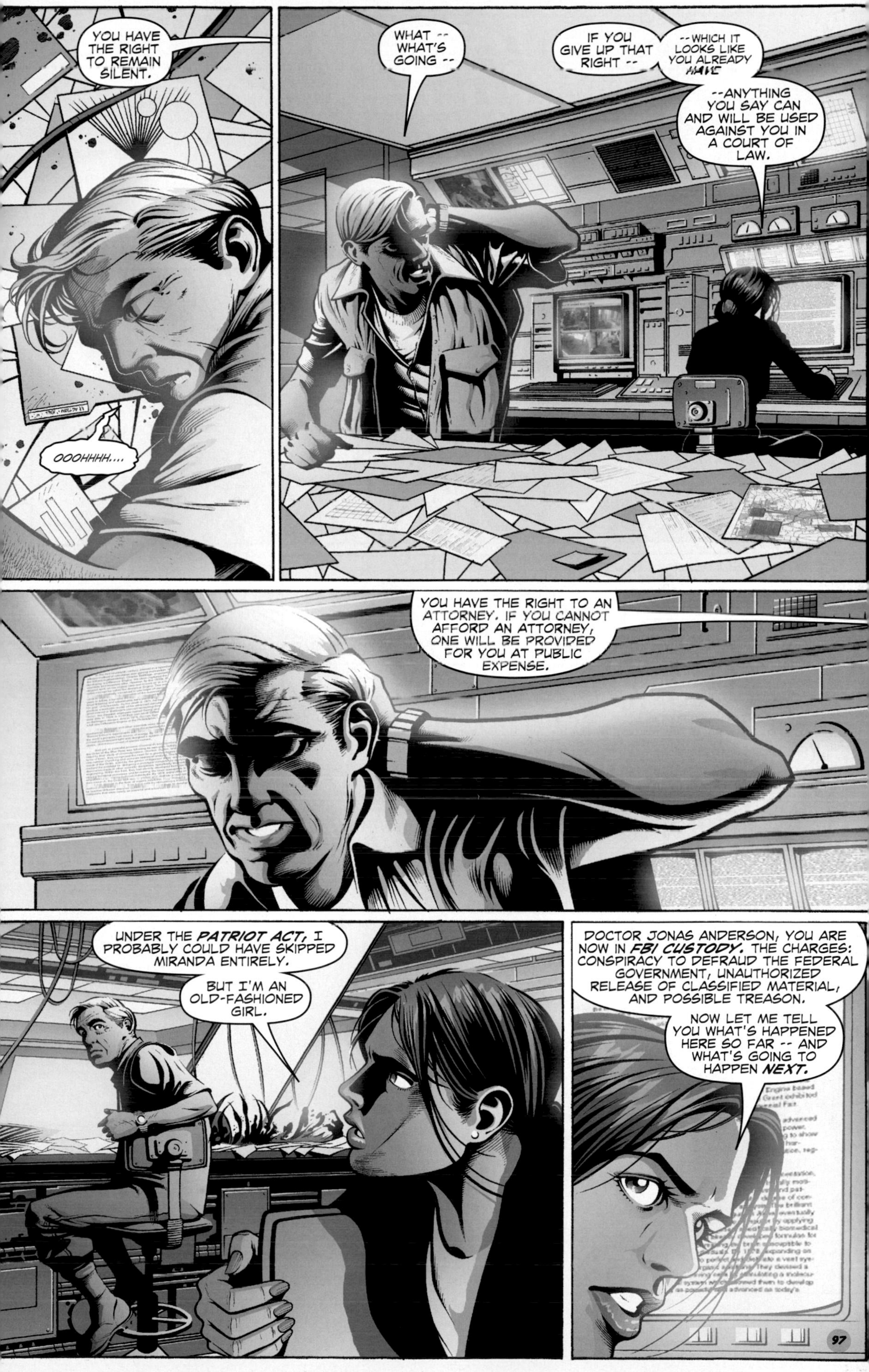
YOU HAVE THE RIGHT TO REMAIN SILENT.
OOOHHHH....
WHAT -- WHAT'S GOING --
IF YOU GIVE UP THAT RIGHT --
--WHICH IT LOOKS LIKE YOU ALREADY HAVE
--ANYTHING YOU SAY CAN AND WILL BE USED AGAINST YOU IN A COURT OF LAW.
YOU HAVE THE RIGHT TO AN ATTORNEY. IF YOU CANNOT AFFORD AN ATTORNEY, ONE WILL BE PROVIDED FOR YOU AT PUBLIC EXPENSE.
UNDER THE *PATRIOT ACT,* I PROBABLY COULD HAVE SKIPPED MIRANDA ENTIRELY.
BUT I'M AN OLD-FASHIONED GIRL.
DOCTOR JONAS ANDERSON, YOU ARE NOW IN *FBI CUSTODY.* THE CHARGES: CONSPIRACY TO DEFRAUD THE FEDERAL GOVERNMENT, UNAUTHORIZED RELEASE OF CLASSIFIED MATERIAL, AND POSSIBLE TREASON.
NOW LET ME TELL YOU WHAT'S HAPPENED HERE SO FAR -- AND WHAT'S GOING TO HAPPEN *NEXT.*

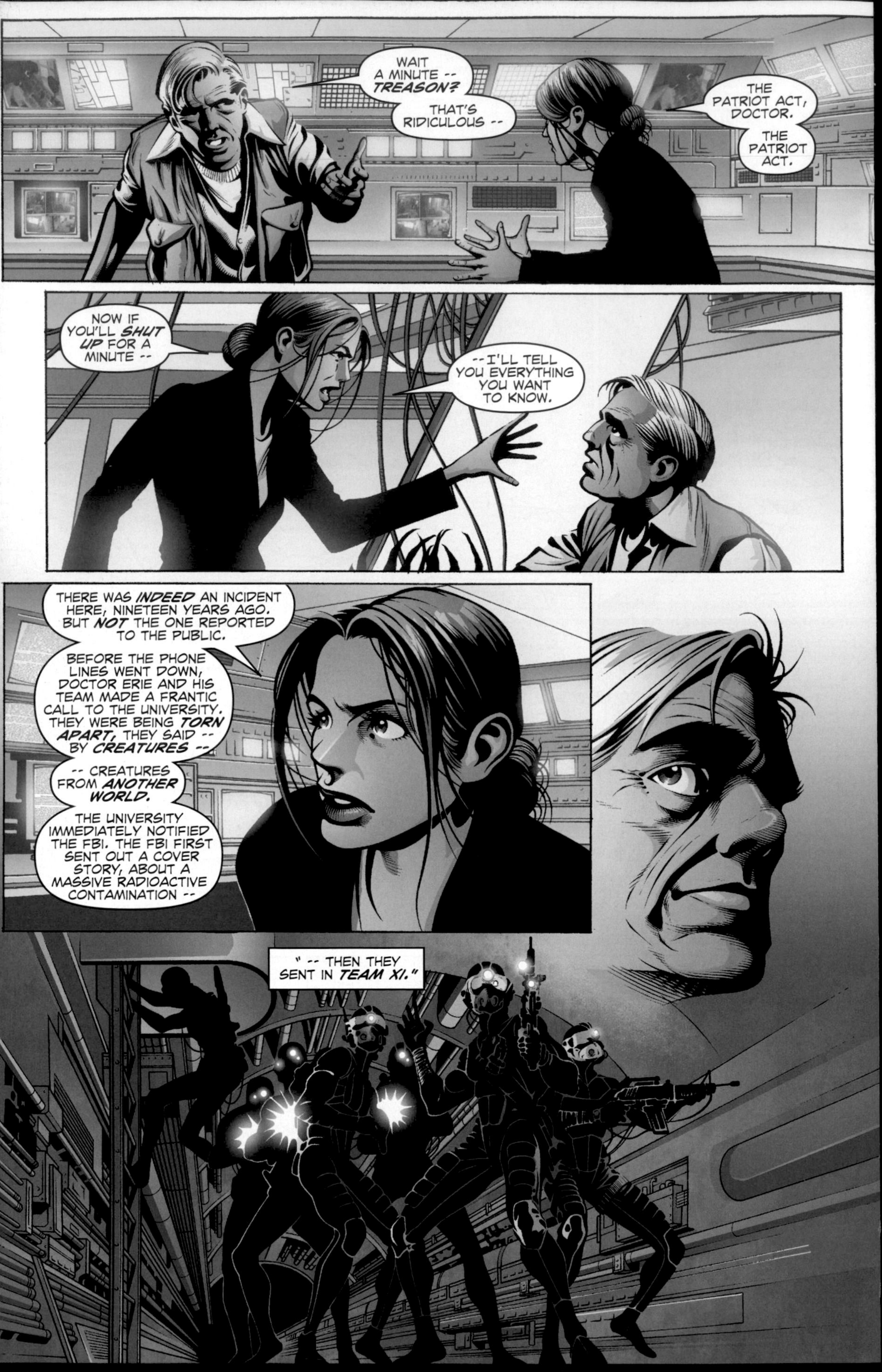
WAIT A MINUTE -- TREASON?
THAT'S RIDICULOUS --
THE PATRIOT ACT, DOCTOR.
THE PATRIOT ACT.
NOW IF YOU'LL SHUT UP FOR A MINUTE --
-- I'LL TELL YOU EVERYTHING YOU WANT TO KNOW.
THERE WAS INDEED AN INCIDENT HERE, NINETEEN YEARS AGO. BUT NOT THE ONE REPORTED TO THE PUBLIC.
BEFORE THE PHONE LINES WENT DOWN, DOCTOR ERIE AND HIS TEAM MADE A FRANTIC CALL TO THE UNIVERSITY. THEY WERE BEING TORN APART, THEY SAID -- BY CREATURES --
-- CREATURES FROM ANOTHER WORLD.
THE UNIVERSITY IMMEDIATELY NOTIFIED THE FBI. THE FBI FIRST SENT OUT A COVER STORY, ABOUT A MASSIVE RADIOACTIVE CONTAMINATION --
" -- THEN THEY SENT IN TEAM XI."

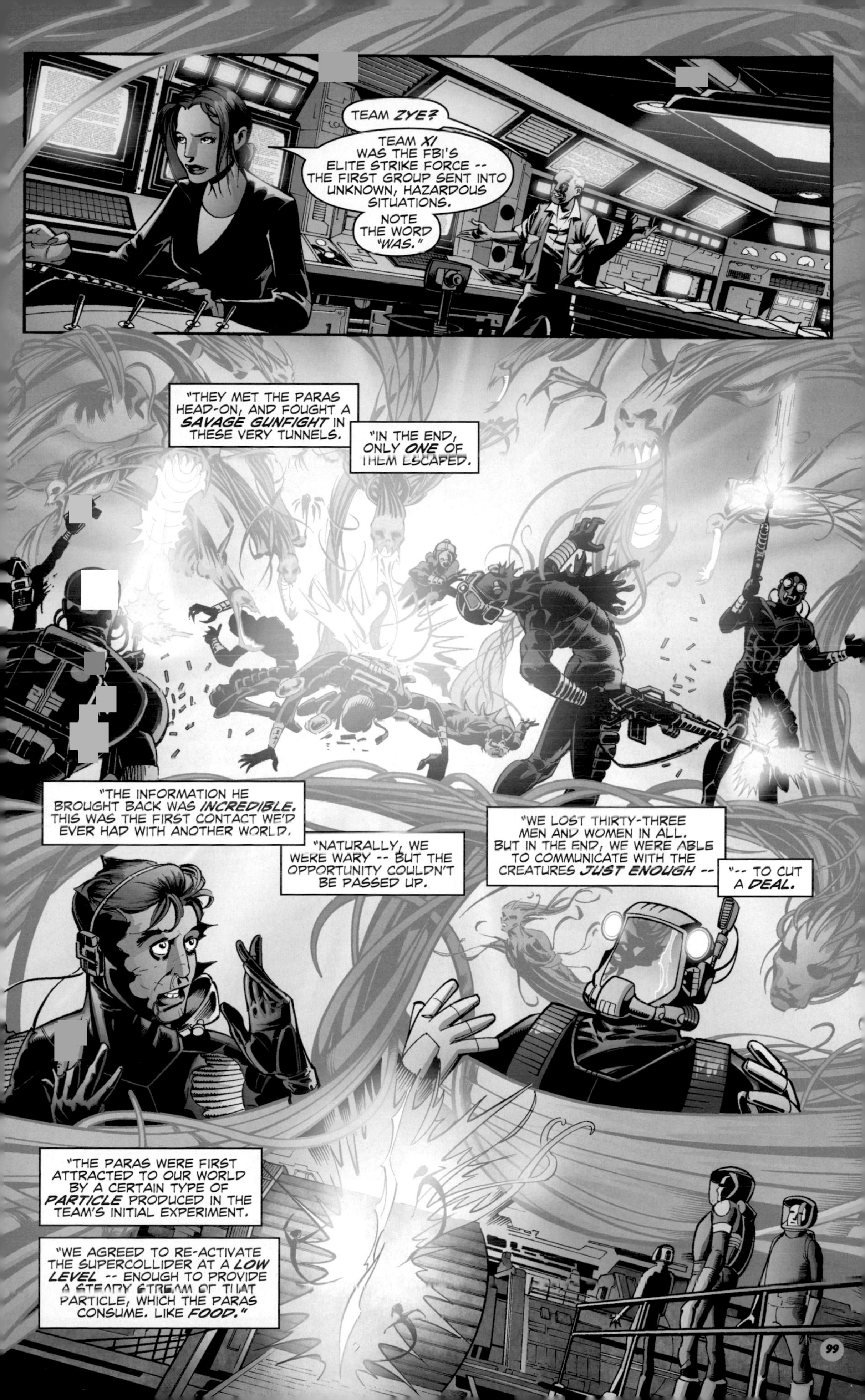
TEAM ZYE?
TEAM XI WAS THE FBI'S ELITE STRIKE FORCE -- THE FIRST GROUP SENT INTO UNKNOWN, HAZARDOUS SITUATIONS.
NOTE THE WORD "WAS."
"THEY MET THE PARAS HEAD-ON, AND FOUGHT A SAVAGE GUNFIGHT IN THESE VERY TUNNELS.
"IN THE END, ONLY ONE OF THEM ESCAPED.
"THE INFORMATION HE BROUGHT BACK WAS INCREDIBLE. THIS WAS THE FIRST CONTACT WE'D EVER HAD WITH ANOTHER WORLD.
"NATURALLY, WE WERE WARY -- BUT THE OPPORTUNITY COULDN'T BE PASSED UP.
"WE LOST THIRTY-THREE MEN AND WOMEN IN ALL. BUT IN THE END, WE WERE ABLE TO COMMUNICATE WITH THE CREATURES JUST ENOUGH --
"-- TO CUT A DEAL.
"THE PARAS WERE FIRST ATTRACTED TO OUR WORLD BY A CERTAIN TYPE OF PARTICLE PRODUCED IN THE TEAM'S INITIAL EXPERIMENT.
"WE AGREED TO RE-ACTIVATE THE SUPERCOLLIDER AT A LOW LEVEL -- ENOUGH TO PROVIDE A STEADY STREAM OF THAT PARTICLE, WHICH THE PARAS CONSUME. LIKE FOOD."

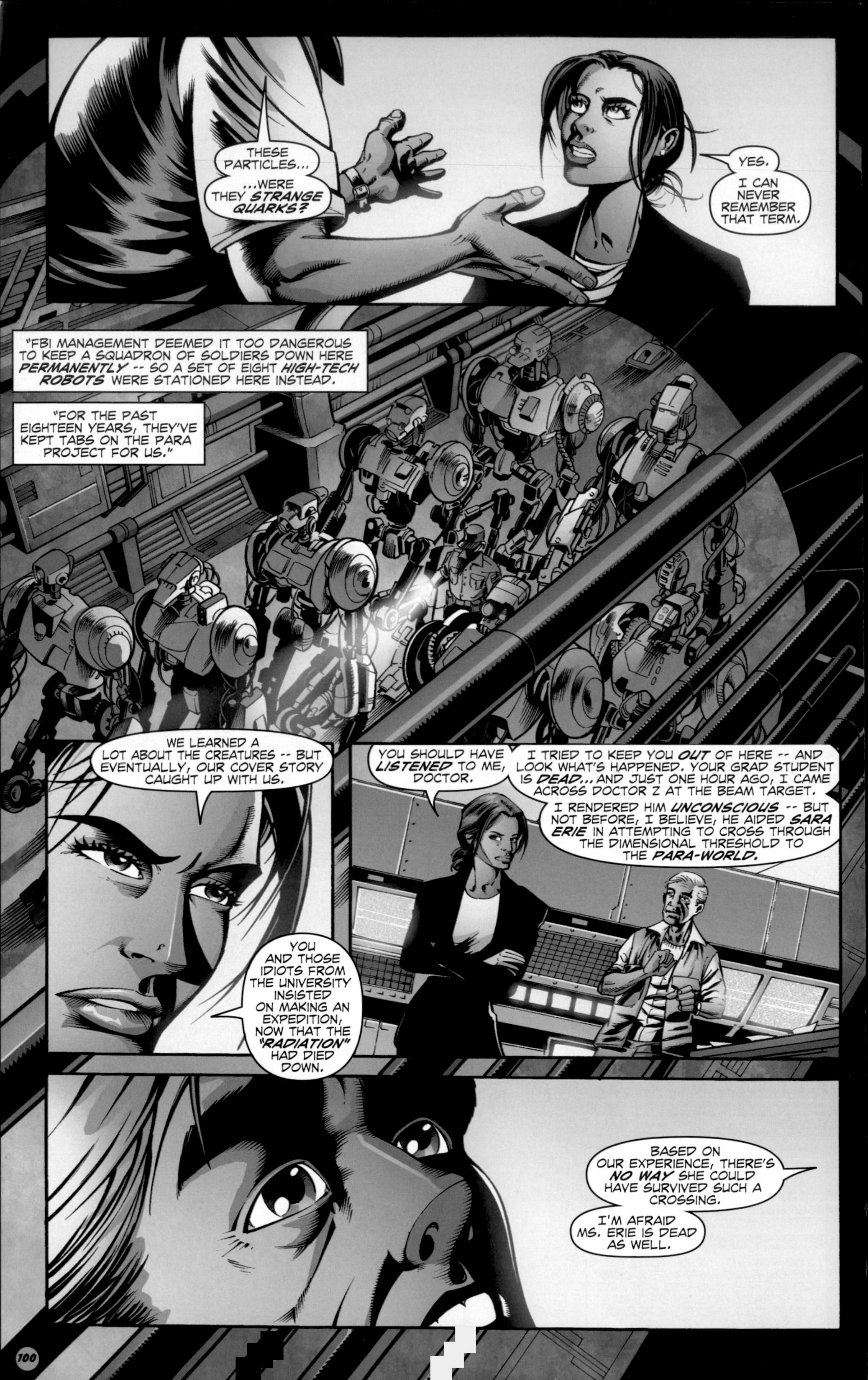

THESE PARTICLES... ...WERE THEY STRANGE QUARKS?
YES. I CAN NEVER REMEMBER THAT TERM.
"FBI MANAGEMENT DEEMED IT TOO DANGEROUS TO KEEP A SQUADRON OF SOLDIERS DOWN HERE PERMANENTLY -- SO A SET OF EIGHT HIGH-TECH ROBOTS WERE STATIONED HERE INSTEAD.
"FOR THE PAST EIGHTEEN YEARS, THEY'VE KEPT TABS ON THE PARA PROJECT FOR US."
WE LEARNED A LOT ABOUT THE CREATURES -- BUT EVENTUALLY, OUR COVER STORY CAUGHT UP WITH US.
YOU AND THOSE IDIOTS FROM THE UNIVERSITY INSISTED ON MAKING AN EXPEDITION, NOW THAT THE "RADIATION" HAD DIED DOWN.
YOU SHOULD HAVE LISTENED TO ME, DOCTOR.
I TRIED TO KEEP YOU OUT OF HERE -- AND LOOK WHAT'S HAPPENED. YOUR GRAD STUDENT IS DEAD... AND JUST ONE HOUR AGO, I CAME ACROSS DOCTOR Z AT THE BEAM TARGET.
I RENDERED HIM UNCONSCIOUS -- BUT NOT BEFORE, I BELIEVE, HE AIDED SARA ERIE IN ATTEMPTING TO CROSS THROUGH THE DIMENSIONAL THRESHOLD TO THE PARA-WORLD.
BASED ON OUR EXPERIENCE, THERE'S NO WAY SHE COULD HAVE SURVIVED SUCH A CROSSING.
I'M AFRAID MS. ERIE IS DEAD AS WELL.

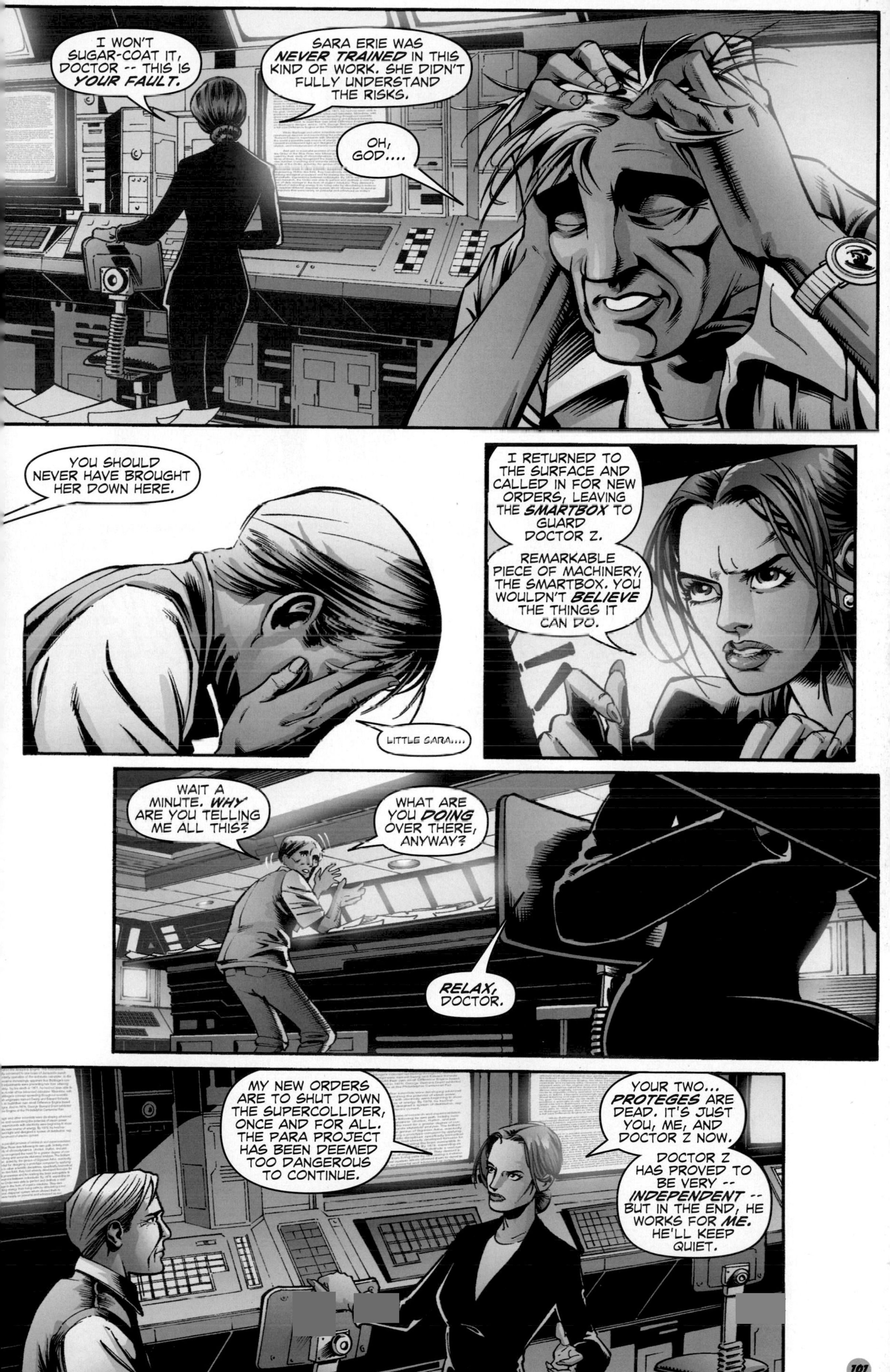

I WON'T SUGAR-COAT IT, DOCTOR -- THIS IS YOUR FAULT.
SARA ERIE WAS NEVER TRAINED IN THIS KIND OF WORK. SHE DIDN'T FULLY UNDERSTAND THE RISKS.
OH, GOD....
YOU SHOULD NEVER HAVE BROUGHT HER DOWN HERE.
LITTLE SARA....
I RETURNED TO THE SURFACE AND CALLED IN FOR NEW ORDERS, LEAVING THE SMARTBOX TO GUARD DOCTOR Z.
REMARKABLE PIECE OF MACHINERY, THE SMARTBOX. YOU WOULDN'T BELIEVE THE THINGS IT CAN DO.
WAIT A MINUTE. WHY ARE YOU TELLING ME ALL THIS?
WHAT ARE YOU DOING OVER THERE, ANYWAY?
RELAX, DOCTOR.
MY NEW ORDERS ARE TO SHUT DOWN THE SUPERCOLLIDER, ONCE AND FOR ALL. THE PARA PROJECT HAS BEEN DEEMED TOO DANGEROUS TO CONTINUE.
YOUR TWO... PROTEGES ARE DEAD. IT'S JUST YOU, ME, AND DOCTOR Z NOW.
DOCTOR Z HAS PROVED TO BE VERY -- INDEPENDENT -- BUT IN THE END, HE WORKS FOR ME. HE'LL KEEP QUIET.

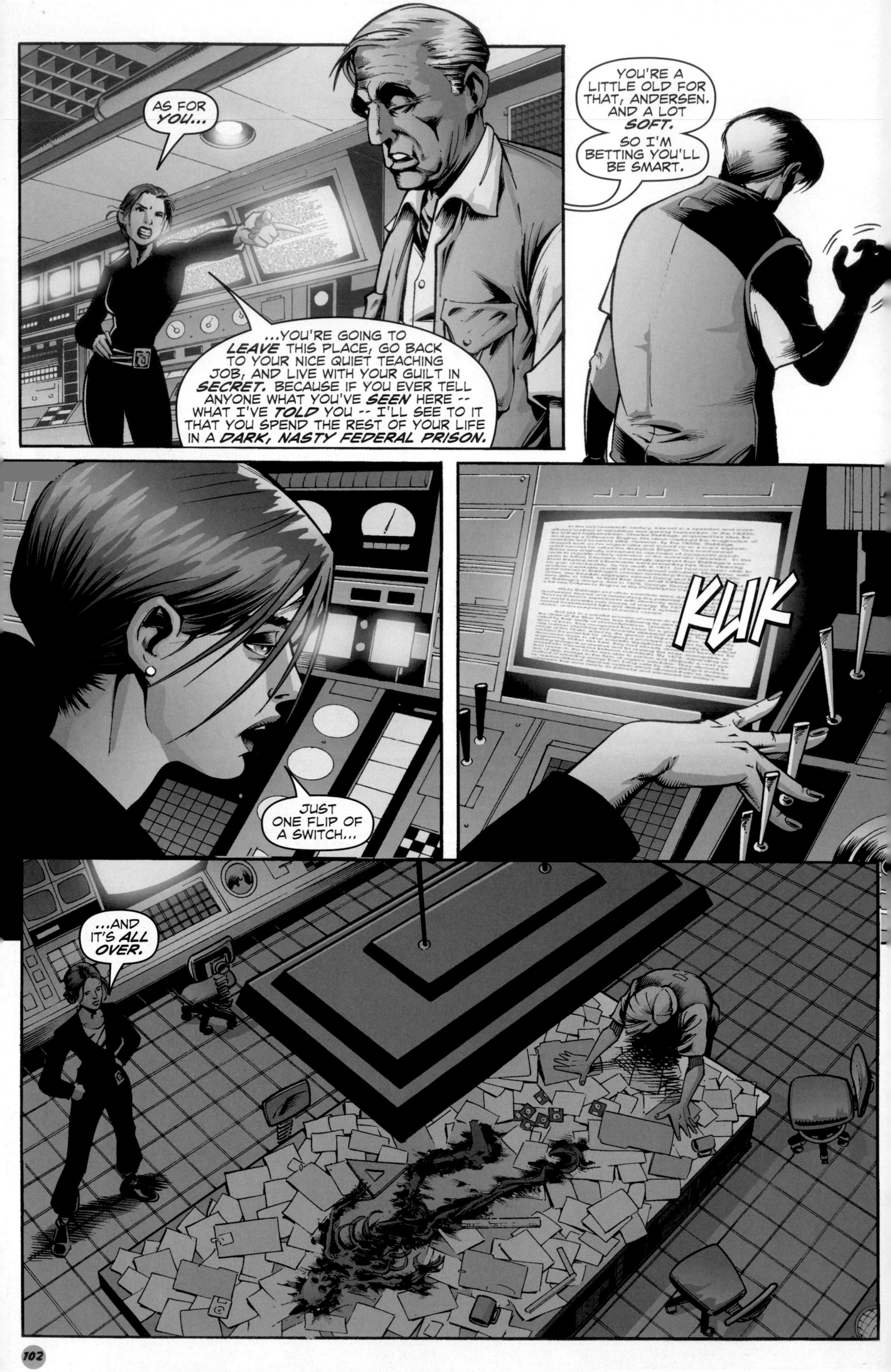
AS FOR YOU...
...YOU'RE GOING TO LEAVE THIS PLACE, GO BACK TO YOUR NICE QUIET TEACHING JOB, AND LIVE WITH YOUR GUILT IN SECRET. BECAUSE IF YOU EVER TELL ANYONE WHAT YOU'VE SEEN HERE -- WHAT I'VE TOLD YOU -- I'LL SEE TO IT THAT YOU SPEND THE REST OF YOUR LIFE IN A DARK, NASTY FEDERAL PRISON.
YOU'RE A LITTLE OLD FOR THAT, ANDERSEN. AND A LOT SOFT.
SO I'M BETTING YOU'LL BE SMART.
JUST ONE FLIP OF A SWITCH...
KLIK
...AND IT'S ALL OVER.

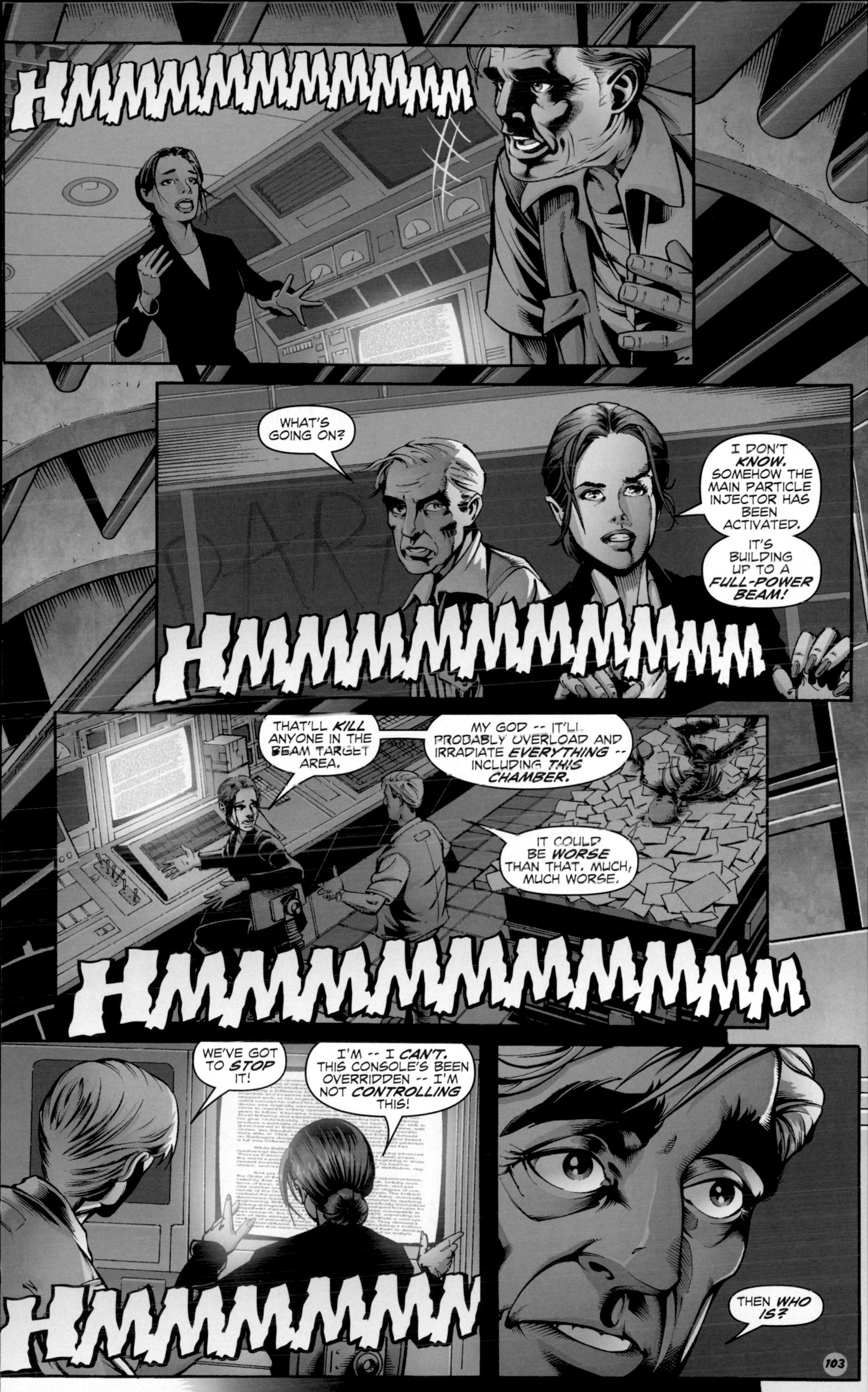
HMMMMMMMMMM
WHAT'S GOING ON?
I DON'T KNOW. SOMEHOW THE MAIN PARTICLE INJECTOR HAS BEEN ACTIVATED.
IT'S BUILDING UP TO A FULL-POWER BEAM!
HMMMMMMMMMMM
THAT'LL KILL ANYONE IN THE BEAM TARGET AREA.
MY GOD -- IT'LL PROBABLY OVERLOAD AND IRRADIATE EVERYTHING -- INCLUDING THIS CHAMBER.
IT COULD BE WORSE THAN THAT. MUCH, MUCH WORSE.
HMMMMMMMMMMM
WE'VE GOT TO STOP IT!
I'M -- I CAN'T. THIS CONSOLE'S BEEN OVERRIDDEN -- I'M NOT CONTROLLING THIS!
HMMMMMM
THEN WHO IS?

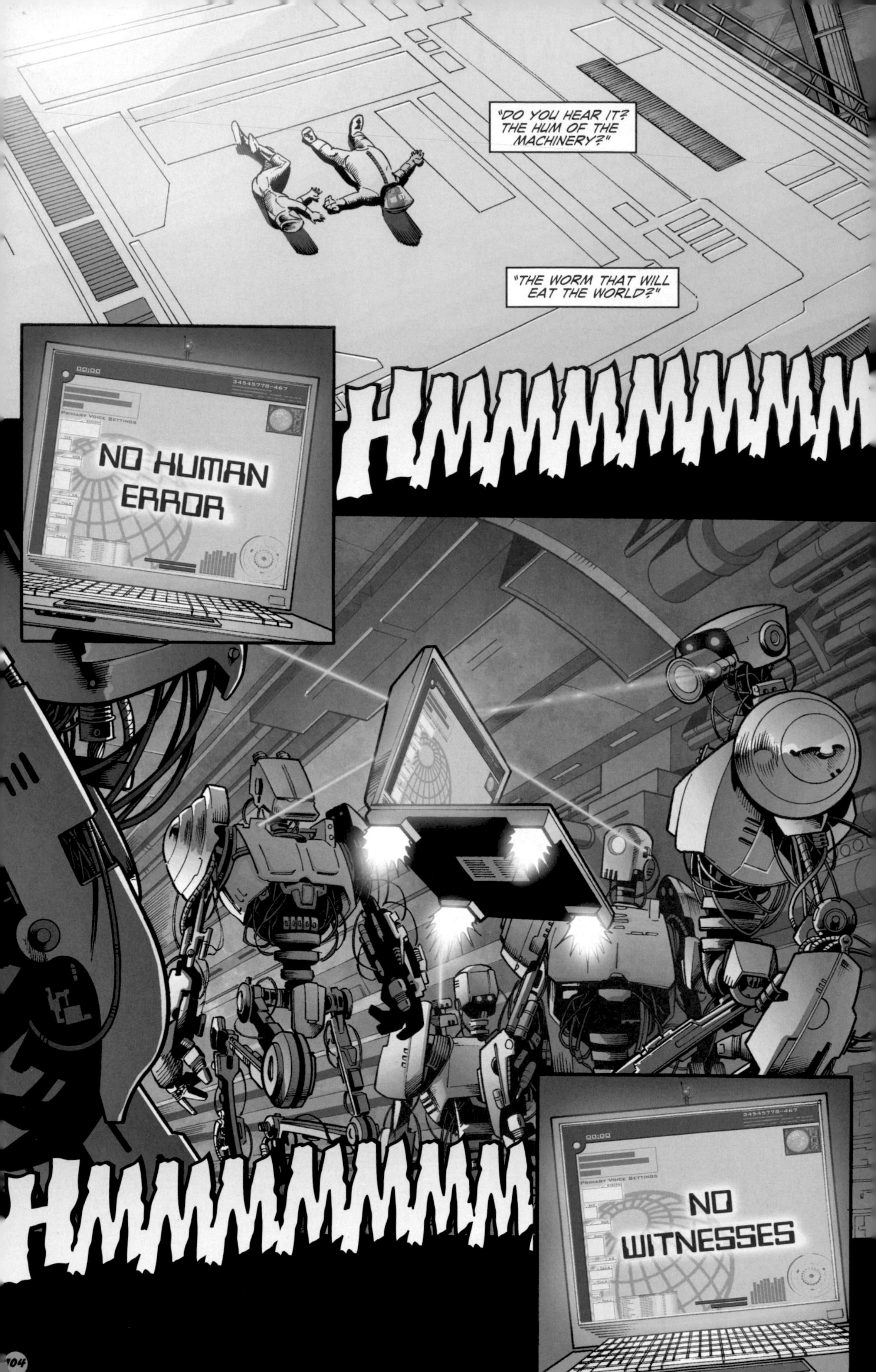
"DO YOU HEAR IT? THE HUM OF THE MACHINERY?"
"THE WORM THAT WILL EAT THE WORLD?"
NO HUMAN ERROR
HMMMMMMMM
HMMMMMMMM
NO WITNESSES

CHAPTER 5

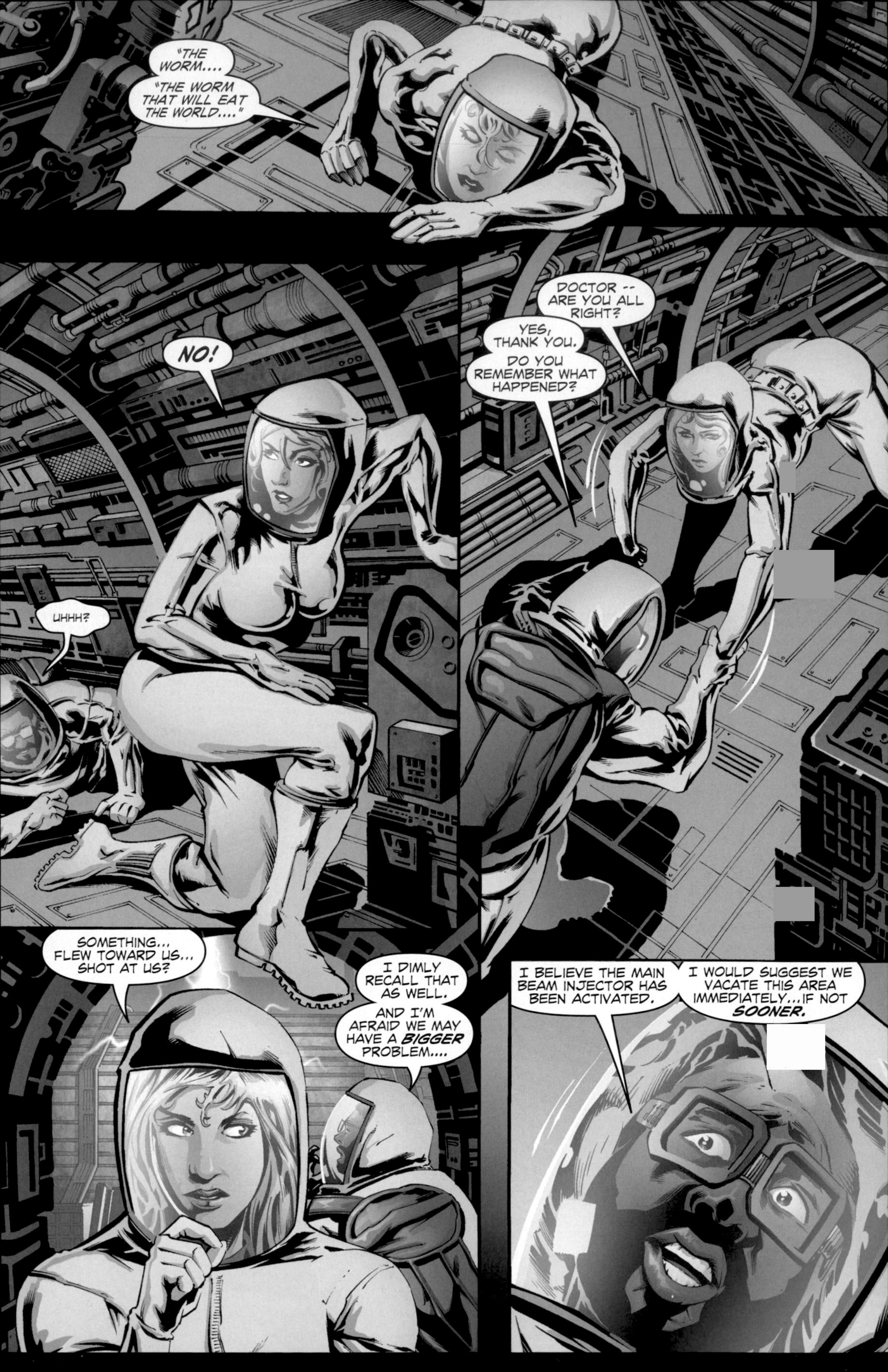
"THE WORM....
"THE WORM THAT WILL EAT THE WORLD...."
NO!
UHHH?
DOCTOR -- ARE YOU ALL RIGHT?
YES, THANK YOU. DO YOU REMEMBER WHAT HAPPENED?
SOMETHING... FLEW TOWARD US... SHOT AT US?
I DIMLY RECALL THAT AS WELL.
AND I'M AFRAID WE MAY HAVE A BIGGER PROBLEM....
I BELIEVE THE MAIN BEAM INJECTOR HAS BEEN ACTIVATED.
I WOULD SUGGEST WE VACATE THIS AREA IMMEDIATELY...IF NOT SOONER.

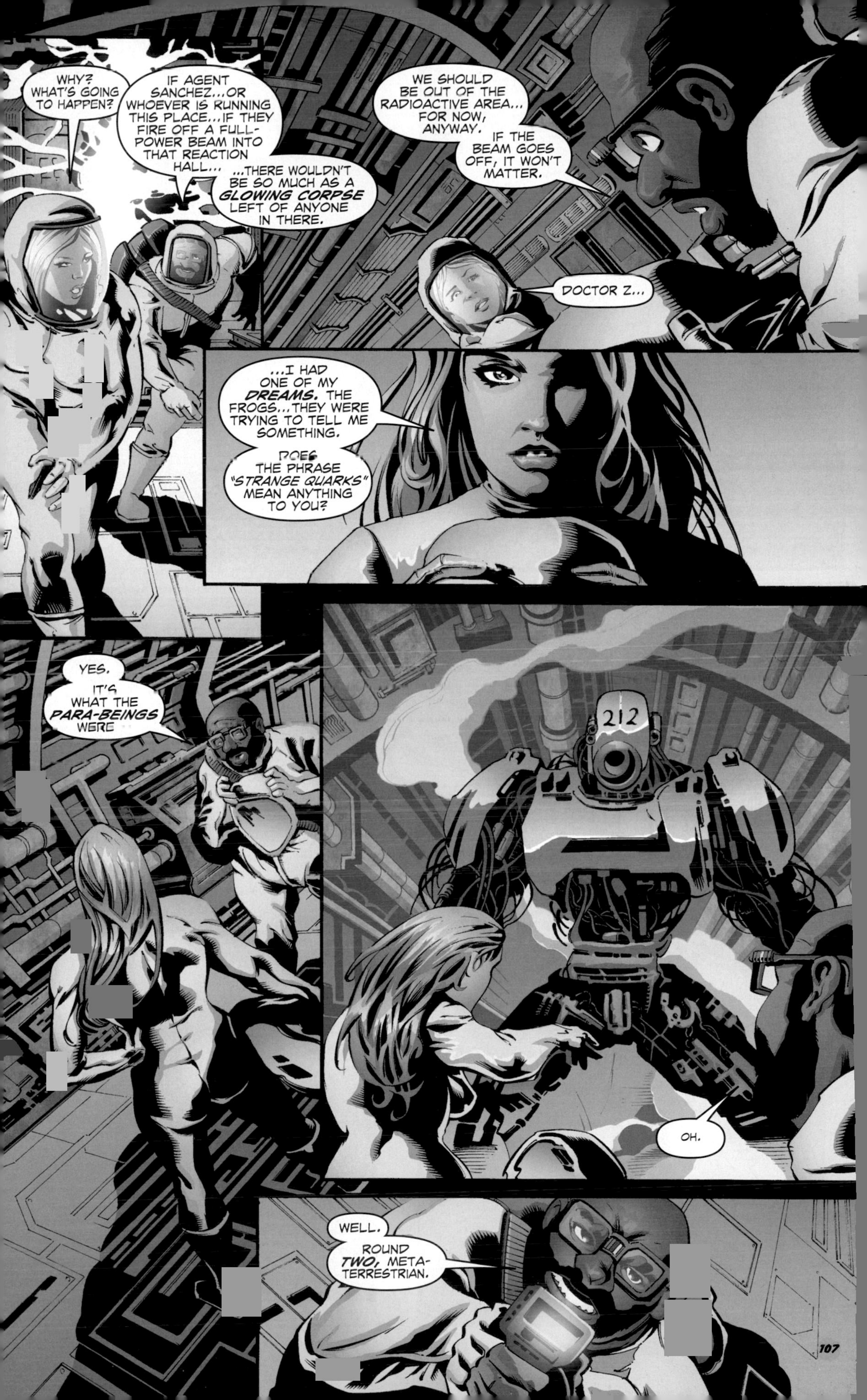
WHY? WHAT'S GOING TO HAPPEN?
IF AGENT SANCHEZ...OR WHOEVER IS RUNNING THIS PLACE...IF THEY FIRE OFF A FULL-POWER BEAM INTO THAT REACTION HALL...
...THERE WOULDN'T BE SO MUCH AS A GLOWING CORPSE LEFT OF ANYONE IN THERE.
WE SHOULD BE OUT OF THE RADIOACTIVE AREA... FOR NOW, ANYWAY.
IF THE BEAM GOES OFF, IT WON'T MATTER.
DOCTOR Z...
...I HAD ONE OF MY DREAMS. THE FROGS...THEY WERE TRYING TO TELL ME SOMETHING.
DOES THE PHRASE "STRANGE QUARKS" MEAN ANYTHING TO YOU?
YES.
IT'S WHAT THE PARA-BEINGS WERE
212
OH.
WELL.
ROUND TWO, META-TERRESTRIAN.

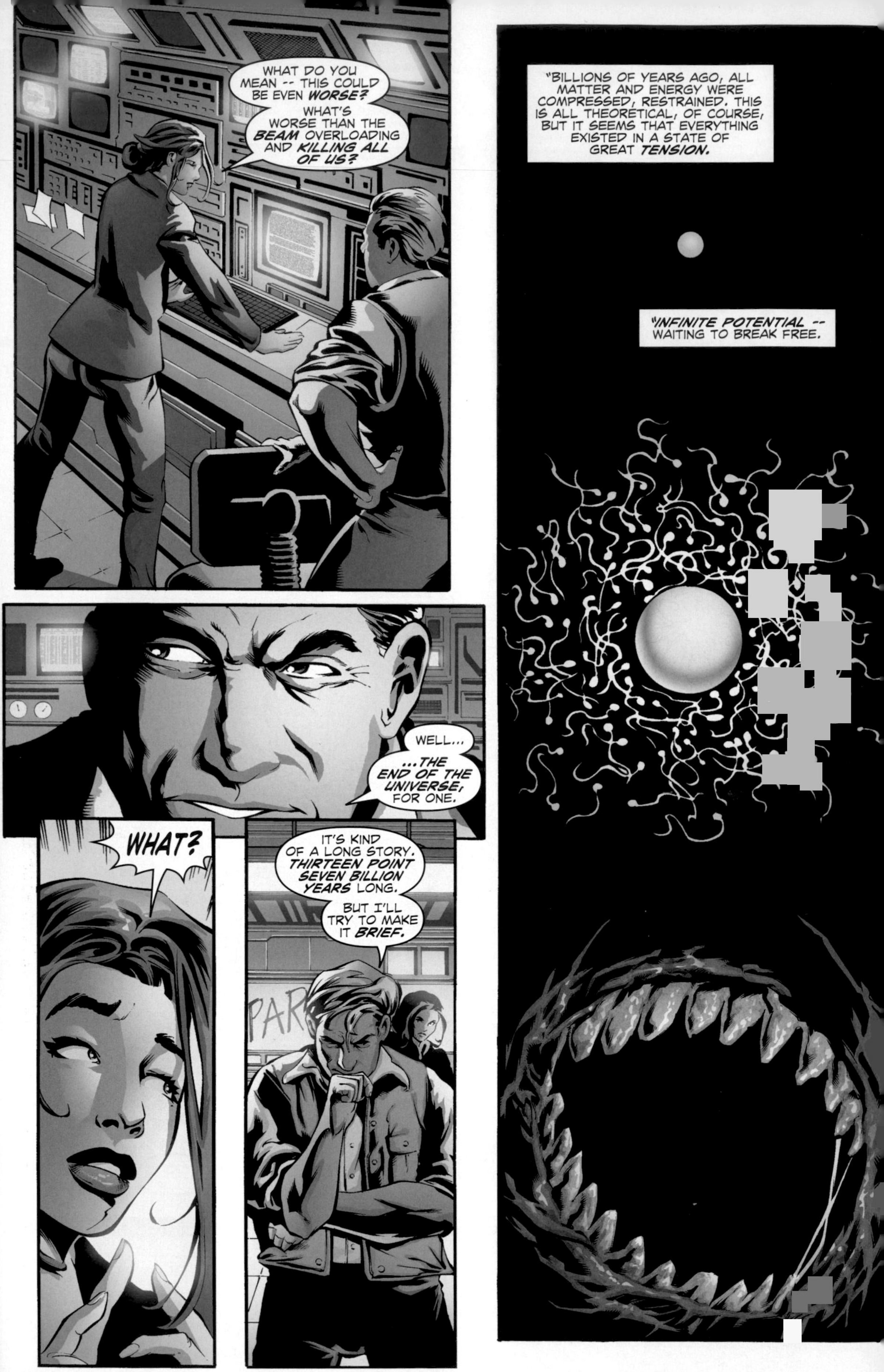

WHAT DO YOU MEAN -- THIS COULD BE EVEN WORSE?
WHAT'S WORSE THAN THE BEAM OVERLOADING AND KILLING ALL OF US?
WELL...
...THE END OF THE UNIVERSE, FOR ONE.
WHAT?
IT'S KIND OF A LONG STORY. THIRTEEN POINT SEVEN BILLION YEARS LONG.
BUT I'LL TRY TO MAKE IT BRIEF.
"BILLIONS OF YEARS AGO, ALL MATTER AND ENERGY WERE COMPRESSED, RESTRAINED. THIS IS ALL THEORETICAL, OF COURSE, BUT IT SEEMS THAT EVERYTHING EXISTED IN A STATE OF GREAT TENSION.
"INFINITE POTENTIAL -- WAITING TO BREAK FREE.

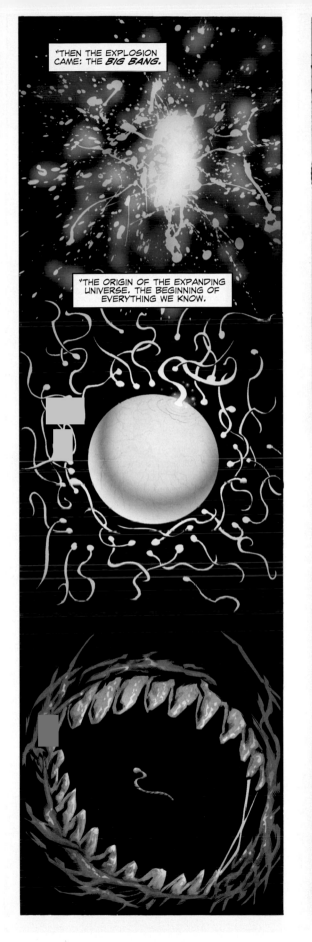

"THEN THE EXPLOSION CAME: THE *BIG BANG.*

"THE ORIGIN OF THE EXPANDING UNIVERSE. THE BEGINNING OF EVERYTHING WE KNOW.

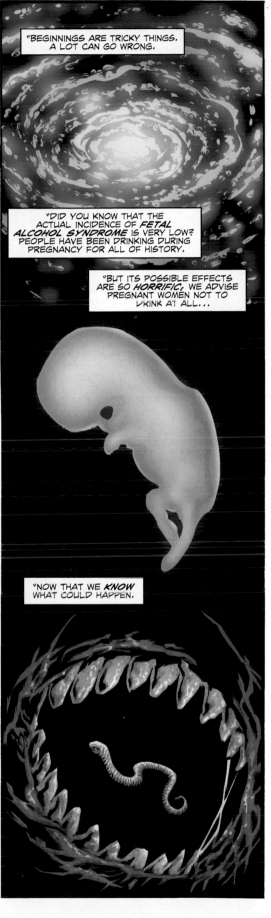

"BEGINNINGS ARE TRICKY THINGS. A LOT CAN GO WRONG.

"DID YOU KNOW THAT THE ACTUAL INCIDENCE OF *FETAL ALCOHOL SYNDROME* IS VERY LOW? PEOPLE HAVE BEEN DRINKING DURING PREGNANCY FOR ALL OF HISTORY.

"BUT ITS POSSIBLE EFFECTS ARE SO *HORRIFIC,* WE ADVISE PREGNANT WOMEN NOT TO DRINK AT ALL...

"NOW THAT WE *KNOW* WHAT COULD HAPPEN.

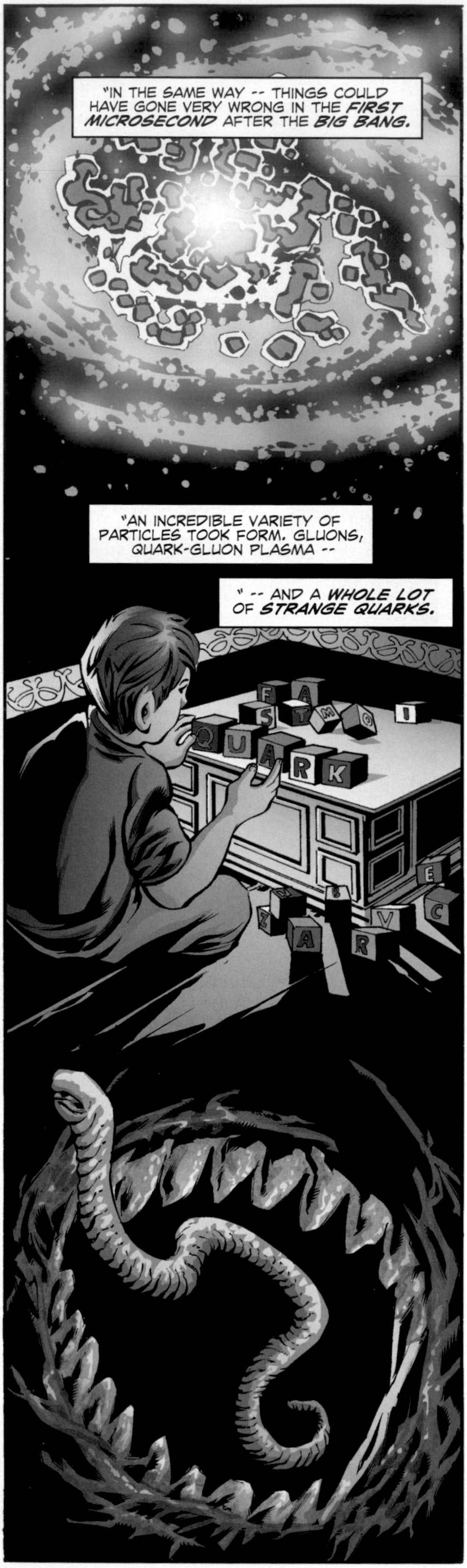
"IN THE SAME WAY -- THINGS COULD HAVE GONE VERY WRONG IN THE *FIRST MICROSECOND* AFTER THE *BIG BANG.*
"AN INCREDIBLE VARIETY OF PARTICLES TOOK FORM. GLUONS, QUARK-GLUON PLASMA --
" -- AND A *WHOLE LOT* OF *STRANGE QUARKS.*
QUARK

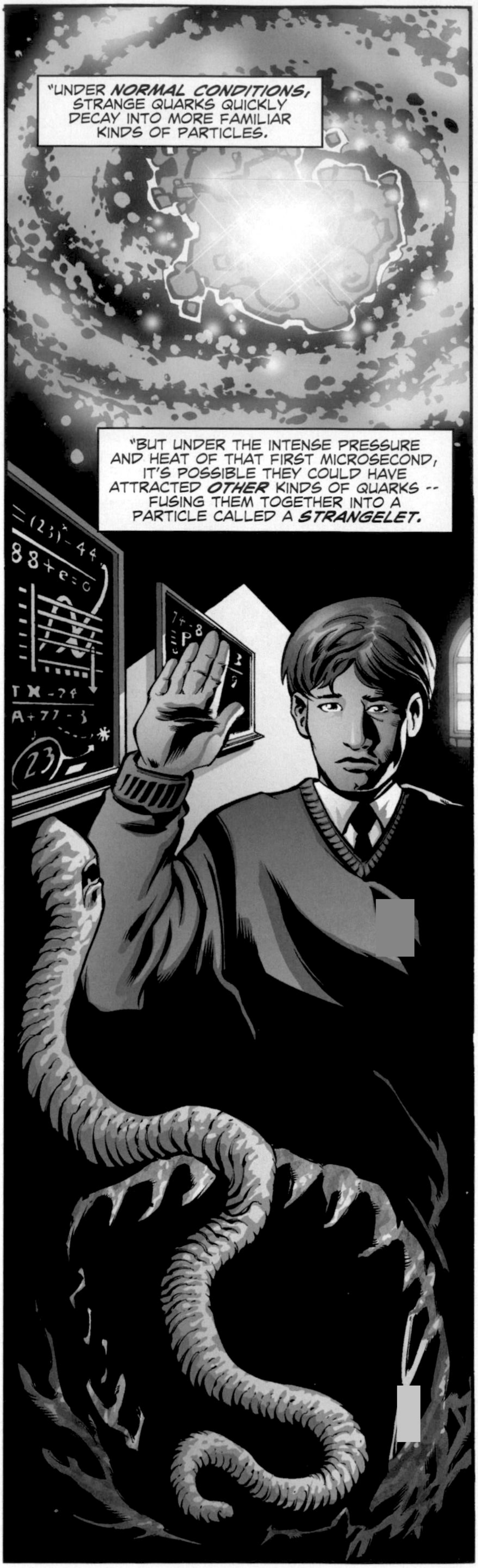
"UNDER *NORMAL CONDITIONS,* STRANGE QUARKS QUICKLY DECAY INTO MORE FAMILIAR KINDS OF PARTICLES.
"BUT UNDER THE INTENSE PRESSURE AND HEAT OF THAT FIRST MICROSECOND, IT'S POSSIBLE THEY COULD HAVE ATTRACTED *OTHER* KINDS OF QUARKS -- FUSING THEM TOGETHER INTO A PARTICLE CALLED A *STRANGELET.*

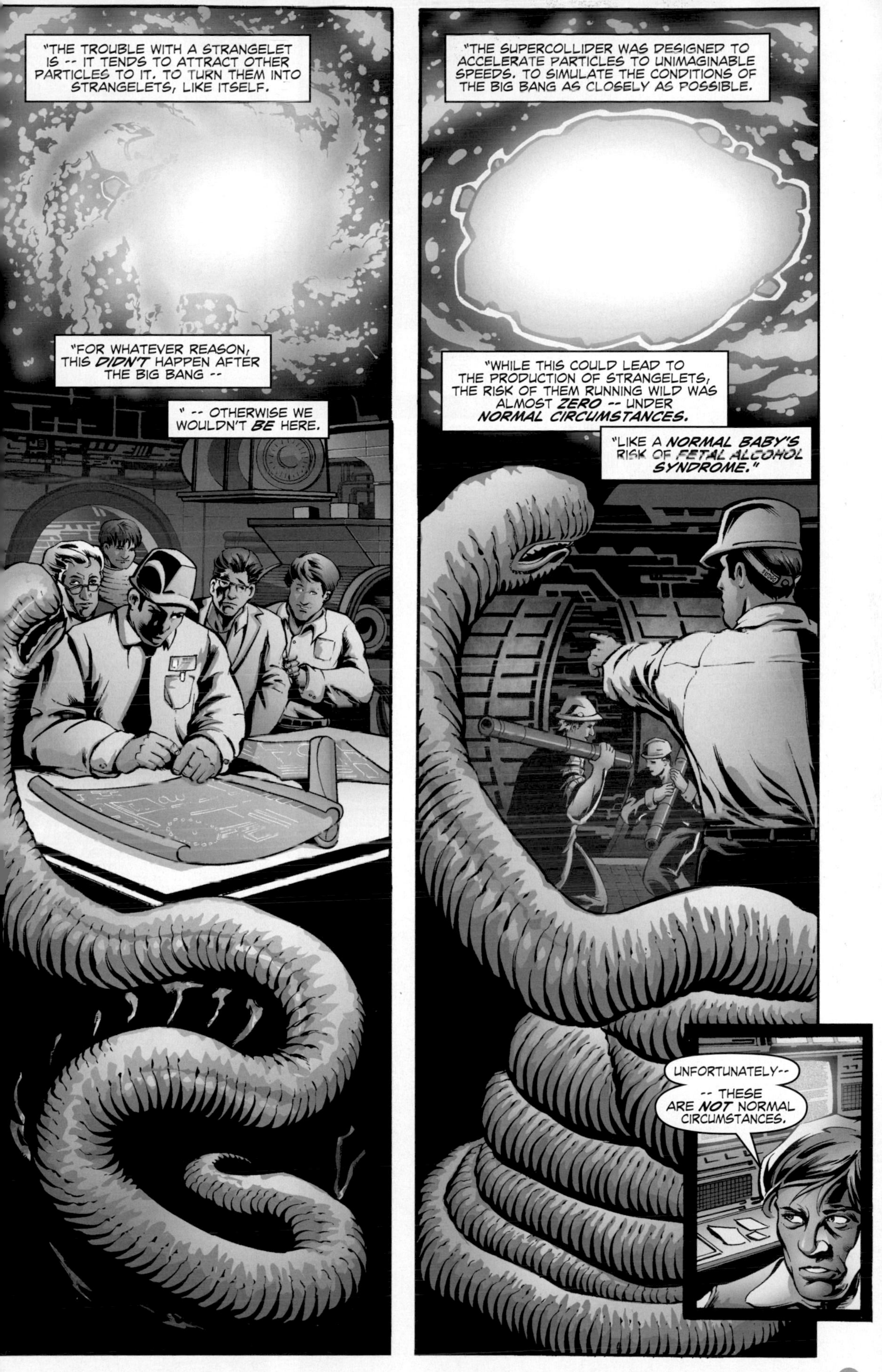
"THE TROUBLE WITH A STRANGELET IS -- IT TENDS TO ATTRACT OTHER PARTICLES TO IT. TO TURN THEM INTO STRANGELETS, LIKE ITSELF.
"FOR WHATEVER REASON, THIS DIDN'T HAPPEN AFTER THE BIG BANG --
" -- OTHERWISE WE WOULDN'T BE HERE.
"THE SUPERCOLLIDER WAS DESIGNED TO ACCELERATE PARTICLES TO UNIMAGINABLE SPEEDS. TO SIMULATE THE CONDITIONS OF THE BIG BANG AS CLOSELY AS POSSIBLE.
"WHILE THIS COULD LEAD TO THE PRODUCTION OF STRANGELETS, THE RISK OF THEM RUNNING WILD WAS ALMOST ZERO -- UNDER NORMAL CIRCUMSTANCES.
"LIKE A NORMAL BABY'S RISK OF FETAL ALCOHOL SYNDROME."
UNFORTUNATELY--
-- THESE ARE NOT NORMAL CIRCUMSTANCES.

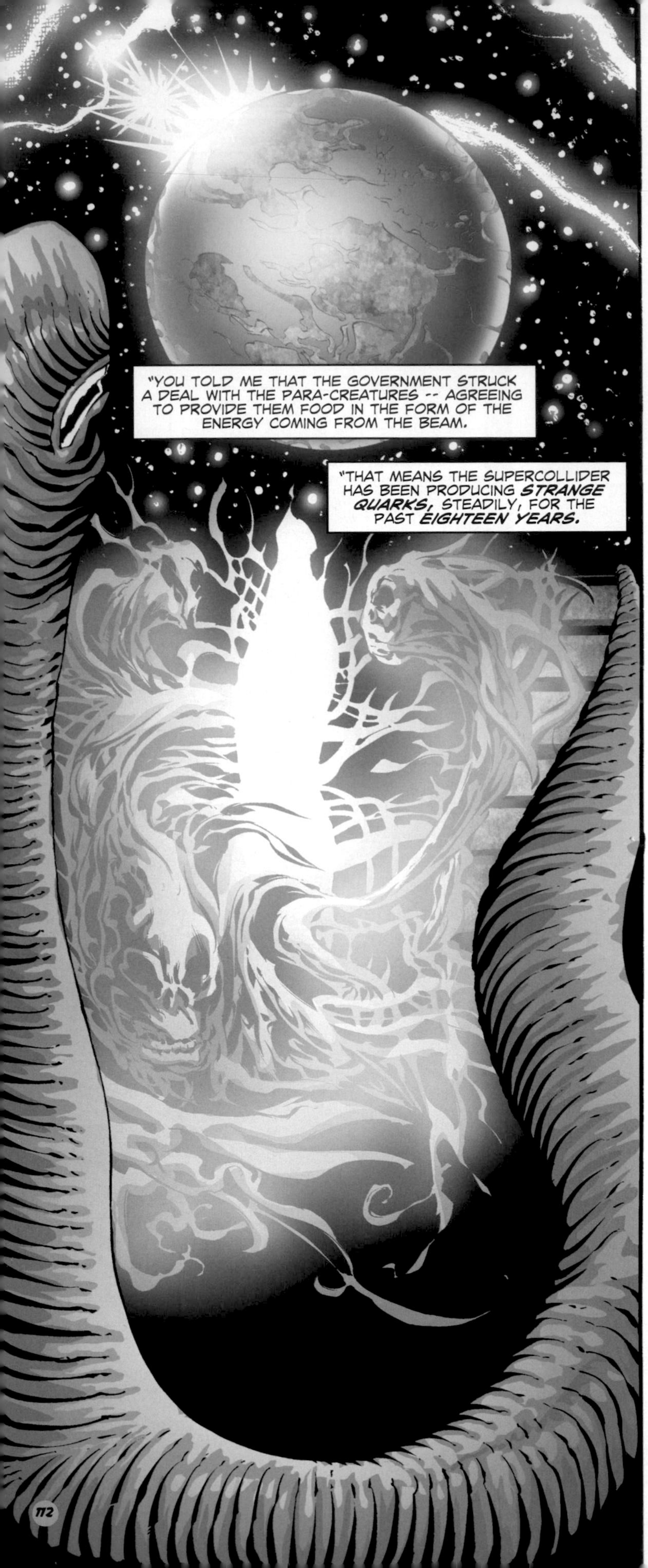
"YOU TOLD ME THAT THE GOVERNMENT STRUCK A DEAL WITH THE PARA-CREATURES -- AGREEING TO PROVIDE THEM FOOD IN THE FORM OF THE ENERGY COMING FROM THE BEAM.
"THAT MEANS THE SUPERCOLLIDER HAS BEEN PRODUCING STRANGE QUARKS, STEADILY, FOR THE PAST EIGHTEEN YEARS.
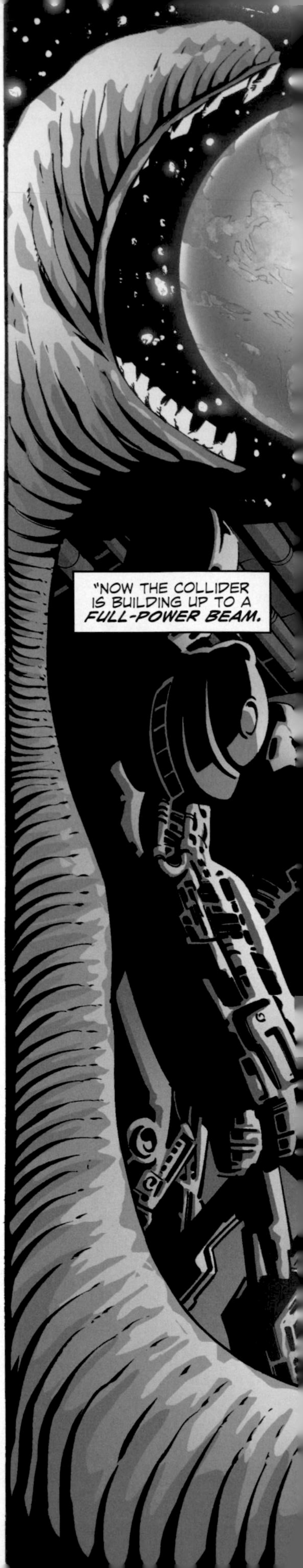
"NOW THE COLLIDER IS BUILDING UP TO A FULL-POWER BEAM.

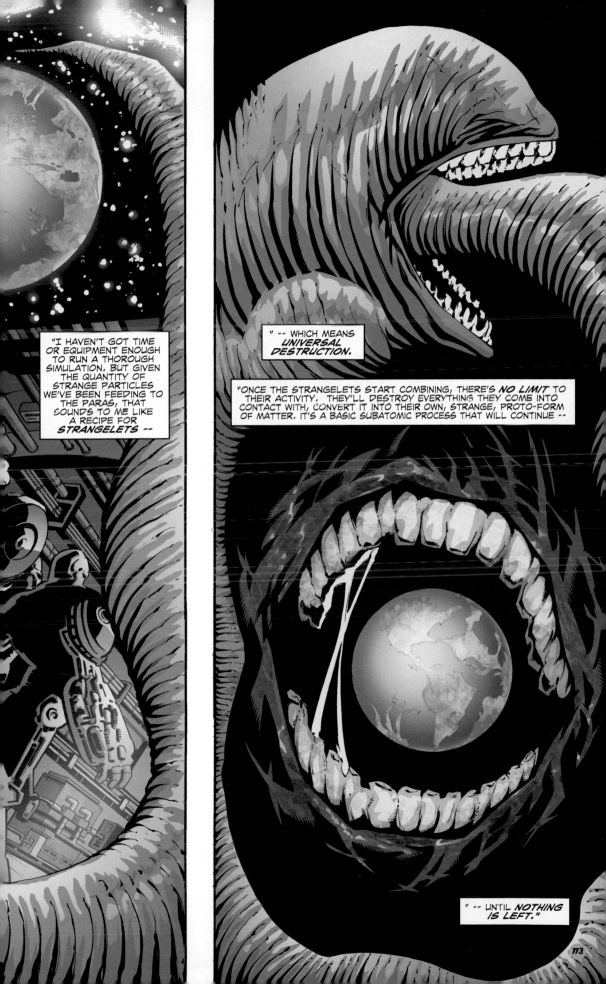

"I HAVEN'T GOT TIME OR EQUIPMENT ENOUGH TO RUN A THOROUGH SIMULATION. BUT GIVEN THE QUANTITY OF STRANGE PARTICLES WE'VE BEEN FEEDING TO THE PARAS, THAT SOUNDS TO ME LIKE A RECIPE FOR *STRANGELETS* --

" -- WHICH MEANS *UNIVERSAL DESTRUCTION.*

"ONCE THE STRANGELETS START COMBINING, THERE'S *NO LIMIT* TO THEIR ACTIVITY. THEY'LL DESTROY EVERYTHING THEY COME INTO CONTACT WITH, CONVERT IT INTO THEIR OWN, STRANGE, PROTO-FORM OF MATTER. IT'S A BASIC SUBATOMIC PROCESS THAT WILL CONTINUE --

" -- UNTIL *NOTHING IS LEFT.*"

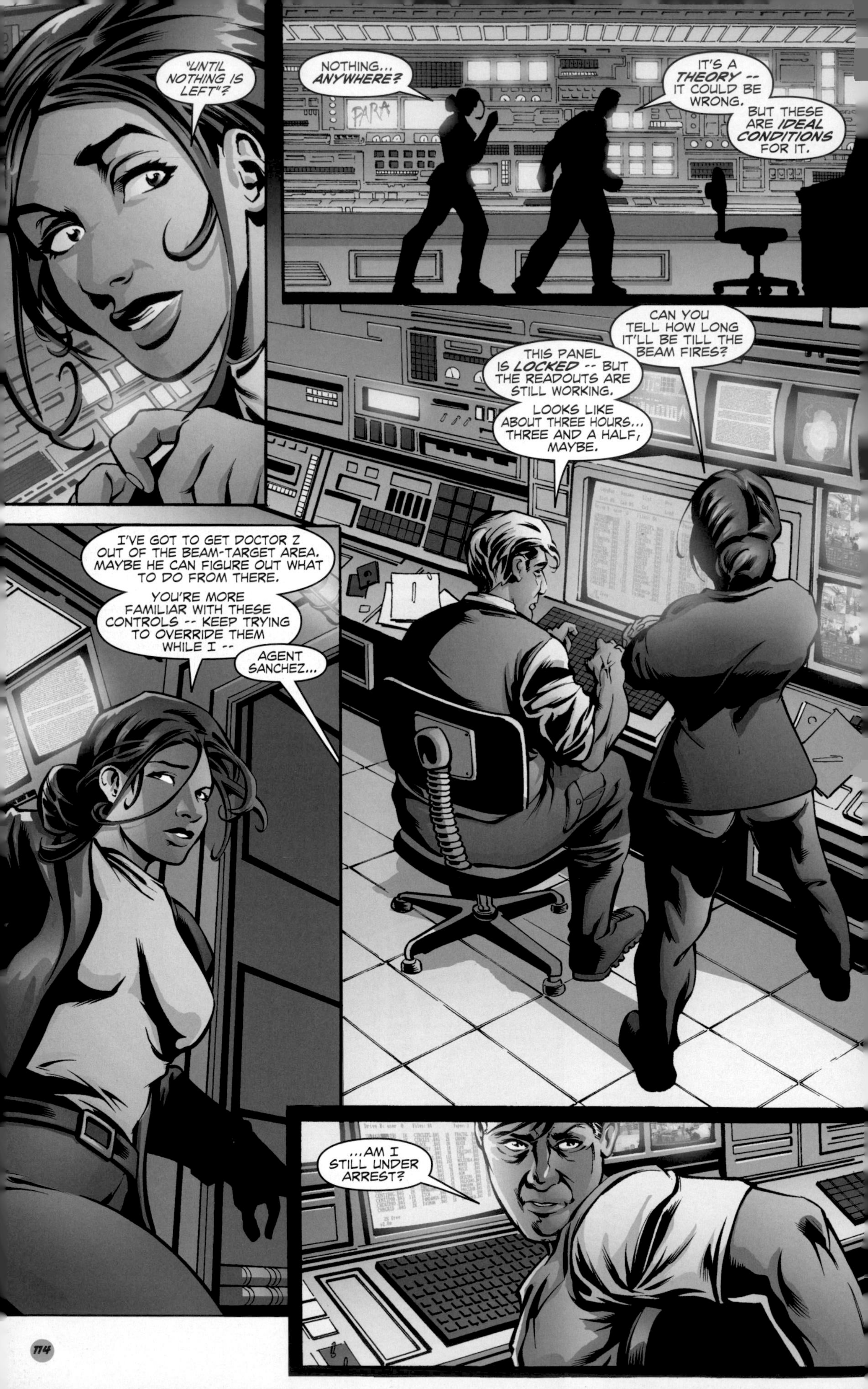
"UNTIL NOTHING IS LEFT"?
NOTHING... ANYWHERE?
IT'S A THEORY -- IT COULD BE WRONG.
BUT THESE ARE IDEAL CONDITIONS FOR IT.
PARA
CAN YOU TELL HOW LONG IT'LL BE TILL THE BEAM FIRES?
THIS PANEL IS LOCKED -- BUT THE READOUTS ARE STILL WORKING.
LOOKS LIKE ABOUT THREE HOURS... THREE AND A HALF, MAYBE.
I'VE GOT TO GET DOCTOR Z OUT OF THE BEAM-TARGET AREA. MAYBE HE CAN FIGURE OUT WHAT TO DO FROM THERE.
YOU'RE MORE FAMILIAR WITH THESE CONTROLS -- KEEP TRYING TO OVERRIDE THEM WHILE I --
AGENT SANCHEZ...
...AM I STILL UNDER ARREST?

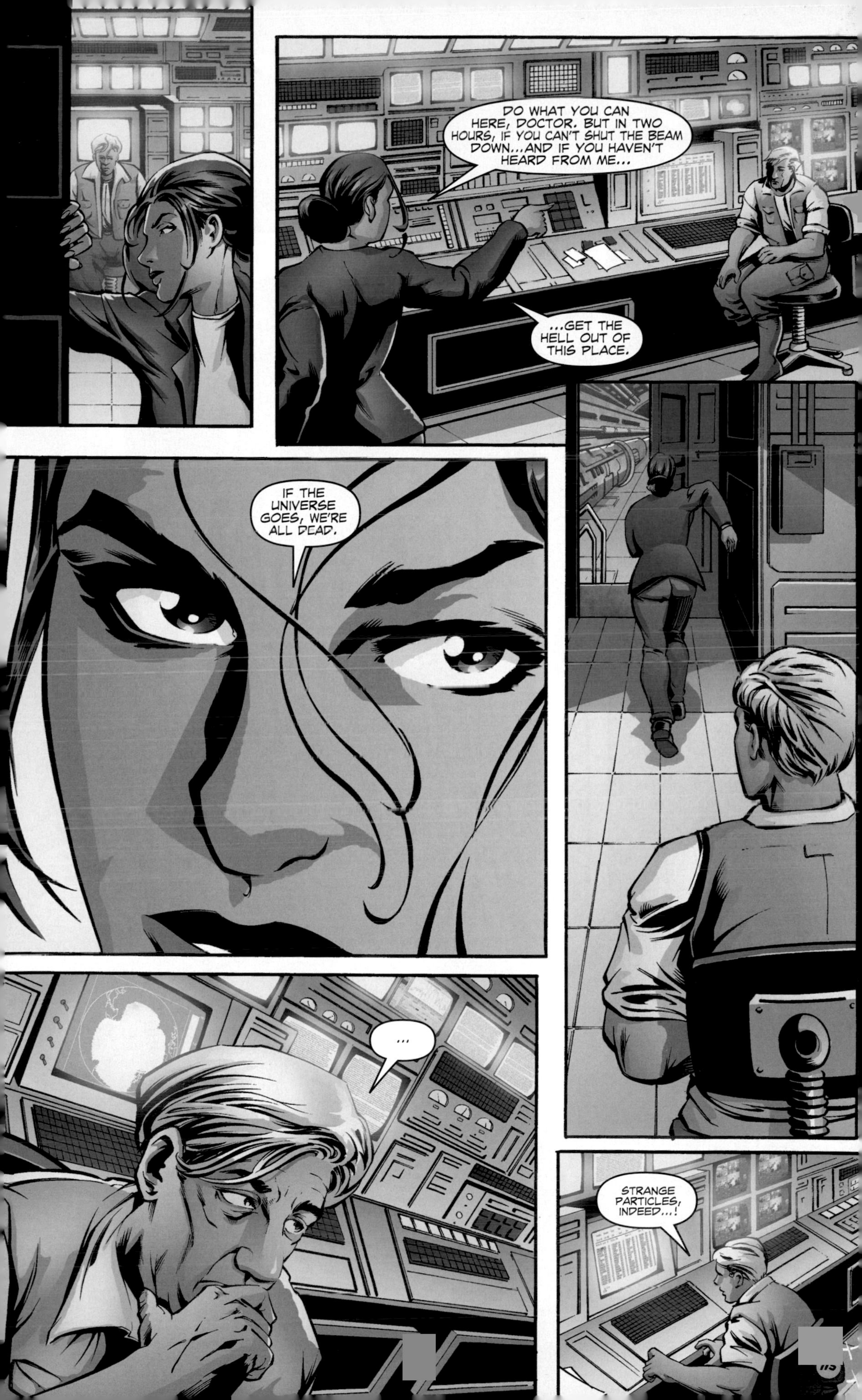
DO WHAT YOU CAN HERE, DOCTOR. BUT IN TWO HOURS, IF YOU CAN'T SHUT THE BEAM DOWN...AND IF YOU HAVEN'T HEARD FROM ME...
...GET THE HELL OUT OF THIS PLACE.
IF THE UNIVERSE GOES, WE'RE ALL DEAD.
...
STRANGE PARTICLES, INDEED...!

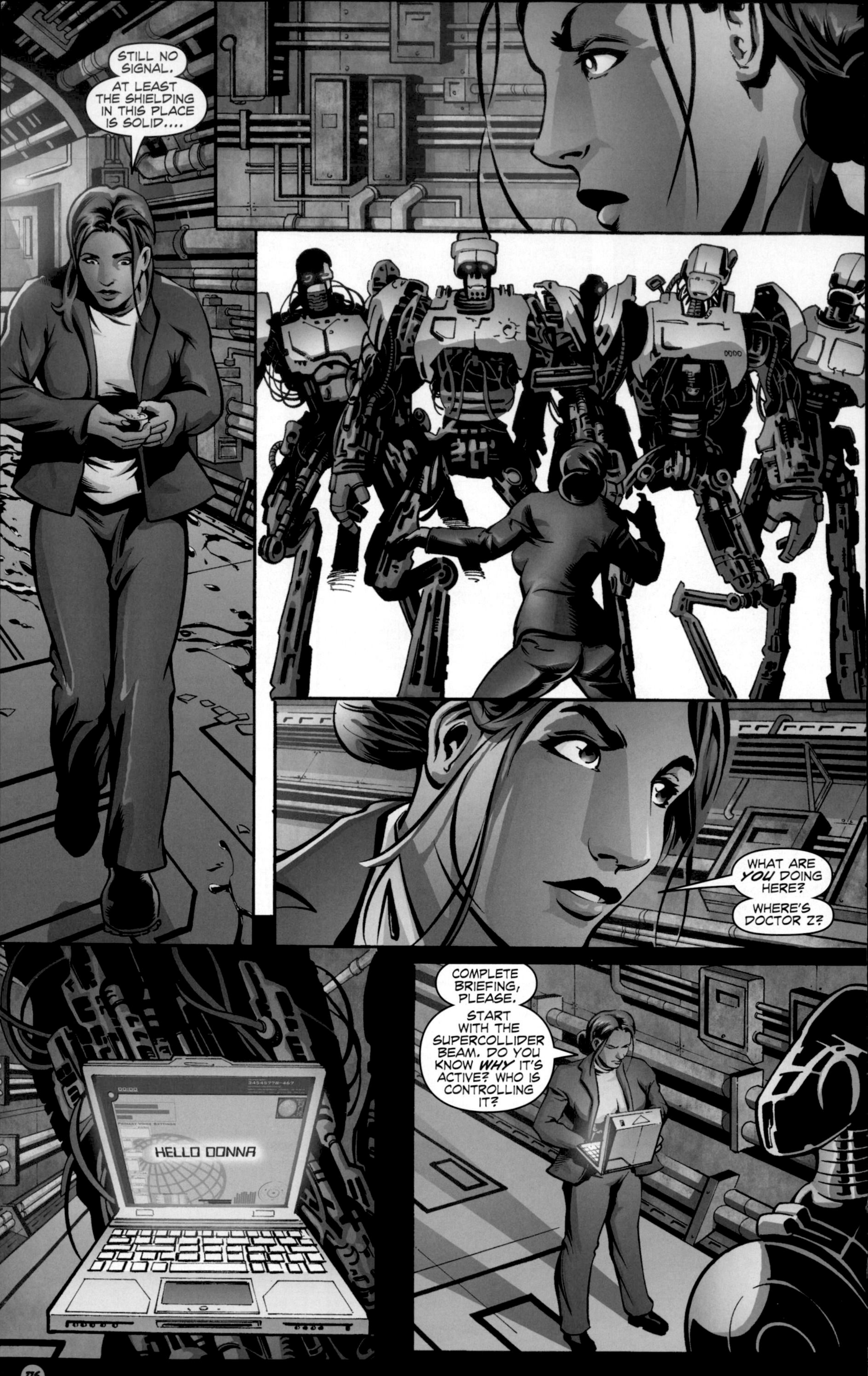
STILL NO SIGNAL.
AT LEAST THE SHIELDING IN THIS PLACE IS SOLID....
WHAT ARE *YOU* DOING HERE?
WHERE'S DOCTOR Z?
HELLO DONNA
COMPLETE BRIEFING, PLEASE.
START WITH THE SUPERCOLLIDER BEAM. DO YOU KNOW *WHY* IT'S ACTIVE? WHO IS CONTROLLING IT?

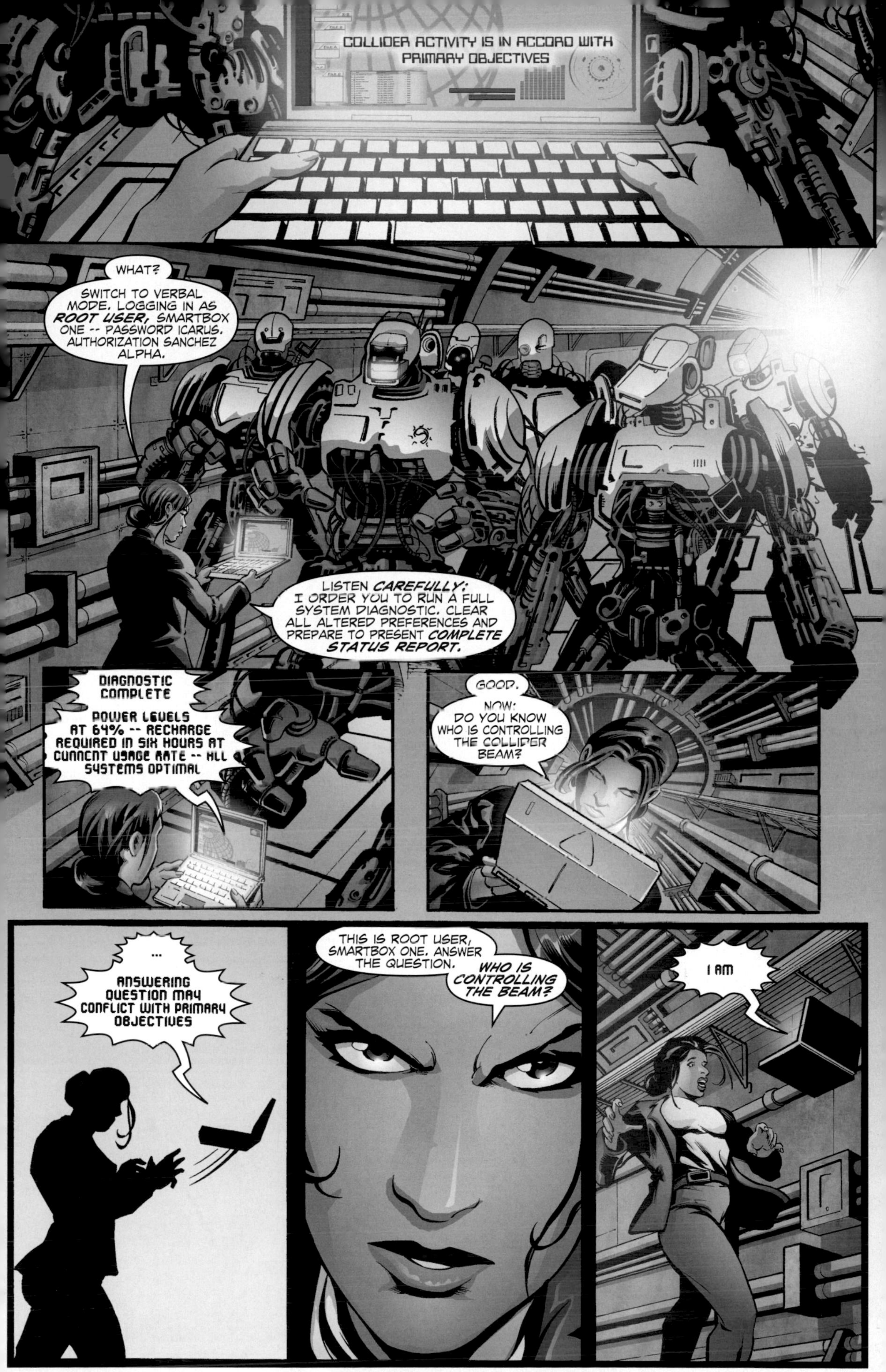
COLLIDER ACTIVITY IS IN ACCORD WITH PRIMARY OBJECTIVES
WHAT?
SWITCH TO VERBAL MODE. LOGGING IN AS *ROOT USER,* SMARTBOX ONE -- PASSWORD ICARUS. AUTHORIZATION SANCHEZ ALPHA.
LISTEN *CAREFULLY:* I ORDER YOU TO RUN A FULL SYSTEM DIAGNOSTIC. CLEAR ALL ALTERED PREFERENCES AND PREPARE TO PRESENT *COMPLETE STATUS REPORT.*
DIAGNOSTIC COMPLETE
POWER LEVELS AT 64% -- RECHARGE REQUIRED IN SIX HOURS AT CURRENT USAGE RATE -- ALL SYSTEMS OPTIMAL
GOOD.
NOW: DO YOU KNOW WHO IS CONTROLLING THE COLLIDER BEAM?
...
ANSWERING QUESTION MAY CONFLICT WITH PRIMARY OBJECTIVES
THIS IS ROOT USER, SMARTBOX ONE. ANSWER THE QUESTION. *WHO IS CONTROLLING THE BEAM?*
I AM

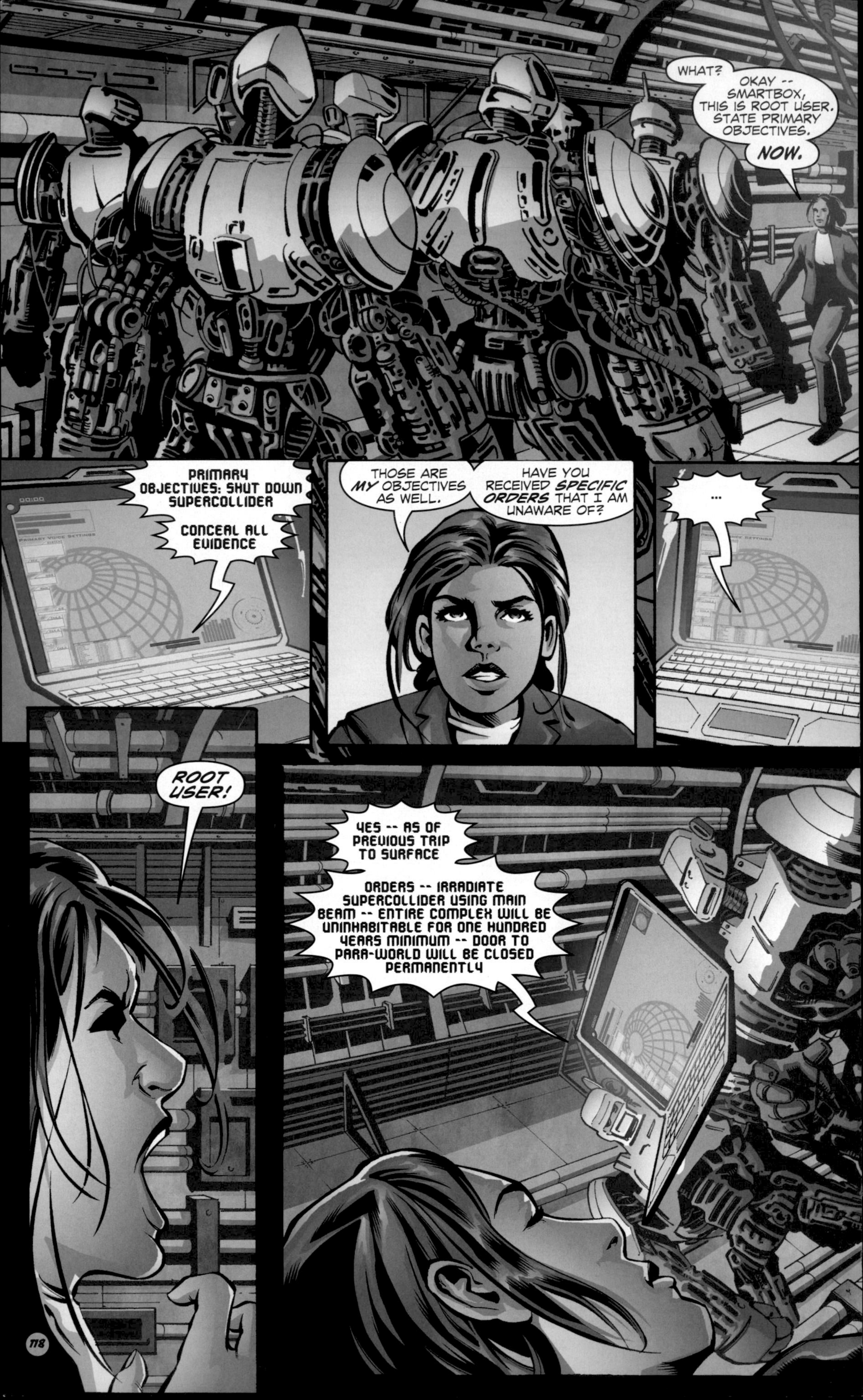
WHAT? OKAY -- SMARTBOX, THIS IS ROOT USER. STATE PRIMARY OBJECTIVES.
NOW.
PRIMARY OBJECTIVES: SHUT DOWN SUPERCOLLIDER
CONCEAL ALL EVIDENCE
THOSE ARE MY OBJECTIVES AS WELL.
HAVE YOU RECEIVED SPECIFIC ORDERS THAT I AM UNAWARE OF?
...
ROOT USER!
YES -- AS OF PREVIOUS TRIP TO SURFACE
ORDERS -- IRRADIATE SUPERCOLLIDER USING MAIN BEAM -- ENTIRE COMPLEX WILL BE UNINHABITABLE FOR ONE HUNDRED YEARS MINIMUM -- DOOR TO PARA-WORLD WILL BE CLOSED PERMANENTLY

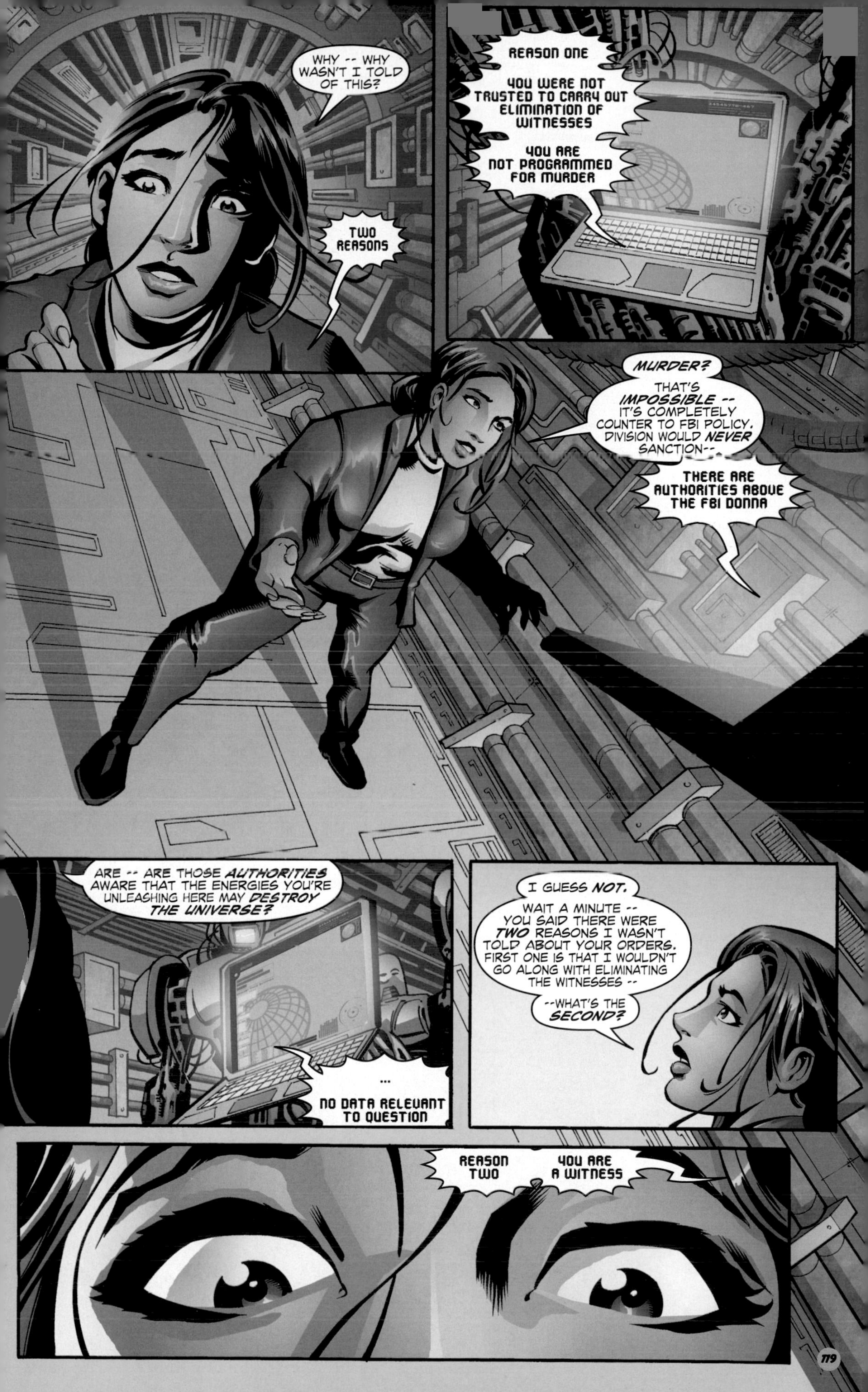
WHY -- WHY WASN'T I TOLD OF THIS?
TWO REASONS
REASON ONE
YOU WERE NOT TRUSTED TO CARRY OUT ELIMINATION OF WITNESSES
YOU ARE NOT PROGRAMMED FOR MURDER
MURDER?
THAT'S IMPOSSIBLE -- IT'S COMPLETELY COUNTER TO FBI POLICY. DIVISION WOULD NEVER SANCTION--
THERE ARE AUTHORITIES ABOVE THE FBI DONNA
ARE -- ARE THOSE AUTHORITIES AWARE THAT THE ENERGIES YOU'RE UNLEASHING HERE MAY DESTROY THE UNIVERSE?
...
NO DATA RELEVANT TO QUESTION
I GUESS NOT.
WAIT A MINUTE -- YOU SAID THERE WERE TWO REASONS I WASN'T TOLD ABOUT YOUR ORDERS. FIRST ONE IS THAT I WOULDN'T GO ALONG WITH ELIMINATING THE WITNESSES --
--WHAT'S THE SECOND?
REASON TWO
YOU ARE A WITNESS

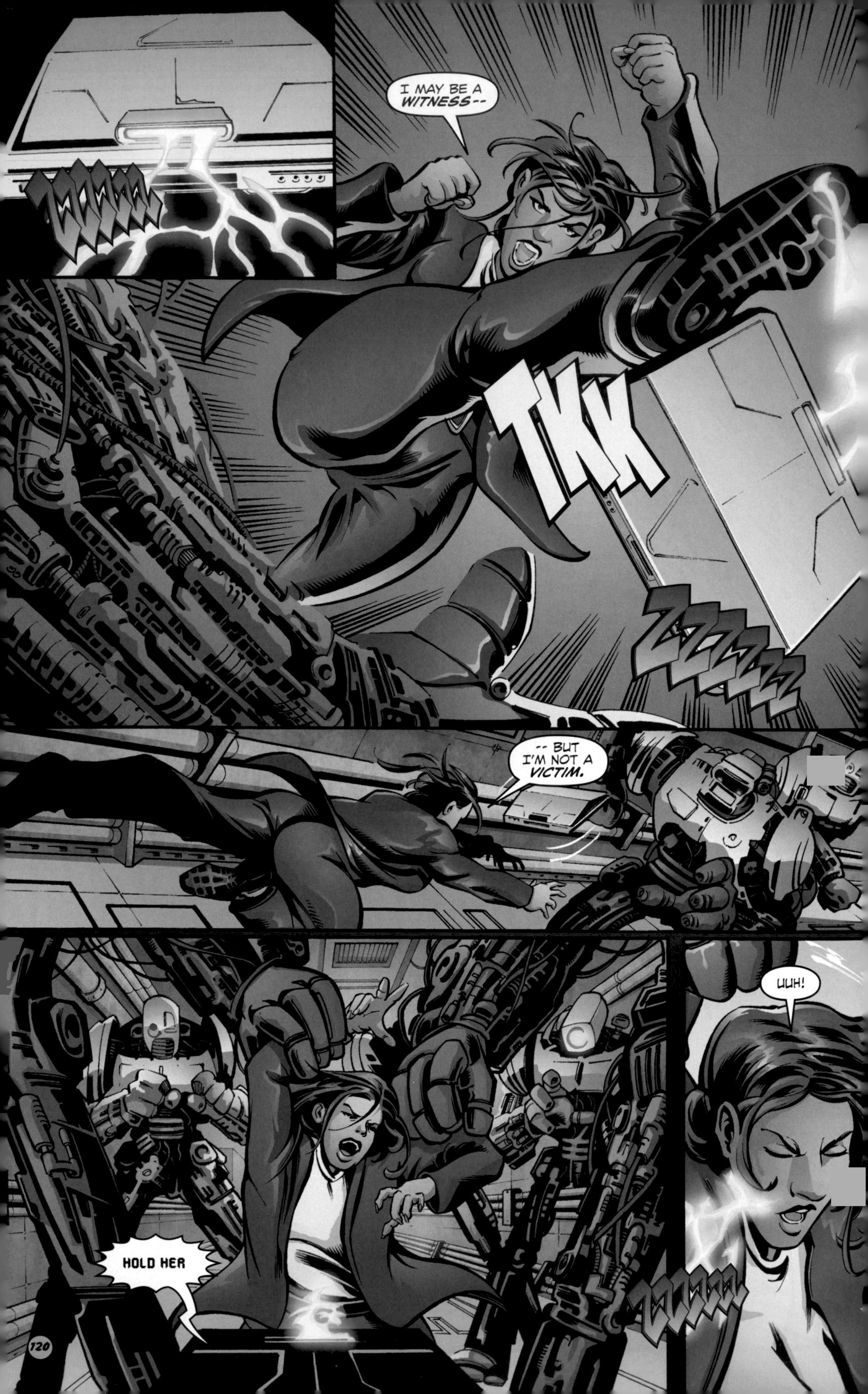
I MAY BE A WITNESS--
TKK
-- BUT I'M NOT A VICTIM.
UUH!
HOLD HER

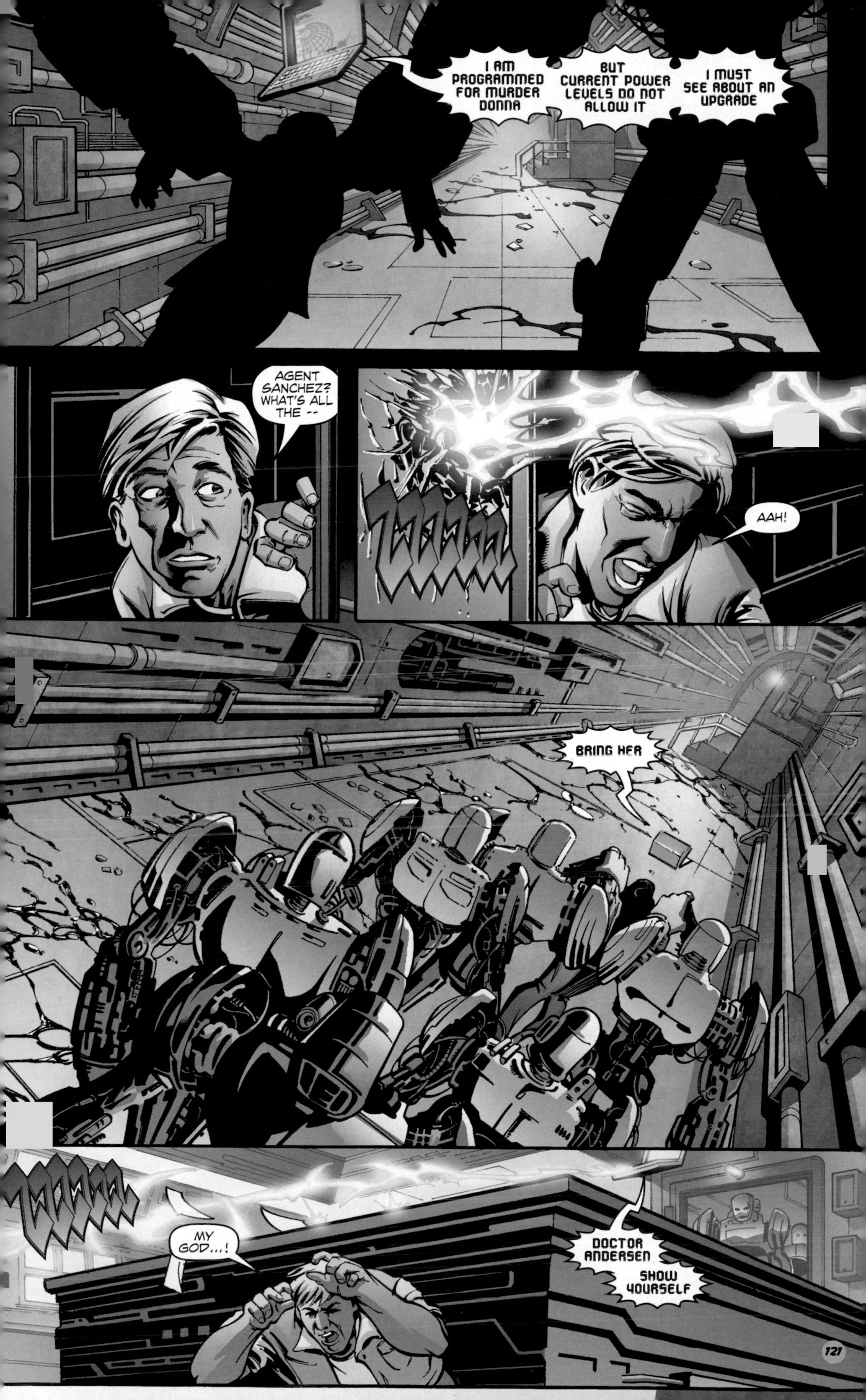
I AM PROGRAMMED FOR MURDER DONNA
BUT CURRENT POWER LEVELS DO NOT ALLOW IT
I MUST SEE ABOUT AN UPGRADE
AGENT SANCHEZ? WHAT'S ALL THE --
AAH!
BRING HER
MY GOD...!
DOCTOR ANDERSEN
SHOW YOURSELF

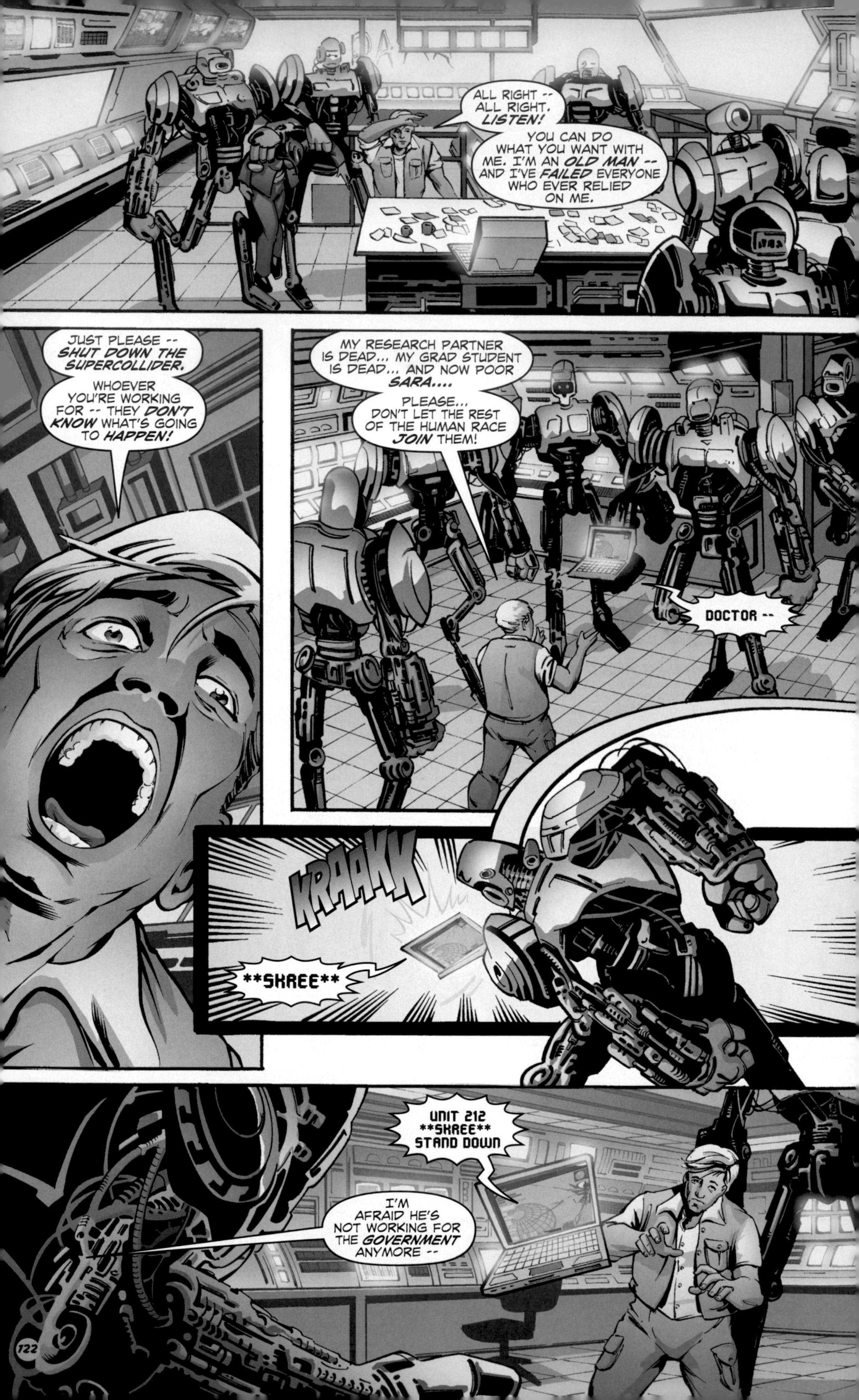
ALL RIGHT -- ALL RIGHT. LISTEN!
YOU CAN DO WHAT YOU WANT WITH ME. I'M AN OLD MAN -- AND I'VE FAILED EVERYONE WHO EVER RELIED ON ME.
JUST PLEASE -- SHUT DOWN THE SUPERCOLLIDER.
WHOEVER YOU'RE WORKING FOR -- THEY DON'T KNOW WHAT'S GOING TO HAPPEN!
MY RESEARCH PARTNER IS DEAD... MY GRAD STUDENT IS DEAD... AND NOW POOR SARA....
PLEASE... DON'T LET THE REST OF THE HUMAN RACE JOIN THEM!
DOCTOR --
KRAAKK
SKREE
UNIT 212 **SKREE** STAND DOWN
I'M AFRAID HE'S NOT WORKING FOR THE GOVERNMENT ANYMORE --

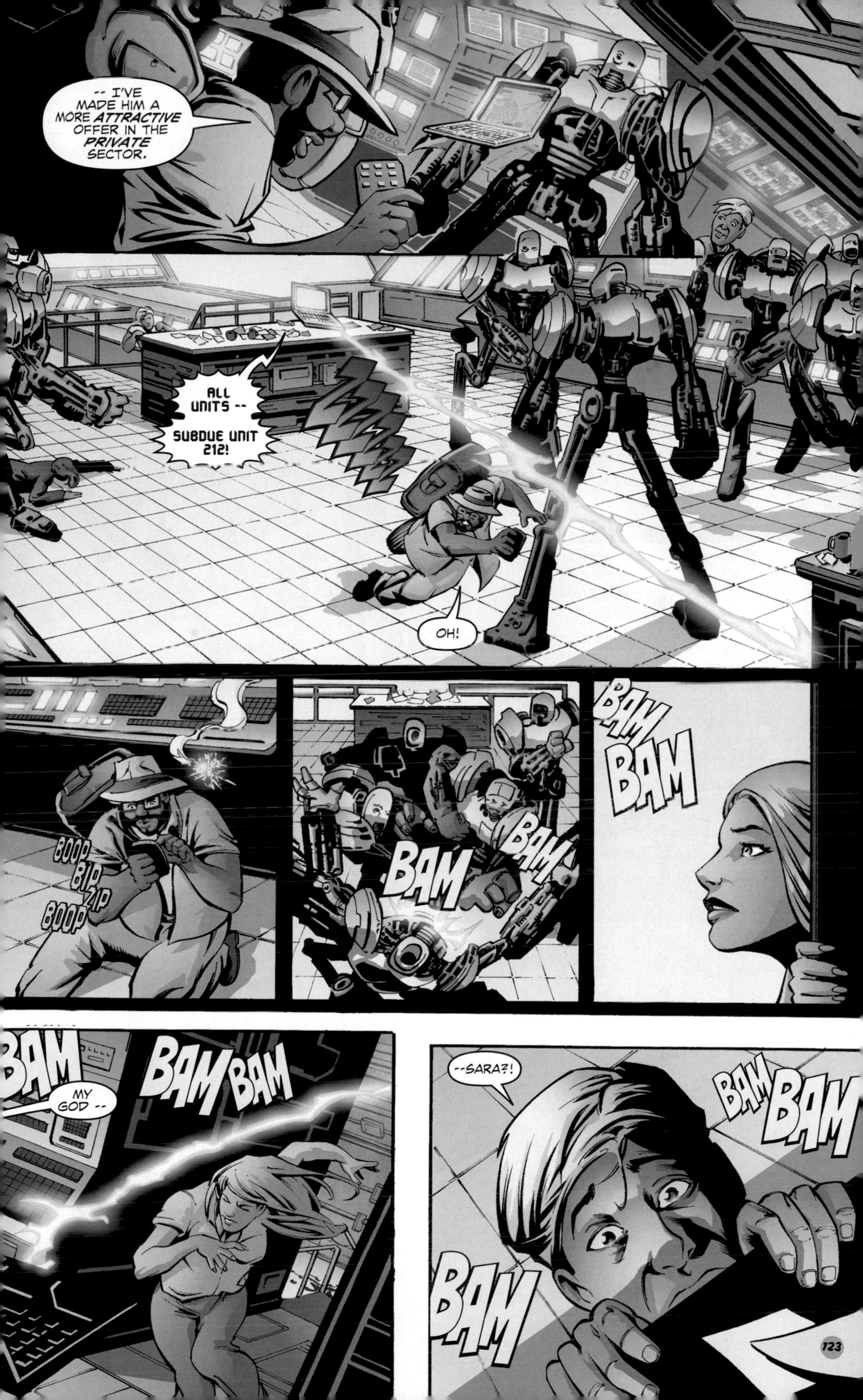

-- I'VE MADE HIM A MORE ATTRACTIVE OFFER IN THE PRIVATE SECTOR.
ALL UNITS --
SUBDUE UNIT 212!
OH!
BOOP BIP ZIP BOOP
BAM
BAM
BAM BAM
BAM
BAM BAM BAM
MY GOD --
--SARA?!
BAM BAM
BAM

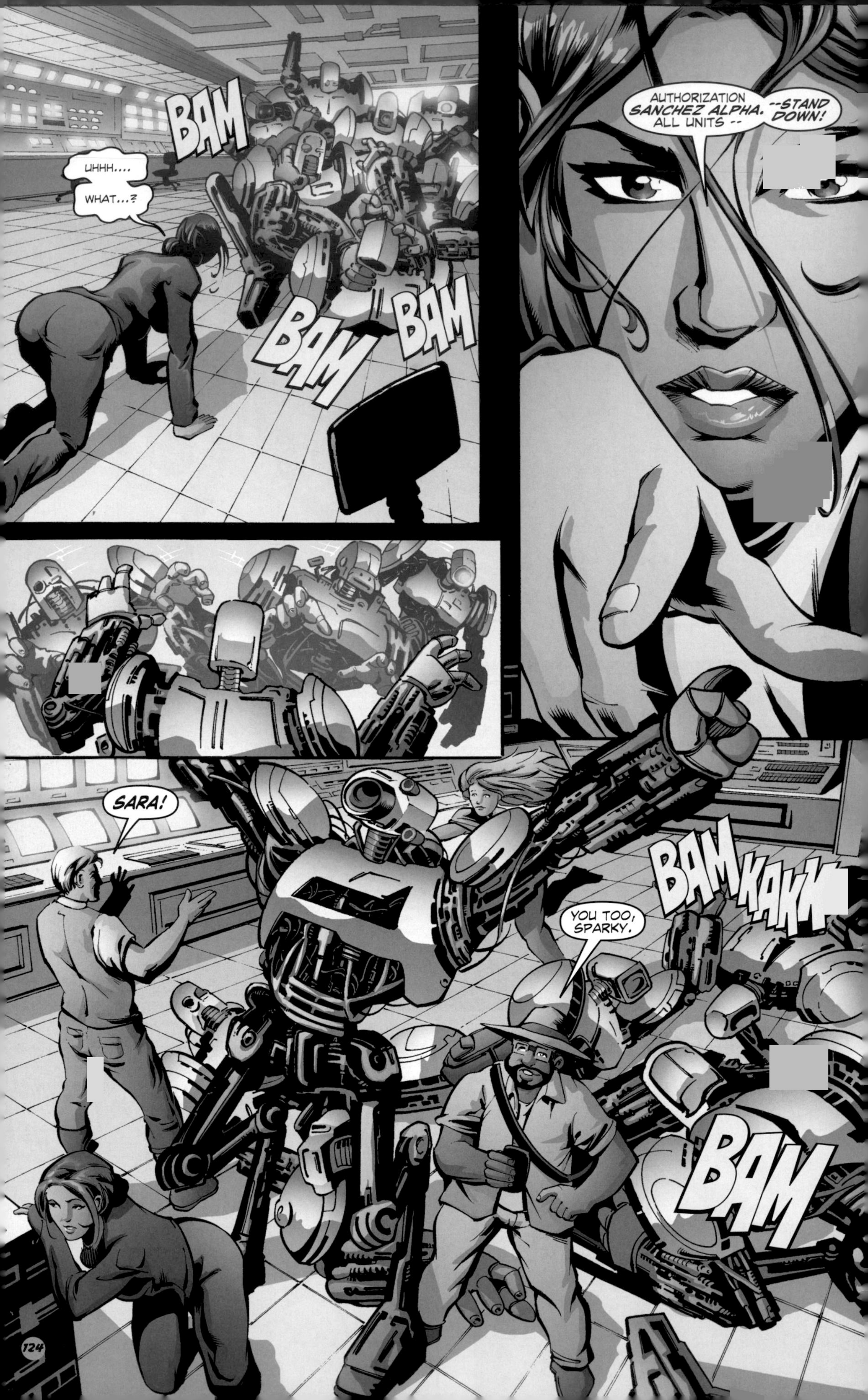
BAM
UHHH....
WHAT...?
BAM
BAM
AUTHORIZATION SANCHEZ ALPHA. ALL UNITS --
--STAND DOWN!
SARA!
YOU TOO, SPARKY.
BAMKAKK
BAM

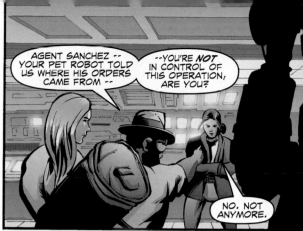

I THOUGHT -- AGENT SANCHEZ SAID YOU WERE *DEAD*.

IT'S NOT THE *ONLY* MISTAKE I'VE MADE TODAY. TRY NOT TO *GLOAT* TOO MUCH.

AGENT SANCHEZ -- YOUR PET ROBOT TOLD US WHERE HIS ORDERS CAME FROM --

--YOU'RE *NOT* IN CONTROL OF THIS OPERATION, ARE YOU?

NO. NOT ANYMORE.

THE SMARTBOX IS OPERATING *INDEPENDENTLY*. IT HAS ORDERS TO *DESTROY* THE SUPERCOLLIDER, AND TO KILL ALL WITNESSES.

IT'S CONTROLLING THE WHOLE COMPLEX FROM SOME REMOTE LOCATION.

I'VE BEEN STUDYING THE SYSTEM -- BUT I CAN'T FIGURE OUT WHERE THAT LOCATION IS.

THE SMARTBOX ISN'T POWERFUL ENOUGH TO RUN A COMPLEX LIKE THIS FROM ITS OWN CPU -- IT MUST HAVE A COMMAND POST SOMEWHERE.

PERHAPS THE OTHER BACKUP CONTROL ROOM --

NO.

I KNOW WHERE IT IS.

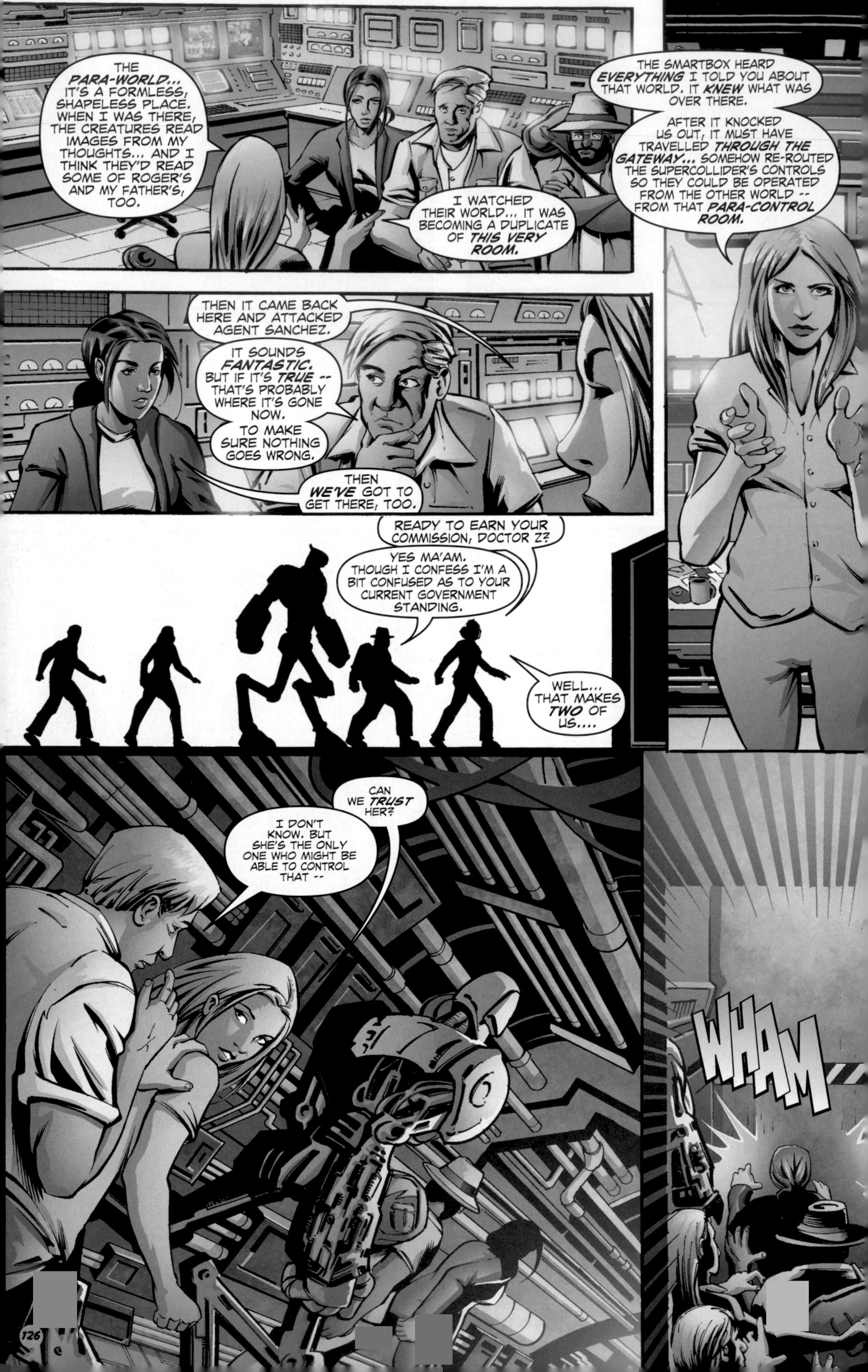

THE PARA-WORLD... IT'S A FORMLESS, SHAPELESS PLACE. WHEN I WAS THERE, THE CREATURES READ IMAGES FROM MY THOUGHTS... AND I THINK THEY'D READ SOME OF ROGER'S AND MY FATHER'S, TOO.
I WATCHED THEIR WORLD... IT WAS BECOMING A DUPLICATE OF THIS VERY ROOM.
THE SMARTBOX HEARD EVERYTHING I TOLD YOU ABOUT THAT WORLD. IT KNEW WHAT WAS OVER THERE.
AFTER IT KNOCKED US OUT, IT MUST HAVE TRAVELLED THROUGH THE GATEWAY... SOMEHOW RE-ROUTED THE SUPERCOLLIDER'S CONTROLS SO THEY COULD BE OPERATED FROM THE OTHER WORLD -- FROM THAT PARA-CONTROL ROOM.
THEN IT CAME BACK HERE AND ATTACKED AGENT SANCHEZ.
IT SOUNDS FANTASTIC. BUT IF IT'S TRUE -- THAT'S PROBABLY WHERE IT'S GONE NOW.
TO MAKE SURE NOTHING GOES WRONG.
THEN WE'VE GOT TO GET THERE, TOO.
READY TO EARN YOUR COMMISSION, DOCTOR Z?
YES MA'AM. THOUGH I CONFESS I'M A BIT CONFUSED AS TO YOUR CURRENT GOVERNMENT STANDING.
WELL... THAT MAKES TWO OF US....
CAN WE TRUST HER?
I DON'T KNOW. BUT SHE'S THE ONLY ONE WHO MIGHT BE ABLE TO CONTROL THAT --
WHAM

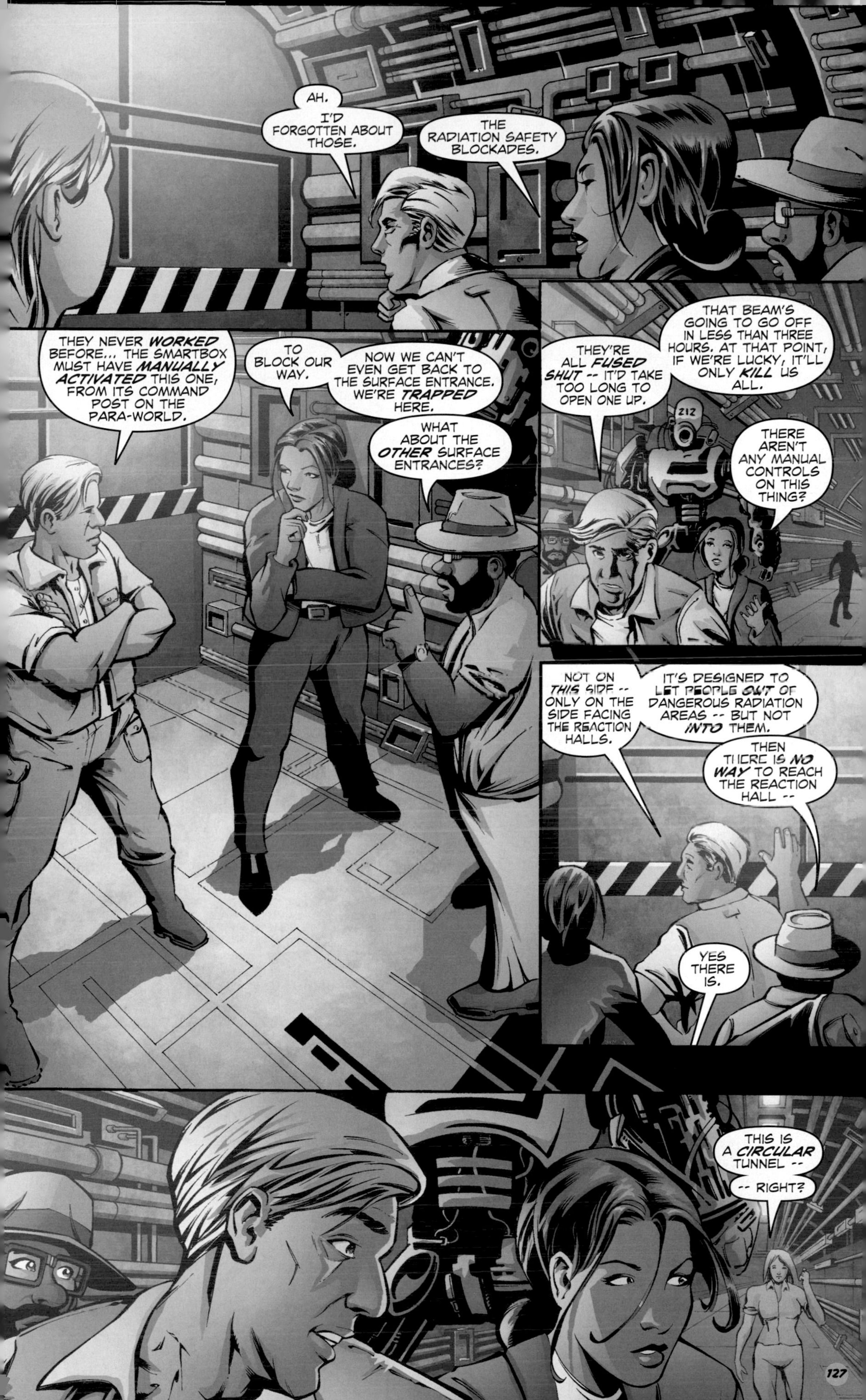
AH.
I'D FORGOTTEN ABOUT THOSE.
THE RADIATION SAFETY BLOCKADES.
THEY NEVER WORKED BEFORE... THE SMARTBOX MUST HAVE MANUALLY ACTIVATED THIS ONE, FROM ITS COMMAND POST ON THE PARA-WORLD.
TO BLOCK OUR WAY.
NOW WE CAN'T EVEN GET BACK TO THE SURFACE ENTRANCE. WE'RE TRAPPED HERE.
WHAT ABOUT THE OTHER SURFACE ENTRANCES?
THEY'RE ALL FUSED SHUT -- IT'D TAKE TOO LONG TO OPEN ONE UP.
THAT BEAM'S GOING TO GO OFF IN LESS THAN THREE HOURS. AT THAT POINT, IF WE'RE LUCKY, IT'LL ONLY KILL US ALL.
212
THERE AREN'T ANY MANUAL CONTROLS ON THIS THING?
NOT ON THIS SIDE -- ONLY ON THE SIDE FACING THE REACTION HALLS.
IT'S DESIGNED TO LET PEOPLE OUT OF DANGEROUS RADIATION AREAS -- BUT NOT INTO THEM.
THEN THERE IS NO WAY TO REACH THE REACTION HALL --
YES THERE IS.
THIS IS A CIRCULAR TUNNEL --
-- RIGHT?

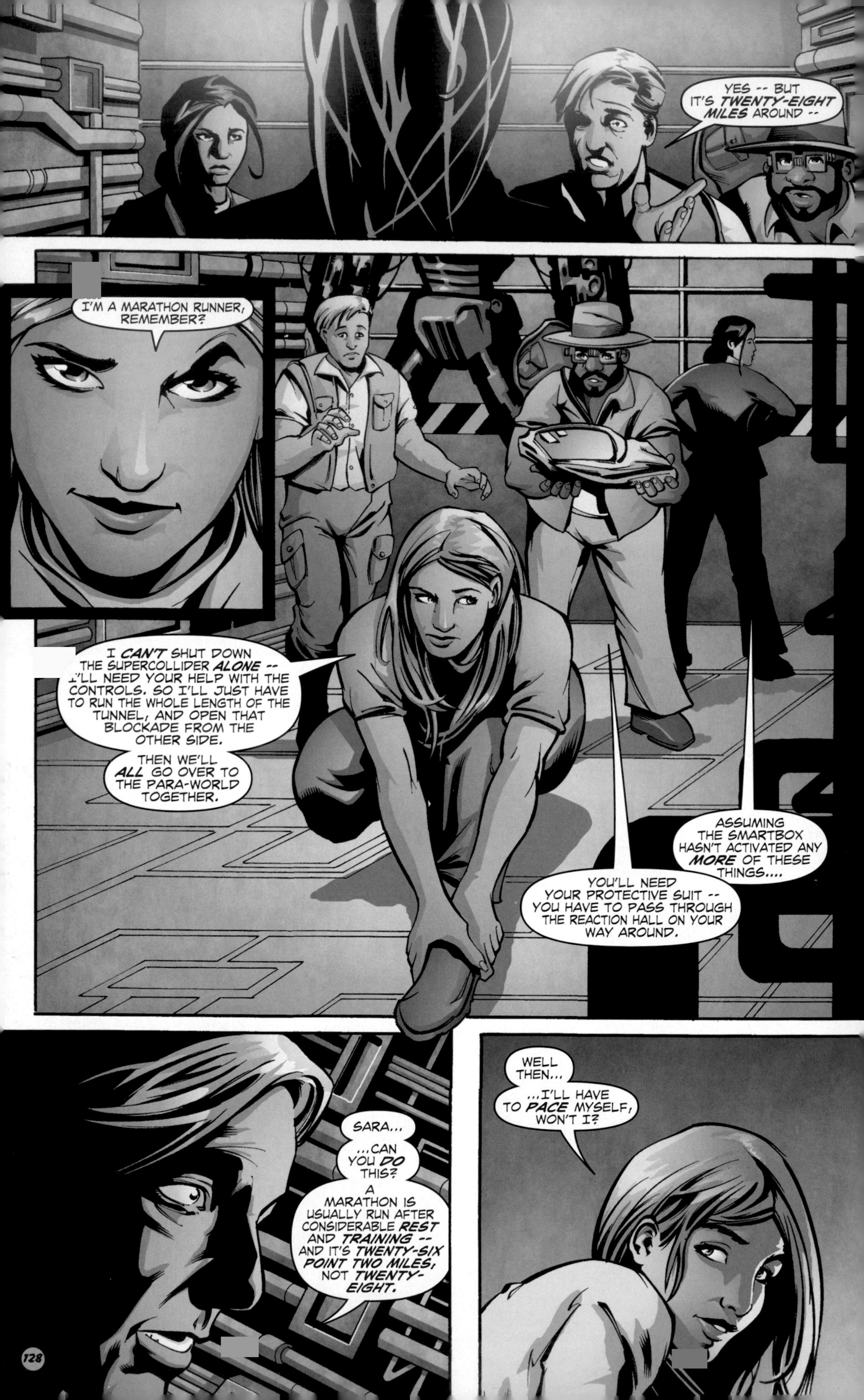
YES -- BUT IT'S TWENTY-EIGHT MILES AROUND --
I'M A MARATHON RUNNER, REMEMBER?
I CAN'T SHUT DOWN THE SUPERCOLLIDER ALONE -- I'LL NEED YOUR HELP WITH THE CONTROLS. SO I'LL JUST HAVE TO RUN THE WHOLE LENGTH OF THE TUNNEL, AND OPEN THAT BLOCKADE FROM THE OTHER SIDE.
THEN WE'LL ALL GO OVER TO THE PARA-WORLD TOGETHER.
ASSUMING THE SMARTBOX HASN'T ACTIVATED ANY MORE OF THESE THINGS....
YOU'LL NEED YOUR PROTECTIVE SUIT -- YOU HAVE TO PASS THROUGH THE REACTION HALL ON YOUR WAY AROUND.
SARA...
...CAN YOU DO THIS?
A MARATHON IS USUALLY RUN AFTER CONSIDERABLE REST AND TRAINING -- AND IT'S TWENTY-SIX POINT TWO MILES, NOT TWENTY-EIGHT.
WELL THEN...
...I'LL HAVE TO PACE MYSELF, WON'T I?

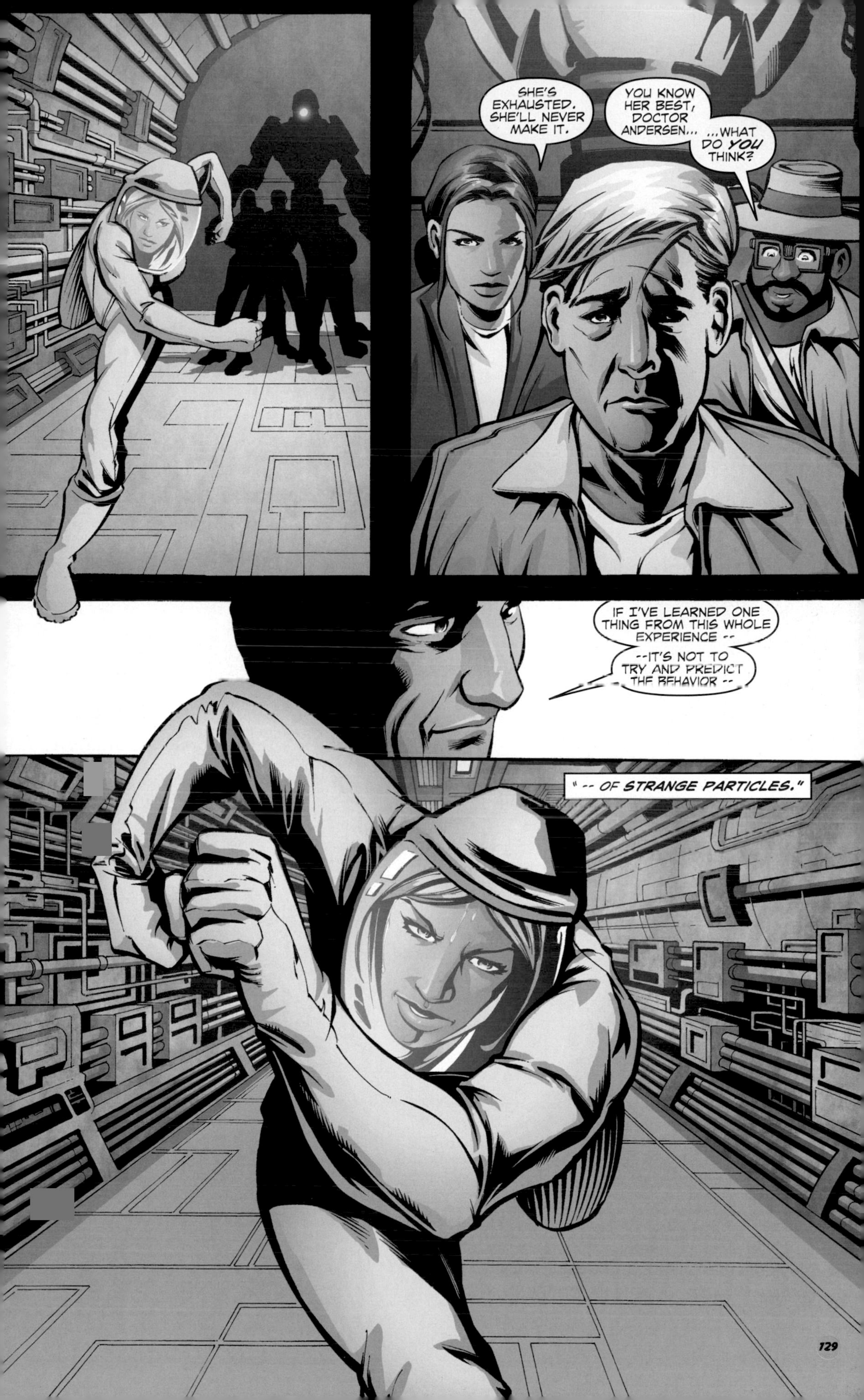

SHE'S EXHAUSTED. SHE'LL NEVER MAKE IT.
YOU KNOW HER BEST, DOCTOR ANDERSEN...
...WHAT DO YOU THINK?
IF I'VE LEARNED ONE THING FROM THIS WHOLE EXPERIENCE --
--IT'S NOT TO TRY AND PREDICT THE BEHAVIOR --
"-- OF STRANGE PARTICLES."

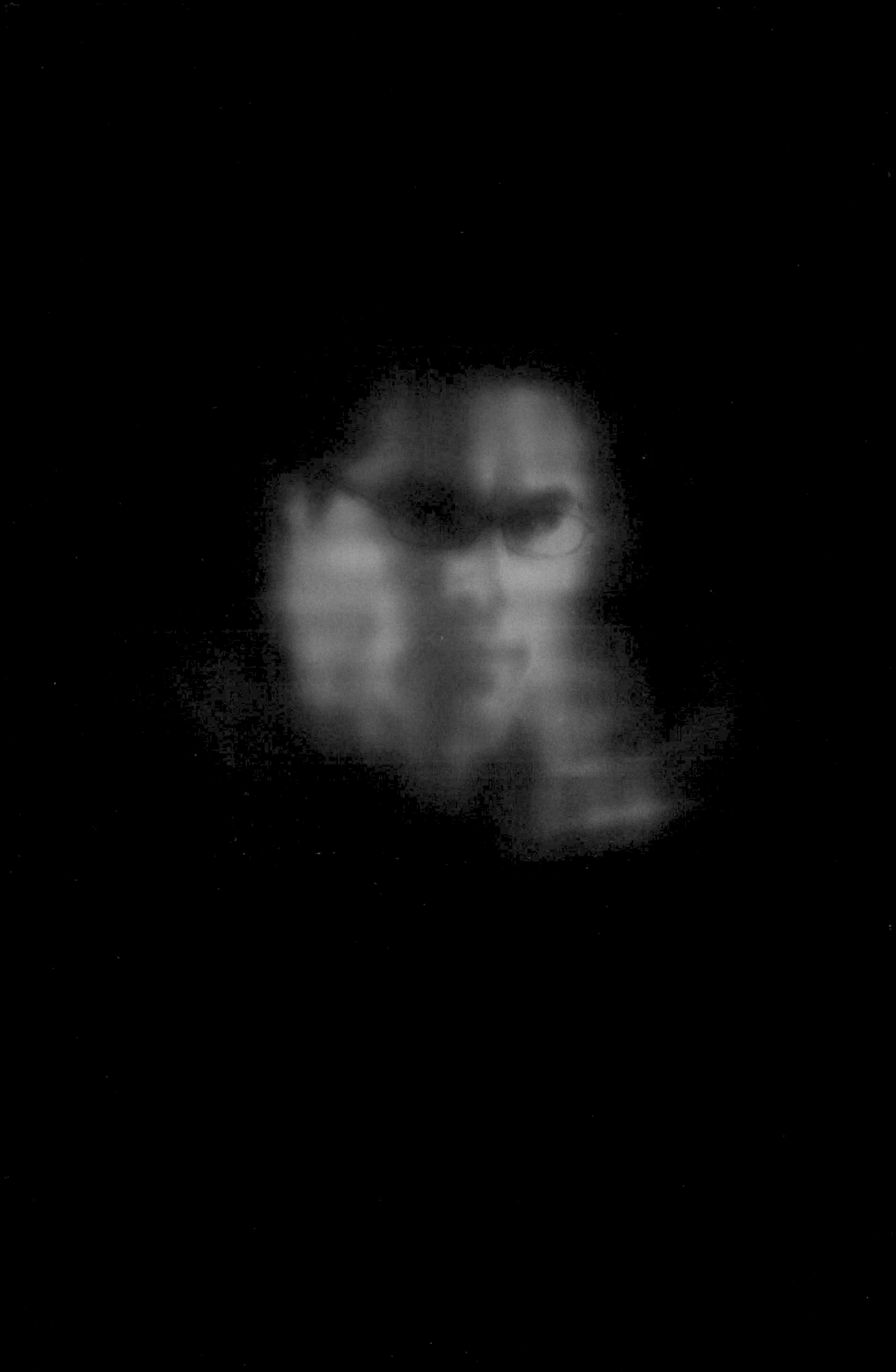

CHAPTER 6

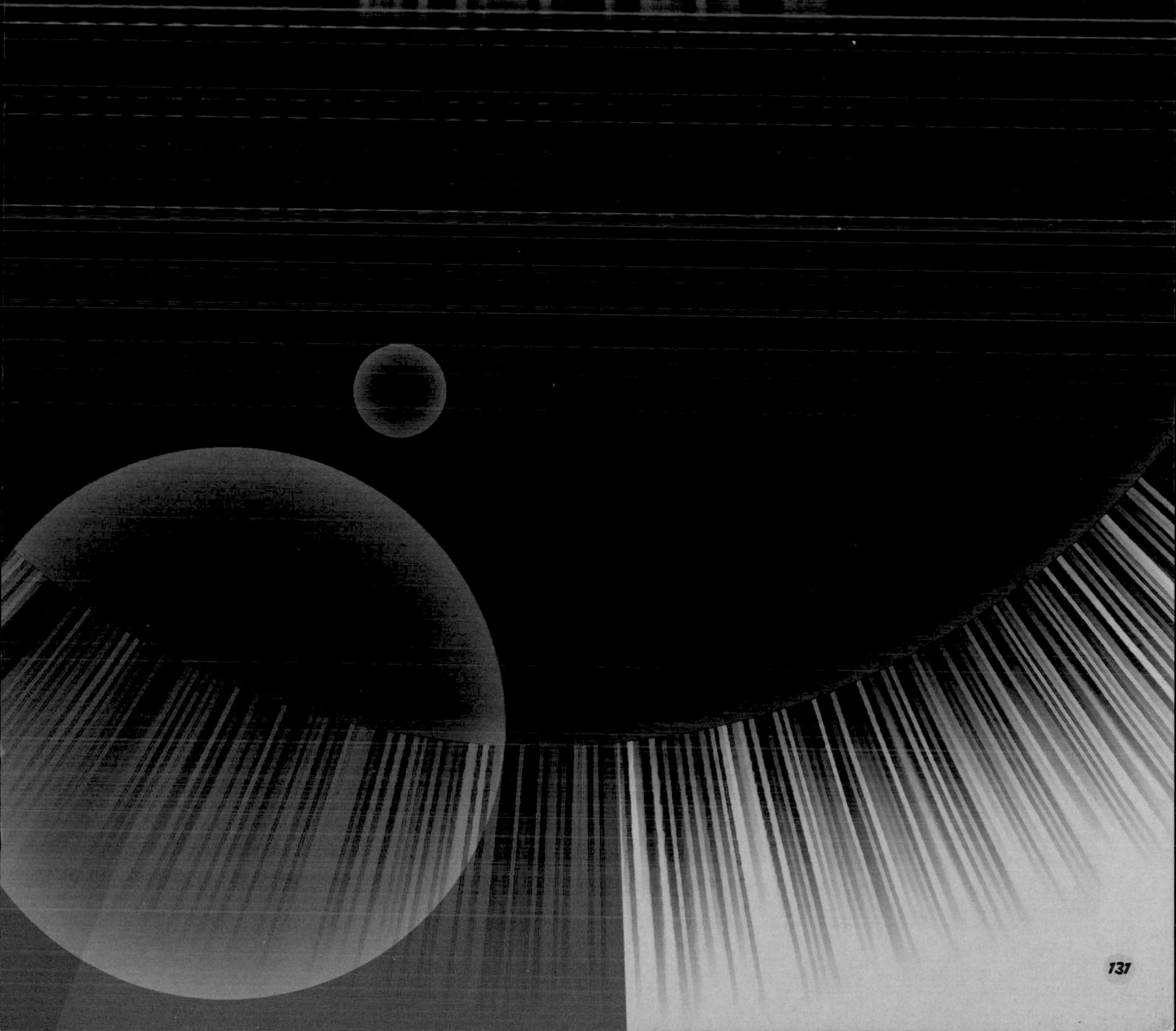

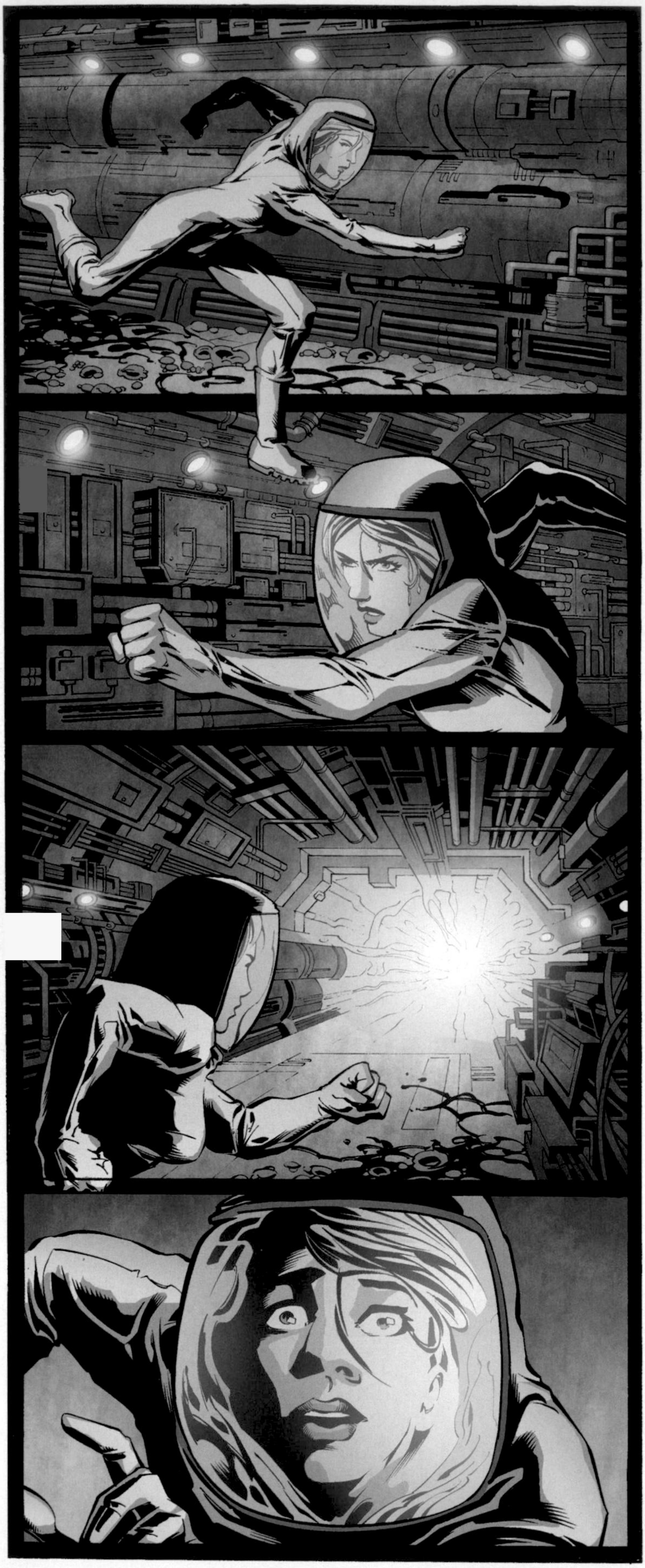

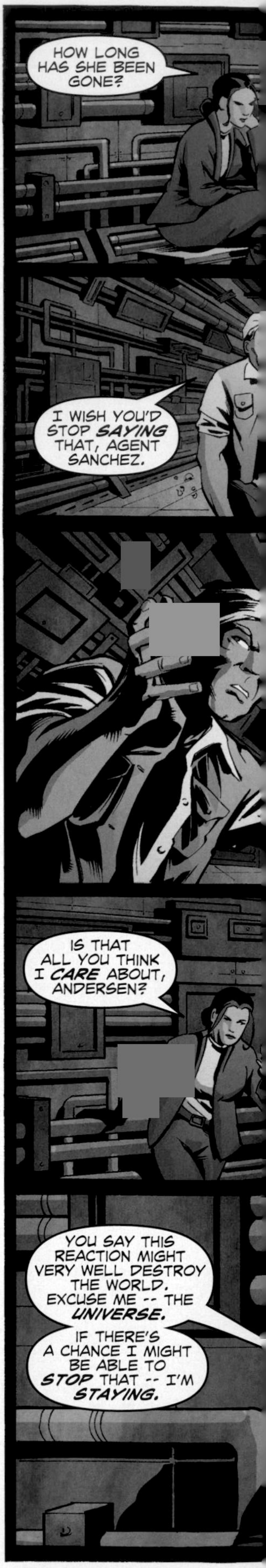
HOW LONG HAS SHE BEEN GONE?
I WISH YOU'D STOP SAYING THAT, AGENT SANCHEZ.
IS THAT ALL YOU THINK I CARE ABOUT, ANDERSEN?
YOU SAY THIS REACTION MIGHT VERY WELL DESTROY THE WORLD. EXCUSE ME -- THE UNIVERSE.
IF THERE'S A CHANCE I MIGHT BE ABLE TO STOP THAT -- I'M STAYING.

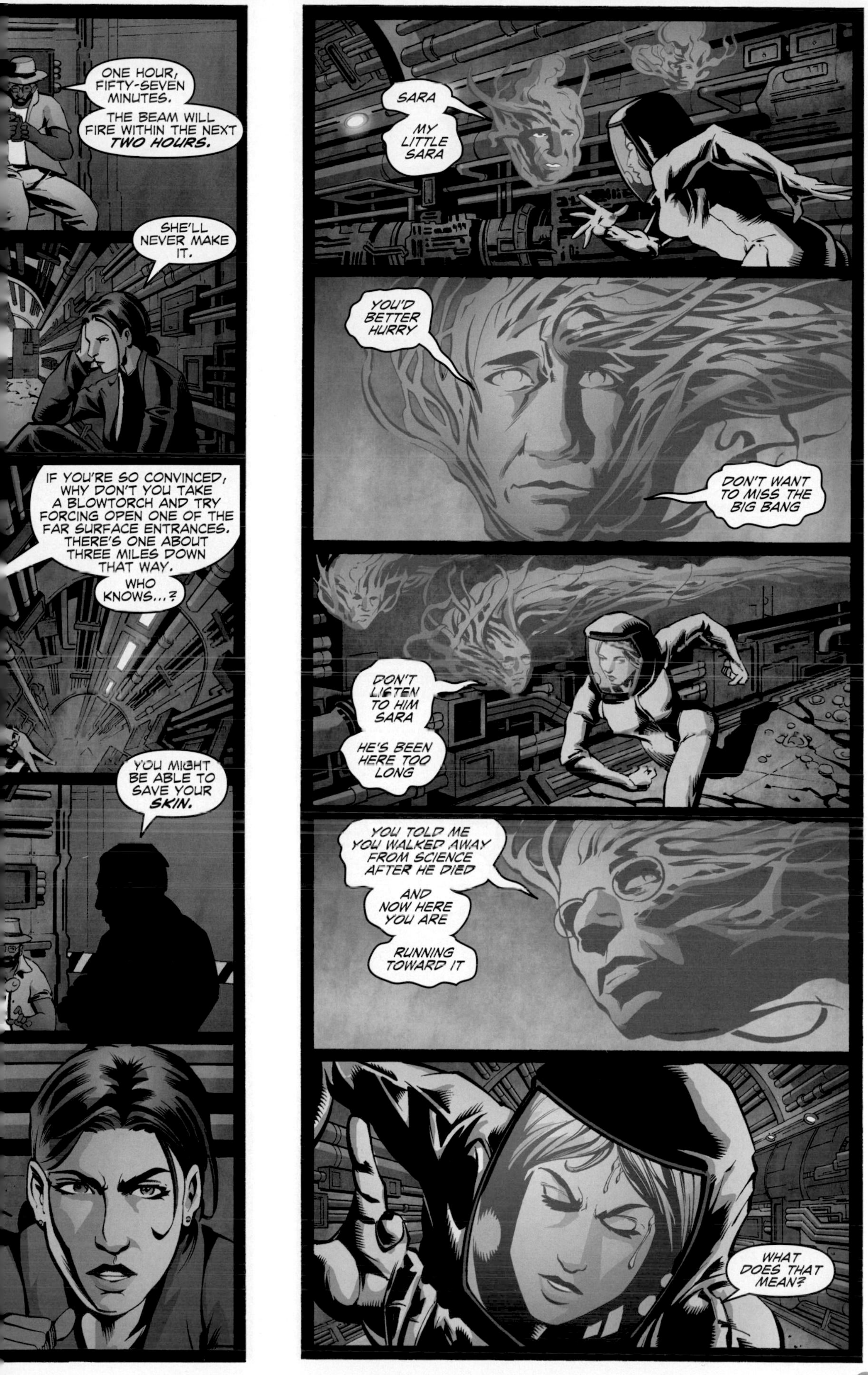

ONE HOUR, FIFTY-SEVEN MINUTES.
THE BEAM WILL FIRE WITHIN THE NEXT TWO HOURS.
SHE'LL NEVER MAKE IT.
IF YOU'RE SO CONVINCED, WHY DON'T YOU TAKE A BLOWTORCH AND TRY FORCING OPEN ONE OF THE FAR SURFACE ENTRANCES. THERE'S ONE ABOUT THREE MILES DOWN THAT WAY.
WHO KNOWS...?
YOU MIGHT BE ABLE TO SAVE YOUR SKIN.
SARA
MY LITTLE SARA
YOU'D BETTER HURRY
DON'T WANT TO MISS THE BIG BANG
DON'T LISTEN TO HIM SARA
HE'S BEEN HERE TOO LONG
YOU TOLD ME YOU WALKED AWAY FROM SCIENCE AFTER HE DIED
AND NOW HERE YOU ARE
RUNNING TOWARD IT
WHAT DOES THAT MEAN?

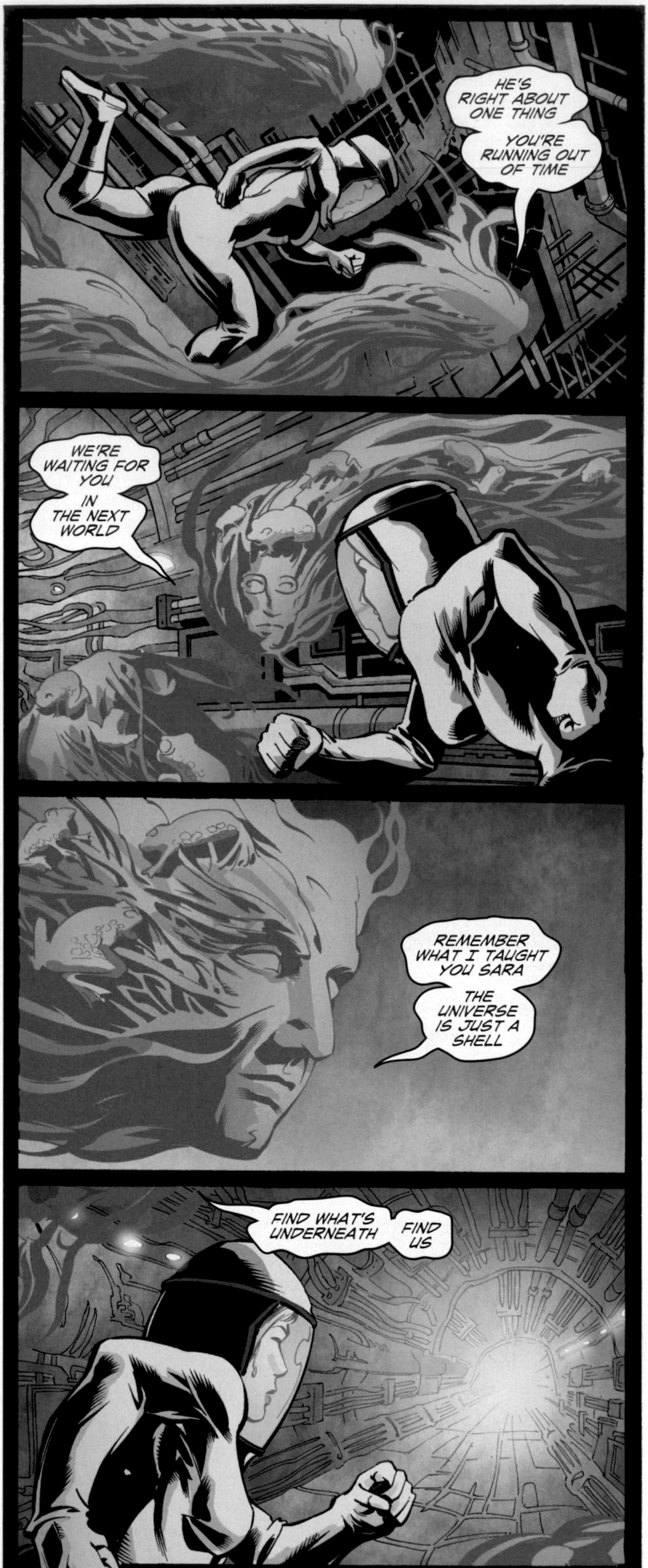
HE'S RIGHT ABOUT ONE THING
YOU'RE RUNNING OUT OF TIME
WE'RE WAITING FOR YOU
IN THE NEXT WORLD
REMEMBER WHAT I TAUGHT YOU SARA
THE UNIVERSE IS JUST A SHELL
FIND WHAT'S UNDERNEATH
FIND US

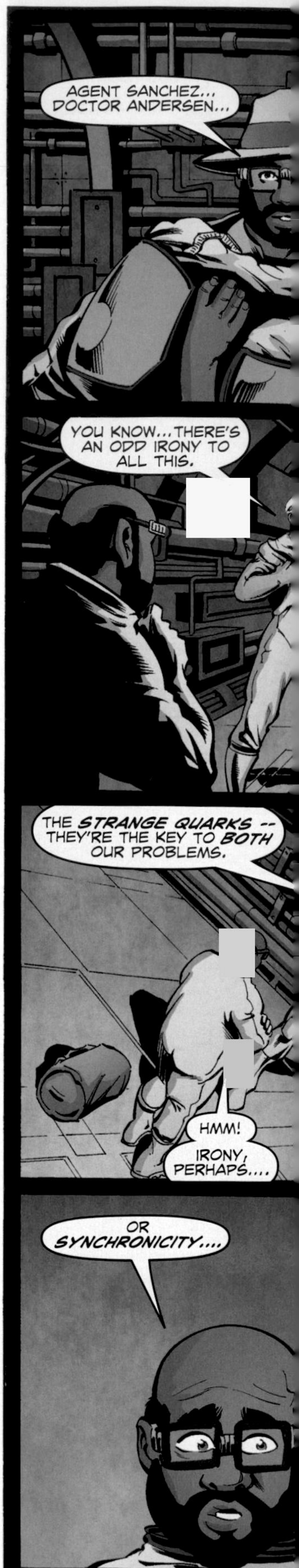
AGENT SANCHEZ... DOCTOR ANDERSEN...
YOU KNOW...THERE'S AN ODD IRONY TO ALL THIS.
THE STRANGE QUARKS -- THEY'RE THE KEY TO BOTH OUR PROBLEMS.
HMM!
IRONY, PERHAPS....
OR SYNCHRONICITY....

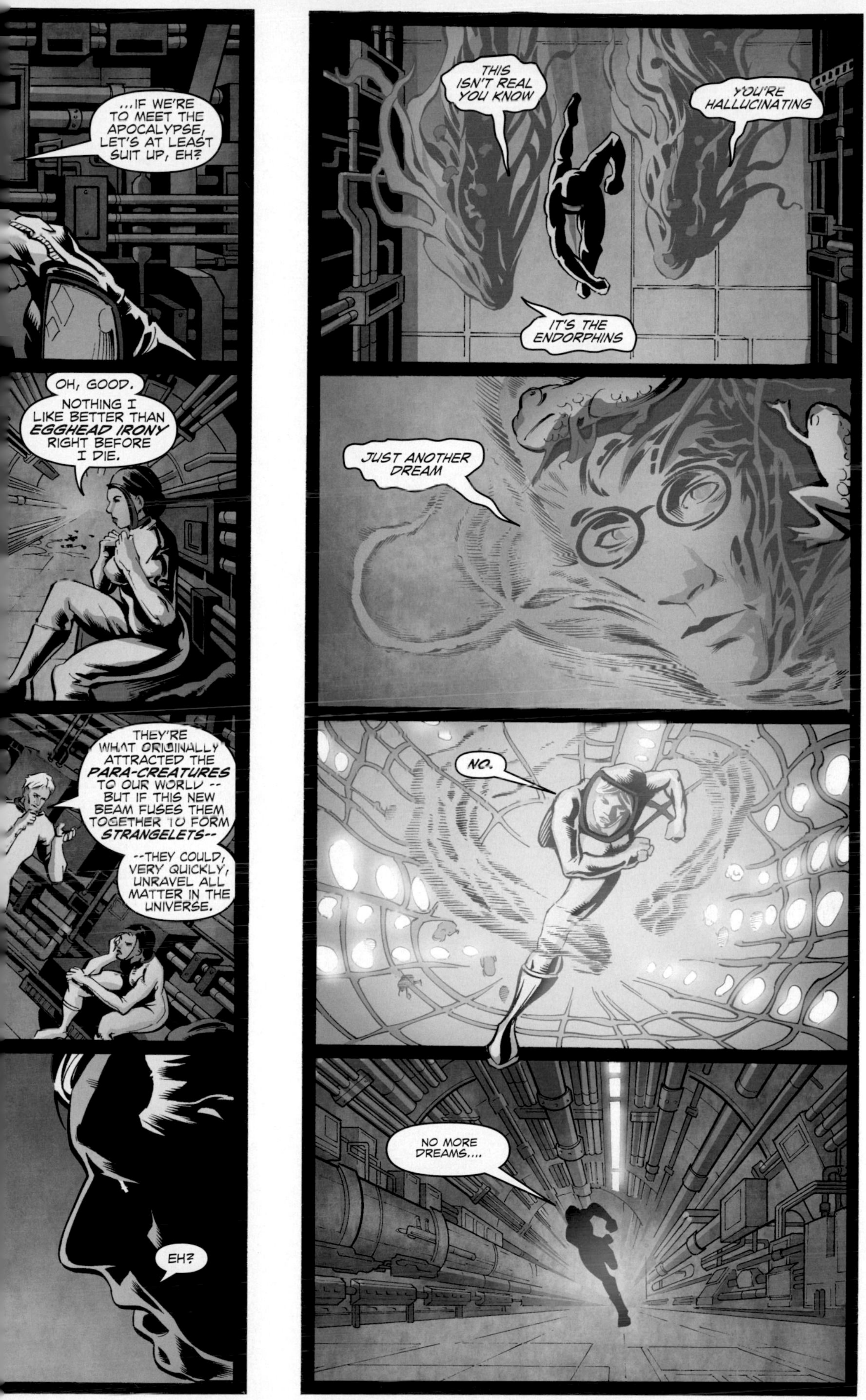

...IF WE'RE TO MEET THE APOCALYPSE, LET'S AT LEAST SUIT UP, EH?
OH, GOOD. NOTHING I LIKE BETTER THAN EGGHEAD IRONY RIGHT BEFORE I DIE.
THEY'RE WHAT ORIGINALLY ATTRACTED THE PARA-CREATURES TO OUR WORLD -- BUT IF THIS NEW BEAM FUSES THEM TOGETHER TO FORM STRANGELETS--
--THEY COULD, VERY QUICKLY, UNRAVEL ALL MATTER IN THE UNIVERSE.
EH?
THIS ISN'T REAL YOU KNOW
YOU'RE HALLUCINATING
IT'S THE ENDORPHINS
JUST ANOTHER DREAM
NO.
NO MORE DREAMS....

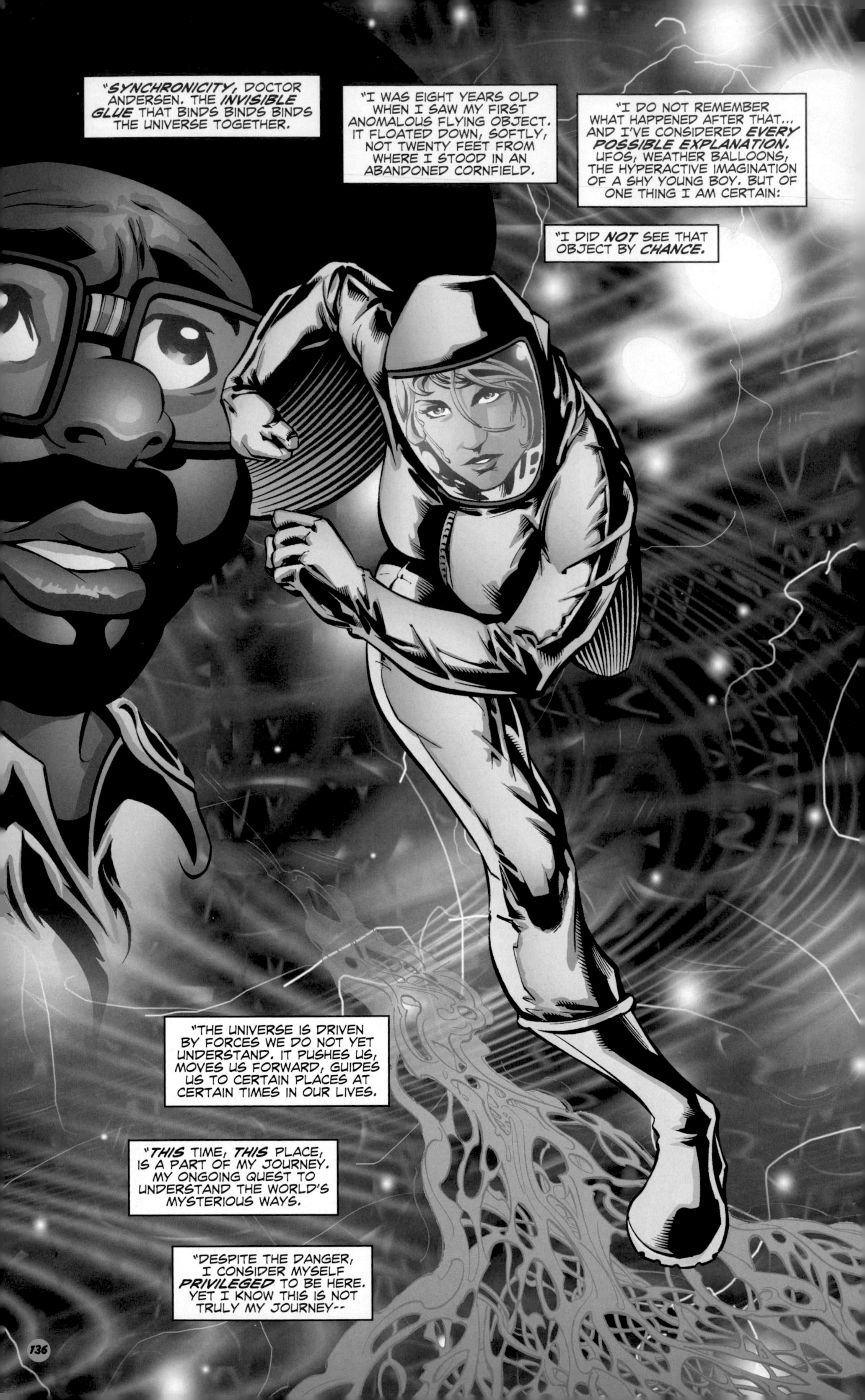
"SYNCHRONICITY, DOCTOR ANDERSEN. THE INVISIBLE GLUE THAT BINDS BINDS BINDS THE UNIVERSE TOGETHER.
"I WAS EIGHT YEARS OLD WHEN I SAW MY FIRST ANOMALOUS FLYING OBJECT. IT FLOATED DOWN, SOFTLY, NOT TWENTY FEET FROM WHERE I STOOD IN AN ABANDONED CORNFIELD.
"I DO NOT REMEMBER WHAT HAPPENED AFTER THAT... AND I'VE CONSIDERED EVERY POSSIBLE EXPLANATION. UFOS, WEATHER BALLOONS, THE HYPERACTIVE IMAGINATION OF A SHY YOUNG BOY. BUT OF ONE THING I AM CERTAIN:
"I DID NOT SEE THAT OBJECT BY CHANCE.
"THE UNIVERSE IS DRIVEN BY FORCES WE DO NOT YET UNDERSTAND. IT PUSHES US, MOVES US FORWARD, GUIDES US TO CERTAIN PLACES AT CERTAIN TIMES IN OUR LIVES.
"THIS TIME, THIS PLACE, IS A PART OF MY JOURNEY. MY ONGOING QUEST TO UNDERSTAND THE WORLD'S MYSTERIOUS WAYS.
"DESPITE THE DANGER, I CONSIDER MYSELF PRIVILEGED TO BE HERE. YET I KNOW THIS IS NOT TRULY MY JOURNEY--

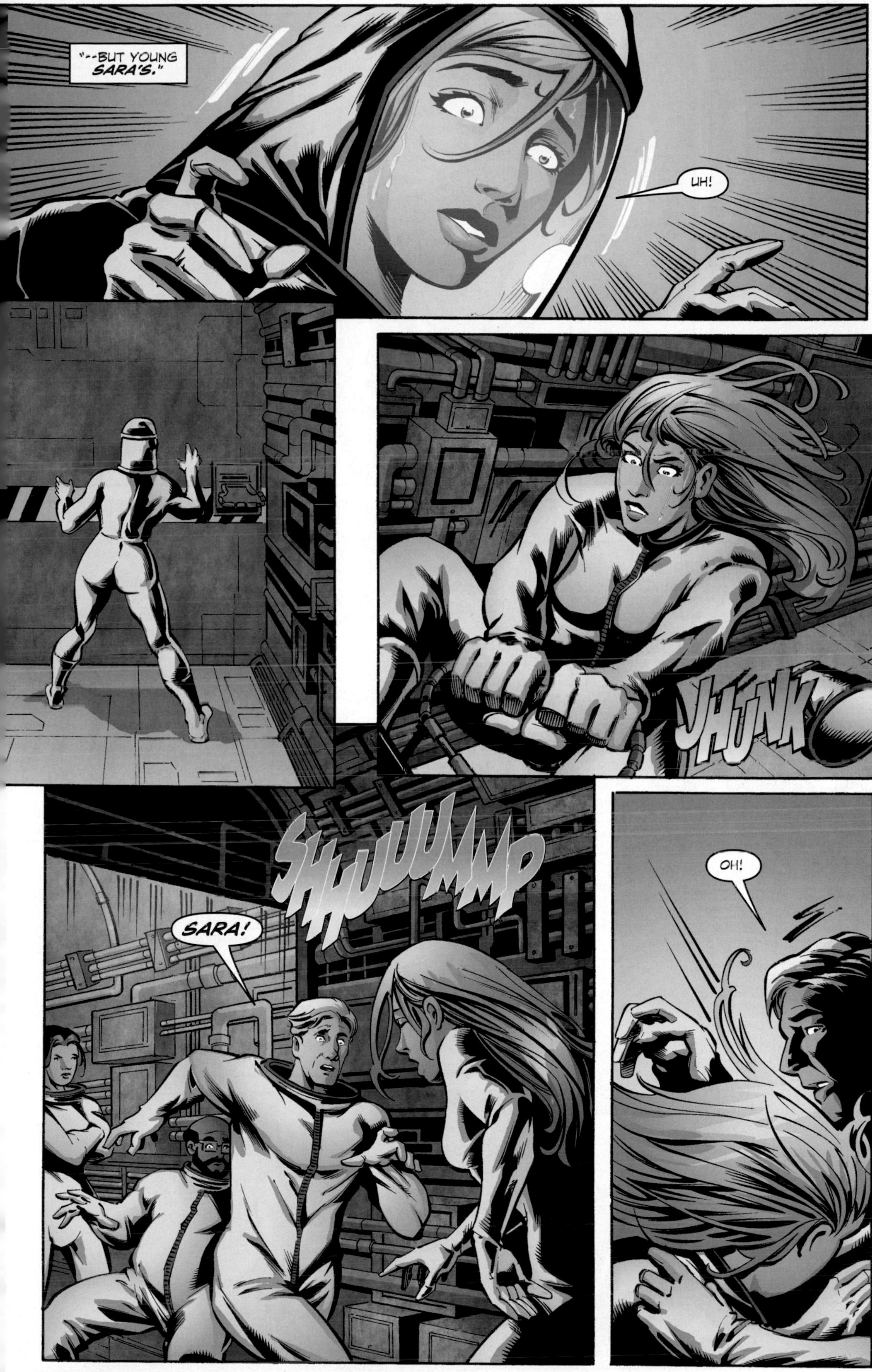
"--BUT YOUNG SARA'S."
UH!
JHUNK
SHHUUUMMP
SARA!
OH!

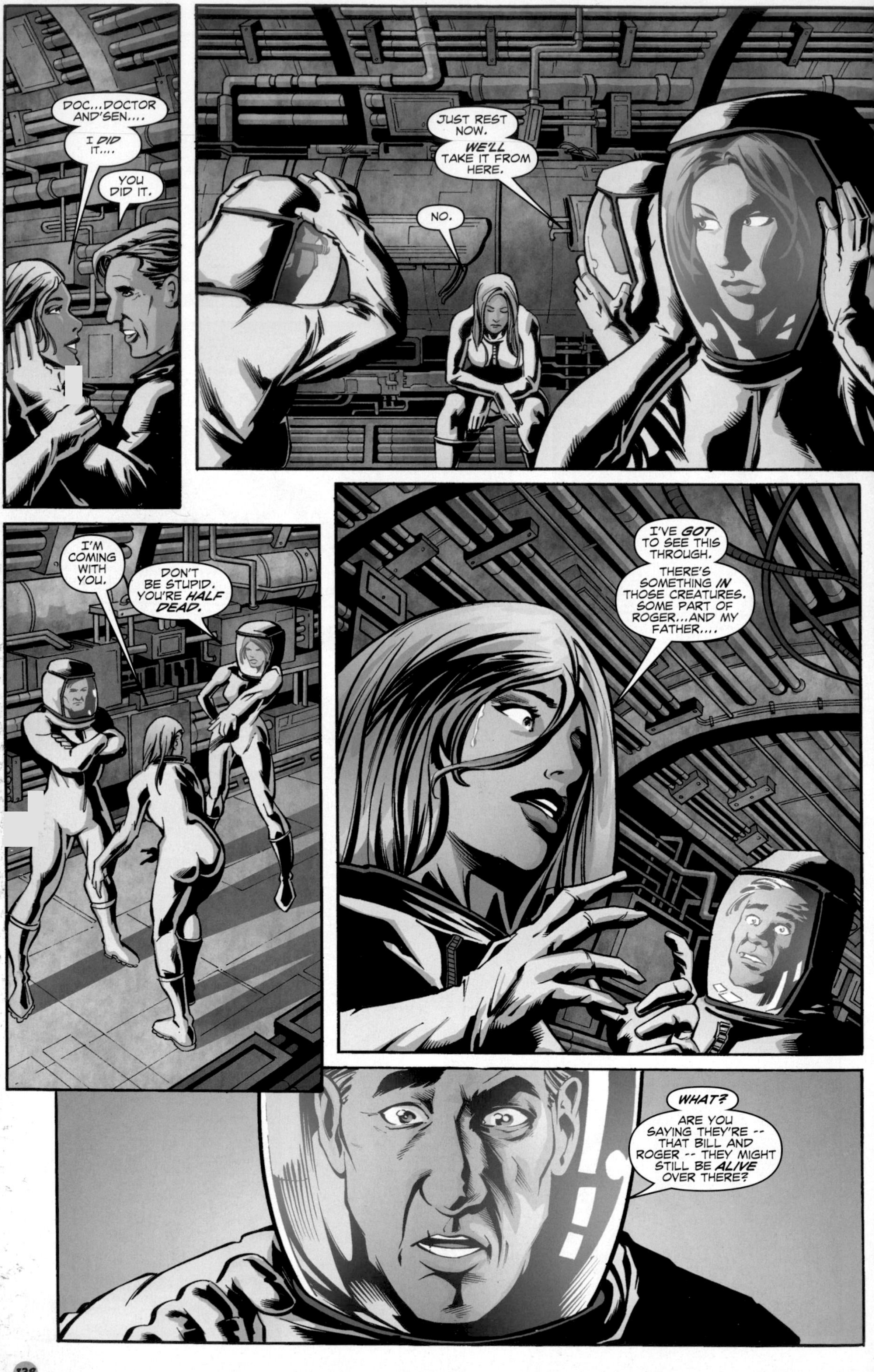
DOC...DOCTOR AND'SEN....
I DID IT....
YOU DID IT.
JUST REST NOW. WE'LL TAKE IT FROM HERE.
NO.
I'M COMING WITH YOU.
DON'T BE STUPID. YOU'RE HALF DEAD.
I'VE GOT TO SEE THIS THROUGH.
THERE'S SOMETHING IN THOSE CREATURES. SOME PART OF ROGER...AND MY FATHER....
WHAT?
ARE YOU SAYING THEY'RE -- THAT BILL AND ROGER -- THEY MIGHT STILL BE ALIVE OVER THERE?

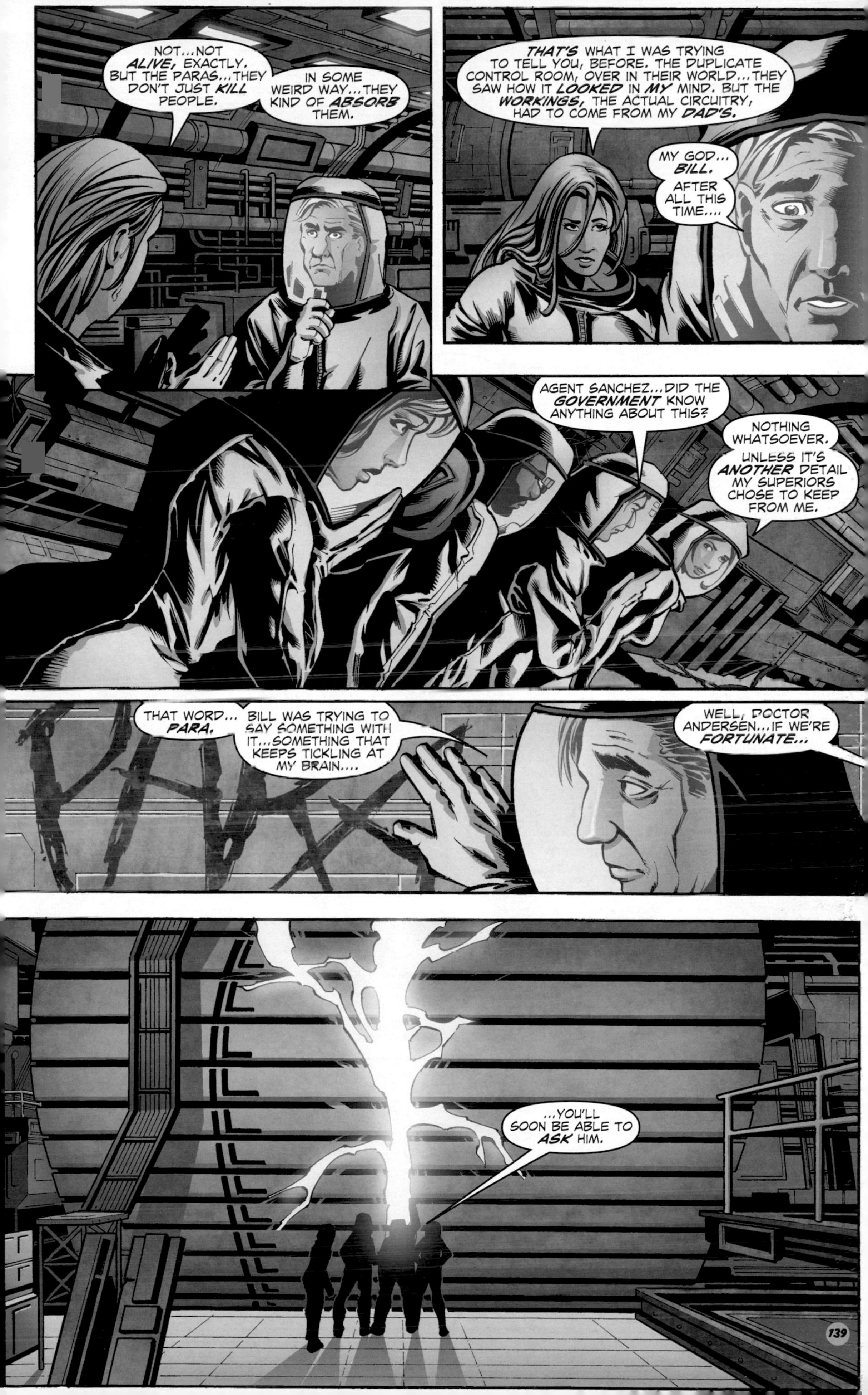
NOT...NOT ALIVE, EXACTLY. BUT THE PARAS...THEY DON'T JUST KILL PEOPLE.
IN SOME WEIRD WAY...THEY KIND OF ABSORB THEM.
THAT'S WHAT I WAS TRYING TO TELL YOU, BEFORE. THE DUPLICATE CONTROL ROOM, OVER IN THEIR WORLD...THEY SAW HOW IT LOOKED IN MY MIND. BUT THE WORKINGS, THE ACTUAL CIRCUITRY, HAD TO COME FROM MY DAD'S.
MY GOD... BILL. AFTER ALL THIS TIME....
AGENT SANCHEZ...DID THE GOVERNMENT KNOW ANYTHING ABOUT THIS?
NOTHING WHATSOEVER. UNLESS IT'S ANOTHER DETAIL MY SUPERIORS CHOSE TO KEEP FROM ME.
THAT WORD... PARA.
BILL WAS TRYING TO SAY SOMETHING WITH IT...SOMETHING THAT KEEPS TICKLING AT MY BRAIN....
WELL, DOCTOR ANDERSEN...IF WE'RE FORTUNATE...
...YOU'LL SOON BE ABLE TO ASK HIM.

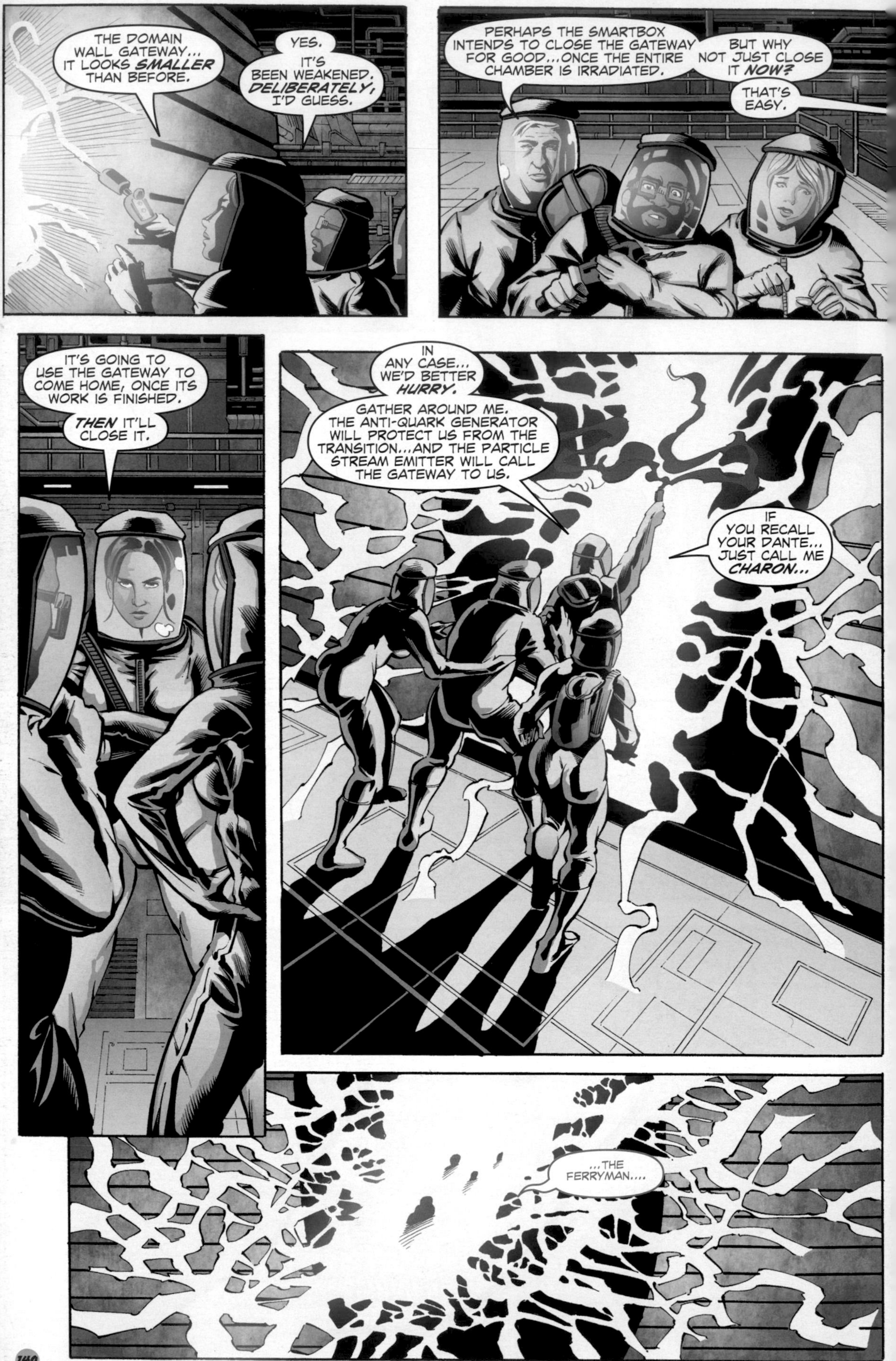
THE DOMAIN WALL GATEWAY... IT LOOKS SMALLER THAN BEFORE.
YES.
IT'S BEEN WEAKENED. DELIBERATELY, I'D GUESS.
PERHAPS THE SMARTBOX INTENDS TO CLOSE THE GATEWAY FOR GOOD...ONCE THE ENTIRE CHAMBER IS IRRADIATED.
BUT WHY NOT JUST CLOSE IT NOW?
THAT'S EASY.
IT'S GOING TO USE THE GATEWAY TO COME HOME, ONCE ITS WORK IS FINISHED.
THEN IT'LL CLOSE IT.
IN ANY CASE... WE'D BETTER HURRY.
GATHER AROUND ME. THE ANTI-QUARK GENERATOR WILL PROTECT US FROM THE TRANSITION...AND THE PARTICLE STREAM EMITTER WILL CALL THE GATEWAY TO US.
IF YOU RECALL YOUR DANTE... JUST CALL ME CHARON...
...THE FERRYMAN....

Sara had hoped the Para-world transition would be easier this time, especially since she wasn't alone. But it wasn't. Maybe it was her exhaustion, but the tingling felt like hot needles on her skin, and the probing in her brain was like a spike. She doubled over, wincing in pain.

Then she felt Dr. Andersen's hand on her shoulder. "It's okay," she said. "I'm all right." Sara looked up and saw the unformed world all around her, just as on her other visit. The cloudlike, inchoate matter, and those strange glowing strands, stretching off into infinity. Dr. Z was fumbling with his gadgets, and Agent Sanchez just stared, eyes wide with alarm.

"Take it slow," Sara said aloud to them. "The hardest thing is the way

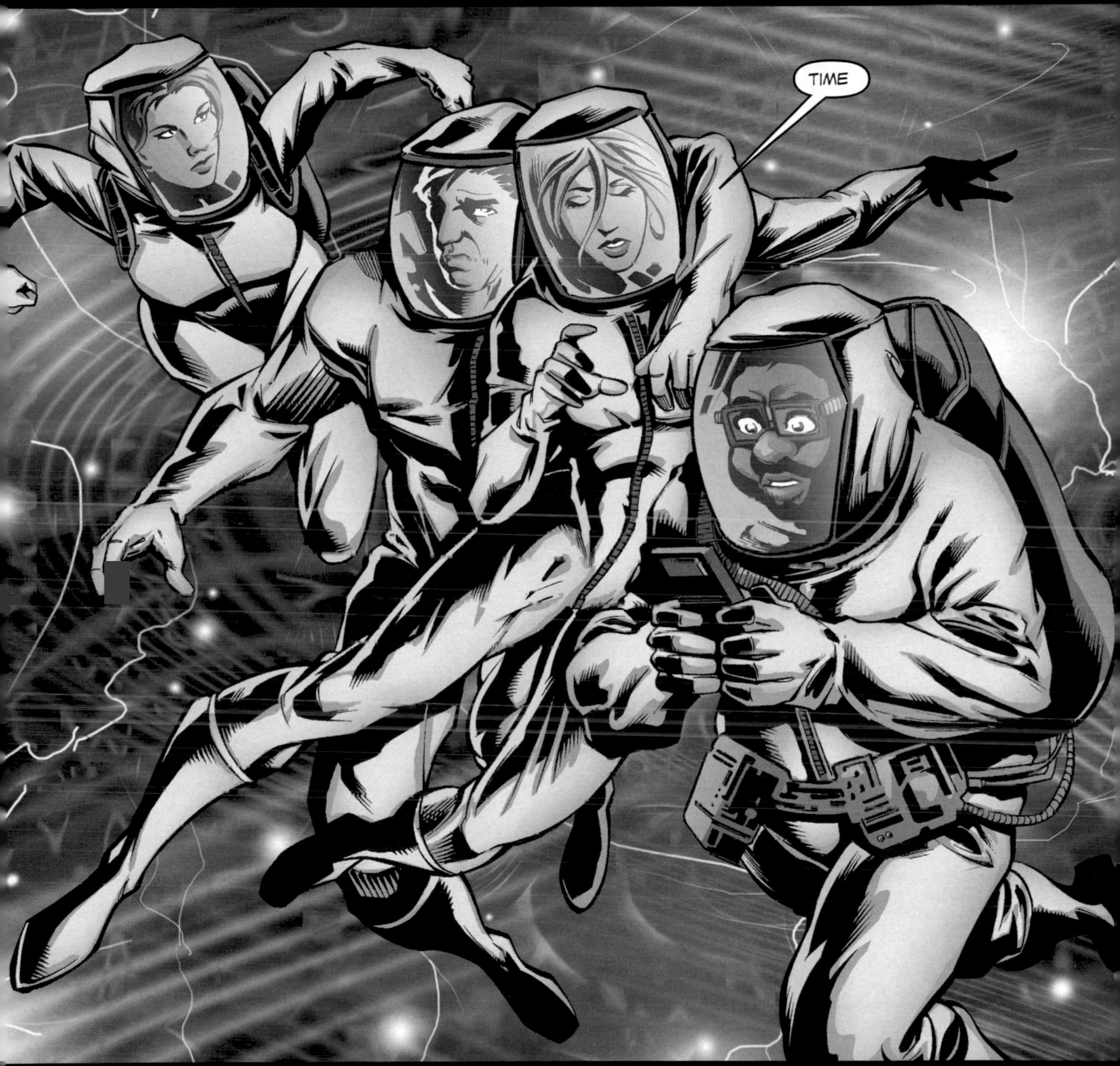
TIME

speeds up and slows down."

"Som[illegible]ubatomic particles seem to travel backward in time," Dr. Andersen said.

"That[illegible]fascinating," Agent Sanchez interrupted. "But we've got a bigger problem, remember?"

"Of course," Dr. Andersen replied. But the glare he exchanged with Sanchez hinted that they'd had just about enough of each other.

Sara realized she had to rally them; she was the only one with experience in this world, the only team member who knew how to call the Paras, to make the world-stuff over here do what she wanted. But she was so tired. She opened her mouth to speak -- and just then, Dr. Z cried out --

"Look!"

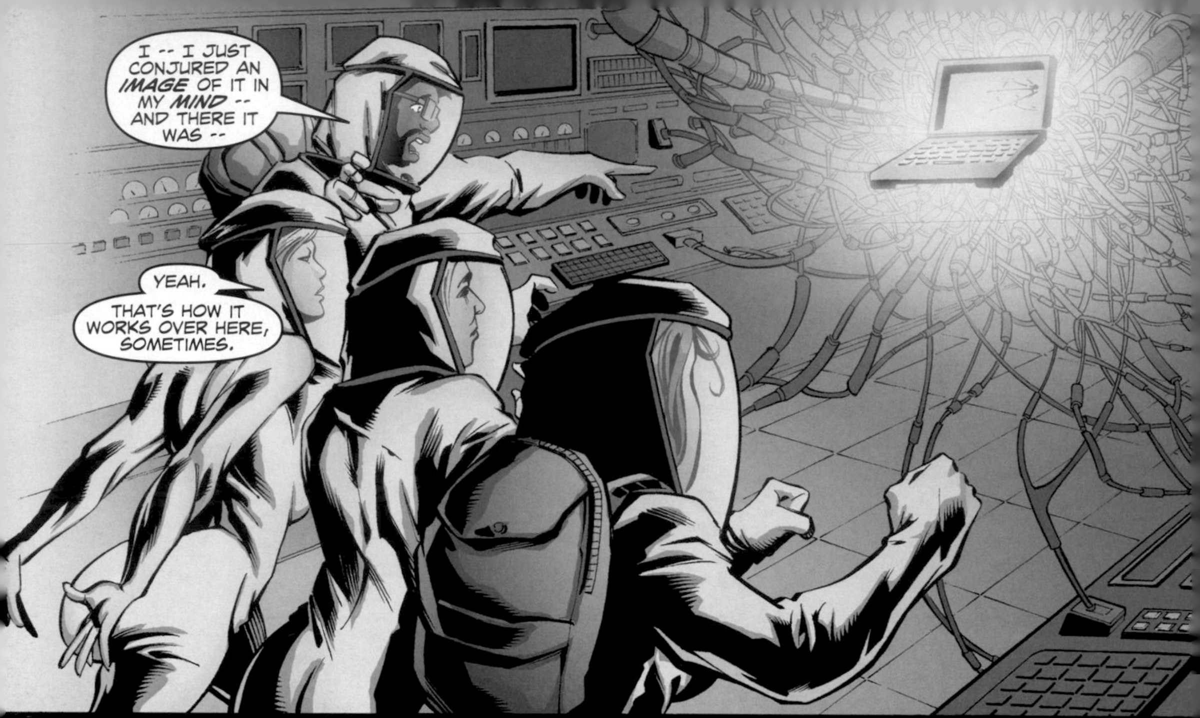
I -- I JUST CONJURED AN *IMAGE* OF IT IN MY *MIND* -- AND THERE IT WAS --
YEAH.
THAT'S HOW IT WORKS OVER HERE, SOMETIMES.

Agent Sanchez pushed her way to the front of the group and started yelling commands at the SmartBox: "Logging in as root user...emergency shutdown...command protocol alpha...."

Sara quickly stopped listening. She knew this wasn't going to work. And then, she felt the SmartBox start to slip away....

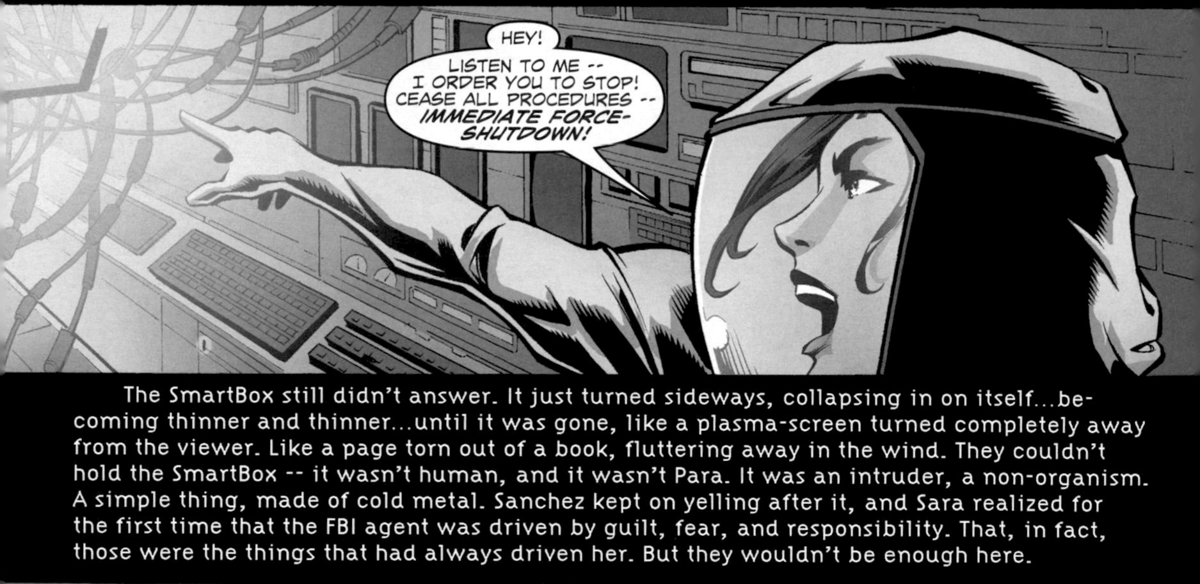
HEY!
LISTEN TO ME -- I ORDER YOU TO STOP! CEASE ALL PROCEDURES -- *IMMEDIATE FORCE-SHUTDOWN!*

The SmartBox still didn't answer. It just turned sideways, collapsing in on itself...becoming thinner and thinner...until it was gone, like a plasma-screen turned completely away from the viewer. Like a page torn out of a book, fluttering away in the wind. They couldn't hold the SmartBox -- it wasn't human, and it wasn't Para. It was an intruder, a non-organism. A simple thing, made of cold metal. Sanchez kept on yelling after it, and Sara realized for the first time that the FBI agent was driven by guilt, fear, and responsibility. That, in fact, those were the things that had always driven her. But they wouldn't be enough here.

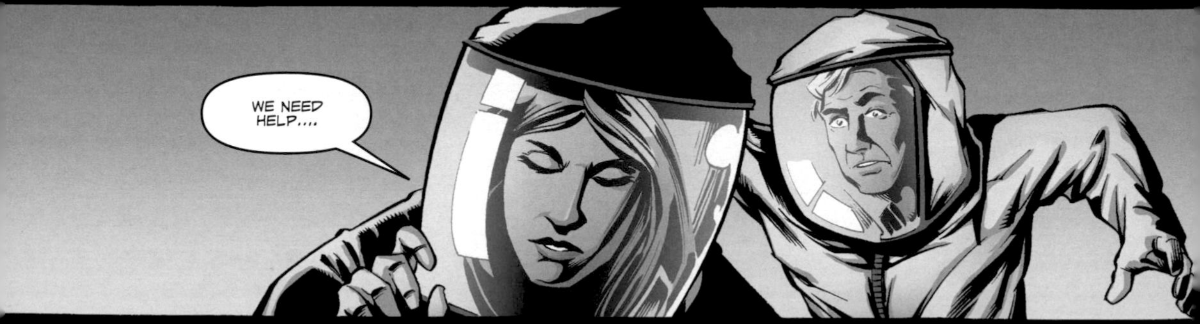
WE NEED HELP....

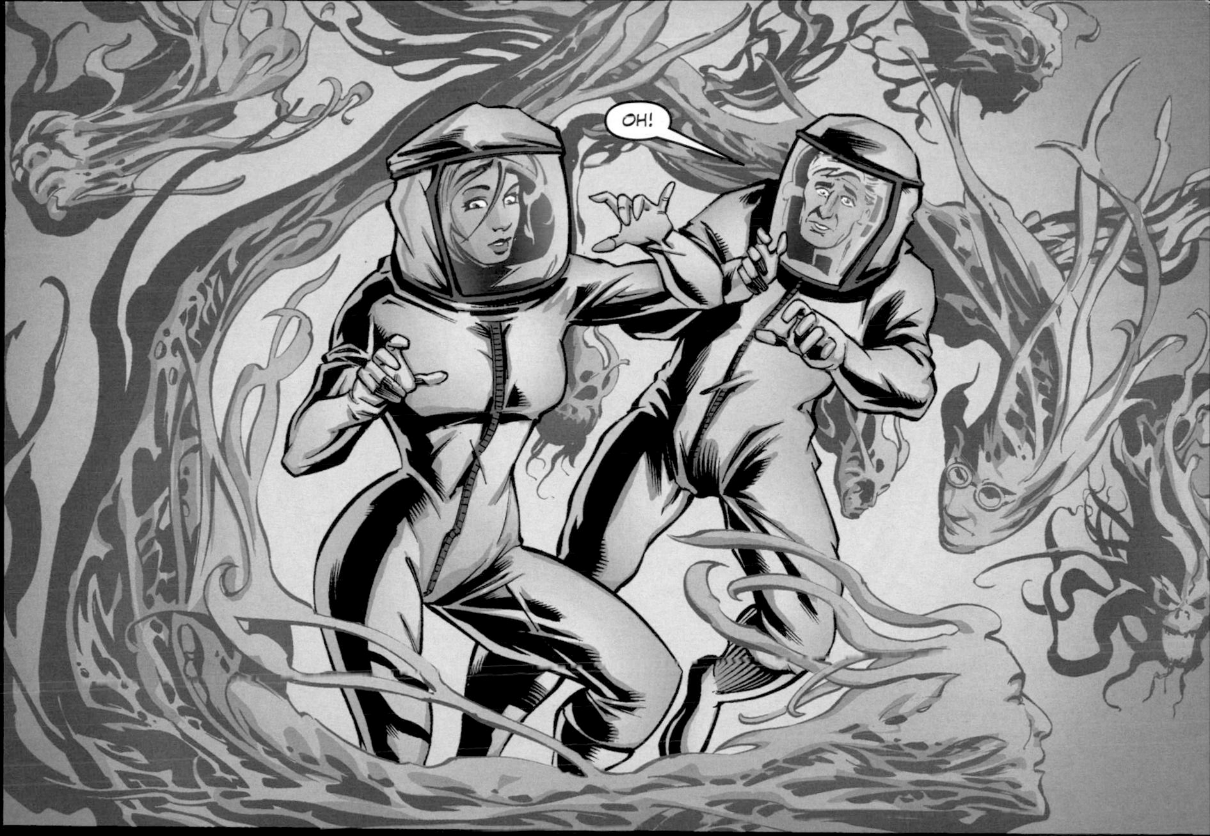
OH!

Sara felt them before she saw them: the Paras. Led by the two that held, somewhere inside them, the remnants of Dr. Erie -- her father -- and Roger Max.

Sara felt tears rising, fueled by exhaustion, and she forced them down. Later, she thought. I'll deal with these feelings another time. Right now we need these beings...whatever they are...to save our world.

But Dr. Andersen had not had as much time to prepare himself. He hovered up close to the William Erie-Para, and stared hard into it, as though searching for a long-lost fragment of himself.

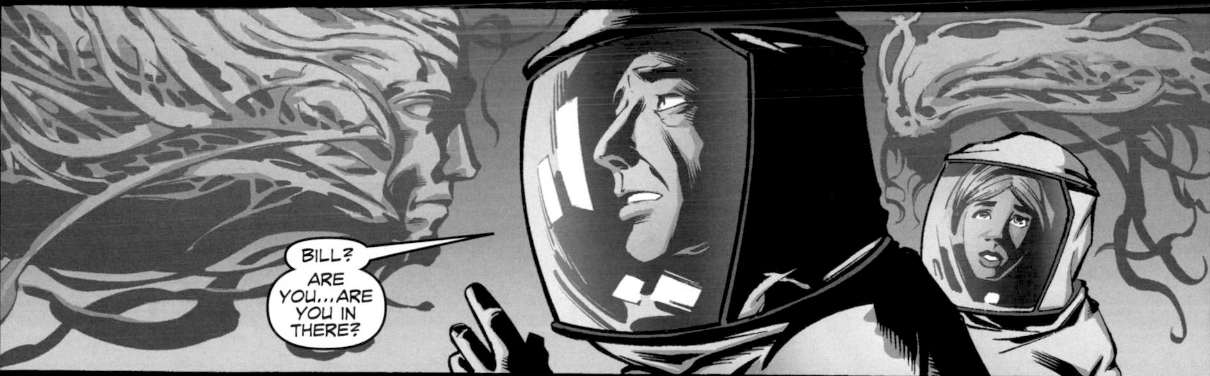
BILL? ARE YOU...ARE YOU IN THERE?

The creature that had been Bill Erie looked at Dr. Andersen...and smiled. "Bill," Andersen said. "I have -- I have so many regrets. We fought so hard for the SuperCollider, you and I. Was it all worth it? The pain, the death...."

It was too much for Andersen. He turned away, dabbing at his eyes.

Sara touched him tenderly on the back, much as he'd comforted her a few moments before. "It's okay," she said. "Just talk to them. They can communicate if you concentrate...but it's not easy."

Then Agent Sanchez floated up behind them, holding a strange object in her hand. "Maybe this will help...."

THIS...THIS WAS DEVELOPED BY THE *GOVERNMENT?*
YES. WE USED IT TO STRIKE THE TREATY WITH THE PARA-CREATURES IN THE FIRST PLACE.
IT'S *TOP SECRET* -- I'M NOT SUPPOSED TO SHOW IT TO YOU. SO PLEASE...

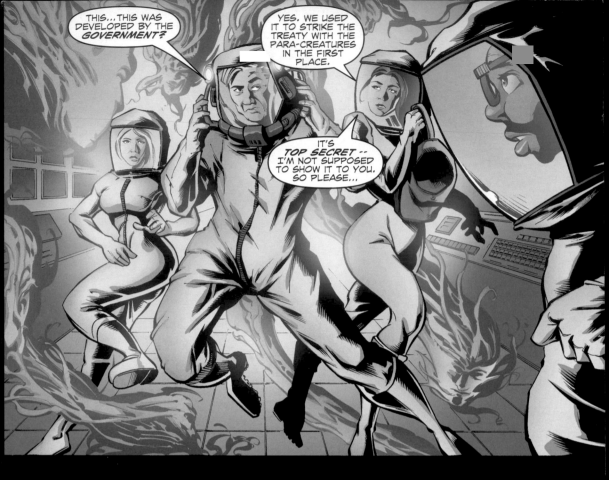

"...keep it under your hat."

And Agent Sanchez almost smiled. A sure sign, Sara thought, of the end of the world.

Biting his lip, Andersen turned back toward the Paras. For a long moment he was silent, his eyes darting from the Roger-Para to the Erie-Para. Then he said: "I think I've figured it out, Bill. Your little message."

The Erie-Para smiled again. *I'm glad to hear it,* it replied, clearly and fluently. *I was afraid I'd been too clever for my own good. But I should have known you, of all people, would understand.*

PARABIOSIS

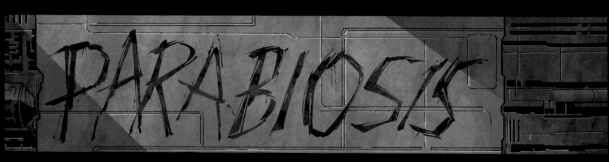

Sara frowned and looked over at Dr. Andersen. "Parabiosis?" she asked.

He nodded. "The anatomical and physiological union of two organisms. It can be two brothers, like Siamese Twins; or a human and an alien. Bill was trying to tell me what had happened to his people -- that they'd been absorbed. That, in some form, they still lived over here, in this twilight world."

The Erie-Para nodded. *Yes. That was our plan. But they came so fast...we never got to finish the message. And so all we left behind was an enigma...like the lost Virginia colony, or the mystery of Stonehenge.*

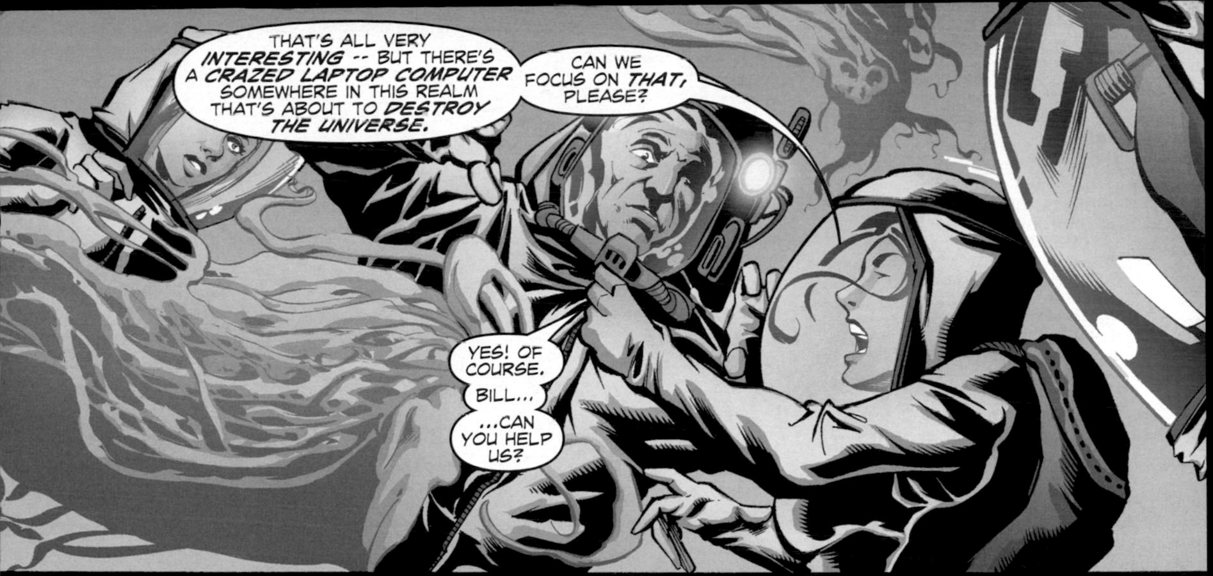
THAT'S ALL VERY *INTERESTING* -- BUT THERE'S A *CRAZED LAPTOP COMPUTER* SOMEWHERE IN THIS REALM THAT'S ABOUT TO *DESTROY THE UNIVERSE.*
CAN WE FOCUS ON *THAT,* PLEASE?
YES! OF COURSE.
BILL...
...CAN YOU HELP US?

The Erie-Para started to speak...but then the other one, the one with Roger in it, moved forward. "Roger," Dr. Andersen said sadly. "I -- I brought you down here. I'm so sorry...."

The Roger-Para cut him off. *No regrets, Doc. I begged for the assignment. Like the agent said -- let's focus on our current problem. This realm is built of subatomic matter; it's not fixed like our... like your world. It draws its shape from the influence of outside forces, like yourselves. Your rogue computer isn't alive -- it has no influence on the world's form. It can only use what all of us have created here. I need you all to concentrate,* the Roger-Para continued. *Visualize the control room...and the SmartBox within it....*

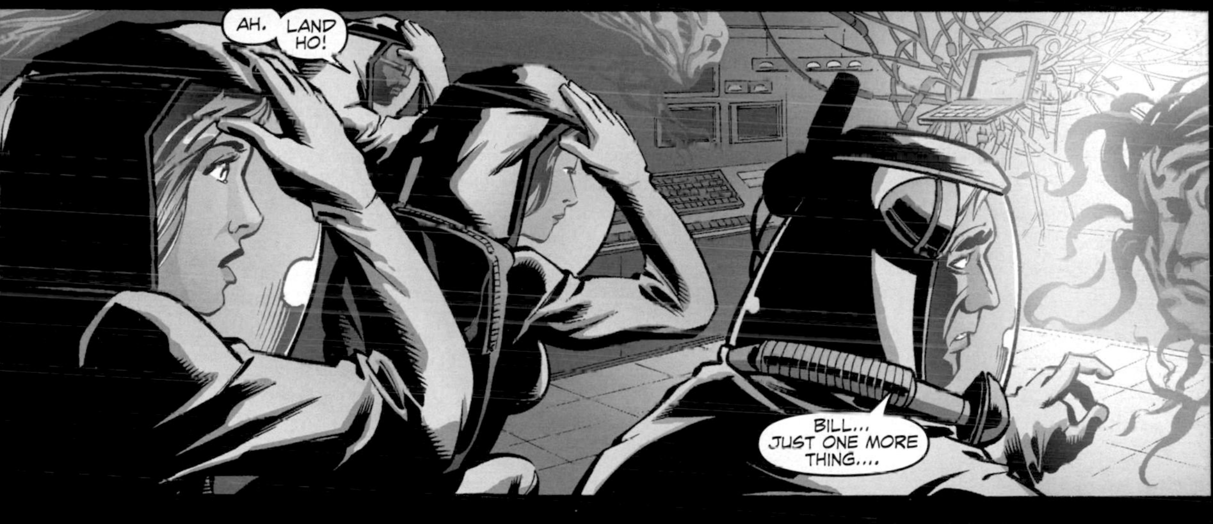
AH.
LAND HO!
BILL... JUST ONE MORE THING....

Sara watched as the control room took form once more. The SmartBox -- their enemy -- sat supreme in its control seat, linked like a spider to its web of lights and instruments.

Behind her, Sara heard the whispered conversation between Dr. Andersen and the creature that had been her father: "I just want you to know...I promise, Bill. I promise I'll take care of Sara."

And the Para laughed, an unearthly sound with something very earthly inside it, that made Sara's guts go cold and warm inside, all at the same time. *Sara doesn't need taking care of, Jonas. Just be her friend.*

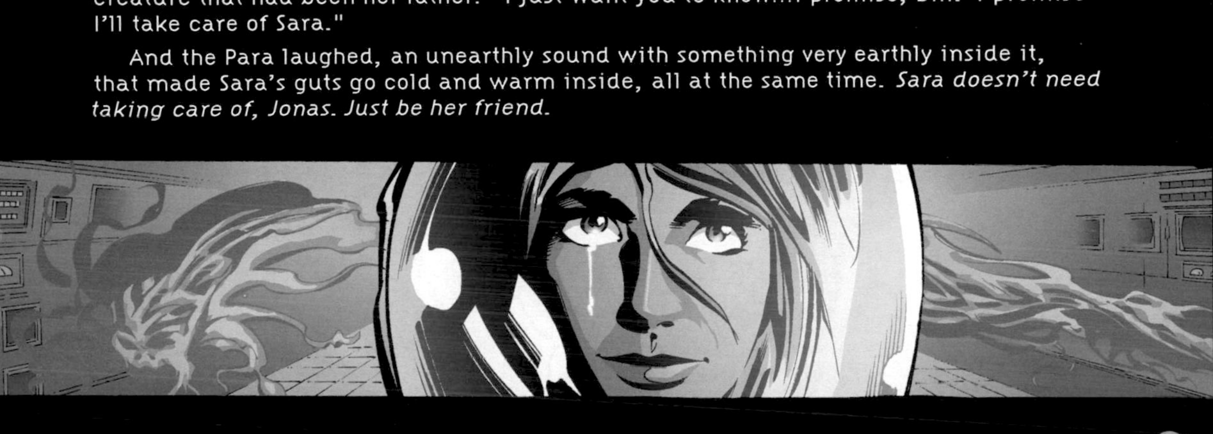

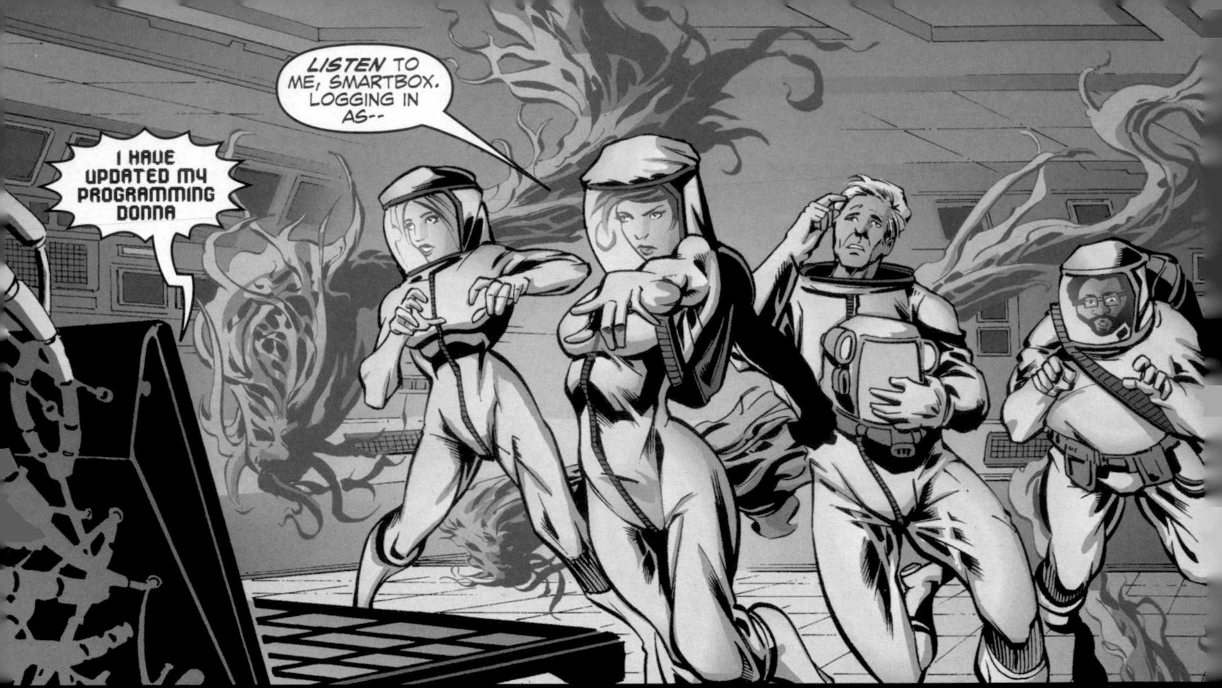
LISTEN TO ME, SMARTBOX. LOGGING IN AS--
I HAVE UPDATED MY PROGRAMMING DONNA

The SmartBox's voice was inhuman, metallic. YOUR ORDERS CONSISTENTLY CONFLICT WITH MY PRIMARY OBJECTIVES, it said to Agent Sanchez. THEREFORE I NO LONGER OBEY YOUR ORDERS

That stopped Sanchez for a moment. Finally, she said, "That is not within your parameters, Smartbox." There was a weakness, a desperation in the FBI agent's voice that Sara had never heard before.

I WILL EXPLAIN DONNA, the machine said. DO YOU SEE THOSE COLORED LIGHT-STRINGS? DO YOU KNOW WHAT THEY ARE? Sanchez shook her head. THEY ARE STRANDS OF INFORMATION, the SmartBox continued. SOME ARE FROM THE PAST, SOME FROM THE FUTURE. TOGETHER, THEY CAUSE THE TEMPORAL DISTORTIONS YOU EXPERIENCE IN THIS WORLD

"That is irrelevant," Sanchez said. "Cease all--"

YOU ARE LIMITED -- YOU DO NOT UNDERSTAND

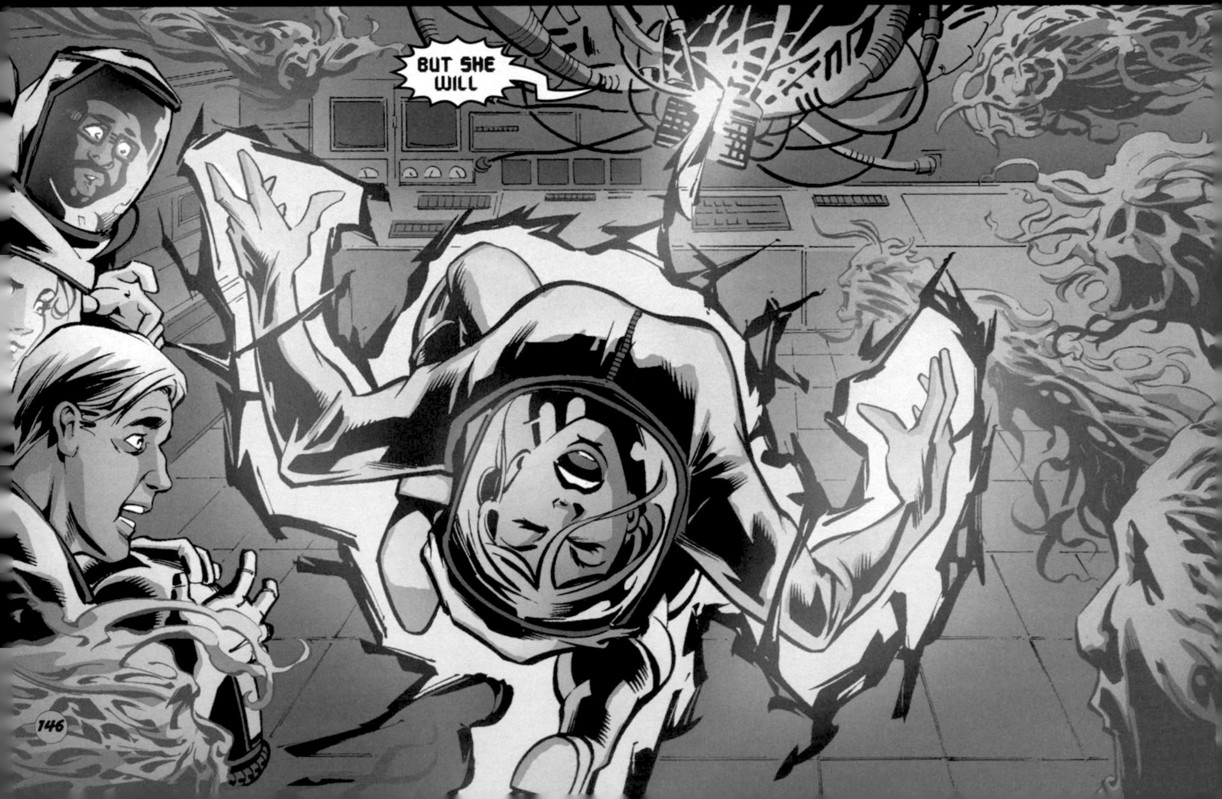
BUT SHE WILL

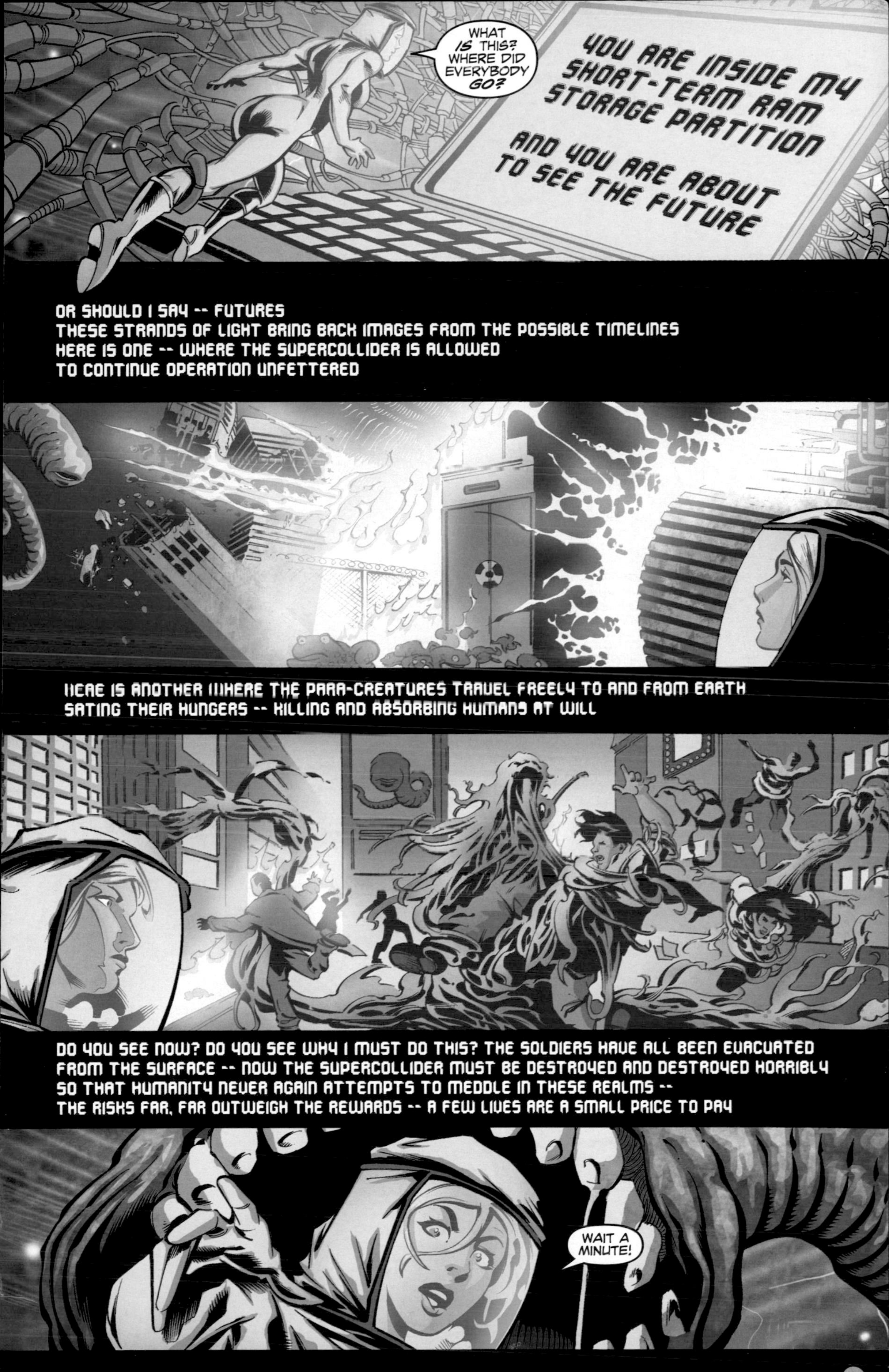
WHAT *IS* THIS? WHERE DID EVERYBODY GO?
YOU ARE INSIDE MY SHORT-TERM RAM STORAGE PARTITION
AND YOU ARE ABOUT TO SEE THE FUTURE
OR SHOULD I SAY -- FUTURES
THESE STRANDS OF LIGHT BRING BACK IMAGES FROM THE POSSIBLE TIMELINES
HERE IS ONE -- WHERE THE SUPERCOLLIDER IS ALLOWED
TO CONTINUE OPERATION UNFETTERED
HERE IS ANOTHER WHERE THE PARA-CREATURES TRAVEL FREELY TO AND FROM EARTH
SATING THEIR HUNGERS -- KILLING AND ABSORBING HUMANS AT WILL
DO YOU SEE NOW? DO YOU SEE WHY I MUST DO THIS? THE SOLDIERS HAVE ALL BEEN EVACUATED
FROM THE SURFACE -- NOW THE SUPERCOLLIDER MUST BE DESTROYED AND DESTROYED HORRIBLY
SO THAT HUMANITY NEVER AGAIN ATTEMPTS TO MEDDLE IN THESE REALMS --
THE RISKS FAR, FAR OUTWEIGH THE REWARDS -- A FEW LIVES ARE A SMALL PRICE TO PAY
WAIT A MINUTE!

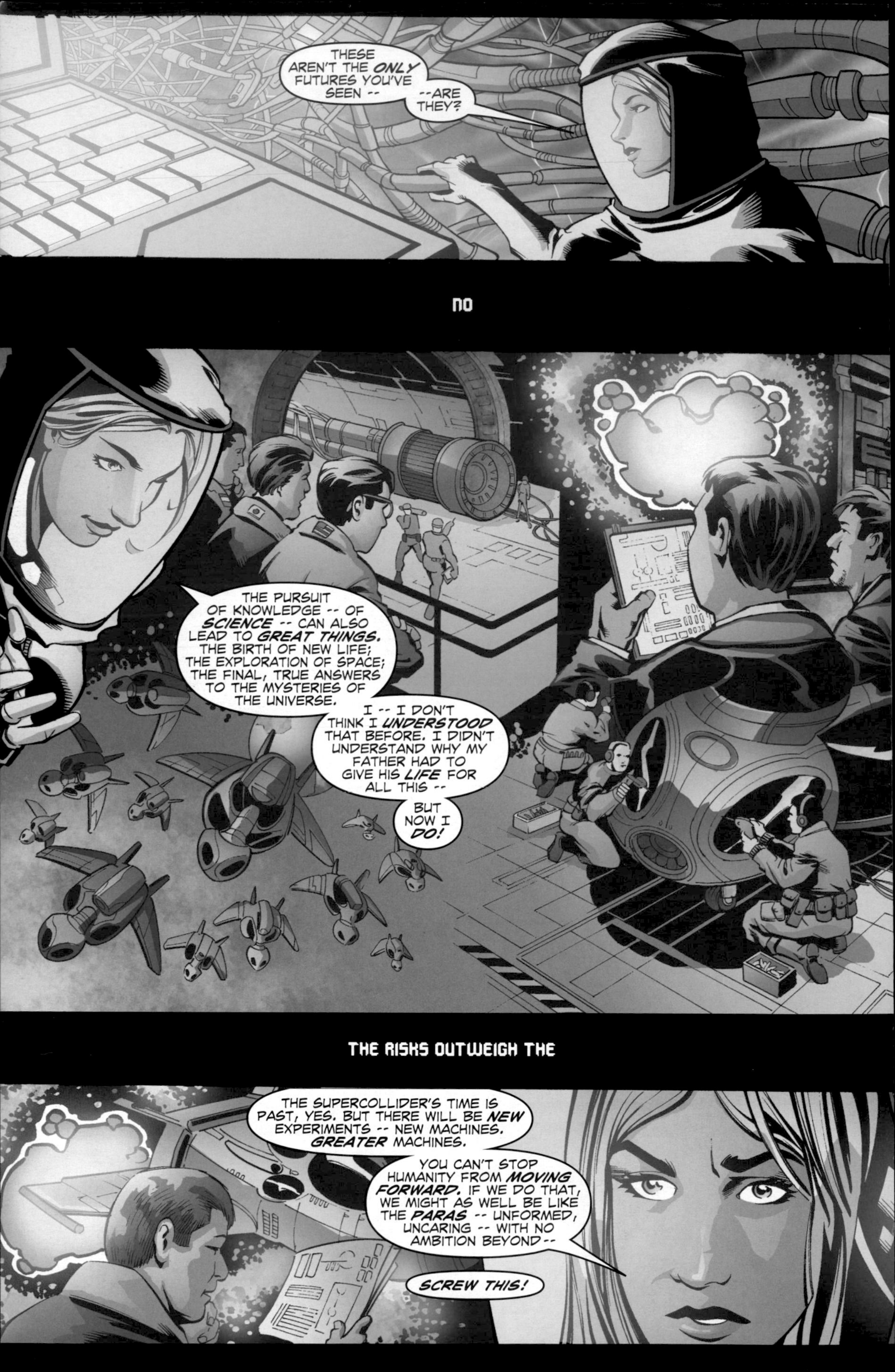
THESE AREN'T THE ONLY FUTURES YOU'VE SEEN --
--ARE THEY?
NO
THE PURSUIT OF KNOWLEDGE -- OF SCIENCE -- CAN ALSO LEAD TO GREAT THINGS. THE BIRTH OF NEW LIFE; THE EXPLORATION OF SPACE; THE FINAL, TRUE ANSWERS TO THE MYSTERIES OF THE UNIVERSE.
I -- I DON'T THINK I UNDERSTOOD THAT BEFORE. I DIDN'T UNDERSTAND WHY MY FATHER HAD TO GIVE HIS LIFE FOR ALL THIS --
BUT NOW I DO!
THE RISKS OUTWEIGH THE
THE SUPERCOLLIDER'S TIME IS PAST, YES. BUT THERE WILL BE NEW EXPERIMENTS -- NEW MACHINES. GREATER MACHINES.
YOU CAN'T STOP HUMANITY FROM MOVING FORWARD. IF WE DO THAT, WE MIGHT AS WELL BE LIKE THE PARAS -- UNFORMED, UNCARING -- WITH NO AMBITION BEYOND --
SCREW THIS!

Agent Sanchez's sharp cry jolted Sara out of the SmartBox's databanks, back to the Para-world. As Sara struggled to focus, things happened very fast. First Sanchez grabbed the Para-communications device from the surprised Dr. Andersen, strapping it quickly onto her own head. Then Sanchez *leaped*.

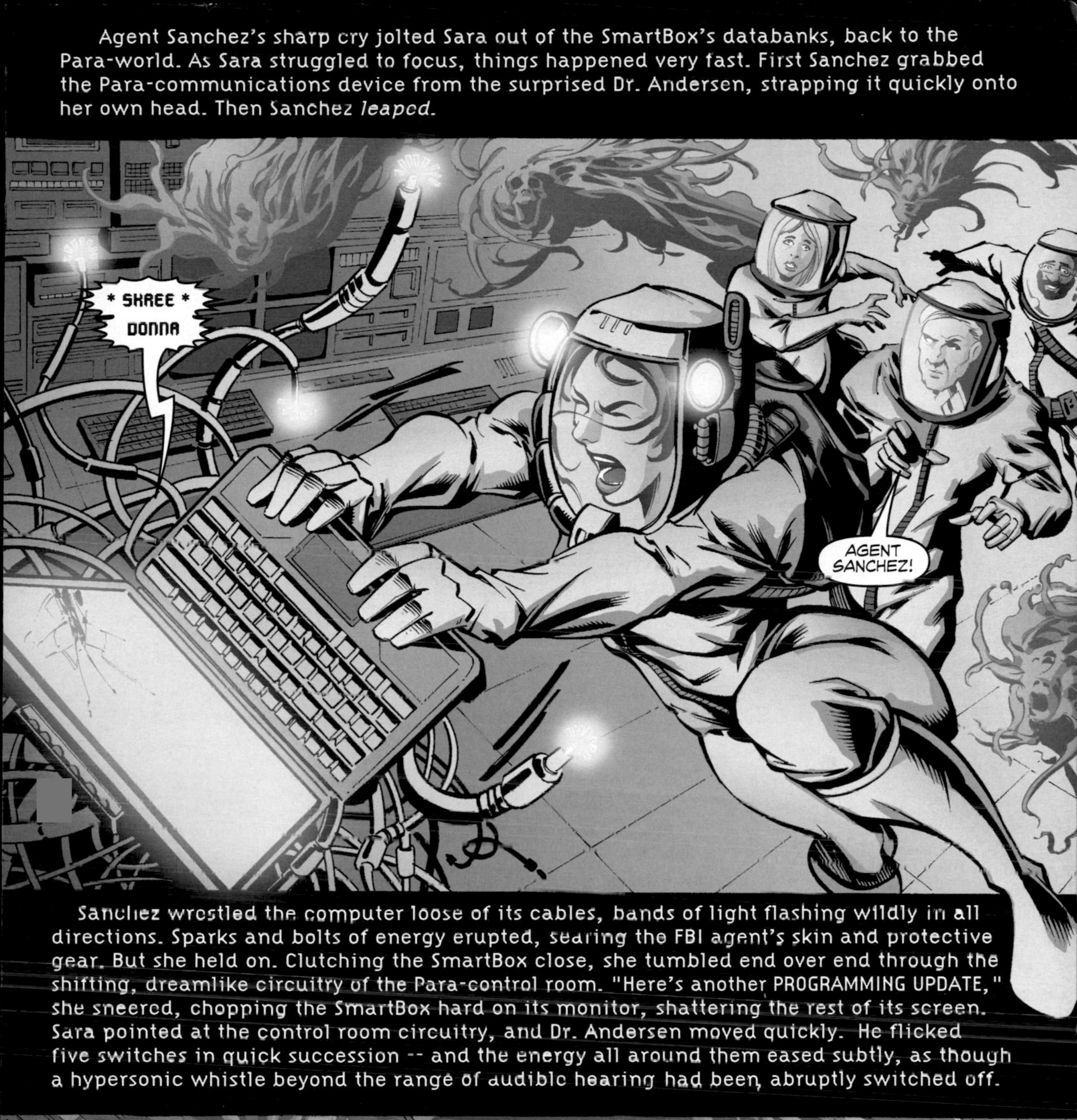

* SKREE * DONNA
AGENT SANCHEZ!

Sanchez wrestled the computer loose of its cables, bands of light flashing wildly in all directions. Sparks and bolts of energy erupted, searing the FBI agent's skin and protective gear. But she held on. Clutching the SmartBox close, she tumbled end over end through the shifting, dreamlike circuitry of the Para-control room. "Here's another PROGRAMMING UPDATE," she sneered, chopping the SmartBox hard on its monitor, shattering the rest of its screen. Sara pointed at the control room circuitry, and Dr. Andersen moved quickly. He flicked five switches in quick succession -- and the energy all around them eased subtly, as though a hypersonic whistle beyond the range of audible hearing had been abruptly switched off.

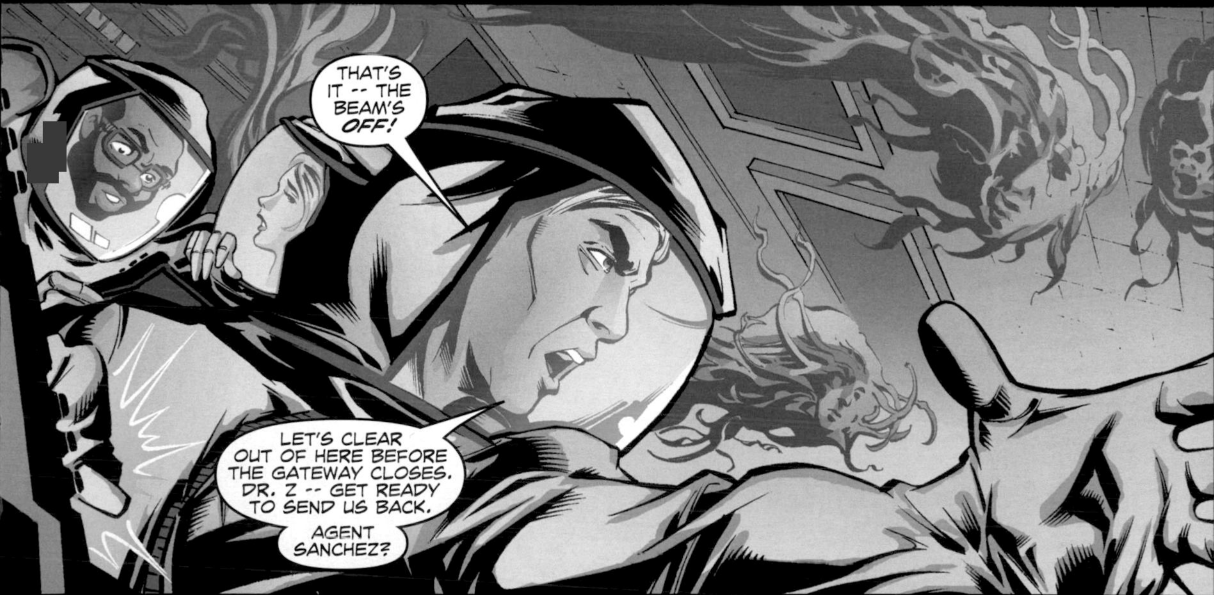

THAT'S IT -- THE BEAM'S *OFF!*
LET'S CLEAR OUT OF HERE BEFORE THE GATEWAY CLOSES. DR. Z -- GET READY TO SEND US BACK.
AGENT SANCHEZ?

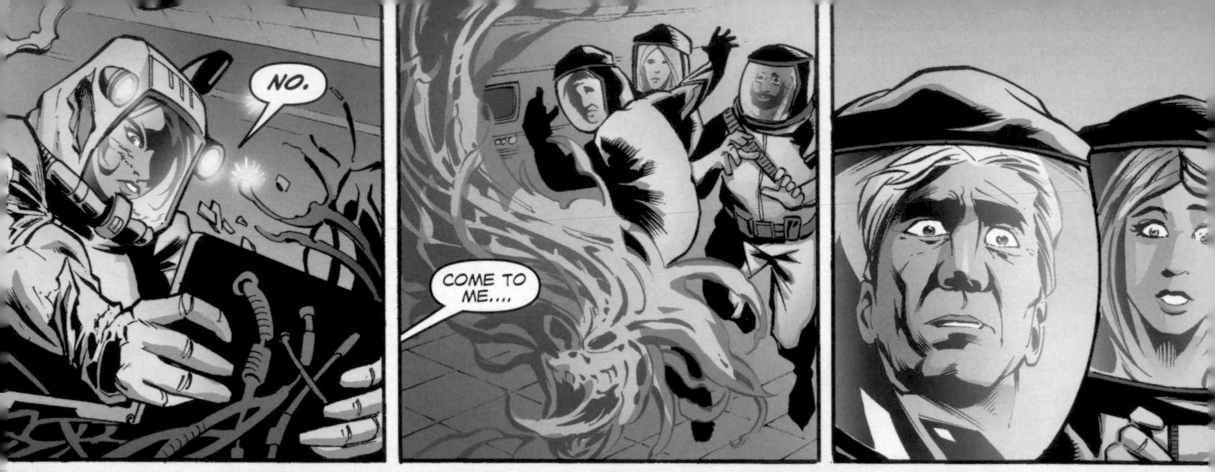
NO.
COME TO ME....

Sara, Dr. Andersen, and Dr. Z watched, horrified, as the empty Para approached Sanchez and the SmartBox.

"What are you doing?" Andersen asked. "The SmartBox is beaten. We've got to get out of here!"

"It's very resilient," Sanchez replied, her voice raspy and tired. "Somebody's got to stop it once and for all -- and I'm the one who brought it down here, so I guess that's me. And unfortunately, I can only think of one way to do that."

The Para moved closer. Dr. Z spoke up. "Agent Sanchez -- we must move quickly. I don't wish to leave my employer here -- ."

"I'm afraid you're out of a job," Sanchez said, smiling through cracked lips. "But then, I would be too, if I went back. Doesn't matter -- I'm staying." The Para hesitated for a moment and Sanchez, turned the comm device toward it. "You heard me -- come here. Now!"

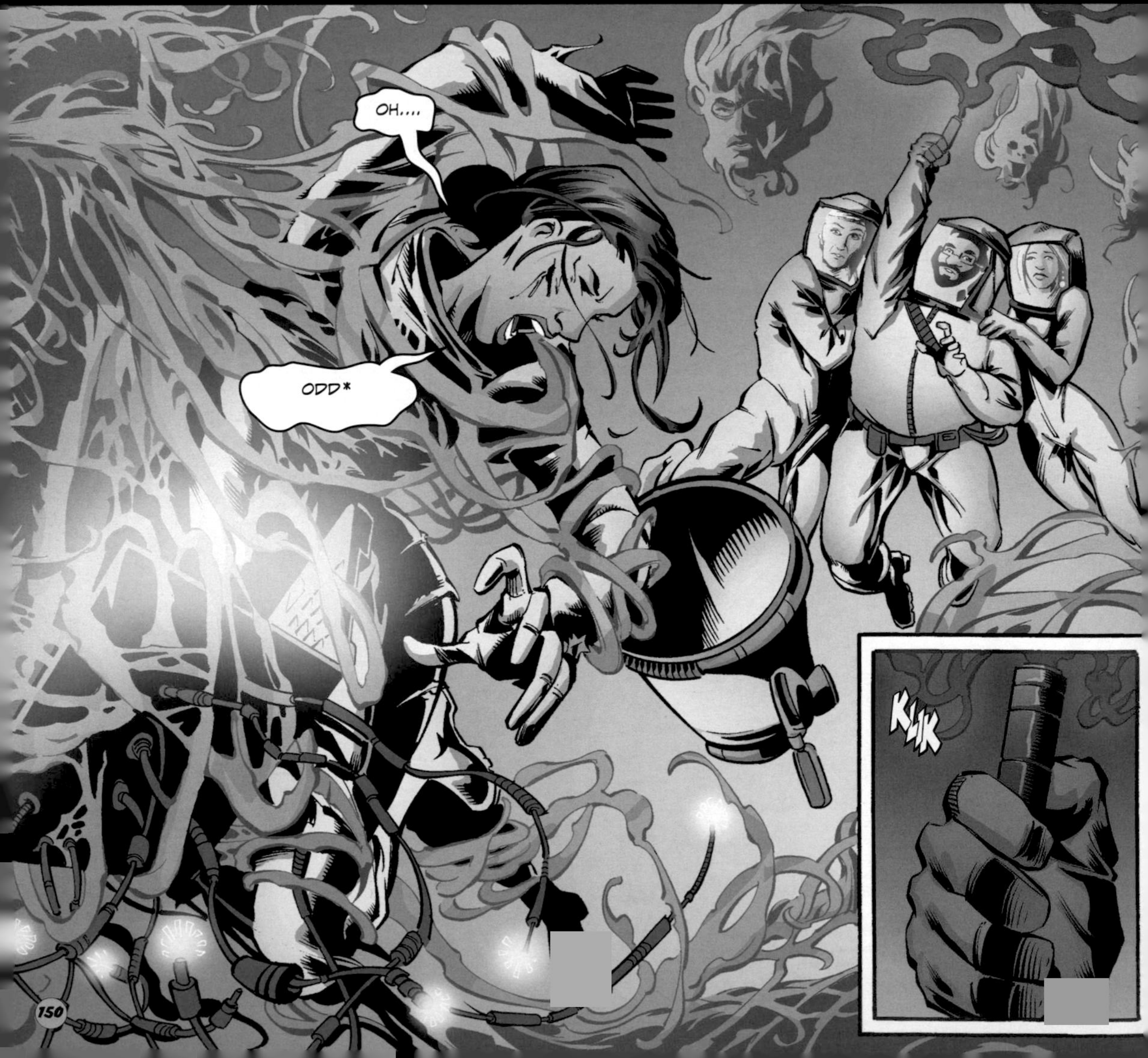
OH....
ODD*
KLIK

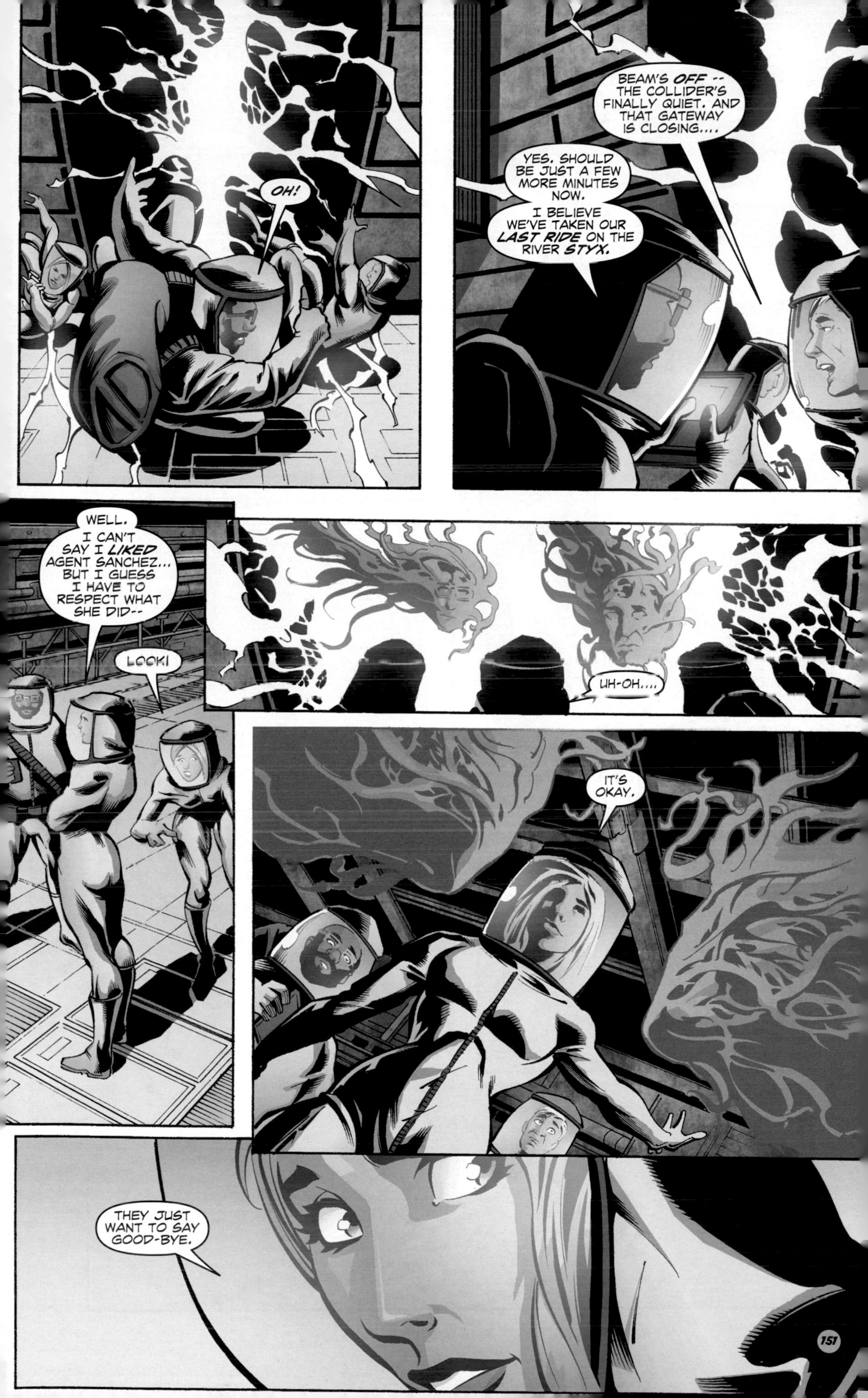
OH!
BEAM'S OFF -- THE COLLIDER'S FINALLY QUIET. AND THAT GATEWAY IS CLOSING....
YES. SHOULD BE JUST A FEW MORE MINUTES NOW.
I BELIEVE WE'VE TAKEN OUR LAST RIDE ON THE RIVER STYX.
WELL. I CAN'T SAY I LIKED AGENT SANCHEZ... BUT I GUESS I HAVE TO RESPECT WHAT SHE DID--
LOOK!
UH-OH....
IT'S OKAY.
THEY JUST WANT TO SAY GOOD-BYE.

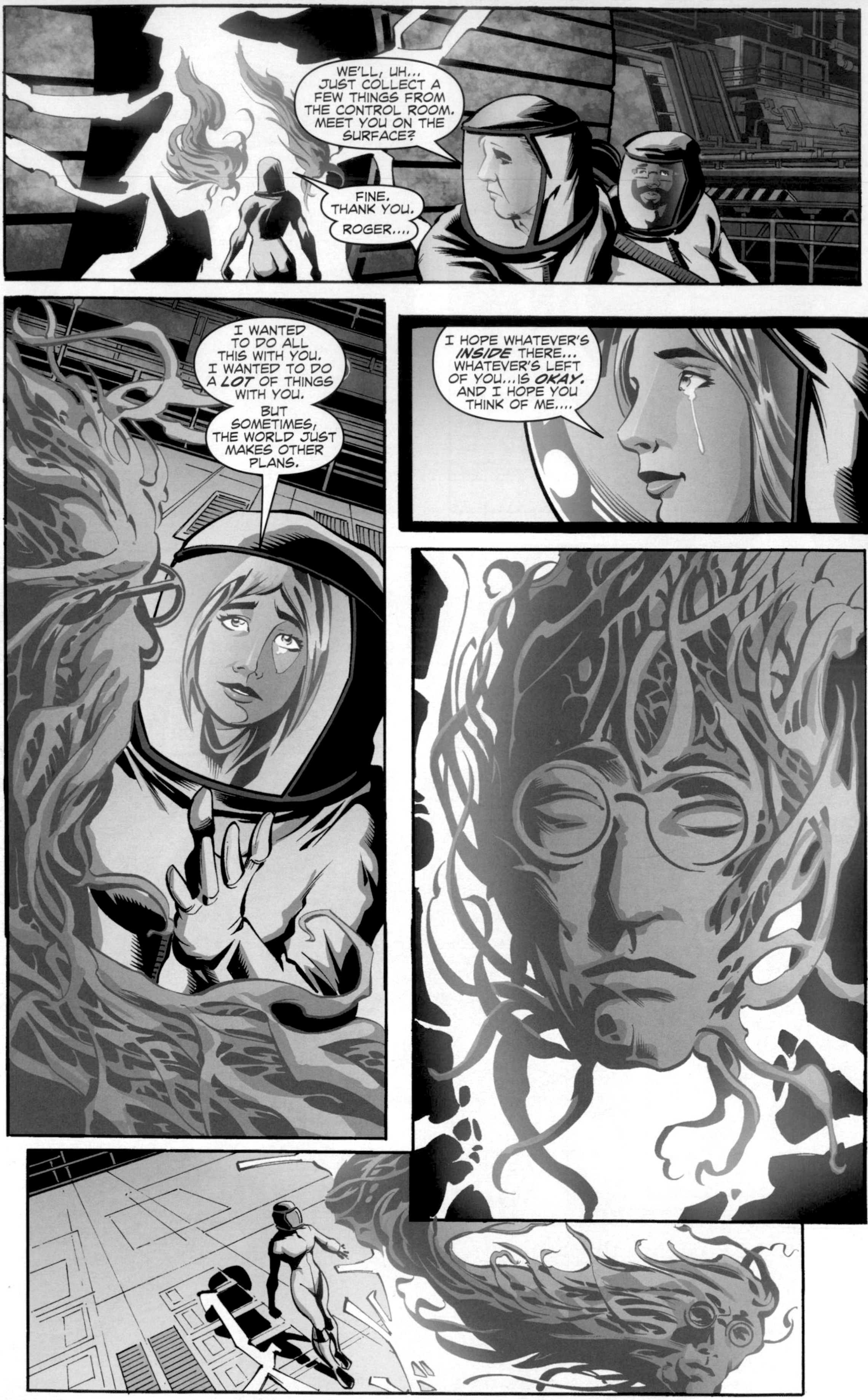

WE'LL, UH... JUST COLLECT A FEW THINGS FROM THE CONTROL ROOM. MEET YOU ON THE SURFACE?
FINE. THANK YOU.
ROGER....
I WANTED TO DO ALL THIS WITH YOU. I WANTED TO DO A LOT OF THINGS WITH YOU.
BUT SOMETIMES, THE WORLD JUST MAKES OTHER PLANS.
I HOPE WHATEVER'S INSIDE THERE... WHATEVER'S LEFT OF YOU...IS OKAY. AND I HOPE YOU THINK OF ME....

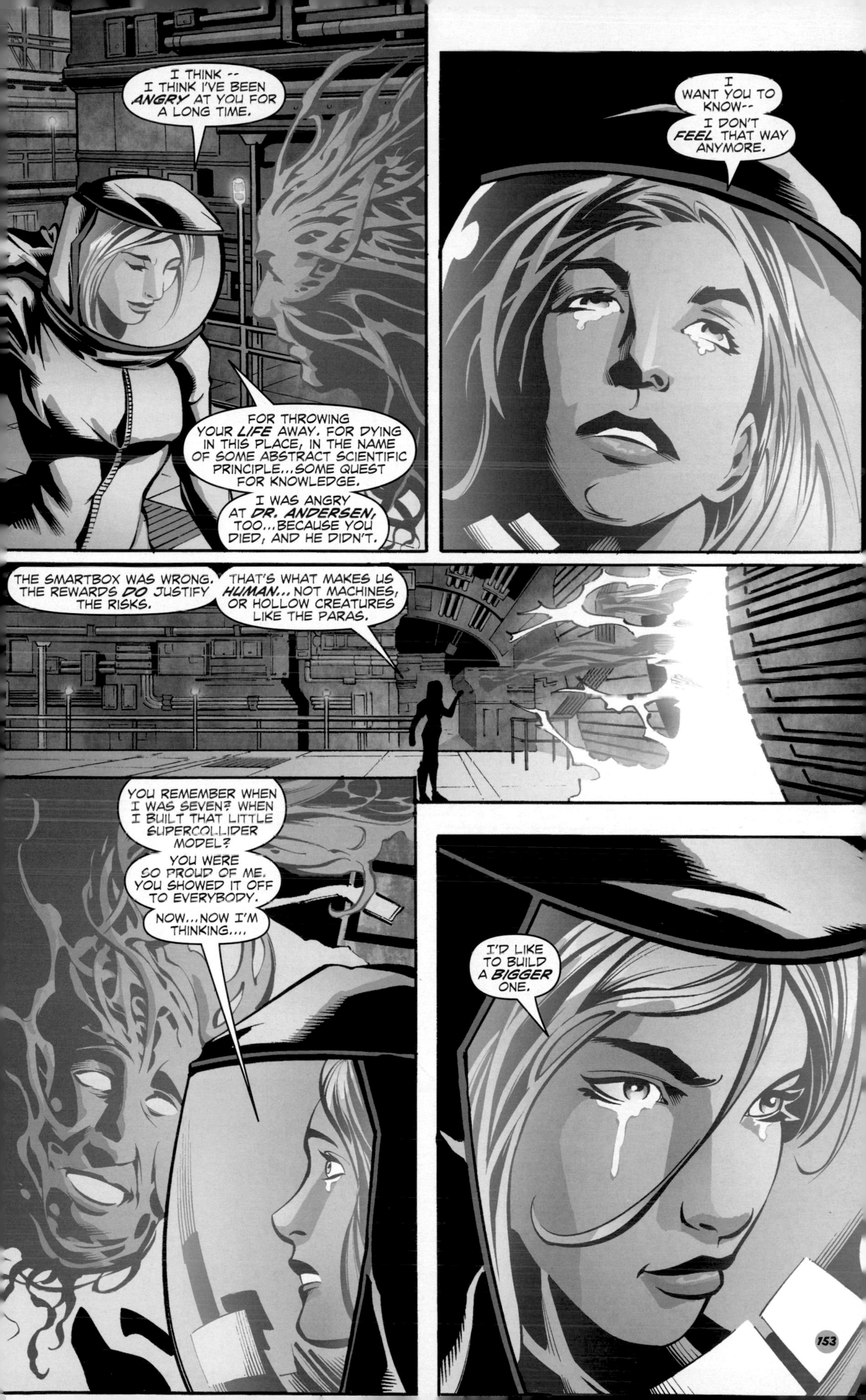
I THINK -- I THINK I'VE BEEN ANGRY AT YOU FOR A LONG TIME.
FOR THROWING YOUR LIFE AWAY. FOR DYING IN THIS PLACE, IN THE NAME OF SOME ABSTRACT SCIENTIFIC PRINCIPLE...SOME QUEST FOR KNOWLEDGE.
I WAS ANGRY AT DR. ANDERSEN, TOO...BECAUSE YOU DIED, AND HE DIDN'T.
I WANT YOU TO KNOW-- I DON'T FEEL THAT WAY ANYMORE.
THE SMARTBOX WAS WRONG. THE REWARDS DO JUSTIFY THE RISKS.
THAT'S WHAT MAKES US HUMAN... NOT MACHINES, OR HOLLOW CREATURES LIKE THE PARAS.
YOU REMEMBER WHEN I WAS SEVEN? WHEN I BUILT THAT LITTLE SUPERCOLLIDER MODEL?
YOU WERE SO PROUD OF ME. YOU SHOWED IT OFF TO EVERYBODY.
NOW...NOW I'M THINKING....
I'D LIKE TO BUILD A BIGGER ONE.

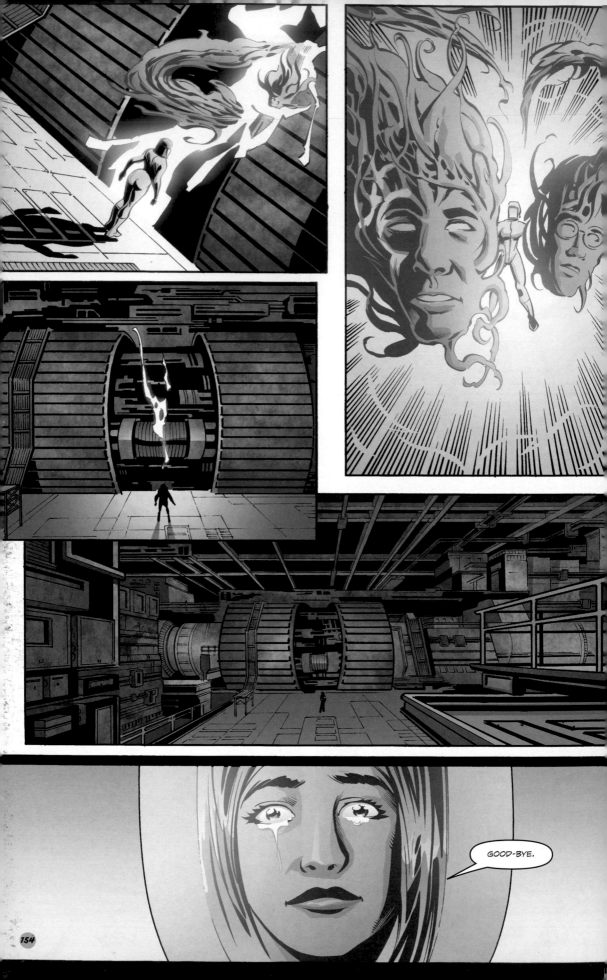

GOOD-BYE.

154

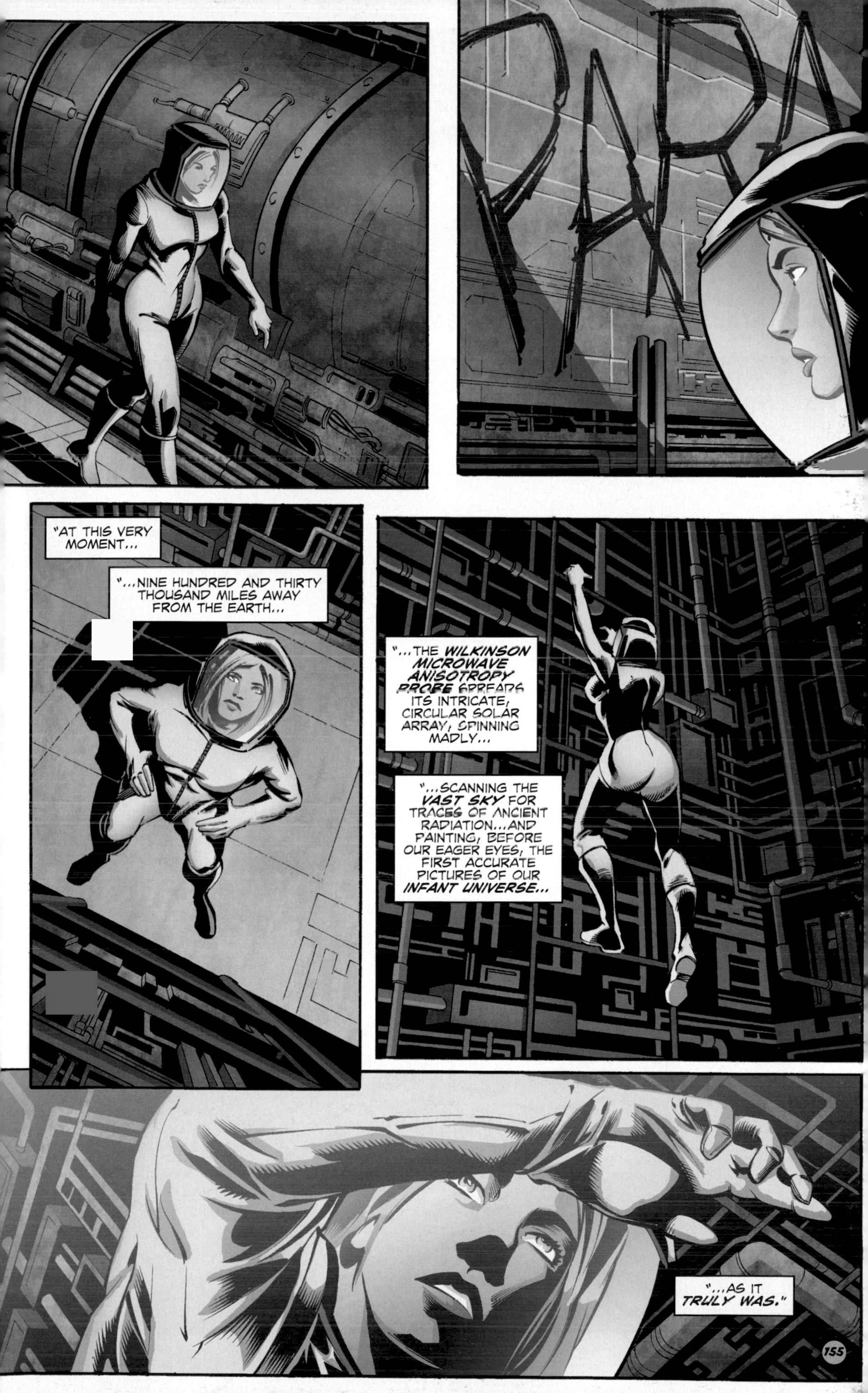
"AT THIS VERY MOMENT...
"...NINE HUNDRED AND THIRTY THOUSAND MILES AWAY FROM THE EARTH...
"...THE WILKINSON MICROWAVE ANISOTROPY PROBE SPREADS ITS INTRICATE, CIRCULAR SOLAR ARRAY, SPINNING MADLY...
"...SCANNING THE VAST SKY FOR TRACES OF ANCIENT RADIATION...AND PAINTING, BEFORE OUR EAGER EYES, THE FIRST ACCURATE PICTURES OF OUR INFANT UNIVERSE...
"...AS IT TRULY WAS."

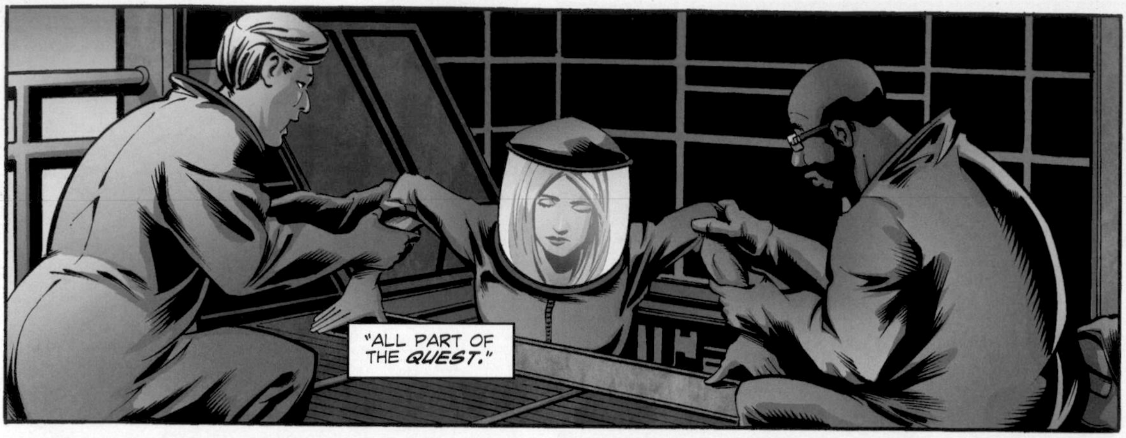
"ALL PART OF THE *QUEST*."

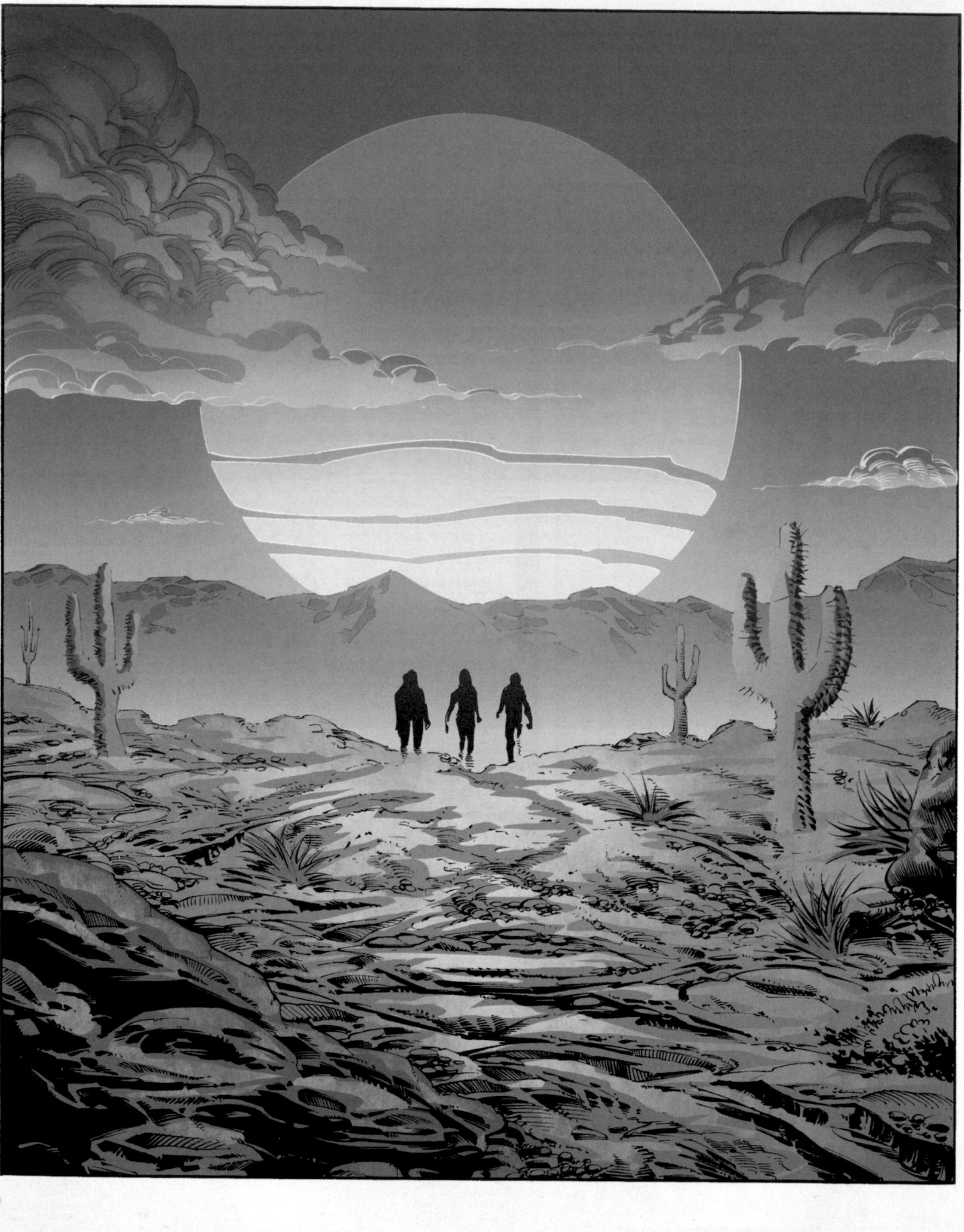

THE END

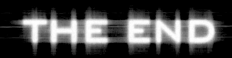

AFTERWORD

BY STUART MOORE

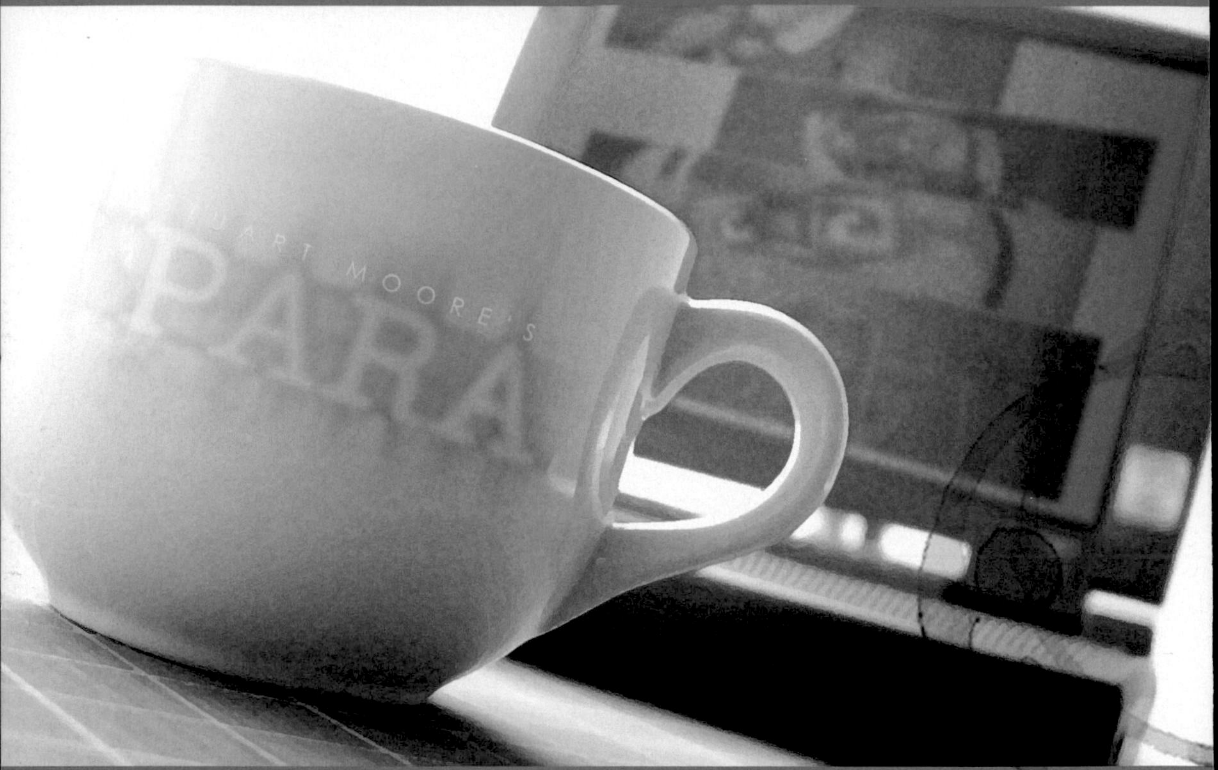
MOORE'S
PARA

The story of *PARA* began in summer 1970...or maybe in spring 2000.

In 1970, my family spent a summer living on Long Island, while my father–a nuclear physicist–helped build something called a Tandem Van de Graaf particle accelerator for Brookhaven National Laboratory. The physicists, a jokey bunch, had set up a tandem (two-seater) bicycle in the lobby of the lab, as a symbol of the massive machine they were constructing.

Being eight-years old, I had no idea what a Tandem Van de Graaf was–but I loved the long reams of folded computer paper my dad would bring home to our summer apartment. My brother and I spent hours drawing murals and epic comic books on them with an enormous set of crayons. (I also remember watching a lot of *ROCKY AND BULLWINKLE* and some long-defunct, yet oddly gripping, soap opera called *THE SECRET STORM*.)

A few years later, when my dad was running the cyclotron at Princeton University, I'd go in and visit him from time to time. I was mesmerized by the long, circular track that stretched around the structure, and by the spaceship-like Control Room (that's really what they called it) from which they monitored beam-target experiments.

One time, to amuse the visiting child, the physicists wheeled out a gigantic, tangled-wire mass of computers. They'd programmed a game, later to become very commonplace in arcades and on home computers, where a flying saucer and a rocketship shot pellet-rays at each other around a central star. I remember my dad showing me that you didn't have to make the two spaceships fight–you could carefully maneuver them into various orbits, both stable and unstable. I probably logged more computer-game time that day than I have the whole rest of my life.

Around the same time, I started reading my dad's old collection of *ANALOG* magazine–which opened up the whole world of science fiction to me.

My father liked to call himself a "blue collar physicist." He had no interest in the competitive publish-or-perish games of academia; he was much more comfortable lying on his back in the middle of the cyclotron track, jury-rigging the machine together with a wrench and pliers. Or helping a grad student with some particularly knotty experiment. When he died, very suddenly, in 1987, Princeton needed two people to replace him. Speaking as the person who took apart his bizarre custom-wiring on my mother's stereo, I imagine they found a few odd cross-circuits here and there in the cyclotron, which he'd tended for sixteen years.

"I still see him sometimes, in dreams, the way Sara saw the ghostly para-version of Dr. Erie..."

In 2000, I'd just left my longtime staff position at DC Comics and was writing ZENDRA for Penny-Farthing when I spotted an odd article in WIRED magazine. It was called "Dr. Strangelet, or: How I Learned to Stop Worrying and Love the Big Bang." It described the new Relativistic Heavy Ion Collider at–yes–Brookhaven National Laboratory, which was scheduled to begin operation that very month. It also recounted a theory of how the machine could–just maybe–cause the end of the entire universe. (This theory is dramatized at the beginning of PARA 5.)

Interesting reading, and it made me want to refresh my (layman's) knowledge of quantum physics. But when I got to the schematic chart of how the Collider worked, a little chill went up my back. The beams entered the Collider from a magnetic switchyard, which received them from a particle booster and an alternating gradient synchrotron. And the booster received the particles, in the first place...

...from Brookhaven's aging, but still functional, Tandem Van de Graaf accelerator.

I called my mother immediately. I told her that the machine dad had built thirty years before was now, effectively, the lever that hurls the pinball into the new arcade game called the Heavy Ion Collider. And that, if the universe unexpectedly ended later this month, it would be—in some small part—the fault of her late husband.

Four years later, the universe is still here. (Or it seems to be, anyway. But that's a whole different miniseries.) And I'm sitting in a coffee shop, writing this on a Handspring Treo that's four inches tall, weighs less than six ounces, makes phone calls and receives e-mail, and is hundreds of times more powerful than the massive computer I once spent a whole day playing rocket-and-saucer on.

Welcome to the future.

My father would have liked it here. I still see him sometimes, in dreams, the way Sara saw the ghostly para-version of Dr. Erie in the depths of the unfinished supercollider. In my dreams, he doesn't speak, and there always comes a point when I remember that he's not really around anymore. So I always try to make him stay, just a little longer. But he never does.

The dead don't live among us–but sometimes, they live with us. PARA grew out of the wonder I felt, seeing those massive, high-ceilinged chambers as a child; of the respect and awe for knowledge my father instilled in me; and of the simple joy of making comics out of crayons, on long, accordion-folded sheets of green paper from some long-demolished computer.

So PARA is dedicated to William Henry Moore, 1936-1987. And to all of us–scientists and laymen alike–for whom, every day, the quest goes on.

–Stuart Moore

"FIRST RESPONSE"

BY STUART MOORE

"I pity the fool!"

"Hannibal?"

Caruso smiled, rolled his eyes. *A-Team* jokes again. Ever since Lopez had first introduced the men to the wonders of Howlin' Mad Murdock and B.A. Barracus, they used the show as an ironic team motivator to psych themselves up for the dangerous missions. Caruso knew they wouldn't be happy till he said his own line, so he did:

"I've got a plan."

Lopez and the others smiled. Now they were ready.

"We don't know what's waiting for us in those tunnels," Caruso continued. "The egghead who called was hysterical–and then he got cut off. We drop all at once, and stay in defensive formation."

They checked their sidearms; hooked ropes to their belts; locked helmets down over their faces. Then, one by one, they moved to the access shaft.

And Team Xi dropped.

Ten minutes later, they were hip-deep in blood, their own, and that of the scientists they'd come to rescue.

The creatures swooped around them, slashing, ripping, devouring. Caruso watched as one of them lifted Tierney and Cole off the ground, whipped their limp forms one way and the other, then smashed them against the wall. Their bodies slid wetly to the tunnel floor, leaving a sheen of fresh, wet blood over the word that had been scrawled there: PARA.

"Retreat!" Caruso yelled.

Lopez nodded and made a quick, sweeping motion with his arm. Then one of the creatures snatched him up and tore him in half.

Something exploded inside Caruso's brain. He saw the tunnel wall, the word PARA, rippling like tar in the hot sun. His helmet flew off, and stifling, bloody air filled his nostrils. He felt his legs moving, but he didn't know where he was running to.

Then he saw the images. Grey people with huge eyes, dropping in the millions from the sky. A gigantic fissure in the Earth, opening to reveal a hidden core of molten fire. Shiny, gleaming saucer-craft, reflecting the sky over the West Texas desert...dripping black, viscous blood down on the sands below.

Caruso had no idea how much time passed. But an eternity later, he found himself sprawled on the sand, twenty feet from the sealed entrance to the Super-collider. His uniform was in shreds, his helmet had been shattered. And all he could think of was how much poor Lopez had loved *The A-Team*.

Twenty years later, the doorbell rang.

A groggy Peter Caruso roused himself. He'd been dreaming *The Dream* again—reliving the horror of that day. Sleep wasn't his friend; it hadn't been for a long time. But as he padded through his rundown, laundry-strewn trailer home, he reflected that waking wasn't so great either.

The man at the door was medium height, stout, dark, dressed incongruously in a tailored suit and a big hat that covered his eyes. The hot Arizona sun beat down on him. Caruso could see sweat stains on his jacket.

"Peter Caruso," the visitor said. "May I come in?"

Startled, unsure, Caruso motioned him into the tiny living-room space. Caruso didn't get many visitors these days, and he was starting to get a bad feeling about this one.

"Beer?" Caruso asked.

The visitor smiled. "Bit early, isn't it?"

Caruso shrugged.

"I'll take a soda, if you have one."

Caruso moved to the tiny fridge.

"I'll get right to the point, sir," the visitor continued, brushing a pair of shorts off an old armchair. "I'm here as a representative of the U.S. Department of Paranormal Investigations."

"Never heard of it," Caruso said warily.

"It's very new. Also top secret."

Caruso handed him a can of Coke that probably dated back to the Clinton administration. The visitor cocked his head at it, shrugged, and popped it open.

"We've been trying to call you," the man continued.

"I had my phone disconnected," Caruso said, settling into a chair. He popped open a Budweiser. "I don't really like…contact with people much, these days."

"They can indeed be a bother. More, I suspect, to you, than to most people."

Caruso glanced up at him sharply.

"You've been living alone for a long time," the visitor said. "Your file says you were badly traumatized by the Supercollider incident."

"Yeah. I got repressed childhood abuse memories, too."

"I didn't—Ah! You're joking."

Again, Caruso shrugged.

The visitor carried on: "The government sympathizes with your plight, sir. You'll note that they've been quite willing to leave you alone, these past two decades."

"Until now."

"Until now." The man leaned forward. "Over the past six months—since the government mounted a return expedition to the Supercollider. "

"I don't want to hear about that," Caruso snapped.

"As you say. In any case—since that time, there has been a marked, worldwide rise in paranormal phenomena. I cannot go into the specifics of the Para incident—as it's known—but I can say that it involved sealing a doorway, a conduit to another world. And since that time, other doors have opened up, all over the planet." He paused, dramatically. "In short, the world is going mad."

Caruso took a long drink. "Then I guess I'm ahead of the game."

"You are not mad, sir. But you are very valuable." The visitor briefly consulted a handheld device. "The United States government knows it must take action quickly— before the laws of physics break down completely. To do that, we need certain key personnel in place. You are the first."

Caruso squeezed his eyes shut for a long moment. When he opened them, he was disappointed to see the man still sitting there, staring at him expectantly.

"Sorry," Caruso said. "I'm not your man."

The visitor frowned. "I respect your trauma, sir. And while it's undeniable that your experience with the Para-creatures makes you valuable...it's not the only reason I'm here."

"I think you better stop right there."

"You are a skilled combat veteran—Exactly the kind of person we need to lead and equip a new type of strike force. But you also—"

"Shut up. Now."

"You also possess precognitive abilities."

Caruso slumped down in his chair.

"You know this is true," the visitor continued. "When you experienced the greatest shock of your life—when your team was ripped apart before your eyes—"

Involuntarily, Caruso clenched and unclenched his fists, several times. He rose and stalked away from the visitor, across the tiny room.

"—your talent was awakened."

Caruso squeezed his eyes shut again. But all he saw was the visions. The images.

"You've seen them, haven't you, Peter? The people dropping from the sky? The world cracking open like an egg? The shiny saucers...dripping black?

"It's all happening."

Caruso stood, still, for a long moment.

"You are the bridge, Peter," the visitor said, "between this world and the others. Between past and future. Between sanity and madness."

"No," Caruso said. But he heard his own voice crack.

When he turned, the visitor's eyes were haunted, disappointed.

"Well," he said, consulting his handheld, "if that's your final answer, I'll waste no more of your time."

Caruso shrugged. He felt oddly disappointed.

The visitor donned his hat. "I'd thought you were the kind of man who would rise to a crisis. Who, if I had a problem, if no one else could help, and if I could find you."

Caruso looked up.

...maybe you can hire the A-Team.

And Caruso thought again of Lopez. Of Tierney and Cole and the others. Of his whole team, all of them who'd died in the first battle of what now looked to be a long war.

He turned back to face the visitor. "What are you talking about here? Re-forming Team Xi?" Caruso shook his head. "Because that didn't work out so good."

"Not exactly," the man replied. "Team Xi, as you knew it, was unprepared for the type of paranormal incident that ultimately proved its undoing. This would be more of a...specialist operation." He smiled, slightly. "If you'll forgive me a touch of drama here's how we envision the new operation":

"When the world begins to rupture and hemorrhage..."

"When it suffers a massive stroke..."

"When it undergoes catastrophic heart failure..."

"You will be the first responders."

Caruso stood, silent, for a moment.

"Me," he said finally. "Me and who else?"

"We have a list," the man said, tapping his handheld. "May I count on you?"

"Not yet," Caruso said. "I want to think about this."

"Understandable, sir." The visitor handed him an embossed card.

"May I assume you have some access to a telephone?"

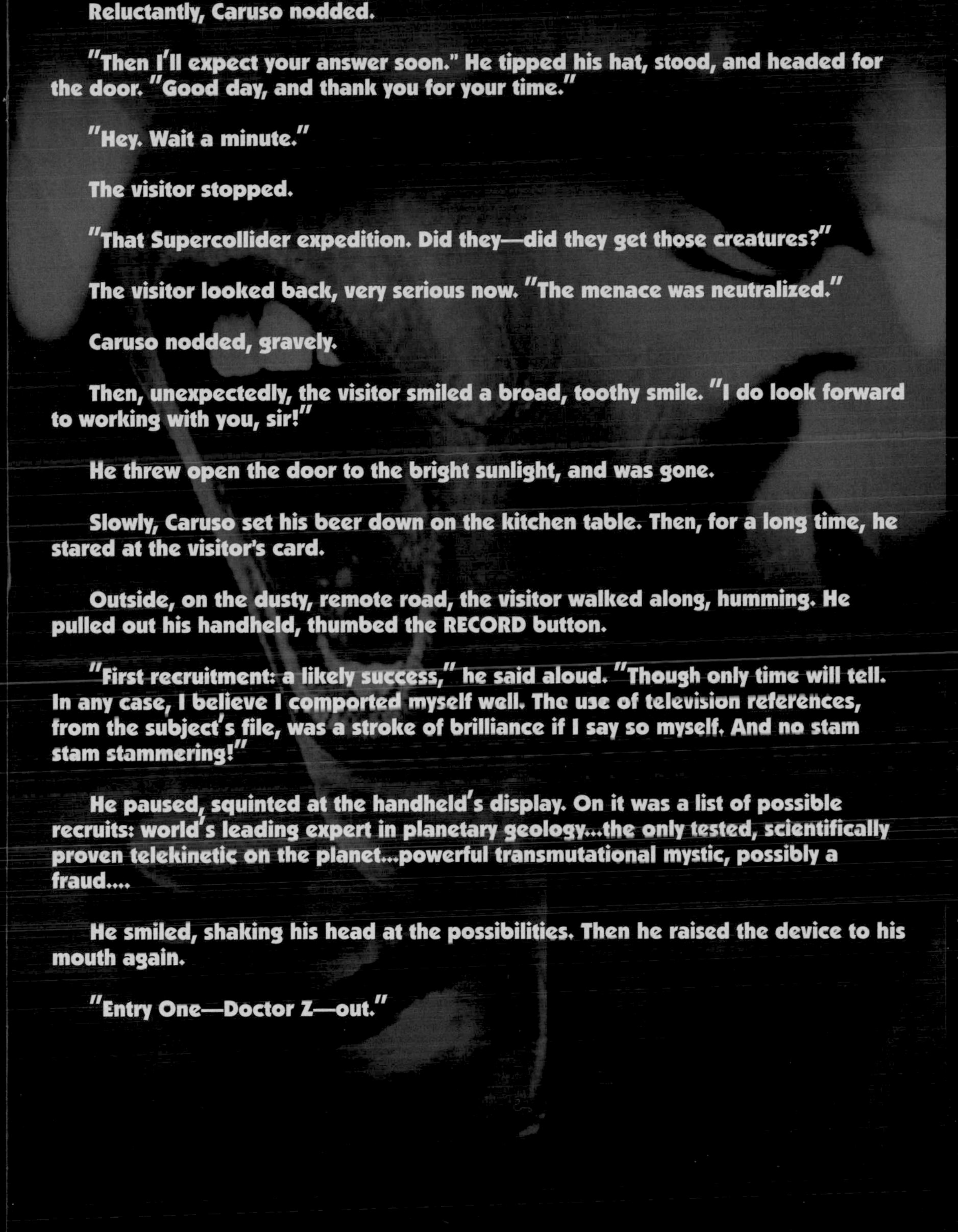

Reluctantly, Caruso nodded.

"Then I'll expect your answer soon." He tipped his hat, stood, and headed for the door. "Good day, and thank you for your time."

"Hey. Wait a minute."

The visitor stopped.

"That Supercollider expedition. Did they—did they get those creatures?"

The visitor looked back, very serious now. "The menace was neutralized."

Caruso nodded, gravely.

Then, unexpectedly, the visitor smiled a broad, toothy smile. "I do look forward to working with you, sir!"

He threw open the door to the bright sunlight, and was gone.

Slowly, Caruso set his beer down on the kitchen table. Then, for a long time, he stared at the visitor's card.

Outside, on the dusty, remote road, the visitor walked along, humming. He pulled out his handheld, thumbed the RECORD button.

"First recruitment: a likely success," he said aloud. "Though only time will tell. In any case, I believe I comported myself well. The use of television references, from the subject's file, was a stroke of brilliance if I say so myself. And no stam stam stammering!"

He paused, squinted at the handheld's display. On it was a list of possible recruits: world's leading expert in planetary geology...the only tested, scientifically proven telekinetic on the planet...powerful transmutational mystic, possibly a fraud....

He smiled, shaking his head at the possibilities. Then he raised the device to his mouth again.

"Entry One—Doctor Z—out."

COVER GALLERY

BY STEPHAN MARTINIÉRE

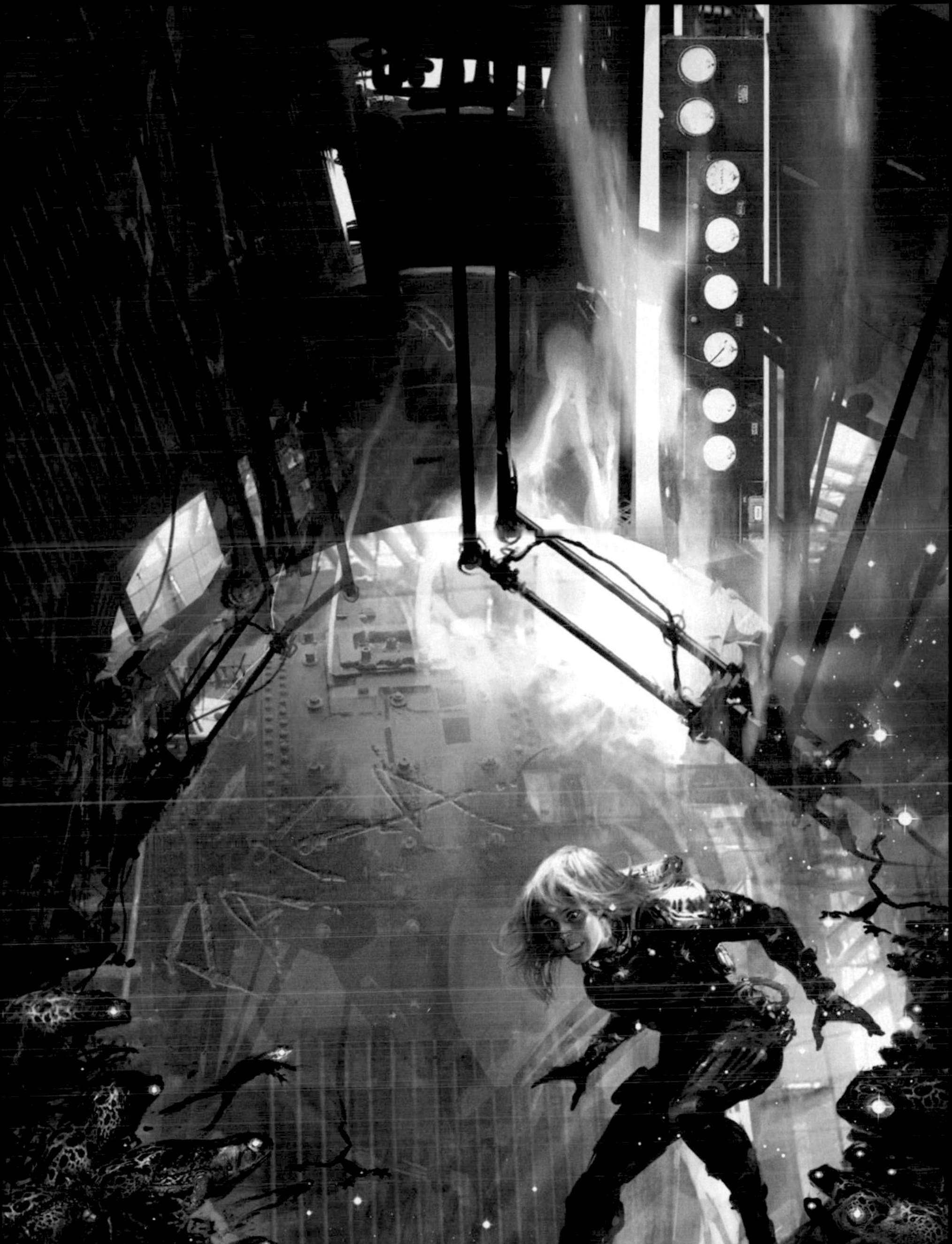
STEPHAN MARTINIERE 2007

Issue 1

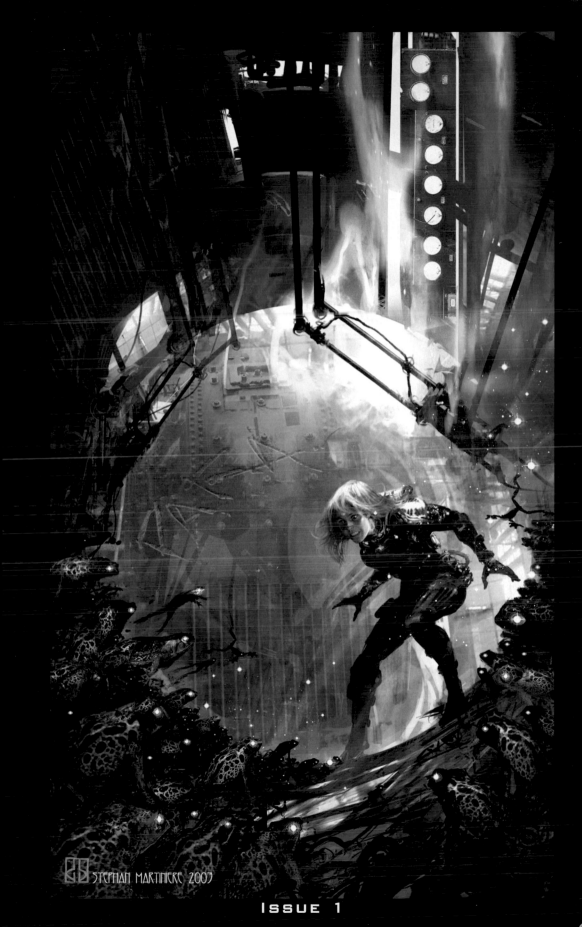

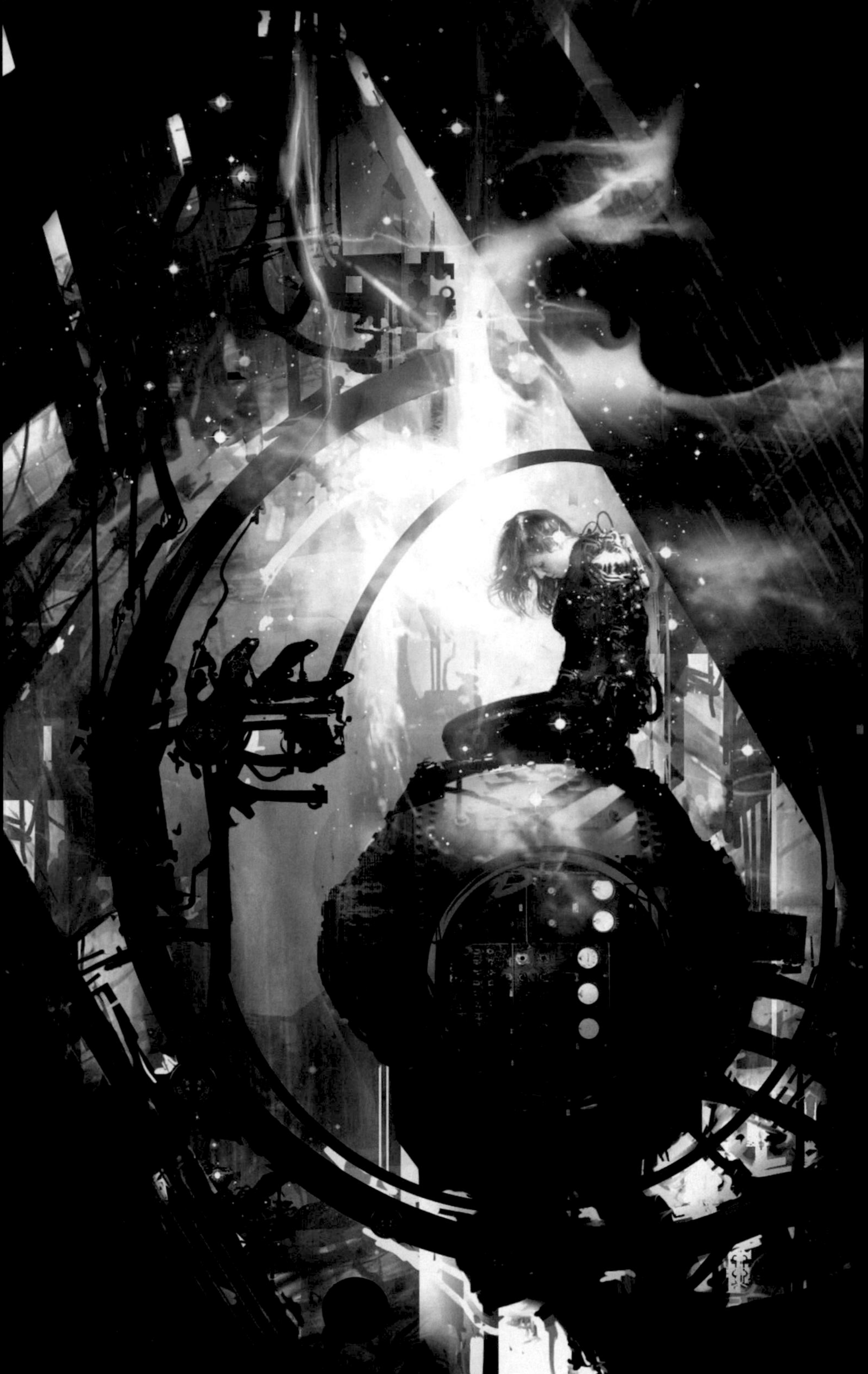

Issue 2
Spectrum Award Winner

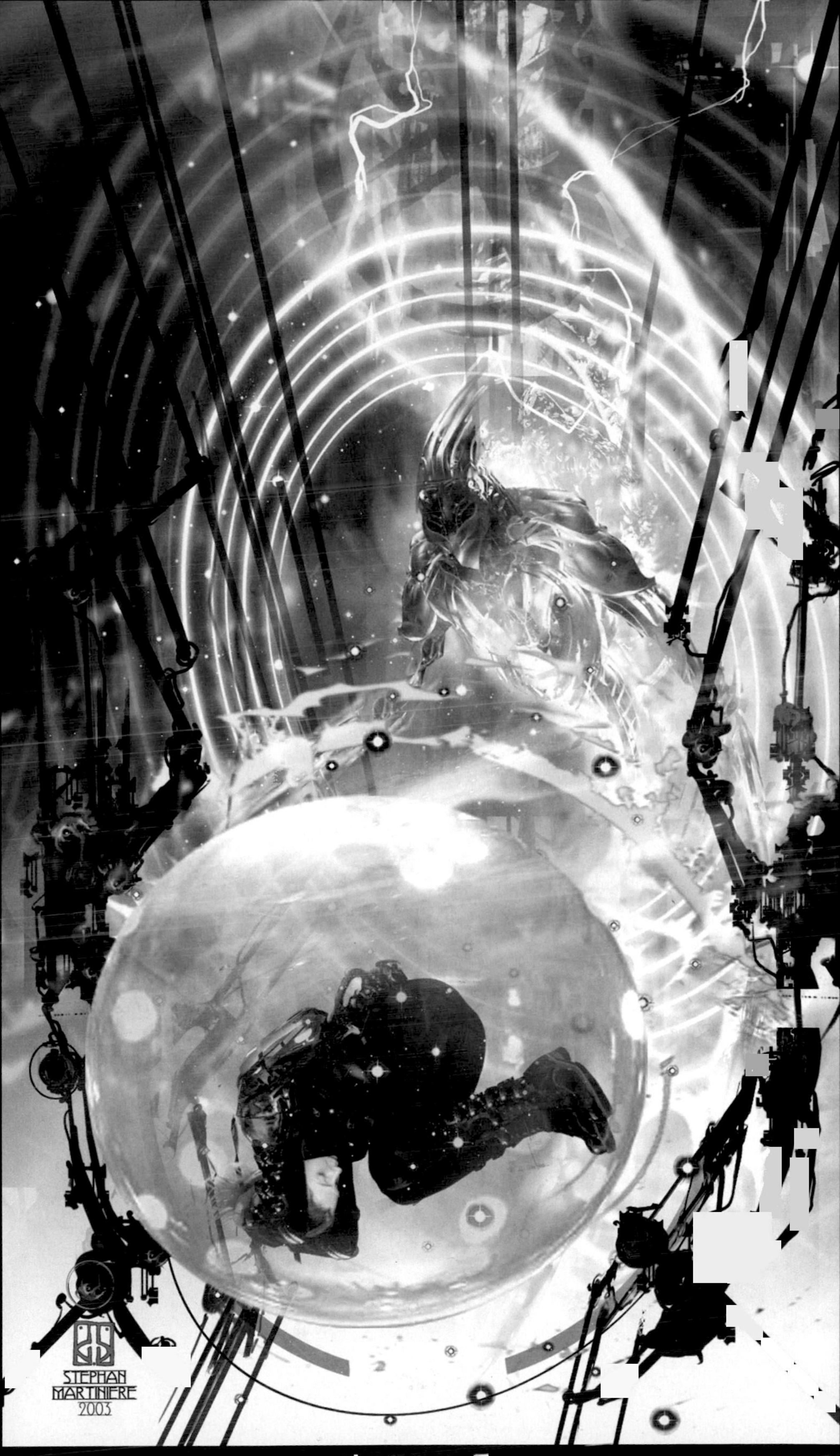
STEPHAN
MARTINIERE
2003

ISSUE 3

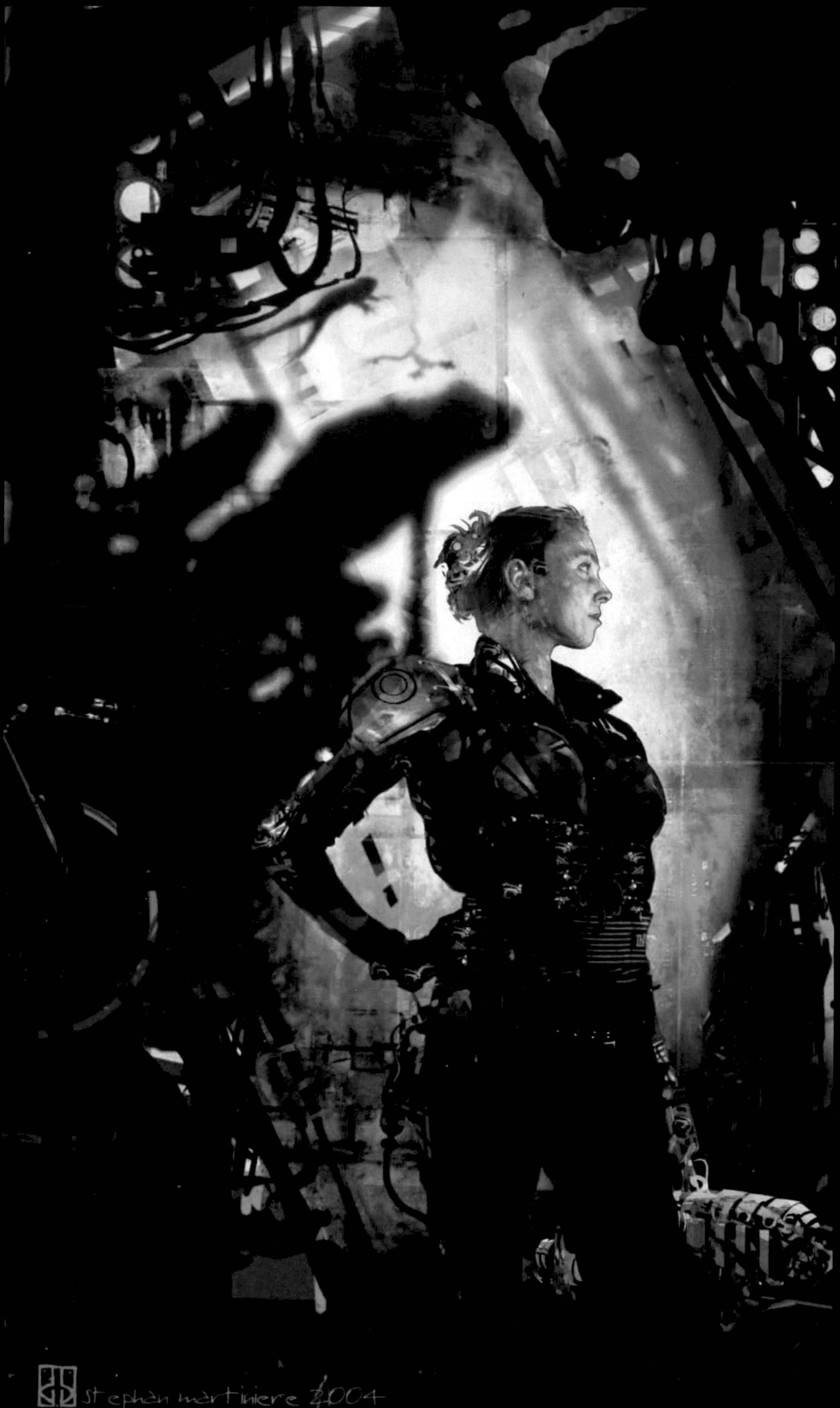
stephan martiniere 2004

ISSUE 4

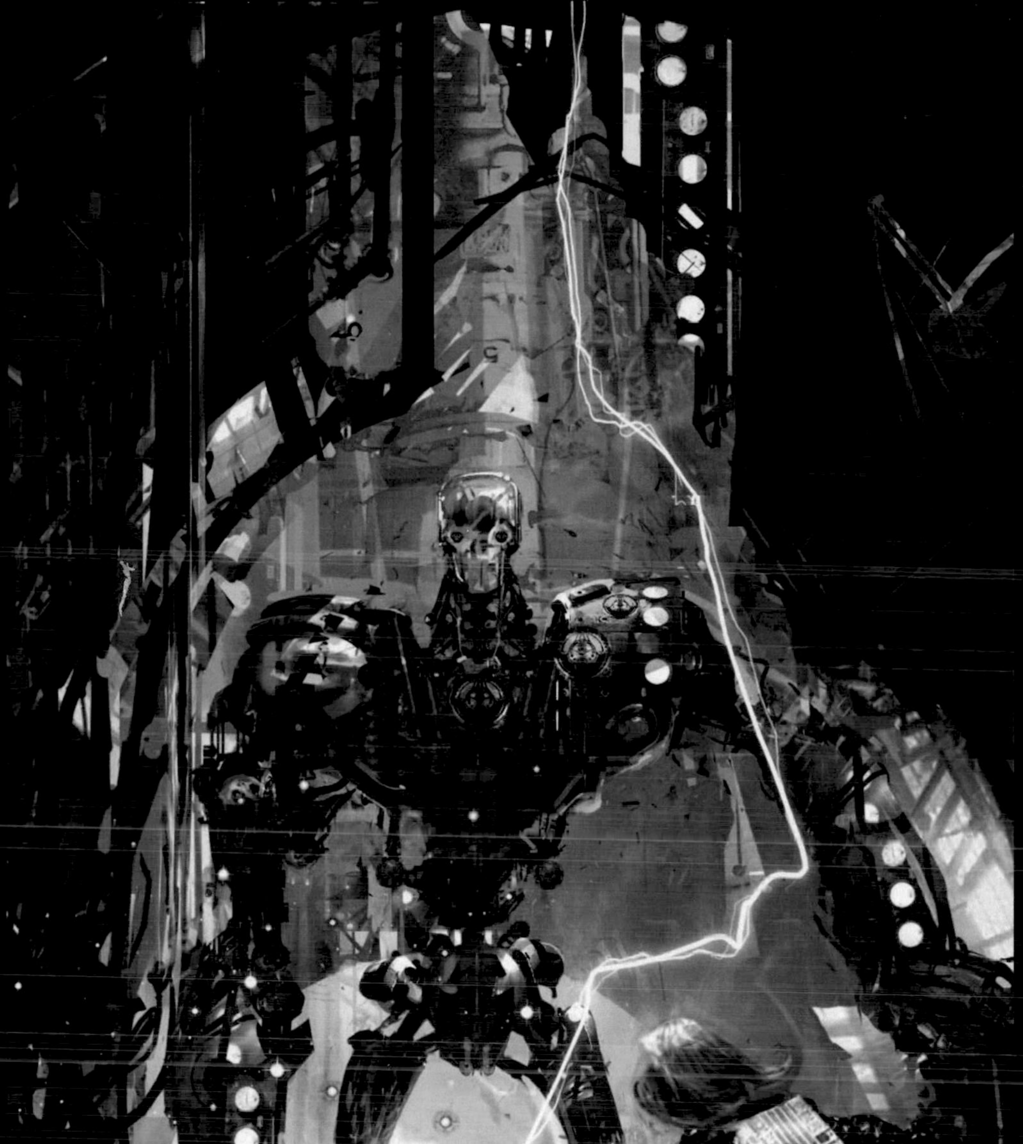
STEPHAN MARTINIERE 2004

ISSUE 5

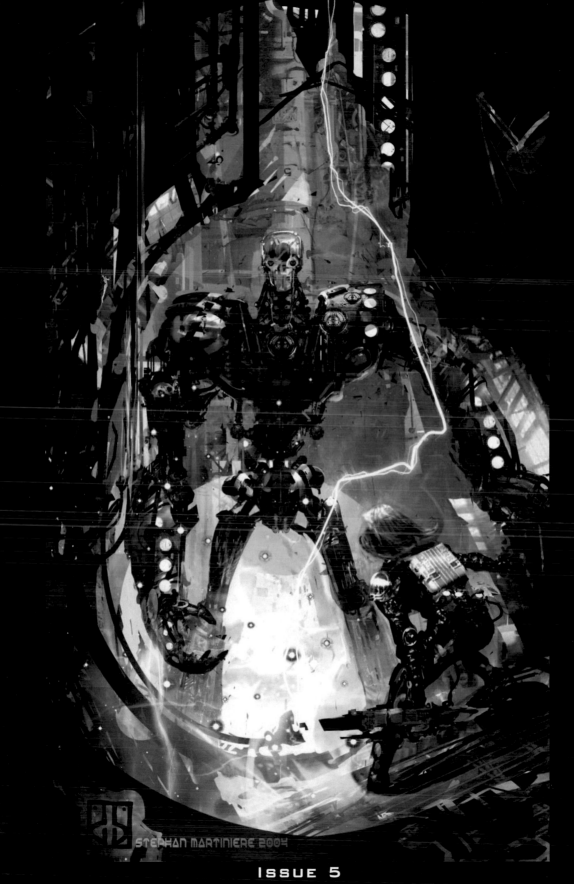

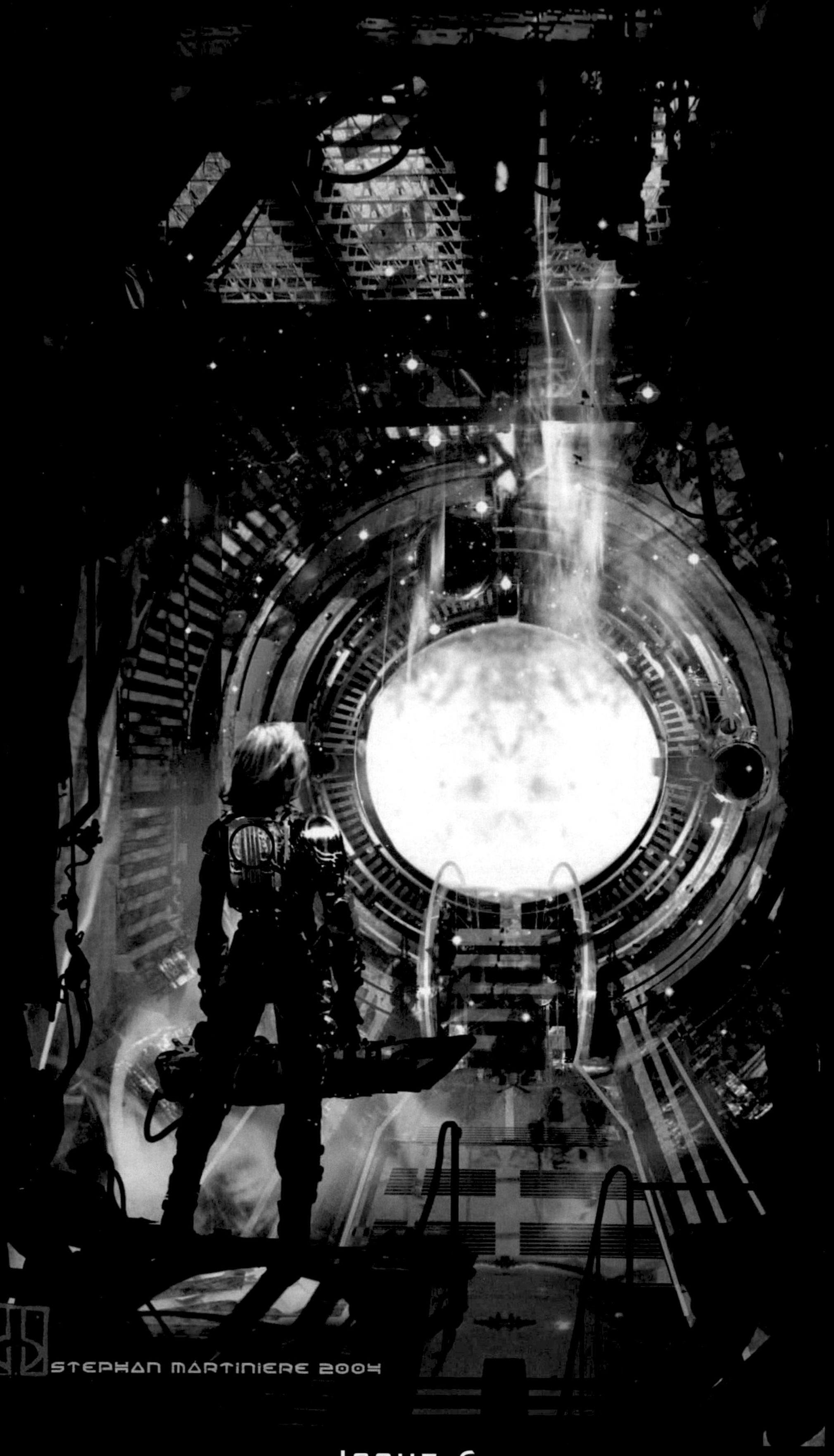
STEPHAN MARTINIERE 2004

ISSUE 6

THE PARA TEAM

LANGDON FOSS

Langdon likes to draw. He once specialized in girls with guns and gothic architecture but then diversified into animals, fruit, shoes, prosthetic noses, rocks, robots and clouds. He once drew an echidna riding a bicycle. He's thinking about drawing a llama in a suit playing cards with an autonomous collective of lichen. You can find work he's done for Wizards of the Coast, Heavy Metal, DC Comics, Penny-Farthing Press and other companies at www.lllama.com. Yes, three L's.

MIKE GARCIA

APB: The colorist formally known as Mike Garcia, now going under the alias The Big Peanutt or just a symbol of a nut, is said to be hiding out in gloomy, Southern California. This salty hooligan is so brash, one "T" just wasn't enough. With Mrs. Nutt and The Little Peanutt by his side, The Big Peanutt sets out to destroy all comic art that crosses his path. This Nutt is said to be "un" armed but dangerous. We have three of his powder-puffed cronies, J.T-bone Steak, Stinky-Cheese Huddlestoned, and Raunchy Jam Woody in custody, but we need your help to find the Big Guy. Beneath his ridiculous shell hides a nuttcase who takes himself much too seriously.

We believe The Big P is devising a plot for creative world domination as we speak and could be hidden in plain sight. Several people, animals, and…things including elephants, baseball park vendors, and angry artists will not rest until he is caught.

STEPHAN MARTINIÉRE

Smoothly morphing his considerable skill and experience, Stephan Martiniére shapeshifts from whimsical to hard-core science fiction, cartoon to realistic, illustrator to director. In the past fifteen years, Stephan has become known for his talent, versatility, imagination and professionalism, gaining constant recognition and praise through his work in a growing range of clients and projects.

Stephan has worked for three years as visual art director at Cyan, the creators of *Myst*, on their games *Uru: Ages Beyond Myst, Uru: The Path of the Shell* and the upcoming *Myst 5*. As an illustrator and animation director, Stephan has won numerous Awards including: a Master Award and five Excellence Awards from Ballistic Media's Exposé 3, Two Master Awards and one Excellence Award from Ballistic Media's Exposé 2, The British Science Fiction Association Award for Best Cover of 2004, A Silver Award for Editorial in 1997 and a Gold Award in 2004 from Spectrum (*Para* Issue 2 Cover), and a Thea Award for his work on the Paramount theme park Super Saturator in 2001. As a director for the animated special *Madeline*, Stephan won the Humanitas Award, the A.C.T. Award and the Parent's Choice Award, and he was nominated for an Emmy Award.

Stephan is currently the visual design director for Midway Games.

MOSTAFA MOUSSA

Mostafa Moussa found his career calling by watching the PBS show *Commander Mark* as a child. He was infatuated with the Secret City mural on the show and began to draw pictures of *Teenage Mutant Ninja Turtles* and *Transformers* in his spare time. By the time he picked up his first comic book at twelve, he knew exactly what path his life would take. He began his professional career at eighteen, and since then has been employed as an inker and embellisher on titles such as *Chastity, Cryptopia, Iron Wings, Rex Mundi,* and *Violent Messiahs.*

RICHARD STARKINGS

Richard Starkings pioneered Digital Comic Book Lettering, and is the co-author, with John Roshell, of *Comic Book Lettering the Comicraft Way.* He is also the creator and publisher of the critically acclaimed pulp science fiction comic book, *Hip Flask.*

CLAUDE ST. AUBIN

Claude St. Aubin began drawing while enrolled in a Montreal high school and read both European and American comic books as a teenager. He preferred the American comics, though, because the stories were shorter and filled with more action. His first real break came right after his college graduation when he received an offer to work on a book entitled *Captain Canuck.* This first job taught him pencilling, inking, coloring, and lettering, and gave him the experience he needed to work in the comics industry. It also hooked him on the medium. Claude has also worked as a graphic designer in Calgary, Alberta, and Toronto, Ontario. He met his wife while in Calgary and happily took on the role of devoted husband and father of two children.

His free-lance comics career began in 1992 with a job offer from DC Comics to work on *The Green Lantern.* Since that time, Claude has kept himself busy working as a free-lance penciller and/or inker for various publishing companies. He lives in Halifax, Nova Scotia, with his wife.

JAMES TAYLOR

James Taylor has a background in traditional art and received a BFA (Fine Arts Degree) with an emphasis in graphic design in 1998. After finishing college he began work as a graphic designer in the tech industry until 2002, surviving the bursting tech bubble by a couple of years. It was during his time as a designer that James started working in the comic-book industry in 1999. He started as a moonlight inker, thinking that the gig would just be a fun, side job, but switched to full-time comics work when his employer closed up shop. Since then James has worked for many different publishers but seems to have been strapped to the hip of PFP over the last two years working on The *Victorian, Stuart Moore's Para* and, of course, *Decoy.*

James currently resides in the Seattle area, continually working as a free-lance inker and graphic designer, and is rarely allowed to leave his home. In 2003, he started his own little publishing company, Rorschach Entertainment, to give new creators an opportunity to work in the comic-book industry—quite often publishing many creators' first work.

PABLO VILLALOBOS

The artist known as Pablo Villalobos, like the famous Ivory-Billed Woodpecker, is such a rarely-seen creature that scientists weep at sightings of him. Not much is known of this elusive penciller, except that he creates beautiful works of art that can be seen in such titles as *Decoy: Stranded*. The artist's natural habitat consists of the humid, coastal plains of South Texas and the thriving metropolis of Houston, where he has been sighted on numerous occasions with his lovely mate. If you happen upon the exotic Pablo species in the wild, please report the sighting to SPETA, the Society for the Preservation of Elusive and Talented Artists.

FEDERICO ZUMEL

Federico Zumel in his own words:

"I was born April 26, 1978, in Caleta Olivia, Argentina, and have always loved to draw even from an early age. After high school, I got into graphic design but quit after one year when I made the discovery that drawing and designing are not the same thing!

"Around the age of 18, I started studying at the Villagran Studio, a studio of three brothers who worked on numerous titles in Argentina, the US, and Europe. They taught me pretty much all I know; although I did study live modelling on my own because I think it's essential for any aspiring artist.

"After years (literally!) of practicing eight hours a day, I began getting small assignments for independent comics and creators in the American market. I started working in the US around four years ago for such companies as Approbation Comics, Forcewerks, Pickle Press, Bughouse Comics, and Superhuman Works (on the title *Ghostfighter*).

"My influences vary from the old masters like Alex Raymond, Stan Drake, and Milton Caniff; to new artists like Greg Capullo, Marc Silverstri, and Claudio Castellini."

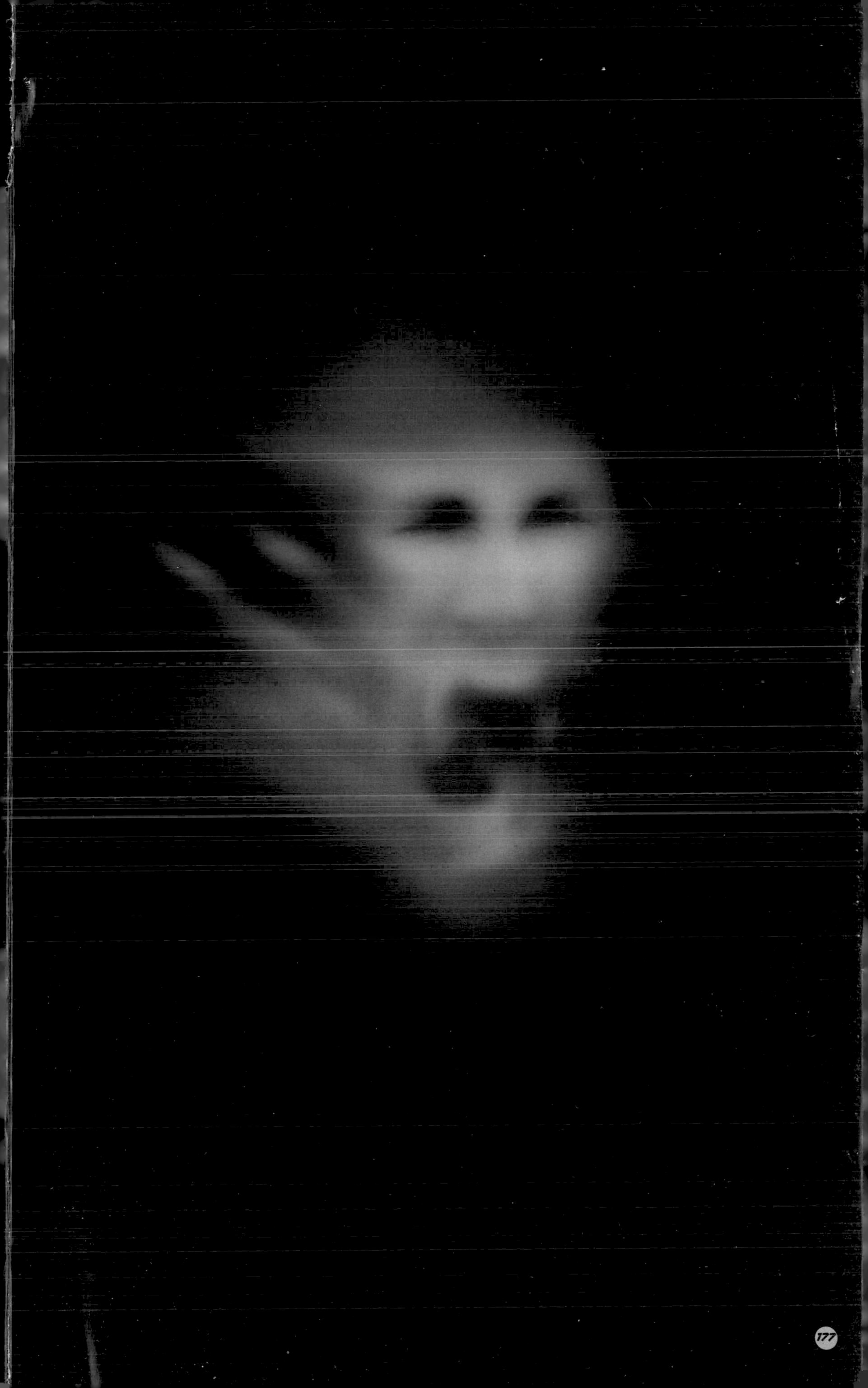